The Big Foundations

THE BIG FOUNDATIONS

Waldemar A. Nielsen

A TWENTIETH CENTURY FUND STUDY

 *New York and London*

COLUMBIA UNIVERSITY PRESS / 1972

LIBRARY OF CONGRESS CATALOGING IN PUBLICATION DATA

Nielsen, Waldemar A.
    The big foundations.

    Includes bibliographical references.
    1. Endowments—United States.   I. Title.
HV97.A3N5   361.7'6'0973   72-3676
ISBN 0-231-03665-5

To the memory of my mother

Foreword

DESPITE THEIR MATERIAL RESOURCES and multiple activities there has been comparatively little independent research on foundations in the United States. This neglect is understandable. Since foundations are a frequent source of financial support for research, scholars are somewhat reluctant to subject them to scrutiny; foundations for their part, with a few notable exceptions, have been inhibited about funding independent examinations of their roles and impact. Yet fresh analysis is needed because foundations as a group constitute a significant institution in the United States and, as such, cannot claim immunity from public interest and scrutiny. It also is needed because without adequate knowledge and understanding, there is a danger that criticism will be uninformed and that governmental action to control or regulate foundations could be inappropriate or counterproductive.

Aware of these needs for increased philanthropic research, the Trustees of the Twentieth Century Fund decided to support this study of the nation's major foundations by Waldemar A. Nielsen. Their decision was preceded by considerable debate over the propriety of the Fund's sponsoring a project that dealt with other foundations, those with assets of $100 million or more. Both the importance of the subject and Mr. Nielsen's credentials for carrying it out overcame all doubts.

During the course of the study, Congress enacted the Tax Reform Act of 1969. Many of its provisions have a definite effect on foundations, large and small. In his analysis Mr. Nielsen discusses the changes that the legislation has brought about. But he goes beyond its impact to consider the future of foundations. He recognizes that if foundations lived what amounted to a charmed life in the past, they must now expect continued questioning and criticism, and should take steps to assure that they will have a vital role to play in the future.

Like all other Fund research directors, Mr. Nielsen has enjoyed complete independence in his analysis, in the conclusions he has reached, and in the recommendations he has made. His study reveals an extraordinary diversity in the objectives and operations of the big foundations. These organizations may share a common heritage in large-scale wealth, but in almost every other respect their dominant characteristic is their intense individualism, more so perhaps than almost any other institution coming under examination by Fund research directors in recent years. This trait springs, in part at least, from their origins as the creations of rich philanthropists or philanthropic families, but it also makes it difficult to formulate uniform measures of their competence and value.

Mr. Nielsen, however, makes an attempt to provide a relative appraisal of foundation performance. His assessment is both useful and provocative, and should stimulate foundations to self-examination. It also should spur other research efforts. Foundations should not be self-conscious and need not be self-serving in sponsoring further independent investigation. It is my hope that Mr. Nielsen's study will be the beginning of a systematic and sustained examination, inside and outside, of all foundations.

M. J. ROSSANT, DIRECTOR
The Twentieth Century Fund

February 1972

Preface

THE WRITING OF THIS BOOK is primarily the result of a desire to produce some plain honest talk about foundations and their problems. Any one who has had the unfortunate task—or the curious taste—to read most of the material which has been available about foundations, knows that it is divided roughly into two equally tiresome parts: the self-congratulatory output of foundations themselves; and the ill-informed screeds of the Old Right on the one extreme, the New Left on the other, and the neo-Know-Nothings like George Wallace in between. The reality of the institution as perceived by anyone who has worked in it or who has been closely associated in it, is virtually impossible to discern in such writings. To get at this reality, however, is not easy. The reluctance—even the fear—of individuals in the tight little world of philanthropy to talk about the inner workings and problems of foundations is suggested by the number of respondents listed in the bibliography to this volume who were willing to provide data only on condition that they remain unidentified.

The second purpose has been to attempt to achieve some understanding of the nature and role of foundations in the larger context of the institutional structure of American life. In this regard, I have become increasingly impressed by the fact that important as they are in themselves, foundations are equally important for what they make it possible for us to understand about such problems as institutional "relevance" and adaptation; the changing relationship between government and the private sector, including profit and non-profit organizations; and the prospects for pluralism in the era of the advanced Welfare State. They also provide an unusually clear optic through which to view the values and behavior patterns of our reigning elite, namely the leaders of the business and financial community, who happen also to be the dominant forces in the governance of foundations. The picture that emerges is not necessarily pretty, but it is an important one with enormous implications for the American future.

My third objective in preparing this volume has been a highly practical one: to try, by holding a mirror up to the leading foundations, to show their trustees and officers the urgent need to initiate procedures for self-reform and self-renewal. I believe that this hope is not as vain today as it seemed two years ago when my research began. The dramatic events in Washington in connection with the passage of the 1969 Tax Reform Act have so shaken the complacency of foundation leaders that they may be finally in a mood to look candidly at themselves, and to do something about what they see.

Despite the many weaknesses of foundations, I remain a strong believer in their potential importance: they embody an idea absolutely vital to American democracy, namely the need for independent centers of initiative to challenge, criticize and provide a creative spark for the massive governmental, economic, social and religious institutions which increasingly dominate our national life.

This study of foundations has been financed by a foundation—The Twentieth Century Fund—and I want to acknowledge the scrupulous respect the fund and its director, M. J. Rossant, have consistently shown for my freedom in the design of the study and the formulation of findings.

I would also like to acknowledge the help I have received in this project from dozens of people in the foundation world, and particularly from my closest collaborators: Elliott Abrams, Neil Gluckin, Mary Lynne Bird, Dr. Yole Sills, Dr. Mae Churchill, Joan Titus, and Dr. Frank Husic.

WALDEMAR A. NIELSEN

January 1972
Aspen, Colorado.

Contents

Foreword   vii

Preface   ix

   PART ONE. SETTING AND SCOPE

1. Philanthropy Under Fire   3

2. The Apex of American Philanthropy   21

   PART TWO. A GALLERY OF PORTRAITS

3. Carnegie: Emergence from Elitism   31

4. The Formidable Rockefeller Fleet   47

5. Coming of Age in the Ford Foundation   78

6. Danforth and Kellogg: Fine But Flawed   99

7. Surdna, Bush, Pew, and Irvine: Underachievers and
   Delinquents   119

8. The Ducal Du Ponts   135

9. Texas: Rich Land, Poor Land
   Moody, Houston, Richardson, and Brown   150

10. Lilly, Hartford, and Duke: Birds in Gilded Cages   170

11. Sloan, Kettering, and Mott: GM's Philanthropic Offspring   191

12. The Middling Mellons   207

13. Astor, Woodruff, Kresge, Waterman, and Kaiser:
    Philanthropy Family Style   227

14. Fleischmann and Commonwealth: Two Intriguing Aber-
    rations
    Land: A Gleam of Hope   250

Part Three. Patterns, Processes, and Performance

15. A Profile of Big Philanthropy   273

16. Public Reporting: The Enclave Mentality   295

17. The Determinant Internal Forces: Donors, Trustees, and
    Staff   309

18. Big Philanthropy and the Race Question: A Case Study
    of Performance   332

Part Four. Foundations in the American Context

19. Government and Foundations: The Tightening Embrace
    of Regulation   365

20. Government and Foundation Programs: The Endless,
    Ambiguous Interface   379

21. Summation and Assessment   399

22. Epilogue: A Note on the Prospects for Self-Reform and
    Self-Renewal   431

Appendix: A Note on Foundation Investment Performance   435

Notes   449

Index   457

The Big Foundations

Part One
SETTING AND SCOPE

1.

Philanthropy Under Fire

IN THE GREAT JUNGLE of American democracy and capitalism, there is no more strange or improbable creature than the private foundation. Private foundations are virtually a denial of basic premises: aristocratic institutions living on the privileges and indulgence of an egalitarian society; aggregations of private wealth which, contrary to the proclaimed instincts of Economic Man, have been conveyed to public purposes. Like the giraffe, they could not possibly exist, but they do.

Moreover, they have existed in a great many places and for a very long time. Every major culture and every major religion has in one fashion or another felt the need to encourage and to institutionalize philanthropy. The ancient Chinese, the Indians, the Egyptians, each in their own fashion, possessed their own forms of foundations. Greece and Rome had many. Islam spawned them, called *waqfs*, in profusion. (In Iran, there are more than 20,000 in existence, some several hundred years old; in Teheran alone there are more than 2,500.) In the medieval period in the West, the Catholic Church as well as municipalities and guilds used them extensively to support monasteries, almshouses, orphanages, schools, and hospitals—even to repair bridges and lighthouses and maintain the highroads. In all probability, if the anthropological data were available, it would be found that the red Mayans, the white Norsemen, and the black Benin made their own appropriate arrangements to serve the universal human impulse of altruism.

But the long history of foundations has not been without recurrent dark periods when they have fallen into mismanagement, become sclerotic and outdated, and strayed into politics. Not surprisingly, they have also repeatedly clashed with the authorities, both secular and ecclesiastical. Because of legacy-hunting by the clergy, the Roman Emperor Severus in the second century issued an edict withdrawing the right to will property to the Church. In the fourteenth century, the Council of Vienne cracked down on the corrupt practices of the administrators of Church foundations. In Britain a commission of inquiry was appointed in 1601 to check maladministration among foundations; nearly four centuries later, in our own time, another British select committee was investigating the same kinds of philanthropic abuse that troubled Severus and a long succession of popes, kings, and prime ministers—as well as an eminent line of philosophers, legal theorists, and social critics.

The most visible part of the problem has usually been corruption. But basically it has involved power, both economic and political. By the late Middle Ages, the accumulation of wealth by the Church had reached such proportions that social upheavals and conflicts with the State were repeatedly precipitated. Consequently, the secular authorities sometimes felt impelled to take drastic action—the expropriations during the reign of Henry VIII in England, for example. Henry objected to the religious endowments as obstacles to his efforts of reformation; a century later his royal successors feared private endowments for the opposite reason, as threats to their efforts to block change.[*]

During the French Revolution, resentment against the wealth of foundations resulted in their virtual extermination in that country. And in the twentieth century, fear of their unregulated influence, especially on the part of the new totalitarian regimes, has contin-

[*] Thus W. K. Jordan in his *Philanthropy in England: 1480–1660* (New York, Russell Sage Foundation, 1959), p. 4, writes: "The whole realm stirred as men began to discover that they could create institutions of social change and reformation with their own wealth and charity. . . . The power, the velocity and the direction of movement, which were ordering the basic social institutions of the modern world, were so mighty that they could neither be controlled nor diverted to causes which both James and Charles would have preferred. James was bewildered and his son was not a little alarmed by the vast power and social effectiveness of the huge and carefully devised charitable endowments of the age which were creating an England they did not understand, an England at bottom inimical to their conception of the State."

ued. Foundations were among the first victims of the Bolshevik takeover in Russia and the Nazi rise to power in Germany.

In part, foundations have brought their troubles upon themselves by their own misconduct. But repeatedly throughout history, when nations have been under heavy stress or in the throes of social crisis, foundations have become a favorite target of official frustration and popular anxiety. By some perverse pathology linked to processes of political polarization, nations, when they most need the ameliorative efforts of foundations, tend to become most hostile to them.

The United States, although unique in the modern world for the encouragement it still accords to private philanthropy, is no exception to this universal pattern. In the years before World War I, when the number of foundations was just beginning to swell following an era of great economic growth, they became a focus of bitter controversy between the forces of reckless capital and radical labor. In the agony of the great depression of the 1930s they again became a favorite object of attack, and in the hysteria of the McCarthy period after World War II they suffered the same fate.

Not surprisingly, therefore, as another massive social crisis began to unfold during the 1960s, foundations again found themselves caught in the political crossfire. The shooting came from all ideological directions.

The old Left has long seen them as the center of a powerful apparatus of capitalist domination. More than half a century ago Basil Manly, research director of the U.S. Commission on Industrial Relations, charged:

The domination by the men in whose hands the final control of a large part of American industry rests is not limited to their employees, but is being rapidly extended to control the education and social survival of the Nation.

This control is being extended largely through the creation of enormous privately managed funds for indefinite purposes, hereafter designated "foundations," by the endowment of colleges and universities, by the creation of funds for the pensioning of teachers, by contributions to private charities, as well as through controlling or influencing the public press. . . .

As regards the "foundations" created for unlimited general purposes

and endowed with enormous resources, their ultimate possibilities are so
grave a menace, not only as regards their own activities and influence
but also the benumbing effect which they have on private citizens and
public bodies, that if they could be clearly differentiated from other
forms of voluntary altruistic effort, it would be desirable to recommend
their abolition.[1]

Ferdinand Lundberg in 1968 was echoing the same theories:

The general panorama revealed by [Congressman Wright] Patman was that
through the foundation device this privileged part of the American capitalist structure has been able to move itself back into the earlier
position of unregulated, uncontrolled, untaxed capitalism. Through the
foundations, unless they are restrained by law or public criticism, the
old unregulated capitalism may well be restored." [2]

The deadly enemies of the old Left—the old Right—are
strangely not in disagreement about the nature and the extent of
danger posed by the foundations. René Wormser, a lawyer and
professional anti-Communist who first came to a tawdry prominence as counsel to a congressional committee that investigated
foundations in the mid-1950s, says:

The grant-making [foundation] can exercise enormous power through
the direct use of its funds. Moreover, it materially increases its power
and its influence by building collateral alliances which serve greatly to
insulate it against criticism. . . . These dangers [to our society] relate
chiefly to the use of foundation funds for political ends; they arise out of
the accumulation of substantial economic power and of cultural influence
in the hands of a class of administrators of tax-exempt funds established
in perpetuity. An "elite" has thus emerged, in control of gigantic financial resources operating outside of our democratic processes, which is
willing and able to shape the future of this Nation and of mankind in the
image of its own values and concepts. An unparalleled amount of power
is concentrated increasingly in the hands of an interlocking and self-perpetuating group. Unlike the power of corporate management, it is unchecked by the people; unlike the power of Churches, it is unchecked by
any firmly established canons of value.[3]

The New Left, in its eclectic fashion, has borrowed freely from
both ends of the ideological spectrum in mounting its attack on
foundations. It sees their origins in the rapacity, hypocrisy, and
corruption of the corporate Establishment. The political power of

foundations, however, derives only in part from the volume of their assets. Even more pernicious is the concept of "strategic philanthropy" by which they:

sustain the complex nerve centers and guidance mechanism for a whole system of institutional power. . . . The Foundations . . . are the base of the network of organizations through which the nerve centers of wealth impress their will on Washington. This network, the ganglia of foundation intelligence, is composed of a panoply of "independent" research and policy organizations, jointly financed and staffed by the foundations and the corporate community, which as a group set the terms and define the horizon of choice for the long-range policies of the United States government. . . . [They have] been nothing less than a means of shifting the balance of political thinking and political power in the United States consistently in the direction of the moderates and those supporting the *status quo* and against those advocating more revolutionary change.[4]

By 1969, foundations were once again under assault not only from the ideological barricades but also in the arena of practical politics. The setting was the U.S. Congress, and the context a debate over tax reform legislation. The leader of the anti-foundation forces was the sturdy old Populist from Texas, Wright Patman, who for more than thirty years—with considerable success—has carried on a personal crusade against Wall Street, chain stores, monopolies, banks, and "greedy millionaires" in general. Patman is a blue-eyed, cherubic-looking man (he has been called a mixture of Father Christmas and Foxy Grandpa) of gentle manner and deceptively quiet voice. But in exposing and condemning what he regards as the evils of Big Money, he is tenacious and tough.

Patman had begun his campaign against the foundations eight years before with a mild speech in the House on May 2, 1961, praising their "wonderful work," but deploring their rapid growth and questioning the motives of some of their donors. In the following months his attacks became less restrained; he made use of all available charges of financial misconduct as well as the contradictory allegations of both capitalistic and communistic bias among foundations. In early 1962, the House Small Business Committee authorized him to hire a staff, conduct studies, and hold hearings. Over the next several years, with unflagging energy, he prepared massive (and not always accurate) compilations of data, on the

basis of which he charged foundations with short sales of securities, speculation in commodity futures and oil wells, manipulation
of stock prices, and the use of their assets to carry on proxy fights
for the control of corporations.

Through his skill in making headlines Patman began to attract
public and congressional attention to the general subject of foundation conduct. He also succeeded in badgering the Treasury
Department and the Internal Revenue Service into more vigorous
surveillance. In July 1964 he held his first series of public hearings,
calling only government witnesses. He charged that the Treasury's
statistics on foundations were totally inadequate and that as a result of its "indefensible apathy and its archaic procedures" it had
actually encouraged abuses by some donors and foundations. At
Patman's demand, the Treasury undertook a new study of foundations and issued a report in 1965 that identified a number of
spreading financial abuses among foundations and analyzed their
basic structural faults, such as the unduly close ties among foundations, donor families, and certain associated companies. For this
major accomplishment the Treasury—and Patman—must be given
full credit.

The recommendations in the report were moderate, but foundation response was divided. A number of the big philanthropies approved them, but rather passively; others, however, immediately
dispatched their lawyers to Washington to try to block any legislative action on the basis of them, which they succeeded in doing.
Nonetheless, the Treasury's report had a deep effect on public
opinion and generally seemed to validate Patman's charges. In a
succession of further reports in 1966, 1967, and 1968, the Texas
congressman presented a stream of new allegations and cases of flagrant foundation misconduct.°

° For example, the Public Health Foundation for Cancer and Blood Pressure Research, created by the late James H. Rand Jr., of Remington-Rand
Corporation, was allegedly involved in the following transactions: Rand sold
his Connecticut house to his foundation for more than $230,000 for use as a
research center—and then continued to live in it, with the foundation paying
the household expenses and salaries of Rand's servants. Nearly $160,000 was
spent to construct a research laboratory in Stuart, Florida, to grow vegetables
—which were then consumed by Rand and his friends.

Nevertheless, it began to appear that Patman's crusade was running out of steam; it had produced no significant legislation, and Congress and the public were becoming fatigued by his antics. But in 1968 it suddenly revived, riding the wave of a spontaneous public revolt against the burdens and injustices of the tax laws, especially their loopholes for the rich. Half the letters then being deposited on congressional desks were taxpayers' protests. The public mood was reflected in the response to a statement late that year by Joseph W. Barr, then secretary of the treasury, to a congressional committee that in 1967 there had been 155 individual tax returns filed with adjusted gross income above $200,000 on which no income tax had to be paid: and 21 returns were filed with incomes above $1 million on which no tax had to be paid.° These startling figures, when reported by the press and television, provoked a new torrent of outraged letters, telegrams, and telephone calls to Washington.

This, then, was the atmosphere in which the House Ways and Means Committee under Chairman Wilbur Mills of Arkansas opened its tax reform hearings on February 18, 1969. It began by taking up the question of tax-exempt foundations and thereby got off to a lively start. The first witness called was Wright Patman, who fired a shotgun blast full into their flank:

Today, I shall introduce a bill to end a gross inequity which this country and its citizens can no longer afford: the tax-exempt status of the so-called privately controlled charitable foundations, and their propensity for domination of business and accumulation of wealth.

Put most bluntly, philanthropy—one of mankind's more noble instincts —has been perverted into a vehicle for institutionalized, deliberate evasion of fiscal and moral responsibility to the nation.

This has been accomplished by tax immunities granted by the U.S. Congress. The use of the tax-free status . . . reveals the continuing de-

---

° Actually the situation was worse than Secretary Barr indicated. Because he used adjusted gross income, his figures did not measure the full degree of escape at the higher levels of income. "Adjusted gross income" does not include tax-exempt interest, the excluded part of capital gains, excess percentage depletion, excess real estate depreciation, or intangible drilling expenses for oil wells. If his figures had been based on total income, the number of people above the $200,000 level who paid no tax in 1967 would have been several times larger.

votion of some of our millionaires to greed, rather than conversion to graciousness.

Mr. Chairman, when a privilege is abused, it should be withdrawn. And the onerous burdens of 65 million taxpayers demand that Congress curb the tax-exempt foundations which, in unwitting good faith, it helped to create.[5]

On the second day of the hearings, the committee heard Representative John J. Rooney, a Democrat from Brooklyn, New York. He told a story to agitate the heart of any politician. Apparently a wealthy opponent of his in the previous primary campaign had used his own private foundation as a weapon of partisan attack. According to Rooney, the Frederick W. Richmond Foundation had swooped into his district just before the election and handed out tax-free gifts to such politically potent groups as the Puerto Rican Trade Committee, the Hispanic Society of the Fire Department, and the Zion Negro Baptist Church. In addition the foundation created Neighborhood Study Clubs, Inc., which Rooney charged was simply a political machine "oiled" by charity dollars. In concluding his testimony he said:

In other words, to sum up my experience in the primary campaign of 1968, for the first time in anyone's knowledge, a congressional political campaign was subsidized by all United States taxpayers and in defiance, if not in violation, of laws governing campaign moneys. . . .

This time, Mr. Chairman, it happened in my district. It can—and probably will—happen in your districts. In fact, the appeal of this political gimmick is a threat to every officeholder, in Congress or elsewhere, who does not have access to a fat bankroll or to a business or to a tax-exempt foundation.[6]

On the third day McGeorge Bundy, president of the Ford Foundation, was the witness before a chamber packed with hundreds of intent spectators. Bundy had left his post as dean of Harvard College to go to Washington in 1961 with President John F. Kennedy and the New Frontier. Over the following five years, under President Kennedy and then under President Lyndon Johnson, he served as the White House assistant for national security affairs. Many in Congress and elsewhere had come to believe that Bundy had played a key role in the Bay of Pigs and the Dominican Republic interventions and in the escalation of the Vietnam War.

In 1966, Bundy moved from the White House to the Ford Foundation, and the hawkish strategic planner seemed almost instantly to be transformed into an activist domestic reformer, a change that some of his liberal critics charged to bad conscience. In any event, the foundation under his leadership began a series of grants that plunged it into sensitive areas (see also chapter 5). In the South, Ford supplemented the funds of the Southern Regional Council to enlarge its voter registration drive for blacks. And as the number of newly registered black voters swelled, many traditional Southern political leaders felt that their power was being undermined by the foundation. In the Southwest, Ford gave help to a militant Mexican-American organization which, brandishing radical slogans, then entered local politics, causing even the leading liberal Democrats of the area to protest Ford's actions.

In Cleveland in 1967, Ford gave substantial funds to the local chapter of the Congress on Racial Equality to be spent, among other things, for a voter registration drive. The preponderance of new voters registered were black—and when a black was elected mayor in the next election, there were charges from both Democratic and Republican party regulars that Ford money had put him in office. In New York City, the foundation financed a school decentralization experiment which, by the time it was over, had detonated black–Jewish tensions in the city, brought about a bitter confrontation between the black community and the powerful United Federation of Teachers, and resulted in a destructive citywide school strike that nearly cost John Lindsay his second term as mayor.

To make the atmosphere at the Washington hearings still more volatile, the New York *Times* just the week before had reported Ford grants to eight prominent members of the staff of the late Senator Robert F. Kennedy. They had received awards aggregating $131,000, personally approved by Bundy. According to a foundation press release issued after the first news stories appeared, "the grants were provided under a foundation program of long standing that aims to ease the transition from public to private life. They provide up to a year of leisure and freedom from immediate financial concern."

The members of the House committee immediately pounced on
Bundy about them. He got off to a bad start because his discursive
defense of the grants as purely "educational" and not tinged with
political or personal favoritism was singularly unpersuasive. His
replies to subsequent questions were equally unconvincing to the
committee. According to private statements made later by five
members who were present, Bundy conveyed a strong impression
of arrogance and condescension. One congressman said, "I went
into that hearing this morning basically friendly to the foundations; I came out feeling that if Bundy represents the prevailing
attitude among them, they are going to have to be brought down a
peg. For all their Ph.D.'s they are not above the law."

John D. Rockefeller 3d appeared a week later—and in so far as
the committee at any point seriously discussed nonpolitical issues
of philanthropy, it was largely in the exchange between him and
Representative John W. Byrnes of Wisconsin, the ranking Republican member.

For example, in reply to Rockefeller's earnest and self-effacing
plea for continued tax inducements for private philanthropy, Representative Byrnes posed some serious questions:

The real problem here . . . is that certain people have a choice as to
how the tax aspect of their income is going to be spent. . . . The great
vast array of the American people do not have this choice. They are not
only paying for things about which some of them are not very enthusiastic, but they must also pay a higher price to carry on these services simply because some people with wealth have said that they do not want to
support any of these services.

Should we permit a segment of our society to set up a government of
its own to render philanthropic services? Our tax laws have given one
group a chance to . . . make their own determination as to what is in
the public good, and to decide how to spend that money.

How do we cope with the choice that we have given to some people
when we haven't given that choice to the great mass of citizens? [7]

But even that interval of sobriety in the proceedings was inter-
rupted by a nerve-jangling distraction. In making his case, the witness had happened to mention, almost in passing, that because of
the unlimited deduction privilege for charitable contributions permitted under existing legislation, he had not had to pay any in-

come tax since 1961. That statement by a Rockefeller in 1969, a year of tax rebellion, brought the committee bolt upright and sent newspapermen racing for the telephones.

Once the hearings were over, the committee and its staff, with the help of a number of Treasury experts, set to work to draft proposals for new legislation. Three months later, in a press release dated May 27, 1969, the committee issued a harsh judgment upon foundations. The foundations were shocked by some of the specific recommendations, but even more so by the evidence of the extent to which they were mistrusted.

Their predicament was made still worse a month later by the disclosure of a relationship between Supreme Court Justice Abe Fortas and the Wolfson Family Foundation, whose donor—the notorious corporation raider and stock manipulator, Louis E. Wolfson—was then under federal indictment. Fortas, it was learned, had agreed to accept a $20,000 annual fee from the foundation after he joined the Supreme Court. Shortly thereafter it was revealved that another member of the Court, Justice William O. Douglas, was on the payroll of the Parvin Foundation, whose donor, Albert Parvin, had extensive holdings in hotels and gambling casinos in Las Vegas. On May 9 the Los Angeles *Times* reported an interconnection between the two cases; Wolfson and Parvin had once been named co-conspirators in a stock manipulation case. In addition, Fortas' wife, Carolyn Agger Fortas, had been retained as an attorney by the Parvin Foundation. A few days later Fortas resigned from the Court—and a new charge had been added against philanthropic foundations, namely that they had become instruments for the corruption of public officials.

As the congressional battle shifted from the House to the Senate the odds against the foundations were heavy. Years of bombardment by Patman, the foundations' stumbling performance before the House Committee, and such incidents as the Fortas case had thrown them on the defensive. More ominous, once it was realized in Washington that the tax reform drive might threaten even such hallowed loopholes as the oil depletion allowance and the excess depreciation rules for real estate, big politics took over. Tax lobbyists representing major industries and interest groups from all over the country began a mass assault on the members of Congress. In this atmosphere, foundations became a convenient scapegoat and even the few political friends on whom they could ordinarily rely suddenly became unwilling to speak up. Southern conservatives, led by George Wallace, were furious about grants for black voter registration and school desegregation, and northern conservatives were equally upset by foundation activism in the ghettos; at the same time the vigorous opposition of the AFL-CIO to foundations as tax shelters for the wealthy undermined the support of a number of liberal congressmen. The large and politically influential state universities, long resentful of foundation favoritism for the Ivy League schools, decided not to exert themselves in behalf of the foundations. And in a few cases, strong opponents of the Vietnam War were put off by the prominence of McGeorge Bundy among the spokesmen for private philanthropy. Most members of Congress, confronted with the necessity of choice, made a simple political calculation: foundations, compared to oil, banking, and real estate, represented a small and weak constituency that presumably could be ignored.*

Another major handicap to the foundations was the contradictory position of the Nixon administration. During his presidential campaign, Nixon had been skeptical of the significance of the tax revolt, and when he took office he put tax reform near the bottom of his priorities. His top appointees in the Treasury, scarcely noted as reformers, did little to persuade him otherwise. Thus both the White House and the Treasury were surprised by the storm that broke over Capitol Hill. Forced to submit legislative proposals, the Treasury did so hurriedly and with little preparation. Later, as the tax fight heated up and the various pressure groups went to work, the White House embarrassed the Treasury by reversing its position even on the mild reforms that had been proposed. Assistant

---

* Nor were some of these interests, particularly the oil lobby, negligent in reminding congressmen that one politically convenient way to take public attention away from the oil depletion allowance was to crack down hard on the foundations and their tax privileges. Lobbyists of two major oil companies reportedly presented detailed memoranda to friendly members of the Senate Finance Committee outlining the tactics to be followed and the political benefits that would accrue.

Secretary Edwin Cohen, the principal Treasury participant in the technical work of the Ways and Means Committee, consistently displayed an anti-foundation bias that by early fall had become so marked that it produced a split within the Administration. The secretary of health, education and welfare, Robert Finch, on September 17, 1969, wrote a strong letter, which he also made public, to Treasury Secretary David M. Kennedy, asserting that the bill approved by the House committee threatened to undermine American foundations and even to destroy them. The gravest dangers, he said, were posed by the provisions—apparently supported by the Treasury—prohibiting any activity by foundations that might influence legislation. In his view the language could be "interpreted in such a way as to preclude any foundation impact on public opinion formation" and render illegal a broad and important range of foundation activities directed to social and educational problems.

Secretary Kennedy, in a superbly bland reply drafted in Cohen's office, said: "While the line between education and the influencing of legislation may not always be easy to draw, I am confident that the Internal Revenue Service will continue to exercise sound discretion in this respect as it has in the past."

Handicapped by a dubious public, an irritated and harassed Congress, and an unsympathetic administration, the foundations in September prepared to face the Senate Finance Committee. A blue-ribbon lineup of leaders from universities, research centers, the business community, and civil rights groups was organized to pay individual calls on key members of the House and the Senate. In addition, a coordinated series of statements was prepared defending the foundation position, and a panel of witnesses was organized consisting of some of the most eminent names in American life. A useful buttress to these efforts was the report issued on October 22 by a private study group headed by Peter G. Peterson, a prominent Chicago businessman.[8] The commission had been organized several months before at the prompting of John D. Rockefeller 3d to make an independent appraisal of foundations, and its findings and recommendations were critical but constructive.

The well-planned testimony of the foundation witnesses certainly did no harm. But how much good it accomplished for their case was difficult to measure because by the time the Senate committee met, the political winds generated by a multitude of aroused interest groups were howling so loudly around the tax bill that the small voice of the pro-foundation spokesmen could scarcely be heard.* In the end the Finance Committee, although it dropped some of the features of the House bill that were most objectionable to the foundations, added a provision putting a mandatory forty-year limitation on their life.

Although the provision was eventually rejected, it produced a lively but bewildering debate on the floor of the Senate which revealed the full depth of congressional division if not confusion regarding philanthropy. Among the liberals, for example, Senator Walter F. Mondale, a Democrat from Minnesota, defended the foundations in these terms: "In health, in education, in the cultural field, in social welfare, in noncommercial television, in legal rights for the poor and the consumer, in civil rights, in social sciences, in the National Merit Scholarships, in population problems— wherever we look, the cutting edge of the liberal dynamic thought in this country today is being supported by the private foundations." [9]

Senator Charles H. Percy, a liberal Republican from Illinois, defended them on opposite grounds, citing their sound traditionality: "The heart of foundation giving is not generally the glamorous, pioneering variety. . . . Instead, grants are made year in and year out to the YMCA, Boys' Clubs, the Cancer Society, educational in-

---

* Also, Congress is not necessarily impressed by the kind of leaders in American life who tend to be foundation trustees and spokesmen. As Richard Rovere noted in his tongue-in-cheek essay *The American Establishment:* "Too many journalists, awed by their observations of the Establishment at work, leap to the conclusion that its power is not only great but invariably decisive. This is by no means the case. There are powerful anti-Establishment forces at work, and frequently they prevail. It seems to me perfectly clear, for example, that the Establishment has never found a way of controlling Congress. Indeed, there are times when Congress appears to be nothing more or less than a conspiracy to louse up the plans of the Establishment. Whatever the Establishment wants, it often seems, Congress mulishly opposes." (Richard H. Rovere, *The American Establishment and Other Reports, Opinions, and Speculations* [New York, Harcourt Brace Jovanovich, 1964; paperback], p. 6)

stitutions and hospitals, symphonies, museums, welfare agencies, and the myriad of other institutions which contribute to the development of a better society.[10]

A dean of the liberal group, Senator Albert Gore, Democrat of Tennessee, then attacked the liberal defenders of foundations: "One of the strangest anomalies in our history is that my liberal friends think this is a liberal cause for which they are fighting. They are fighting for the vested interest of this country, for the vested wealth of this country, to be tied up in perpetuity for the descendants of a few people who have waxed rich, sometimes by chance or inheritance, from this society of ours." [11]

After the Senate passed the tax bill without the forty-year "death sentence," the conference committee of the two houses under Chairman Mills worked long hours on the final compromises. At 3:30 Tuesday afternoon, December 23, the cluster of lobbyists and newspapermen outside the committee room knew from a burst of applause inside that the Tax Reform Act of 1969 needed only President Nixon's signature to become reality.

Thus came to an end a Pinteresque drama susceptible of many interpretations. The foundations were seemingly in as much confusion and disagreement as everyone else about the significance of what had happened. During the heat of the congressional battle, Alan Pifer of the Carnegie Corporation took a dark view. In a speech in November 1969 he said: "From what I have witnessed in Washington in recent months, it is my sad conclusion that the role played by free private institutions as a bulwark of the American democratic system may be in jeopardy." The new law rested, in his view, on untested assumptions and was little more than an overreaction by Congress to the public disclosure of a few abuses. He called it "an almost classical example of legislating in the dark," and said that "its broad, sweeping provisions, the fallacious concepts which inform it, and the ignorance and myths on which it is based add up to nothing less than a vast disservice to the nation."

McGeorge Bundy, in the Annual Report of the Ford Foundation for 1970, was more sanguine: "We must defer final judgment until the statute is fully developed in regulations and by interpretations, but my current belief is that the new law will permit and protect

the effective continuation of all of the basic programs of this foundation. I believe it is essentially right that foundations as a class
should have the framework of permanent safeguards against abuse
which the new law aims to provide. Our main task is to make the
new law work." To many of his peers it looked as though Bundy,
having brought down congressional wrath on all of the foundations
by his errors and insensitivity, was now being conciliatory if not
contrite.

But by 1972, after the new Tax Reform Act had been in operation for some two years and the Treasury had had opportunity to
draft detailed administrative regulations and interpretations, there
was basis for at least a preliminary appraisal of the more important
consequences of those portions of the legislation relating to foundations.

On the positive side, Representative Patman by his years of
effort—and despite the sneers and hostility of the foundations—
had clearly rendered a major national service by forcing correction
of a number of the worst of their financial abuses. He had obliged
them to increase their contributions to charity by hundreds of millions of dollars and subjected them to painful pressure to make
their investment portfolios more productive and in some cases to
begin the long overdue process of divestiture. He had forced them
to pay the costs of the federal government in maintaining surveillance over them. And he had forced them to report more fully to
the general public on their activities.

On the other hand, it was apparent even in 1969 that many elements of the Congress were more interested in crippling foundations than in correcting their abuses.*

In the general atmosphere of public suspicion which Patman's
attacks had created and with the help of a set of intricate and

---

* Regarding the odor of reaction and racism given off by the congressional
proceedings, the late Whitney M. Young Jr., executive director of the National
Urban League, remarked at the hearings of the Senate Finance Committee:
"There are features in the bill that are making the Black Community feel that
it is a hostile bill, a bill . . . with a purpose as much to intimidate as to legis-
late, a bill designed to discourage foundations who have belatedly found the
field of social reform to be one in which they might tenderly tread, a bill to
caution and warn them. Already there is evidence that just the introduction of

somewhat dubious distinctions developed by Treasury experts between "private" foundations and "operating" foundations, these antagonists found it easy to add a number of provisions to the legislation which have now clearly proven harmful to philanthropy: the surveillance tax was set at such a high level for example, that it is partly punitive in effect. The sharp reduction in tax inducements to donors to establish foundations combined with a sharp increase in inducements to these same individuals to make their gifts directly to universities, hospitals, churches, and other "operating" charitable institutions has now demonstrably had not only the effect of a "birth control" measure on the establishment of new foundations but has also resulted in the decision of a good number of living donors to close down existing foundations and henceforth make their charitable contributions directly to operating institutions.

Most damaging of all, the Congress—both by the tenor of its debates and by certain provisions of the 1969 Tax Reform Act— singled out for attack those few foundations in the United States that had been attempting to deal with such controversial problems as race relations, the urban crisis, and governmental inadequacies. Conversely, it had allowed the orthodox, conservative foundations —however inert—and the foundations that shelter themselves in the safe areas of science and medicine to get off scot-free.

For example, previous legislation prohibited foundations from devoting any "substantial" part of their outlays to "political or propagandistic activity." The 1969 tax law imposed a flat ban on any such difficult-to-define grants.

The paralyzing effect of the new provision on innovativeness by

---

the bill has caused some foundations to again become very cautious and turn toward those absolutely noncontroversial things they feel will remove them from any threat of punitive action.

"For years the White Community has been able to organize different ethnic groups and regional groups to use the resources of the private sector, through foundations, to address themselves to their problems as they see them. Only recently has the Black Community acquired the kind of sophistication and know-how to make it possible to organize and to make its request for resources to help itself, to meet its needs. To have at this point in the game suddenly to be told that the rules are changing seems to the Black people to be saying all over again 'the rules are changing only when you are about to be benefited.' "

even the most courageous of the large foundations has already been considerable. Their typically conservative boards have developed a new preoccupation with the possible reaction of Congress and the Internal Revenue Service to their grant decisions. This in turn has led to two common results: a greatly increased reliance on lawyers and legal advice in all program matters; and a tendency to restrict the latitude of discretion of typically more liberal staff members in dealing with grant proposals. In addition, because of the severe "expenditure responsibility" requirement of the new law, it is now considered extremely risky for a foundation to make a grant to other than a well-established institution. The lack of adequate accounting procedures, for example, on the part of a newly formed environmental group, or a ghetto welfare rights organization, can now virtually bar it from obtaining a foundation grant.

These seemingly small, procedural changes appear in combination to be having major consequences in diverting foundation funds from controversial but creative recipients to those of the most traditional and often backward-looking kind.

Even Congressman Patman himself by mid-1971 seemed to be aware that program restrictions on foundations contained in the 1969 Tax Act had gone too far: to continue to deserve their privileges and justify these costs, he declared, they must "develop innovative and forward looking programs as well as significant technical expertise." [12]

But however confused the proceedings and however debatable the significance of what Congress did, it nevertheless could be sensed that something at the very core of the American idea had been touched and tampered with and that somehow this curious creature, the private philanthropic foundation, was fatefully intertwined with the great issues of the nation's future. It could also be sensed from the statements both of its detractors and defenders that they were much firmer in their convictions than in their facts. This institution, so distinctively American, was still curiously unknown.

2.

The Apex of American Philanthropy

IN ITS STATISTICAL SILHOUETTE, American philanthropy displays an exaggerated case of megalocephaly. As with the structure of economic power generally and the distribution of corporate assets, the resources of the large and growing number of private foundations are heavily concentrated in the top few. In 1968, some 25,000 foundations of all sizes controlled assets estimated at $20.5 billion. More than half this total was owned by thirty-three general-purpose, grant-making foundations, each with assets of $100 million or more.

This group of big foundations symbolizes modern philanthropy in its most advanced form. They incarnate its possibilities and its limitations and epitomize the major issues of public policy which it presents. They are therefore the focus of the present study. Table 1 lists these foundations by rank order of size.

A number of major foundations are excluded from this list of thirty-three. The criteria for excluding them must be explained as well as the major qualifications regarding the financial data presented.

First, several special types of foundations with assets over $100 million have been excluded because they present basically different and more limited problems from the viewpoint of public policy than the "general purpose" foundations. These excluded categories include "operating" foundations, whose assets and income are used principally or entirely for the maintenance of their own laboratories, hospitals, and so on. Examples are the Battelle Institute, a major research facility based in Columbus, Ohio, with assets ap-

Table 1. The Big Foundations by Rank Order of Size

Name	Year Established	Headquarters	Assets (at market, 1968)
Ford Foundation	1936	New York	$3,661,000,000
Rockefeller Foundation	1913	New York	890,000,000
Duke Endowment	1924	New York	629,000,000
Lilly Endowment	1937	Indianapolis	579,000,000
Pew Memorial Trust	1948	Philadelphia	437,000,000
W. K. Kellogg Foundation	1930	Battle Creek	435,000,000
Charles Stewart Mott Foundation	1926	Flint	413,000,000
Nemours Foundation °	1936	Jacksonville	400,000,000
Kresge Foundation	1924	Detroit	353,000,000
John A. Hartford Foundation	1929	New York	352,000,000
Carnegie Corporation of New York	1911	New York	334,000,000
Alfred P. Sloan Foundation	1934	New York	329,000,000
Andrew W. Mellon Foundation †	1969	New York	273,000,000
Longwood Foundation	1937	Wilmington	226,000,000
Rockefeller Brothers Fund	1940	New York	222,000,000
Houston Endowment	1937	Houston	214,000,000
Moody Foundation	1942	Galveston	191,000,000
Danforth Foundation	1927	St. Louis	173,000,000
Emily & Ernest Woodruff Foundation	1938	Atlanta	167,000,000
Richard King Mellon Foundation	1947	Pittsburgh	162,000,000
Sarah Mellon Scaife Foundation	1941	Pittsburgh	145,000,000
Commonwealth Fund	1918	New York	142,000,000
Irvine Foundation	1937	San Francisco	119,000,000
Haas Community Fund ‡	1945	Philadelphia	115,000,000
Brown Foundation Inc.	1951	Houston	108,000,000
Edwin H. and Helen M. Land Foundation	1961	Cambridge	107,000,000
Henry J. Kaiser Family Foundation	1948	Oakland	106,000,000
Sid W. Richardson Foundation	1947	Fort Worth	106,000,000
Surdna Foundation	1917	Yonkers	105,000,000
Vincent Astor Foundation	1948	New York	103,000,000
Charles F. Kettering Foundation	1927	Dayton	103,000,000
Max C. Fleischmann Foundation	1952	Reno	102,000,000
A. G. Bush Foundation	1953	St. Paul	100,000,000

° See chapter 8 for explanation of relationship between the Alfred I. du Pont Estate, which owns the bulk of these assets, and the Nemours Foundation, the beneficiary of the estate.

† Created in 1969 out of merger of pre-existing Old Dominion Foundation and Avalon Foundation established in 1941 and 1940 respectively.

‡ Formerly the Phoebe Waterman Foundation.

proaching $250 million; the Howard Hughes Medical Center in Miami, Florida, with assets of more than $150 million; and the Carnegie Institution of Washington, D.C., with assets of nearly $125 million.

Also among those excluded are "corporate" foundations, which are created and directed by individual profit-making corporations, of which at least one, the Alcoa Foundation in Pittsburgh, has assets of $100 million; and "community" foundations, that is, those whose corpus is composed of gifts from a number of donors administered through a unified local staff—of which one, the Cleveland Foundation in Ohio, has combined assets in excess of $112 million.*

Second, the list does not include those foundations which were once among the top few in size but have now expired or largely exhausted their resources. Among them are the General Education Board, financed with Rockefeller funds and dissolved after sixty-two years of operation in 1964; the Rosenwald Fund which, in accordance with the donor's conviction that perpetual endowments were unhealthy, closed after thirty years in 1946 (see chapter 18 for a discussion of these foundations' grants to minorities); and the A. W. Mellon Educational and Charitable Trust, which used most of its resources for building the National Gallery of Art in Washington and now operates as a smaller foundation.

Finally, the list does not include major new foundations for which operating data are not yet available, such as the Robert Wood Johnson Foundation of New Brunswick, New Jersey, and the Edna McConnell Clark Foundation of New York. The Johnson Foundation, established in 1936, operated on a very limited basis until late 1971, when it received more than $1 billion in securities from the estate of the donor, a founder of Johnson and Johnson Company, manufacturers of surgical dressings, who died in January 1968. It is now, therefore, the second wealthiest foundation, led

* Also excluded is the huge Bernice P. Bishop Estate in Honolulu, created by a Hawaiian princess in the late nineteenth century. The estate owns more than 10 percent of the land area of the islands, with a value of more than $500 million. By a ruling of the Internal Revenue Service in 1969, it is no longer a foundation, having been reclassified as an educational institution on grounds that its principal activity is the operation of two schools for children of Hawaiian ancestry.

only by the Ford Foundation; its grants in the future as in the past will be concentrated in the field of medical care. The Clark Foundation was created in 1969 with a gift of $146 million in shares of Avon Products, Inc., the world's largest door-to-door cosmetics sales organization. Nor does the list attempt to anticipate the creation of major new foundations. H. L. Hunt, the reputed Texas billionaire, now in his eighties and with a political bias for the extreme Right, may be one upcoming donor; another may be J. Paul Getty, supposedly the world's richest man. Among other potential donors are Daniel K. Ludwig, the shipping magnate; the family of Thomas J. Watson of International Business Machines; the DeWitt Wallaces of *Reader's Digest;* and John Erik Jonsson of Texas Instruments.° About all that can be said with reasonable certainty is that there are more Americans today with assets in excess of $100 million than ever before, and that despite the new provisions of the 1969 Tax Reform Act, a fair proportion of these fortunes will eventually be transformed into new philanthropies.†

These qualifications underscore the fact that big philanthropy is a rapidly changing institution directly correlated to the scale and distribution of private wealth in American society. The picture of those in the top category of size in any year is but a snapshot of a moving and growing procession. For example, of the thirty-three largest foundations in 1968, only five were on a comparable list of the top twenty-five in 1937.‡

° *Fortune* magazine's periodic listing of "America's Centimillionaires" is probably the best available index to the major private fortunes and therefore to the sources from which major new foundations may arise.

† Obviously, by the cut-off figure for assets that has been chosen, the list excludes a considerable number of foundations whose resources approach, but as of 1968 did not reach, the $100 million level—such as the Robert A. Welch Foundation of Houston, El Pomar of Denver, the Henry F. Luce of New York, the Z. Smith Reynolds of Winston-Salem, the Charles Hayden of New York, and the William R. Kenan of New York, among others. The rate at which the distribution curve of individual foundation assets slopes off is suggested by the fact that there are some 250 foundations with resources over $10 million each, according to the reliable *Foundation Directory* for 1969, published by the Foundation Center in New York. According to an estimate of *Fortune* magazine the same year, some 7 percent of the 22,000 American foundations, or about 1,500, controlled 90 percent of all foundation assets.

‡ The fluidity of the situation is illustrated by comparing the top five in size in 1968 with the same group in 1969. Ford was first both years. But by 1969

Fixing an accurate value on the wealth of the big foundations is also difficult because the data are elusive. Market value will consistently be used in this study (wherever possible from federal tax return data) as a more realistic figure than book value. But market values change, and fluctuations in the stock market affect the assets of some foundations more than others. For example, in 1969–70, the holdings of the Lilly Endowment jumped $177 million; those of the Ford Foundation dropped by about a billion in the same period. The assets of several major foundations are in holdings that defy even approximate market valuation. The extensive real estate holdings of the Irvine Foundation, for instance, are worth somewhere between the $119 million listed here and $1 billion; until all the land is sold, if ever, no one can say for certain. Similarly, any market value for the oil rights of the Sid W. Richardson Foundation and the real estate of the Houston Endowment is impossible to establish with precision.°

Moreover, the assets *owned* by some of the listed foundations are not the total resources from which they draw their income. The Moody Foundation, in addition to its own property and stock holdings, has rights to a substantial portion of the income from the assets of the separate Libbie Shearn Moody Trust, which in 1968 totaled $157 million. The Surdna Foundation, in addition to its own holdings, has a 45 percent claim on the income of three associated family trusts with assets of nearly $500 million. The Kellogg Foundation has assets of its own of $47 million, but it is the income beneficiary of the W. K. Kellogg Foundation Trust, with assets of $388 million. (It normally reports its resources as the total of the two, namely $435 million in 1968.) The Nemours Foundation of Jacksonville, Florida, listed its own assets as $9 million in 1968,

---

Lilly had risen to second position from fourth, Rockefeller had dropped from second to third, Pew had risen to fourth from fifth, and Duke had dropped from third to fifth. Any ranking by size is obviously affected by the fact that the Ford Foundation is the consolidated philanthropy of Henry Ford and his son Edsel; the Rockefellers, however, have created a dozen or more separate foundations; Andrew Carnegie established five of substantial size and divided his gifts among them; and the prolific du Ponts have set up more than twenty.

° Following passage of the 1969 Tax Reform Act the Treasury has now ordered independent appraisals to be made of such foundation assets in order to determine the annual donations they must make to charity.

but at the time it had a 12 percent claim on the income of the Alfred I. du Pont Estate. Since the death of the donor's widow in 1970, it receives all of the income. For purposes of this study, therefore, the "assets" of the Nemours Foundation, to make them comparable with those reported for the Kellogg Foundation and others, have been given as $400 million, a most conservative estimate of the value of the estate.

Since foundations are not required to report the assets of private trusts on whose income they have legal claim, it is also possible that some seemingly small foundations have been omitted from the list of thirty-three which would be among the largest if such associated assets could be taken into account.

The Key Role of the Top Thirty-Three

But if such is the arbitrariness and the fluidity of the category of so-called big foundations, what justification can there be in a detailed study of them? The reasons are four—in addition to the sheer magnitude of their wealth and the fact that many of them are little known:

First, because they are general-purpose, grant-making institutions, they have an impact on a broad band of recipients— universities, hospitals, research centers, and welfare and cultural institutions of all kinds.

Second, these foundations, though similar in a number of fundamental respects, present considerable diversity. Established in different periods of time, they also derive from different regions of the country. They represent varied relationships with donors, donor families, and associated profit-making companies. They have diverse activities, grant-making techniques, and problems of asset management and they differ greatly in their concepts of philanthropic role and responsibility. As a group, therefore, they present all the major public policy issues raised by modern philanthropy.

Third, a range of alternatives is open to them in scope of interest and methods of operation not available to small foundations. They can employ specialized staff, enabling them to work in sophisticated fields such as advanced science and technology. Because of their resources, they can influence entire research fields or whole categories of institutions. They are free to take initiatives, innovate, and affect the practices not only of their private recipients but sometimes of governments as well. They therefore possess the highest potential for social benefit, as well as for social hazard, among all foundations.

Fourth, again because of their size, they are looked upon as the leaders in their fields. They tend to be linked with donor families and associated corporations which are among the dominant forces in the American economic system. In turn, because of the preponderant influence of business leadership in American life, these foundations are at, or near, the center of gravity of the American Establishment. By themselves and also by their position in an intricate web of powerful men and institutions, they have a significance even larger than their huge resources might suggest.

However, to grasp the nature of these institutions, it is not enough to categorize and quantify. They are not indistinguishable units. Each is a living organism unique in its origins and personality, with its own pattern of evolution shaped by its own internal forces and its particular external setting. Thus, to be examined meaningfully, each must be seen in the round. Its qualities and defects must be understood in relation to one another, and in relation to its own life history and environment. As a basis, therefore, for reaching broader conclusions about the problems and prospects of American philanthropy, a set of individual portraits of the big foundations will be drawn in succeeding chapters.

Part Two

A GALLERY OF PORTRAITS

3.

Carnegie: Emergence from Elitism

ANDREW CARNEGIE was the most extraordinary— certainly the most Napoleonic—of the great capitalists who dominated the baroque era of American industrial expansion. And it was largely through his ideas and example that American philanthropy got off to such a bold and brilliant start at the beginning of the twentieth century. He devoted the last thirty years of his life to giving away the fortune he had accumulated in the first fifty. The Carnegie Corporation of New York, founded in 1911, is the largest of the group of important philanthropies he launched. With assets of $334 million in 1968, it ranked eleventh in size among the largest foundations. For its first forty years it was by turn profligate, precious, and meandering. But in the past twenty years, under strong leadership, it has made important contributions to the advancement of higher education; and more recently, turning from its traditional elitism, Carnegie has begun for the first time to display a courageous social concern. It is today probably the best of the large foundations in terms of its independence, the caliber of its professional staff, and the craftsmanship and creativity of its grants.

Andrew Carnegie's impoverished family had emigrated from Scotland to the United States before the Civil War. By the time he was twenty-five, he had progressed from an untutored bobbin boy in a cotton factory to a self-educated and successful railway superintendent. His first small investment, with money obtained by mortgaging the family home, had already made him moderately rich; and at the age of thirty-three he controlled several large companies. But business and money-making were not the only con-

cerns of this complex man. At that early point, according to a note
found among his papers after his death, he had written the following admonition to himself: "Beyond this, never earn—make no effort to increase fortune, but spend surplus each year for benevolent
purposes." [1]

Carnegie might have followed this philanthropic plan or he
might have gone back to Britain to fulfill an old literary ambition
by becoming a magazine editor had he not been introduced in
1872 to Henry Bessemer and his method to mass-produce cheap
steel. Sensing its commercial possibilities, Carnegie returned to
Pittsburgh to organize the company that was to make him a ty-
coon. In the closing quarter of the nineteenth century, by a series
of combinations and mergers, he made his coal-and-steel complex
so powerful that it had no effective competition. The climax of his
business career came after 1900 with his challenge, based on his in-
vulnerable position in steel-making, to the entire banking and industrial empire of J. P. Morgan. In the end, Morgan was forced to
buy out Carnegie virtually on the latter's terms. Carnegie was paid
$492 million for his companies, of which he personally received
more than $225 million in the form of 5 percent gold bonds of the
United States Steel Corporation.

Thereafter, this 5-foot-2-inch dynamo threw his prodigious energies into philanthropy, which proved to be a natural vehicle for
the ambitions he had long harbored to be a force not only in business but in the realms of intellect and social reform as well. Even
in the early phase of his business career he had expended great effort in making the acquaintance of leading artists, scientists, and
philosophers; and by his later years the most illustrious British and
American intellectuals were regular guests at his dinner table.

Highly articulate, he kept extensive diaries throughout his life.
At first he had them privately printed for his friends, but when
Charles Scribner discovered his talents as a writer, he encouraged
him to write for commercial publication. His writings on philanthropy began in 1889 with the publication in the *North American
Review* of "The Gospel of Wealth." In this treatise Carnegie spoke
of the "disgrace" of dying rich and argued that the chief problem
of his era was the proper administration of wealth so that "the ties

of brotherhood may still bind the rich and poor in harmonious relationships."

Thereafter, he righteously pursued his task as moral guide to the rich on all fronts. With equal fervor, he gave his unsolicited advice in a stream of letters to American presidents and other world leaders. Nor was he deterred in his lecturing of others by the occasional inconsistency between his private conduct and his public declarations. An eminently draftable bachelor, he had bought his way out of service in the Civil War; and on his frequent visits to Britain he made vociferously radical speeches, but upon his return to the scene of his business operations in the United States, his rhetoric regularly cooled. During the bloody Homestead strike of 1892, the self-styled "friend of the workingman" remained safely in England and sent back messages of encouragement to Henry Frick, his antilabor partner in Pittsburgh.

Carnegie's saving grace was that he did not moralize grimly. He was an enthusiastic, charming, open man; and if he now seems to have been a somewhat dotty millionaire, he was a refreshingly ebullient one. He also seriously sought to live up to his philanthropic preachings, as shown by the dazzling list of his major gifts:

—He supplied funds for building and equipping public libraries in the United States and other English-speaking countries on the condition that the citizens of each community provide the site and pay the maintenance costs. Over a twenty-year period his personal gifts for this purpose totaled $43 million and led to the construction of more than 2,000 local libraries, firmly implanting the idea of community responsibility for free library service.

—In 1896 he created the Carnegie Institute of Pittsburgh as a civic gallery and museum, and in 1900 founded the Carnegie Institute of Technology (now Carnegie-Mellon University), which became one of the nation's finest technological institutions. The original grants totaled over $12 million.

—In 1901 he created the Carnegie Trust for the Universities of Scotland with a grant of $10 million.

—In 1902 he established the Carnegie Institution of Washington, D.C., with an initial grant of $10 million (later augmented by $12 million) to encourage basic research in scientific fields.

—In 1904 he created the Carnegie Hero Fund, with a grant of $5 million, to reward the heroic deeds of civilians.

—In 1905 he established the Carnegie Foundation for the Advancement of Teaching with an original gift of $10 million to provide retirement pensions for college professors and to conduct studies on the problems of American education. One outgrowth of the foundation's work was the establishment of the Teachers Insurance and Annuity Association in 1918, which has been invaluable to American higher education by providing teachers with greater financial security. The research studies of the foundation, beginning with the famous Flexner report on medical education in the United States in 1906, have also had great influence.*

—In 1910, he founded the Carnegie Endowment for International Peace, with a grant of $10 million.

In addition, he made a large number of other sizable benefactions—a trust for the benefit of his Scottish birthplace, the town of Dunfermline; gifts to various universities and Negro colleges; and even donations to provide churches with pipe organs. (A nonreligious man, Carnegie thought that the only good part of a church service was the music.) To dissuade Princeton students from playing football, he gave the university a lake for rowing. Yet, by 1910, after more than a decade of active giving, his personal fortune still totaled more than $150 million. His thought then was to provide in his will for the creation of a great foundation. But Elihu Root, his lawyer and close friend, advised him to organize a charitable trust during his lifetime, which he did. The Carnegie Corporation was created in 1911, and Carnegie transferred to it the

---

* The foundation and the Carnegie Corporation over the years have worked in close collaboration. Although they now share the same offices and corporate officers, they remain separate corporate entities with separate boards of trustees.

bulk of his wealth, reserving to himself the right to administer it as long as he lived. The purpose of the trust, according to its articles of incorporation, was "the advancement and diffusion of knowledge and understanding" among the people of the United States and the British dominions and colonies. The trustees were restricted to the disposal of its income and were required to keep its capital intact.

In principle, Carnegie believed in the delegation of authority to foundation trustees and recognized the dangers of donor domination. But in the closing years of his life and in the case of his own greatest philanthropic endowment, he behaved in the dictatorial fashion of most elderly philanthropists. Ignoring all advice, he set up a board consisting of men he knew would be receptive to his wishes, including the heads of the five philanthropic institutions bearing his name, as well as his financial and personal secretaries.°

For eight years, until his death in 1919, Andrew Carnegie was the corporation's president. The board usually met once a year to ratify the decisions which he, with the assistance of his two secretaries and sometimes the advice of his counsel, had already taken. Substantial gifts were made to carry on Carnegie's interest in public libraries and church organs and for medical education, but most of its grants went to other Carnegie institutions. Carnegie's impulse to make large donations at times exceeded the corporation's available funds and he was periodically irked by the restriction he had imposed on any invasion of its capital. On one occasion, after promising a multimillion-dollar gift to set up a British foundation, he had to make good his commitment from his personal funds, which by that time had been reduced to relatively moderate dimensions. The episode made him somewhat more cautious thereafter.[2]

° Dr. Henry Pritchett, then president of the Carnegie Foundation for the Advancement of Teaching and former head of the Massachusetts Institute of Technology, argued with Carnegie that the institutional trustees under such an arrangement would be put in a contradictory position because they would be both distributors and beneficiaries of the funds. He also pointed out that they could completely control the board of the corporation should they decide to combine. But Carnegie kept to his intention and the institutional trustees were in the majority.

Following Carnegie's death, the corporation was left with little institutional capability as well as heavy incumbrances on its future income. Its staff consisted of two of Carnegie's business associates (who had been made treasurer and secretary of the corporation, respectively, as well as trustees for life) and the board was dominated by built-in recipients. To make a difficult situation worse, Dr. James R. Angell, an educator from the University of Michigan with no experience in philanthropy, was named president. He served for fifteen months, from July 1, 1920 to October 1, 1921. During his brief tenure, a total of nearly $28 million was appropriated without benefit of long-range planning or serious consideration of the implications of such a spending spree for the foundation's future. Predictably, most of the money went to institutions represented on the corporation's board.

Upon Angell's retirement, the corporation was administered for the next two years by Henry S. Pritchett. But while the search was on for a full-time president, the trustees gave out an additional $10 million for a variety of less than imperative purposes. The end of the corporation's interval of profligacy came with two important steps taken on December 22, 1922. The trustees amended its charter to create seven additional places on the board to be filled by independent trustees elected for five-year terms, thereby reducing the institutional trustees to a minority; and Frederick P. Keppel was named president effective October 1, 1923. Keppel remained on the job for the next nineteen years.

He ran the corporation largely as a one-man show, distrusting a corps of salaried specialists. No matter how high-minded they might be, he thought they tended "to imprison any institution they served within walls of their own creation." The small staff he eventually assembled served him only as helpers. Few letters, regardless of who prepared them, were signed by anyone but him, and he saw all important visitors.

One of those who served him for many years, John M. Russell, observed:

A large and distinguished foundation can easily give the impression of being cold and unfriendly to a person seeking a grant. Elaborate offices with many doors—all closed—and a series of receptionists and secretaries barring the way can discourage the hardiest university president. Some foundations deliberately adopt this austere device as a means of self-protection, but F.P.K. believed in hanging out the latch-string and making the customer feel welcome. Without question, as the customers still testify, F.P.K.'s office was the most informal and friendly in the business. . . .

F.P.K. was one of the most interesting and lovable men with whom I was ever associated. . . . I believe he will be remembered as the man who humanized Columbia College; who humanized the War Department in World War I; who humanized the administration of foundations.

Keppel was also an essayist of graceful and engaging style. In his annual reports, he made it a practice not only to describe the corporation's grants and activities but also to discourse on general educational and other problems, including those of philanthropy. He was among the first to see the modern foundation as a distinctively American institution and to try to define its responsibilities, one of which he felt was public reporting. Many of his phrases have now entered the standard vocabulary of philanthropy and a number of his ideas have become part of its conventional wisdom. Yet intellectually his ideas were thin, and they were profoundly conservative in their social outlook and in their conception of a foundation's proper role.

In any appraisal of Keppel's contribution to the Carnegie Corporation's program, the severe financial restrictions under which he had to operate must be kept in mind. When he took over in 1922, the corporation's obligations against future income (then about $6 million a year) totaled more than $40 million. The liquidation of those obligations was to consume roughly half of its income during most of Keppel's tenure. To compound its financial difficulties, the corporation had to spend several millions of dollars which it had not anticipated to bail out the Carnegie Foundation, which had vastly underestimated the growth of the nation's education apparatus in committing itself to free pensions for all college and university teachers. Accordingly, a policy of strict austerity had to be followed by which new programs could consist only of modest grants for experimentation and demonstration.

With the uncommitted funds at his disposal Keppel led the corporation into two new fields—adult education and the fine arts.
When he proposed them in 1925, after two years of preparatory
study, they broke new philanthropic ground. The adult education
program sponsored several notable projects for the education of
immigrants, blacks, and prison inmates. It also fostered new methods of teaching, particularly the use of radio. The arts program emphasized education rather than aid to creative artists. Several millions were spent to develop courses in art history and appreciation
at colleges and universities and to train college art teachers and
museum personnel.

These programs were unusual for their time, and Keppel considered them to have had great impact. In the annual report of
1931 he wrote, "Adult Education has become permanently a part
of our educational fabric." In 1938, when the corporation decided
to phase out the arts program, he gave this evaluation: "In sharp
contrast to the situation only a few years ago, the place of the arts
in our secondary schools and colleges need no longer be regarded
as an object of foundation solicitude. Certainly there seems little
need here for further direct financial stimulation." [3]

All in all, it now appears in retrospect that the main contributions of Keppel, a much revered figure, were more stylistic than
substantive. He provided philanthropy with a well-modulated public voice and he gave the Carnegie Corporation itself a liveliness of
manner and sensitive human touch in its operations. But most of
the $185 million that the corporation had distributed by 1941, the
year before Keppel's retirement, had gone to sustain Carnegie programs and institutions which the donor had created before Keppel's arrival; and the arts and adult education programs which
aroused his greatest enthusiasm represented hardly more than interesting initial explorations of new philanthropic territory, not
major achievements.

Perhaps one of Keppel's shortcomings was his indiscriminate enthusiasm for trying something new. As trustee Henry James said:

Keppel's tendency to spread himself wide and thin was trying to some of
his trustees. It had the consequence that each meeting of the Board or of

the Executive Committee had to vote upon too many proposals and too many kinds of proposals. To be sure, many votes called for no discussion whatever, but a trustee sometimes had the feeling that he was sharing in the conduct of a retail business involving more particular transactions than he could classify or understand.

The malaise which a trustee then experienced was increased by Keppel's inability to rationalize and formulate his policies. This was, I think, his chief limitation.[4]

His greatest weakness, however, was the narrowness of his social outlook. The 1920s and '30s when he headed the corporation were marked by severe strain and friction in American life, caused by sweeping changes in mores and values and the accelerated pace of an increasingly urbanized, mobile society. By the early 1930s the tensions were exacerbated by a worldwide depression. Keppel's tenure at Carnegie coincided with the Calvin Coolidge and Herbert Hoover years, the depression, and the early days of the New Deal; when he retired World War II was raging in Europe. Yet, his annual reports contain hardly a hint of the great issues and problems of the times. In the isolated environment of the corporation, training for librarians, adult education conferences, and the distribution of art teaching sets were its preoccupations.

Keppel's long career with the corporation ended on a curious note. Perhaps the single most discussed research project sponsored during his regime was *An American Dilemma,* the now classic study of the American Negro directed by the Swedish social scientist Gunnar Myrdal. It had been commissioned in 1938, partly because of the obvious importance of the problem and also, as the corporation announced, to help it in its future program development. Completion of the study was delayed by the outbreak of war, so it was not until 1942, after his retirement, that Keppel wrote his foreword to the two-volume study. In it he cautiously justified the involvement of a foundation with contemporary social issues. "Provided the foundation limits itself to its proper function, namely, to make the facts available and then let them speak for themselves, and does not undertake to instruct the public as to what to do about them, studies of this kind provide a wholly proper and, experience has shown, sometimes a highly important use of their funds."

The next year Keppel died, and his intention, or hope, that the Myrdal study might lead to further research or other projects related to the Negro was left unfulfilled. His successor, Dr. Walter A. Jessup, who was also president of the Carnegie Foundation for the Advancement of Teaching, hastened to point out in the corporation's report for 1944 that it had never had and did not intend to have special programs in behalf of the Negro. Apart from three grants made several years later and totaling $230,000 to the University of Louisville for training Southern police in race relations, almost no mention was ever made thereafter of the Myrdal study, despite its national acclaim and impact. There have been many examples of a foundation's turning its back on its failures; the Carnegie Corporation in the Myrdal study turned its back on a triumph.

In the five-year period 1942–47, the corporation went through a period of reorganization. Jessup died after only two and one-half years in office, much of which had been devoted to a careful review of the corporation's grants and investment policies over thirty years. Most of the new grants made were of a short-term nature to meet emergency wartime needs.

Jessup was succeeded in 1945 by Devereaux Josephs, an investment banker who had been active in the financial management of the several Carnegie philanthropies. He had also served as president of the Teachers Insurance and Annuity Association from 1943 until his appointment. During his four-year period as president he reassembled the corporation's staff after wartime service, enlarged it, and introduced a number of organizational and operational improvements. One of the most important of these took place in January 1946, when the corporation's constitution was modified to provide that when the heads of the other five major U.S. Carnegie trusts retired from the board, they would be replaced by independent trustees elected for five-year terms. Since that time the only *ex officio* member of the board has been the president of the corporation itself.

Josephs' contribution to program development, however, was less consequential. His view in 1946 of the foundation's purposes was strongly colored by a mood of postwar patriotism. "This is an American foundation, most of whose resources are dedicated to the service of the American people. It is operated to promote the American way of life. . . . This corporation should not hesitate to provide funds to those who can show better ways to democracy, to the freedoms of thought, race, religion, and enterprise." In 1947, in a less jingoistic formulation, he stated the corporation's two major program interests to be "an increase of the nation's understanding of its international responsibilities and an increase in the supply of knowledge and training in the practice of government." However, the most important program action taken during his tenure was to establish the Educational Testing Service, whose initial purpose was to help American universities to deal with an avalanche of applications from returning servicemen.

Josephs was succeeded in 1949 by Charles Dollard, who presided for an additional six-year period of low productivity. By this time the corporation's program for libraries had diminished, as had the adult education and the fine arts programs. Dollard, who was a social scientist, gave research projects in that field greater emphasis, but without striking success. The most important grants during his years were for the creation of several university centers for foreign studies, such as the Russian research center at Harvard University. Dollard's period of uninspired leadership came to an end as the postwar crisis in American higher education was just beginning to erupt.

In late 1954 Dollard, seriously ill, relinquished his responsibilities, and in 1955 John W. Gardner, then vice-president, was elected his successor. His first annual report was a tour de force. In a memorable essay, "A Time for Decision in Higher Education," he described the flood of students then beginning to inundate American colleges and universities, analyzed the consequences, and forecast the army of teachers required to cope with them. He examined the issue of who should be encouraged to go to college and the kind of education that should be provided them; and he pointed out the perils of mass education. He concluded with a warning of bankruptcy if the financial needs of educational institutions continued to be neglected.

With Gardner, the second strong president in the history of the corporation had indubitably arrived. His cause would be that of "excellence" in American higher education. He argued that education had always been the unifying theme of the corporation's program and that a shift of emphasis from the peripheral educational structure—such as library development and adult education —to a concern with the formal structure itself was both natural and necessary. Stressing the need to provide more and better information on the basis of which educational leaders could make their decisions, he led the corporation to support educational research at a number of university centers.

The problems of financing universities and of improving their administration and curricula subsequently became major objectives. But gradually the corporation's interest began to extend to the problems of secondary and primary schools. Gardner's particular personal concern throughout was the need to head off "galloping mediocrity" as educational institutions grew in size and to ensure the maintenance of high academic standards. His strategy was comprehensive and with the able assistance of James A. Perkins, who later became president of Cornell University, it was also well executed.

In personality, Gardner was almost the opposite of Keppel, whose warmth and openness had won him countless friends. Gardner was a loner and a perfectionist. Even his colleagues on the staff and the board never felt close to him. Disciplined and ambitious, he studied hard to master the intricacies of higher education and to become its authority among foundation presidents; and having achieved that, he prepared himself to play a still larger national role. He consulted often with men such as Abraham Flexner, who gave him lessons in philanthropic statesmanship, especially in the art of scanning wide horizons and avoiding being mired in daily routine.[5]

The growth of Gardner's own thinking is reflected in his annual reports. Until 1960 his essays dealt primarily with the major issues

of education. But in 1961 he reviewed fifty years of the corporation's work and drew some broad conclusions about philanthropy
in general and about American society and institutions. In 1962 he
examined the problem of decay and self-renewal in men, institutions, and societies. In 1963, returning to his original field of academic interest, he discussed new research developments regarding
learning and thought processes, and in 1964, his last active year as
president, the corporation's annual report featured his essay on
American pluralism and philanthropy, "Private Initiative for the
Public Good."

In the same report, under a subtitle "Opportunity for All," he
noted: "The most important task facing American education today
is to remove the remaining barriers to educational opportunity,
whether the barriers are due to race prejudice, urban slum conditions, economically depressed rural life, or just plain bad education."

That sentence—and the fact that the corporation that year devoted roughly one-quarter of its grants to educational projects for
the poor—reveals Gardner's slow but finally unmistakable shift
from preoccupation with elitist institutions of higher education to
an awareness of the urgent problems of race and poverty in American life.*

In the postwar years, the Carnegie Corporation had brought in a
number of competent young program officers who felt that its educational programs, however much admired, were parochial and es-
capist in the face of the enormous social crisis then beginning to
confront the nation. After the Supreme Court's decision in the
Brown case in 1954, these staff members subjected Gardner to increasing pressure in favor of direct concern with the black commu-

---

* Gardner has described his own evolution in these words: "I started out as
the most academic of academics—the kind of faculty member who never even
bothers to attend faculty meetings. . . . I spent nineteen years in foundation
work, in the conviction that if you understood a problem well enough and
could communicate that understanding, somehow the world would be better. I
believed in education in the broadest, deepest sense. Only when I went to
H.E.W. and then the Urban Coalition Action Council did I come to understand how much could be accomplished by activist groups." (*The New Yorker*,
February 27, 1971, p. 31)

nity, especially in education. But year after year he resisted, holding to the general principle that excellence had to be the criterion and that blue-ribbon institutions such as Harvard and Yale rather than the weak and inferior colleges catering to blacks and other underprivileged groups should receive the corporation's grants.

The fact that Dr. James B. Conant, a former Harvard president, also strongly recommended attention to the problems of "the slums and the suburbs" in his 1961 study financed by the Carnegie Corporation quite possibly helped alter Gardner's views. In any event, by 1965, when Gardner left to join President Johnson's cabinet, he had become the eloquent liberal voice of the Establishment—a role he was to enlarge and develop in his subsequent activities in government and civic affairs.

Gardner was succeeded by Alan Pifer, who had been on the foundation's staff since 1953 in charge of international activities, and whose credentials—Groton, Harvard, and Cambridge—seemed even more elegant than those of his predecessor. But Pifer, whose origins run not to Back Bay but to the impoverished sand flats of Indiana, is a man of markedly different social instincts. Having both the strength of intellect and much of the articulateness of Gardner, plus an activist view of philanthropy's role in dealing with major social issues, Pifer has carried the corporation into its third major period of growth.

Although Pifer was not formally elected president of the corporation until May 1969, he became acting president in 1965 when Gardner took leave to go to Washington. It quickly became apparent that his foresight and sense of timing were not inferior to those qualities in his predecessor.*

* In November 1965, the corporation helped to bring into being the Education Commission of the States and a Commission on Educational Television. In both instances the distinction of the members of the panels, the political skill with which they had been assembled, and the quality of their analyses and recommendations led to important practical results. The former did much to spur action and reforms on a number of urgent educational problems by state governments. The latter led directly to the proposal by President Johnson—and the subsequent creation by Congress—of the Corporation for Public Broadcasting. In January 1967, the corporation made a $1 million grant to the Carnegie Foundation for the Advancement of Teaching to create a new commission to study the problems of higher education. Headed by Clark Kerr,

Pifer's essay in 1968, "Foundations at the Service of the Public,"
is probably the most searching contemporary analysis of the problems and potentialities of American philanthropy. His main conclusion was that foundations should anticipate the strains of social
change and facilitate the adaptation of major institutions to such
change. The corporation's 1968 grant list shows that it tried to live
up to his rhetoric. It gave support to two experimental high
schools in Harlem and Chicago to assist dropouts; it helped
finance community law offices to assist ghetto residents in securing
their legal rights in landlord-tenant disputes, consumer frauds, and
welfare complaints; it supported a training program at the University of Colorado for a new kind of nonphysician medical practi-
tioner to help the American medical system adapt to the needs of
the urban and rural poor; it financed, with the collaboration of the
Ford Foundation, the Children's Television Workshop to produce
new kinds of programs to stimulate the educational and cultural
growth of young viewers, particularly poor children. *Sesame Street,*
the first of the workshop's programs, has since won almost unanimous praise from both television critics and educators.

Under the leadership of Gardner the Carnegie Corporation became a highly professionalized operation. Under Pifer it has now
also become responsive to contemporary social concerns. A "medium-sized" large foundation, it has skillfully defined a set of programs for itself that fall within its financial and other capabilities
and at the same time are of national benefit. Faithful to both Andrew Carnegie and Keppel, it has a less bureaucratic and more
personal approach than many foundations. It has acutely sensed
the possibilities of spurring public action on major national problems through study projects and public commissions. In organizing
these projects it has consistently shown tactical skill and good timing, as well as the ability to attract men of extraordinary competence, from Myrdal in the 1930s to Conant and Kerr in the 1960s.

At the same time it is only fair—particularly since the
corporation has now defined one of its major objectives as facilitat-

the former chancellor of the University of California, the commission has now
issued a series of reports that have had important influence on the thinking of
both university and government policy-makers.

ing the process of institutional change—to point out that until recently Carnegie was itself an example of sluggishness in response
to changing social requirements. In its educational programs it did
not recognize the problem of racial segregation in the nation's
schools until nearly a decade after the federal government began
actively to address itself to it. And it was not until 1968, when the
related problems of urban decay, poverty, and racial tension had
reached explosive proportions, that it was prepared to go beyond
piecemeal grants and formally approve a general program in this
field. Nor was there until recently a black on the corporation's
board or staff.

To what extent the elitism of the corporation's program in the
past has been related to the nature and composition of its board is
problematical. The Carnegie trustees are now an independent
group, free of conflicting interests. But they have been drawn almost exclusively from the ranks of wealthy corporate executives,
financiers, and lawyers in the New York area. To their credit, they
have chosen good men as presidents, particularly in recent years.
They have also given them wide latitude and have backed them
fully in controversies. It might even be argued that as the corporation now moves into more controversial areas a board of powerful
conservatives can be increasingly useful as a shield against political attack. Yet it seems more likely that the board itself will come
to recognize that the soundness of the corporation's new programs,
as well as its "defense" in terms of public support and acceptance,
will require greater diversity among its membership.

Probably the most important quality the Carnegie Corporation
has displayed for more than half a century is its capacity, despite a
few brief downward jiggles in the curve, for sustained growth, or
as John Gardner says, for "self-renewal." In setting up his corporation on a perpetual basis, Andrew Carnegie wrote in 1911 that he
anticipated "as in all human institutions, there will be fruitful seasons and slack seasons. But as long as it exists there will come,
from time to time, men into its control and management who will
have vision and energy and wisdom, and the perpetual foundation
will have a new birth of usefulness and service." His corporation
stands today as a monument to his prescience.

4.

The Formidable Rockefeller Fleet

FROM THE GENEROSITY of four successive generations of Rockefellers a fleet of foundations has been launched: some of them have now disappeared; others have been consolidated into successor institutions; and over the decades new ones have repeatedly been created. At present, the two largest are the Rockefeller Foundation, incorporated in 1913, and the Rockefeller Brothers Fund, established in 1940.*

In the early years of the century, the Rockefeller philanthropies dramatically revealed the potentialities of the modern foundation. Their achievements in those days are still looked upon as American philanthropy's Golden Age. But since then the record of the various Rockefeller foundations has been uneven. Their characteristic strength has been in the sciences and medicine; their characteristic weakness has been a hesitancy and conservatism in dealing with social problems. The Rockefeller Foundation today symbolizes both qualities: it continues to be a powerful and productive force in the advancement of science, but in dealing with other kinds of issues it displays the rigidity and pompousness of a *grande dame.*

---

* The other significant units are the Rockefeller Family Fund, established by the "cousins," the great-grandchildren of John D. Rockefeller Sr., whose primary field of interest is race relations and urban affairs; the Sealantic Fund, now being phased out of existence, whose primary interest has been Protestant theological education and nursing education; the JDR 3d Fund, concerned primarily with Asian culture and Asian-American cultural relations; the Martha Baird Rockefeller Fund for Music; and Jackson Hole Preserve, Inc. Rockefeller University, formerly the Rockefeller Institute, is a major operating nonprofit institution supported by Rockefeller money.

The several existing Rockefeller foundations are legally independent entities, but they often collaborate with one another and their
programs have been developed so as to avoid duplication. Because
they form an intercommunicating whole, the performance of any
one cannot be appraised fairly without taking into account the activities of the others.

The founder of the family's great wealth and philanthropic record was John D. Rockefeller Sr. (1839–1937), who, depending on
one's historian, was either the greatest of the nineteenth-century
entrepreneurs or the most notorious of the great robber barons. Beginning in the late 1870s and for forty years thereafter, his name
was associated with greed, rapacity, cruelty, hypocrisy, and corruption. Attorneys-general of a half-dozen states clamored for his
imprisonment. In her "History of the Standard Oil Company" series in *McClure's* magazine in 1902, Ida Tarbell saw him as the supreme villain of his age, the symbol of all that was wrong with the
process by which America became industrialized. But some recent
historians have come to feel that while the Rockefeller record was
certainly not blameless, his oil fortune was perhaps the least
tainted of the great fortunes of the day and that the constructive
innovations he and his colleagues brought to large-scale corporate
management and organization have gone largely unrecognized.[1]

However contradictory evaluations of Rockefeller as a businessman may be, the scale and effectiveness of his philanthropy is
hardly open to question. A man of strict religious upbringing, from
his youth he gave a portion of his income every month to charity.
Once his riches began to accumulate, his gifts increased propor-
tionately. During the 1870s and 1880s Rockefeller gave to many
small causes, most of them related to his church interests. But it
was haphazard giving through established institutions. In 1892 he
hired Frederick T. Gates, a former Baptist minister, as his adviser
in philanthropic matters. Over the next twenty years Gates, a man
of unusual energy and vision, formulated a policy based on "the
principles of scientific giving" by which "retail" charity was abandoned for institutionalized "wholesale" philanthropy. Their first
great joint undertaking was the creation of the University of Chicago which, by the injection of a total of $35 million, was trans-

formed from a small, third-rate institution under Baptist auspices into one of the nation's great universities.°

By 1896 Rockefeller had given up active management of the Standard Oil Company to devote more of his time and energy to philanthropic matters. In 1897 his only son, John D. Rockefeller Jr., was graduated from Brown University and became his general assistant. The talents of father and son, in combination with the fervor and genius of Gates, resulted in a very productive philanthropic team. Gates and young Rockefeller explored new ideas and picked organizations and individuals to carry them out. The older Rockefeller retained final decision on all matters, including the amount of money to be provided, but he relied heavily on the recommendations of his two collaborators.

The first wholly new enterprise they launched was the Rockefeller Institute for Medical Research in 1901; the second was the General Education Board in 1903; the third was the Rockefeller Sanitary Commission, set up in 1909 to eradicate hookworm in the Southern states. All these enterprises provided the basis of experience on which Rockefeller's greatest venture in the field of philanthropy—the Rockefeller Foundation—was later built. Some notable successes, particularly of the Sanitary Commission, were achieved and several men of exceptional ability were recruited into the Rockefeller philanthropies. They included Simon Flexner of the medical school at Johns Hopkins University, who became the first head of the Rockefeller Institute; Wallace Buttrick, another Baptist minister, who became the first executive head of the General Education Board; and Wickliffe Rose, a former professor of philosophy, who became the first head of the Sanitary Commission. In his methodical and eminently practical way, Rockefeller was marshaling not only the organizational techniques but the invaluable human resources necessary for the next and climactic phase of his philanthropy.

° Dr. William Rainey Harper, its head, introduced a novel approach in fund-raising by requiring Rockefeller, whenever he visited the latter's office, to kneel down on the floor with him to pray for divine guidance in their conversation. Then, after they had regained their chairs, Harper would make his case for more money.

The Rockefeller Foundation

In 1905 Gates wrote a letter to Rockefeller pointing out that his immense fortune was growing far faster than his charitable outlays, and advised him of the dangers this would eventually pose for him and his family. He proposed a series of "great corporate philanthropies" to pursue goals such as the advancement of scientific agriculture, the development of the fine arts and the refinement of taste, and the encouragement of useful citizenship and civic virtue. In the years thereafter Rockefeller deliberated repeatedly with Gates and his son about whether to found one major trust or several, what the scope of the grants program should be, and where the men could be found to administer the work. Finally, on July 29, 1909, he earmarked $50 million worth of shares in the Standard Oil Company of New Jersey for a trust to be known as the Rockefeller Foundation. Its purposes were stated in very broad terms: "To promote the well-being and to advance the civilization of the peoples of the United States and its territories and possessions and of foreign lands in the acquisition and dissemination of knowledge, in the prevention and relief of suffering, and in the promotion of any and all of the elements of human progress."

At the same time, in a singularly ill-timed decision, he directed the trustees to apply to the Congress of the United States or to an appropriate state legislature for a corporate charter. Not until it was obtained would the foundation officially come into being and the funds be transferred. In March 1910 a bill was introduced in the United States Senate to charter the Rockefeller Foundation. The result was three years of uproar. From one point of view it is astonishing that such a storm of protest should have arisen. Rockefeller need not have gone to *any* legislative body for a charter; he could have established his foundation with a simple deed of trust. But he seemed to be seeking public approval of his transfer of private wealth to public purposes, even if the cost should be a degree of government control. The Senate bill provided that the foundation would report annually to the secretary of the interior on its operations. The charter would also be "subject to alteration, amendment, or repeal at the pleasure of the Congress."

At the Senate hearings on the bill, his attorney stated that Rockefeller "was perfectly content to leave this great foundation in the hands of Congress" and that "if at any time in the future this fund should get in the hands of men who might seek to use it for improper purposes, [Congress could] exert its authority and bring this fund back again to the use for which it was intended." Another Rockefeller spokesman reported to the House of Representatives that it was Rockefeller's intent "to make this munificent gift directly to the whole American people, and for ever subject to the control of their elected representatives."

At subsequent stages in the congressional debate Rockefeller accepted additional proposed restrictions: that the foundation's total assets would never exceed $100 million; that there would be no accumulation of income; that Congress might direct the dissolution of the foundation after a hundred years; that not more than one-tenth of its assets would be invested in the securities of any one corporation; and—perhaps the most extraordinary concession of all—that the election of new trustees would be subject to disapproval within sixty days by a majority of the following persons: the president of the United States, the chief justice of the Supreme Court, the president of the Senate, the speaker of the House of Representatives, and the presidents of Harvard, Yale, Columbia, Johns Hopkins, and Chicago universities.

But despite these concessions, Congress and the William Howard Taft administration viewed Rockefeller's proposal as "an indefinite scheme for perpetuating vast wealth." Such mistrust is comprehensible only in terms of the political atmosphere of the time, which had been greatly inflamed by other events involving Rockefeller and his companies. Two years before, Judge Kenesaw Mountain Landis had imposed a $29.2 million fine on the Standard Oil Company of Indiana for monopolistic activities and the corruption of public officials. The company's attorneys had filed their appeal to the Supreme Court just five days after the bill to create the Rockefeller Foundation was introduced into the Senate, and the Court's decision upholding the government and ordering the dissolution of the company was handed down while the question of the charter was still being debated in Congress. In the end, Rockefeller's advisers withdrew their application for federal incorporation and turned their efforts to Albany, New York, where this curious episode came to its curious end. Without hesitation and with little public reaction the state legislature passed an act in 1913 incorporating the foundation, omitting all of the restrictive amendments that had been added during the course of the congressional debates in Washington. Rockefeller then made his first major gift to the foundation and another one the following year. In all, through 1929, he transferred to it more than $182 million.[*]

At the first meeting of the trustees in 1913, John D. Rockefeller Jr. was elected president, and it fell to him to define the mode of operation for the new institution and identify its principal fields of interest. Under the pressure of the war emergency, the foundation sowed its first grants to all winds: millions of dollars were provided for famine relief; gifts were made for the welfare of war prisoners and the morale of the troops; the foundation purchased a bird refuge in Louisiana and presented it to the state; and smaller grants were made to such a diversity of institutions that Gates and some of the other trustees became critical of what they feared was

[*] Rockefeller's total gifts to his four major philanthropies, figured at the market price of the securities on the day on which each was made, amounted over the first three decades of the century to just under $447 million. The Rockefeller Institute for Medical Research received $60.7 million; the General Education Board received a series of gifts amounting in all to $129.2 million; the Laura Spelman Rockefeller Memorial, set up in 1918 in memory of his wife, received $74 million; and the foundation itself was given a total of $182.9 million. The letters accompanying these various gifts followed essentially the same pattern: "It is more convenient for me to provide funds for the foundation by a gift of specific securities than by a gift of cash, and I believe the securities have an intrinsic and permanent value which would justify you in retaining them as investments; but in order to relieve you from any uncertainty or embarrassment with regard to them, I desire to state specifically that you are under no obligation to retain any of these investments, but are at liberty to dispose of them or any of them and change the form of investment whenever in your judgment it seems wise to do so." In this respect as in a number of others, Rockefeller set a high standard for the independence of his foundation and the authority of his trustees—a standard not many other donors have matched.

a drift into a policy of "scatteration." But more consistent patterns quickly emerged.

The elder Rockefeller was convinced that good health was of first importance to human well-being, and this soon became the foundation's main interest. The Sanitary Commission had achieved dramatic success under the leadership of Wickliffe Rose, and it was absorbed into the new International Health Board which the trustees established as one of the Rockefeller Foundation's component divisions. Rose was invited to become director "to extend to other countries and peoples the work of eradicating hookworm disease . . . and to follow up the treatment and cure of this disease with the establishment of agencies for the promotion of public sanitation and the spread of the knowledge of scientific medicine."

As a result of his Baptist missionary contacts, Rockefeller Sr. had also long maintained an interest in China, which was reflected in the foundation's choice of its second major field of action. In 1914 the trustees established a China Medical Board as part of the foundation to carry out a plan for "the gradual and orderly development of a comprehensive system of modern medicine" in that country.

The foundation was obviously moving toward an emphasis on health and medicine on an international basis and toward direct operation of its principal programs by its own staff of experts. But when it attempted to apply the same approach to the study of social and economic issues it got into trouble. In 1914 W. L. Mackenzie King of Canada was hired to direct a research program in the field of industrial relations. But coincidentally a strike erupted in a Rockefeller-controlled company—the Colorado Fuel and Iron Company—which turned into one of the most savage in the history of American industry, culminating in the tragic Ludlow Massacre. Federal troops had to be brought in to control the bloody fighting between the mine workers and the state militia.

In Washington, the U.S. Commission on Industrial Relations, headed by Frank T. Walsh, immediately began an investigation of the foundation to determine its role and relationship to Rockefeller's business interests. The investigation made headlines for weeks, generating great apprehension across the country about the dangers that might result from the foundation's unsupervised power. The Rockefeller trustees were given an unforgettable lesson about the hazards of becoming involved in social and economic issues, especially if the foundation itself undertook to carry out the work. As a matter of policy they decided thereafter to restrict the foundation's direct operations to scientific areas such as public health, medicine, and agriculture. If it supported work in more controversial social fields, it would do so through grants to other independent institutions. From this mixed beginning the Rockefeller Foundation over the next few years went on to achieve a series of notable successes.

THE HEROIC DECADE

In 1917 John D. Rockefeller Jr. was elevated to chairman of the board and was succeeded as president by George E. Vincent, who came to the post from the University of Minnesota. Vincent was an eloquent and persuasive man and a wise administrator not afraid of large ventures. The ten years in which he headed the foundation were a time of daring development. The International Health Board extended its attack on hookworm infection to sixty-two countries on six continents, and as the program moved forward it was followed by another boldly conceived, worldwide enterprise to control malaria. These programs were accompanied by equally successful efforts to build up permanent governmental machinery in the United States and abroad to deal with problems of public health. The first major schools of public health and public health nursing were established in the United States and abroad, and to make this new educational machinery more effective a system of graduate fellowships for students from nearly every country in the world was instituted.

In this same decade the foundation undertook to create the "Johns Hopkins of China," and nearly succeeded. The Peking Union Medical College was constructed in 1921 at a cost of $8 million and, although the college later became a victim of the ravages of war and revolution in China, it was for a time a place of great intellectual ferment. Its graduates made important contributions to medical teaching, hospital administration, and government health services.

The foundation's third major undertaking was based on Abraham Flexner's report on the deficiencies of American medical schools, commissioned in 1910 by the Carnegie Foundation for the Advancement of Teaching. After World War I the Rockefeller Foundation joined with the General Education Board in a large-scale effort to upgrade medical teaching in the United States and abroad. Within the United States the foundation played a secondary role to the GEB, but abroad it took the lead in contributing to the improvement of medical schools in Britain, France, Belgium, Canada, Latin America, the Middle East, Southeast Asia, and the Antipodes.

Between 1917 and 1928 the outlays of the Rockefeller Foundation included $40 million for medical education and science in Europe, Canada, and the United States; $10 million for schools of hygiene and public health in the United States; and $3.7 million for research fellowships in mathematics, science, and medicine. By the late 1920s it could be said that, as a side effect of its successes, the foundation had been captured by the scientists and doctors on its staff. Their achievements had given them worldwide prestige, and within the foundation their influence was predominant. It had committed itself to the proposition that science, especially medicine, offered the surest means of advancing civilization and the well-being of mankind. Frederick Gates put it in these words: "If science and education are the brain and nervous system of civilization, health is its heart. It is the organ that pushes the vital fluid into every part of the social organism, enabling each organ to function and measuring and limiting its effective life. . . . Disease is the supreme ill of life and it is the main source of almost all other human ills—poverty, crime, ignorance, vice, inefficiency, hereditary taint, and many other evils."

Wickliffe Rose, who was likewise not a scientist, also displayed an amateur's fervor in his belief that science held primacy over all other forms of human activity. In his words: "Science is the method of knowledge. It is the key to such dominion as man may ever acquire over his physical environment. Appreciation of its spirit and technique, moreover, determines the mental attitude of a people, affects the entire system of education, and carries with it the shaping of a civilization." [2]

This fundamental commitment gave the Rockefeller Foundation its distinctive character and continuity and in large part led to the success that the foundation has enjoyed. But at the same time it has resulted in a rigidity that has consistently prevented the foundation from achieving comparable successes in other fields—the social sciences, the arts, and humanities—in which it has also professed interest.

THE FIRST TRANSITION

In the years from 1924 to 1928 a degree of confusion and duplication developed among the programs of the four major Rockefeller philanthropies then active: medical education was divided geographically between the General Education Board and the Rockefeller Foundation, the former operating within the United States and the latter internationally. The natural sciences were included in the programs of the General Education Board, the International Education Board which had been created in 1924, and the foundation itself. The humanities and arts were dealt with both by GEB and the Laura Spelman Rockefeller Memorial, which had been set up in 1918. The organizational untidiness was such that it led Rockefeller Sr. to say in a letter to his son dated May 4, 1926: "If the whole thing were to be done today, you have rightly understood me as feeling that it should be done and doubtless could be done through a single organization."

But the separate traditions that had developed and the momentum of activities under way prevented the individual institutions from simply merging into a single new entity. Instead, a more complex pattern of consolidation was adopted. The Laura Spelman Rockefeller Memorial was liquidated and its activities (except for its work in the field of public administration, which was thereafter carried on by the newly created Spelman Fund) were folded into the foundation. The International Education Board was terminated, and the two remaining organizations, the foundation and the GEB, divided their functions in such a way as to consolidate in the foundation all activities relating to "the advancement of human knowledge." This meant transferring to it the natural sciences activities from the GEB and the IEB, medical sciences and medical education from the GEB, and agriculture and forestry from the IEB and the GEB. In addition, the social sciences program of the Laura Spelman Rockefeller Memorial was taken over by the foundation as well as the humanities and arts activities of the GEB. The significance of all these decisions for its subsequent work and character can hardly be overestimated.

There is considerable indirect evidence to suggest that the consolidation of 1928 was preceded and followed by much bitter dispute extending to issues well beyond those of the administrative clarification. Abraham Flexner, in a waspish little volume called *Funds and Foundations* which he wrote a number of years later, called the reorganization on the whole a disaster. The results, in his view, were to ruin the effectiveness of the GEB by destroying its tradition and to turn the Rockefeller Foundation over to new leadership which he considered ignorant, pretentious, and devoted to meaningless "shotgun" efforts in its grant-making.[3]

Beardsley Ruml, then head of the memorial, had grave misgivings about combining its work with the foundation. He had been aware of the conservatism of the foundation in dealing with social issues ever since the Mackenzie King affair in 1914. In 1924, within a year after Ruml had been appointed to direct the memorial, some controversy had already begun to swirl about its projects, whereupon a committee of senior Rockefeller philanthropic advisers was promptly convened to lay down protective guidelines for its future work. This special group—which included Vincent, Rose, Buttrick, and Flexner—produced a memorandum that recommended caution: no attempt was to be made directly to win any social, economic, or political reforms; not more than a minor part of the costs of any organization engaged in direct activity for social welfare would be provided; and all investigations and research on broad social questions would be conducted through other organizations, not directly by the memorial and its staff.

Second, Ruml was uneasy about the growing tendency of the foundation to support basic scientific research and its distaste for projects involving the application of scientific knowledge to contemporary problems. In the memorial's final report in 1928 summing up its work, Ruml pointedly commented: "Each program was dominated by a practical motive, to achieve concrete improvement in the conditions of life and to contribute realistically to the public welfare. The memorial had no interest in the promotion of scientific research as an end in itself; its motive was not sheer curiosity as to how various human and social phenomena came to be and are; the interest in science was an interest in one means to an end, and the end was explicitly recognized to be the advancement of human welfare." Feeling that the environment of the foundation would not be hospitable to social concerns, Ruml resigned.

By 1928 many of the eminent men who had contributed to the first phase of the foundation's development had retired or died—Gates, Buttrick, Rose, and Vincent—and inadequate preparation had been made to groom their successors. Among the important changes affecting the foundation itself was a subtle shift in the balance of authority between the officers and the trustees, a shift that had an enduring effect on its later character and priorities.

Partly because of the expanded range of subject matter over which the trustees felt they would have to deal following the reorganization, and partly because of the prestige of the major program directors, a set of operating principles was agreed upon which in effect gave decisive power to the directors. The board conceded to the heads of the five new divisions that recommendations in their special fields "would carry an initial weight of authority and responsibility," that is to say they would rarely if ever be rejected.

The irresistability of scientific and technical recommendations made to the board of trustees was further increased by the creation of separate boards of scientific advisers, consisting of prominent outside specialists and attached to the individual divisions of the foundation. It may have been the hope of some trustees, in interposing such boards between themselves and the officers, that recommendations of the latter would be more competently screened. In fact, the technical officers and the scientific boards reinforced one another by giving added weight to technical considerations in program decisions. Finally, the trustees agreed to add some specialists to the board—and since these specialists were consistently chosen from the fields of medicine and the physical and natural sciences, their presence gave further emphasis to those programs in the foundations's overall activities.

In 1929 Max Mason, a mathematical physicist and former president of the University of Chicago, succeeded Vincent as president. Under his leadership the foundation during the next decade sustained its remarkable record of scientific achievement. The most prestigious and independent of the foundation's branches, the International Health Division, continued its worldwide campaigns against disease. The Division of Medical Sciences—formerly the Division of Medical Education—emphasized research in physiology, industrial medicine, and physiological optics, and after 1933 it devoted a considerable part of its funds to psychiatry, then a relatively weak, fragmented, and ignored branch of medical science.

The Division of Natural Sciences, especially after 1932 with the appointment of Warren Weaver, former head of the department of mathematics at the University of Wisconsin, as chief, carried on an imaginative and highly productive program in biology and in those border zones where the physical sciences overlap biology.

The Social Sciences Division, under a newly appointed director, Edmund Day, once professor of economics at Harvard University and later dean of the School of Business Administration at the University of Michigan, continued some elements of Ruml's earlier program and made a number of significant grants in international relations, economic research, and public administration. Reflecting the general preferences of the foundation, however, they tended to stress basic research conducted by a small, select group of universities.

The Division of the Arts and Humanities under David H. Stevens inherited a rather academic tradition from its predecessor in the GEB and dutifully perpetuated it. The program continued to emphasize archeology, scholarly research in ancient cultures, and classical humanistic research. The general effect, as various observ-

ers, including the director of the foundation's program himself, remarked was to buttress "scholasticism and antiquarianism in our
universities." [4]

THE INTRUSION OF EVENTS

In retrospect it seems ironic that the Rockefeller Foundation, on
the eve of the great depression and at the beginning of the decade
that was to see the outbreak of the Spanish Civil War, the rise of
Fascism in Europe, and the beginnings of both Japanese and German militarism, should have turned away so decisively in 1928
from social, economic, and international problems. But within a
relatively few years, events at home and abroad caused a number
of the trustees to question the near-sacred notion that the advancement of knowledge was the magic solution to mankind's problems.
Some began to feel that the emphasis on research had led to a sterile fact-collecting program. Others were concerned that the foundation might be failing to make a direct contribution to the solution of the nation's urgent economic and social problems. In 1934
the board therefore established a special committee to reexamine
the foundation's program. As one of its findings, the committee
stated that "large amounts of money are spent by foundations and
universities alike on research projects that are unrealistic, unproductive, and often unrelated to human aspiration or need."

The board then approved a special appropriation of $1.5 million
to find some means of easing the misery and suffering caused by
the financial depression. The lack of results suggest that Beardsley
Ruml's earlier estimate of the foundation's inhospitality to efforts
"to achieve concrete improvement in the conditions of life" was
correct. The staff came forward with a few proposals for research
grants to organizations such as the Brookings Institution, the Social Science Research Council, and the American Public Welfare
Organization. But two years later—when bread lines were a common sight in the United States and the economic collapse had
reached frightening proportions—the staff returned a substantial
portion of the 1934 appropriation to the general funds of the foundation on the grounds that they could not find useful ways of
spending it.

In 1936, Raymond B. Fosdick became president, and for the next twelve years he gave the foundation exceptionally broad-minded direction. Trained as a lawyer, he had served as a trustee of the GEB for twenty-seven years and of the foundation for fifteen years before his election. So he brought to the post a comprehensive background of experience in the various Rockefeller philanthropies, and he took over an institution which, however hesitant in dealing with social issues, was a powerful scientific force.

In 1937 the International Health Division scored a major breakthrough with the development of the first effective yellow fever vaccine.° About the same time an epidemic of a new type of malaria spread in Brazil, which the division managed to bring under control by 1939. In the 1940s it dealt with the danger of international typhus epidemics and significantly reduced them. The division's work not only met high scientific standards but was characterized by high drama in coping with health crises that erupted unexpectedly in all parts of the globe, and the men who participated in its various campaigns came to feel an intense emotional attachment to and pride in the International Health Division. The work of the Medical Sciences Division in upgrading the education of doctors and later in supporting basic research in the medical sciences—though less spectacular in its achievements—was nonetheless impressive. But its director, Dr. Alan Gregg, came to have increasing doubts about its approach. The result, he became convinced, was "exquisite care" for a small segment of the population and neglect of the rest. Although he personally became more interested in the social and economic aspects of medical care, he and his staff were unable to devise projects that could promise significant results and win the support of the trustees.

During the same period, however, the Natural Sciences Division, having foreseen the coming of the "biological age" in science,

° After the outbreak of World War II the foundation produced some 34 million doses of this vaccine in its laboratories for distribution without cost to government health agencies and other official units. After thousands of soldiers of the United States, Britain, and their allies were vaccinated, however, there was an outbreak of jaundice which seemed to be associated with some of the vaccine. A number of men died, and to the embarrassment of the foundation this jaundice earned the nickname "Rockefeller's disease."

achieved notable advances: in the classical field of genetics; in the new hybrid fields of biophysics and biochemistry; and in the development of new research tools and techniques, including spectroscopy, X-ray diffraction, chromatography, and the use of tracer elements. A cyclotron was financed for Dr. Ernest O. Lawrence of the University of California, which in turn played an important part in the development of the atomic bomb in the early years of World War II. In fact, twenty-three of the leaders of the Manhattan Project had been Rockefeller fellows in earlier years. The foundation's major role in the development of nuclear weapons and the nuclear sciences has been acknowledged by staff and trustees with feelings of both pride and apprehension.

In 1941, acting on a suggestion made by U.S. Vice-President Henry A. Wallace, the Natural Sciences Division began a project in Mexico to develop new varieties of corn and wheat to help alleviate chronic food shortages there. The project, directed by the plant pathologist, George A. Harrar, achieved results that were to have major implications for the solution of the world food problem.

However, the foundation's programs in the social sciences and the humanities and arts from the mid-1930s to the 1940s continued to suffer from irresolution and conservatism. Although the trustees had decided in 1934 that the Social Science Division should give greater emphasis to applications of knowledge to contemporary issues, most of its grants continued to flow into familiar channels: fellowship programs for advanced study and the support of general research in university departments and specialized agencies such as the Social Science Research Council. The program acquired a gloss of relevancy by the financing of projects examining such topics as war and peace, demography, civil liberties, and the social implications of atomic energy, but the results were modest at best. In the humanities, the trustees fostered a program of relating the great classical tradition to contemporary problems, not merely for its preservation. Thus experiments were financed to develop educational radio programs and a film library at the Museum of Modern Art in New York. But the major outlays continued to be for institutional development. Not until the mid-1940s did the foundation make its first efforts to stimulate creativity by aiding artists, musicians, and writers directly, but these initiatives were marked by much awkwardness and uncertainty.

The Rockefeller Foundation from the start had been singularly international in its outlook and, as military conflict in Europe rapidly spread in the late 1930s, it was Fosdick, in contrast to most of the other foundation heads at the time, who appropriately began to warn of some of its sinister implications. In his 1937 annual report, he commented on the state of the social sciences in Germany: "In some fields it is now profitless to go where we formerly went. We find ourselves stopped at some frontiers—not because the frontiers have any greater geographical significance than they had a few years ago, but because behind them the search for truth by eager and skeptical minds has been thwarted." Out of his continuing concern came one of the foundation's major contributions to culture and scholarship—its program to assist and relocate European scientists and intellectuals threatened by Hitler. By its substantial and timely response, the Rockefeller Foundation saved the lives of hundreds of outstanding persons.

By the time of Fosdick's retirement, many of the foundation's programs, particularly those in health and the hard sciences, were still vigorous. But it had become so set in its habits—emphasis on pure research, advanced training, institutional development, and working through universities—that the introduction of any basically new programs was made only with great difficulty. To some degree the foundation had become the prisoner of its own past successes. Fosdick's successor, Chester I. Barnard, a prominent public utilities executive, took over in 1948. He had acquired a reputation as the most thoughtful and effective corporate manager in the United States, and it was hoped that he could ease some of the foundation's internal tensions and resolve some of the organizational problems. Particularly serious was the friction between the heads of the Medical Sciences Division and the Natural Sciences Division, and between the heads of the social sciences and the humanities and arts. Barnard remained only four years. During that period, although he brought about some improvements, the strains on the whole became worse. Symptoms of rigidity persisted and other more specific institutional ailments had become manifest.

These could all be ascribed to the corrosive consequences of institutional eminence. In some ways, staff morale, for example, the foundation's status, may have had beneficial effects. Anyone who worked in the foundation at the time became quickly aware of its extraordinary prestige. When Rockefeller representatives arrived in a foreign country they were greeted at the airport by a receiving line of leading local scientists, educators, and officials. A Rockefeller representative in Latin America merely had to pick up the telephone to be put through to a cabinet minister. Each year the list of Nobel prize winners provided additional testimony to the preeminence of the scientists who worked for the foundation or who were the beneficiaries of its grants (and who, in a sense, it felt it had "created").

But this also led to a certain smugness. The staff came to feel that Rockefeller was the "dean" of the major foundations and that no other—with the possible exception of Carnegie—really counted. Within the foundation the atmosphere became pretentious and excessively formal, suffused with a heavy sense of "the obligations of leadership"—a stultifying self-pride that has never been fully overcome.

In 1952, Barnard was succeeded by Dean Rusk, who came to the post after long experience in the State Department. The hope was that Rusk's diplomatic talents might accomplish what Barnard's managerial expertise had not succeeded in doing. But his chances for bringing harmony among the factions of the staff were not improved by the suspicion of a number of them, because of his past association with John D. Rockefeller 3d, that his appointment would have the effect of strengthening family influence over the foundation's affairs—another bone of contention in the organization. The years of Rusk's tenure, which were not the foundation's most distinguished, began with a period of attrition. A number of new governmental organizations, based on Rockefeller models, began to take over and enlarge on the foundation's pioneering work. In 1948 the United Nations had established the World Health Organization, which then began to move into most of the fields occupied by the International Health Division. In 1950 the United States government established the National Science Foundation, whose program was patterned on the Rockefeller Foundation's approach in the support of research, scholarships, and institutional development. The National Institutes of Health were started in the same year and began to imitate and extend the kind of medical programs the foundation had long supported.

The foundation was left with redundant facilities and specialized personnel who had devoted their working lives to the foundation and could hardly be summarily dismissed. But they constituted a heavy cost and hindered the foundation's maneuverability. Finally, in 1951, the venerable International Health Division was closed down. Its famous virus laboratory and the remaining personnel were transferred to Yale University. Some of the principal organizational and personality problems which Rusk had inherited were relieved when Alan Gregg retired in 1952 as head of the Medical Sciences Division and Warren Weaver, who had headed the Natural Sciences Division, also left. The two branches were then merged under Robert S. Morison, a biologist of unusual capability. Joseph H. Willits, head of the social sciences program, retired in 1954, and the head of the humanities and arts program, Charles B. Fahs, retired in 1962, which eliminated the clash between those two divisions. An outstanding man, Norman Buchanan, was brought in to head the social sciences program, and had he not died in 1958 at the age of fifty-three he might well have come to play a leading role in the foundation.

Caught in the vortex of various staff dissensions, and of differences between some members of the board and senior members of the staff, Rusk was cautious and conciliatory. He was, moreover, distracted from the foundation's internal problems by having to defend it in 1952 and 1954 at two congressional investigations. Perhaps his most significant program initiative, though it hardly seemed daring at the time, was to persuade the trustees in 1956 to give greater program emphasis to the underdeveloped countries. During the next four years he gradually expanded the foundation's activities in the Third World, especially in Latin America and India.

But by 1960, when Rusk was named secretary of state by President-elect Kennedy (who simultaneously raided the foundation's board of two of its most influential members, Douglas Dillon and Chester Bowles), the foundation had not yet found its new program bearings, and many of the management problems which had been present at the time of his arrival remained unresolved.

A DECADE OF REDIRECTION

A few months after Rusk's departure in early 1961, George Harrar was named president. A plain-spoken scientist whose forte was neither public relations nor politics, he had been brought to New York a few years earlier as a vice-president after his long and distinguished service in charge of the Mexican agricultural program. Internally the situation at the foundation was still one of tension between the predominant "hard" scientists and the "soft" people in the social sciences and arts. And the staff was still concerned over the danger of donor-family intrusion upon the independent status of the institution.

Harrar's election was the first time a president had been chosen from inside. That, as well as his scientific background, could readily be interpreted as a victory for the scientists and the staff in the quiet but continuing internal struggle for power. But the matter was somewhat more complicated. Although Harrar was a symbol of continuity and of the scientific approach, he was also much concerned with the practical application of scientific findings. Moreover, the principal area of his work and interest was the poorer countries. To some of the "pure" scientists on the foundation's staff, therefore, he was considered to be excessively "service" and "application" oriented.

In the decade of the 1960s, Harrar presided over great changes in the stated goals of the foundation and in its staff. It had the appearance of being a time of profound redirection of effort away from essentially scientific preoccupations of the earlier period and toward the solution of contemporary national and international problems. Yet, looking deeper, there is question whether the appearance was not greater than the reality. There is also question about the extent to which Harrar and the staff led or followed the trustees in bringing about the changes that took place.

In 1962, in anticipation of the foundation's fiftieth anniversary the following year, the board established a special committee to develop guidelines for future programs. Their report began by pointing out that many of the foundation's long-established activities, which had once been ahead of their time, had now been absorbed into the programs of government and international organizations. They therefore concluded that the foundation could and should disengage from them. The committee proposed that in the future there should be greater emphasis placed on the development of interdisciplinary projects, especially in the developing countries. They then identified five priority problems for future action: the conquest of hunger; control of world population; strengthening selected universities and research centers in the underdeveloped countries; achieving equal opportunity for all American citizens; and aiding cultural development.*

What was most striking in the document was this "problem-approach," which was in sharp contrast to the foundation's habitual emphasis on scientific disciplines. Strong accent was also given to "action programs" instead of basic research. Broad policy statements, however, are one thing; the actual administration of a foundation's program is something else.

For the next nine years, Harrar followed the trustees' guidelines, but implemented some of them with greater vigor than others. In programs related to his special field of competence, he provided exceptionally effective leadership. The foundation's most notable success during the period was its contribution to the "green revolution." The new seed varieties that were produced as a result of its agricultural research quickly helped to overcome chronic food shortages in a number of countries. The award of the Nobel Peace Prize in 1970 to Norman Borlaug, a Rockefeller agricultural scientist, symbolized the continuing excellence of the foundation's work in this field. (Incidentally, not a few scientists felt that the award

* Interestingly enough, in the foundation's annual report the previous year, 1961, Harrar had outlined his view of future directions for its program. His list of priorities was similar to that of the trustee committee a year later with one notable omission; the American race problem.

should have gone to the Rockefeller Foundation itself and not to an individual member of the outstanding group of researchers from whose efforts the "green revolution" has sprouted.)

Its program concerning the world population problem (which John D. Rockefeller 3d had urged the foundation to launch in the early 1950s) got off to a delayed start because of staff opposition. But once it was given priority by the trustees in 1963, Harrar drove it forward strongly and intelligently. On the other hand, it would seem that his enthusiasm for cultural activities and the "equal opportunity" program was tepid. Another obstacle to their effectiveness was Harrar's almost pugnacious belief in professionalism. In his view, in order to recruit and hold first-class men, and to facilitate their eventual return to a university or a research institution if they desire, staff members of a foundation should retain their professional identity as biologists, agronomists, sociologists, and so on. In the foundation they should be organized into units under familiar professional headings and should be encouraged to maintain their professional associations and contacts through research and writing.

Consistent with this view, the foundation's divisions are called "the medical and natural sciences division," or "the agricultural sciences division" even though its major program objectives are now stated in "problem" terms, such as "hunger" or "equal opportunity." In university style, each staff member's academic degrees are indicated in the staff listings. There is no division whose name corresponds to a stated program objective. In order to deal with a multifaceted problem such as that of blacks in the United States—which may involve problems of economics, health, cultural development, and education, for example—multidisciplinary "task forces" have to be formed on an ad hoc basis from the several divisions.

It may well be that Rockefeller's great productivity in the advancement and application of scientific knowledge over the years has been due to its disciplinary structure and professionalism. But the same organizational staffing philosophy may explain its inability to achieve similar results in dealing with social issues and creativity in the arts and its inflexibility in changing program direction.

For despite the modernized "problem" terms in which its goals have come to be stated, the substance of the new programs reflects a persistence of older habits. Thus the grants reported under the new population program closely resemble those formerly made in the programs for medicine and the natural sciences for research in reproductive biology and related fields. The program addressed to the problem of world hunger is essentially an extension of earlier work in the agricultural sciences. The program for "cultural development" differs little from the long-established effort of the foundation in the field of the humanities. Even the "equal opportunity" program for several years consisted of little more than traditional university scholarships for young blacks and other minority students. Only slowly and with evident discomfort did Rockefeller become more directly engaged with nonacademic leaders and institutions in the ghettos.

An unusually clear example of the strong tendencies for continuity was the announcement in 1969 by the trustees of a sixth "new" program relating to the problems of the environment. Again, no new division was created nor were any major personnel changes made. In effect, the foundation took a contemporary problem containing a multiplicity of subproblems and chose to stress those with a clearly defined scientific or educational component, rather than those that involved taking a socially activist stance.

No institution of course, can be all things to all men. Its quality has to be measured not by some theoretical standard of perfection but by comparison with other institutions. By this test the Rockefeller Foundation has been a great foundation: it has set high standards for itself; it has preserved its integrity; it has persevered in its efforts to fulfill its objectives; and it has major achievements to its credit. Indeed, judged by the magnitude of its contributions to human well-being over the years, the Rockefeller Foundation has accumulated an unrivaled record. In many ways it has been the standard against which the other "modern" foundations have measured themselves.

On the other hand, although its main dedication has been to "the advancement of knowledge," it has not been content to confine itself to that single activity. For more than forty years it has struggled continuously—often with lackluster results—to develop parallel programs in the social sciences and in the humanities and arts. Although such programs have not prospered in the scientist- and doctor-dominated environment of the institution, the foundation can claim some achievements, such as the creation of the National Bureau of Economic Research and substantial assistance to the Social Science Research Council.

As of 1971 it seemed doubtful that the Rockefeller Foundation would ever be able to break out of its well-set patterns and become a fully problem-oriented, innovative institution in nonscientific areas. With its faith in research and in advanced training it was not unlike a university—with all the assets and liabilities associated with traditional academic institutions. It seemed to many that it would probably be easier, if changes were to be made, for it to convert itself into a university, adding more teaching and research facilities, than to become an unfettered and free-swinging foundation. But in September of that year, as Harrar approached retirement, the trustees surprised the skeptics by announcing that the new president, to take over in July 1972, would be Dr. John H. Knowles, head of the Massachusetts General Hospital. The choice promised important, possibly radical, changes in direction for the staid old battlewagon of the Rockefeller philanthropic fleet. Knowles has been an outspoken liberal on social as well as specifically medical issues. In 1969 he was a highly controversial nominee for the top health post in the Department of Health, Education, and Welfare, but his nomination was withdrawn by the Nixon administration after a five-month dispute in which Dr. Knowles was reportedly opposed by conservative Republicans and the American Medical Association.

Immediately after his designation as president, Knowles made it clear that the foundation in the future would reduce its heavy traditional emphasis on international programs and increase its attention to domestic issues, including such social questions as welfare, employment, and the needs of the aged and the poor. The indications were that he intended, with the backing of the trustees, to give the Rockefeller Foundation a new and less constipated style and its greatest shaking-up in half a century.

THE ROLE OF THE ROCKEFELLER FAMILY

One unique aspect of the Rockefeller Foundation is that it is highly institutionalized and independent and yet the donor and his descendants have played a continuously active role in its affairs. John D. Rockefeller Sr., through his son and his adviser, Gates, had a direct line of influence into the foundation, and in a number of cases he designated how the funds of his substantial gifts were to be used. Still, he chose good men to direct the institution and gave them wide latitude and responsibility. His son, when he became the dominant figure in the family, devised his own formula for influencing the foundation's work without compromising its independence, namely personal persuasiveness, gentle but effective, upon both trustees and staff.

Relationships between the foundation and the donor family in the third generation reveal a greater degree of friction. In the late 1940s, when John D. Rockefeller 3d assumed the chairmanship of the board, some resistance to the patriarchal situation had begun to develop. By personality he was a less commanding figure than his father. Yet he had his own strong ideas (about the urgency of the world population problem, for example) which he persistently attempted to insert into the foundation's static program priorities. But these efforts to stimulate new thinking were initially seen by the staff as an aggressive thrust of family influence and they were resisted.

Nevertheless, after forty years of continuous involvement in the foundation's affairs (including by 1971 eighteen years as chairman of the board), his imprint on the foundation's program is unmistakable. The substantial alteration of its program priorities since the 1950s has on the whole been in the direction of concerns with which he is especially identified: population, the fine arts, and the blacks. Undoubtedly, events in America and the world have helped to bring about the general change in course, as have the efforts of non-Rockefeller trustees and members of the staff. But it would appear that John D. Rockefeller 3d is a much underrated force not only in the affairs of the Rockefeller Foundation but in other aspects of American philanthropy as well.

Despite its changing method and manner from generation to generation, family influence in the foundation's affairs remains considerable and yet is by no means dominant. There have never been more than two members of the Rockefeller family on the board at any time. At present it is probably the most eminent and diversified group of trustees of any foundation in the country. Among its twenty-one members are two foreigners, two blacks, a woman, and a wide variety of educators, businessmen, and public figures. From its earliest years there has never been any question about the professional competence and influence of the staff; if there has been concern it has been over the possible excess of staff influence vis-à-vis the trustees. The foundation holds over 40 percent of its portfolio in shares of three major oil companies—Standard of New Jersey, Standard of Indiana, and Mobil—which are associated with the Rockefeller name. But these shares constitute less than 1.5 percent of the total shares outstanding in these large publicly held companies.

The fourth John D. Rockefeller has now become a member of the board. This young man, who is now launched on a political career in West Virginia, differs greatly in personality and perhaps social outlook from his father. In what direction and in what manner he will begin to help shape the course of the foundation has not yet become evident. But it is certain that the family through him will continue to play an active part in its work.

The Rockefeller Brothers Fund

The Rockefeller Brothers Fund, the second largest of the Rockefeller philanthropies with assets of $222 million, is fully controlled by family members, who constitute the majority of its board. It exemplifies the positive possibilities of the family foundation when the family involved has a genuine interest in its affairs and when the individual members are persons of exceptional standing.

On the fifty-sixth floor of 30 Rockefeller Plaza in New York City are the offices of the principal members of the Rockefeller family and of their financial advisers. This group of sixteen, which han-

dles the investments of many family members and of their foundations, is headed by J. Richardson Dilworth, a little known but immensely powerful man. His counterpart, two floors below, is the
president of the Rockefeller Brothers Fund, Dana Creel. A soft-
spoken and publicity-shy Georgia-born lawyer his influence and
abilities are also little known and greatly underestimated. He in
fact serves as the respected adviser to the family in all their philanthropic activities. The staff of fifteen that works with him can
be deployed with complete flexibility to carry out nonprofit projects for any member of the family or for their personal foundations.

The fund was established in 1940 by the five sons of John D.
Rockefeller Jr. Prior to its creation, the brothers had developed
their own individual programs of charitable giving, which in time
overlapped. Their initial idea was to consolidate their gifts to
agencies of common interest. At the same time it was understood
that each brother would make arrangements apart from the fund to
handle contributions to organizations and activities in which he
had a special interest not shared by the others. The five brothers
constituted the original board. By the terms of the charter, the
fund was given broad powers to apply its income as well as its
principal to charitable purposes. In its first publication, it characterized its program as a "citizenship approach" to giving, as distinct from professionalized foundation programs emphasizing research or specialized fields.

During its first decade it operated on this standard family-fund
basis. No attempt was made to develop a comprehensive or innovative program, and through 1950 its outlays totaled just slightly
over $2 million. Approximately one-half was given to support various
local and national health, welfare, and religious organizations
on a more or less continuing basis. The rest consisted of special non-
recurring gifts largely related to the demands of the war effort;
more than $800,000 was given for relief and rehabilitation and morale
services for the armed forces.

John D. Rockefeller Jr. was highly pleased by his sons' initiative
in carrying on the family tradition of philanthropy; and rarely has
parental pleasure produced a more substantial movement of capi-

tal. During 1950 and 1951, he gave gifts totaling $52 million to the fund to enable it to undertake larger and more creative tasks. The fund enlarged its professional staff, added two nonfamily members to the board of trustees, and gradually began to increase the scale of its program. From a level of about $500,000 a year in 1951, annual outlays grew to nearly $4 million by 1960. In that year, John D. Rockefeller Jr. died and left half his estate to the fund, which eventually added another $75 million to its resources. Since then, the level of its grants has continued to rise, totaling nearly $8 million in 1968.

The five Rockefeller brothers who define the goals and style of the fund are, as a group, men of extraordinary achievement: John 3d, the eldest, has like his father devoted his life primarily to philanthropy; Winthrop was governor of Arkansas from 1967 to 1970; Nelson is currently governor of New York; Laurance is a successful industrialist; and David, with a Ph.D. in economics from Harvard, is chairman of the Chase Manhattan Bank, one of the nation's largest. The range of their intellectual and philanthropic interests is wide. John has been a major mover in the crusade for population control, the strengthening of American relationships with Asian countries, and the development of cultural institutions in the United States. Nelson is a former president of the Museum of Modern Art in New York (of which his mother was a founder), was instrumental in bringing the United Nations to New York, and since his service as a government official in Washington during the war has had a deep interest in Latin America.

David, also an art collector, has played an increasingly active role in recent years in the fields of urban development and international trade policy. Laurance, deeply interested in science and technology, is said to be the kind of man who enjoys a seminar in aerodynamics far more than a Park Avenue dinner party. As the conservationist in the family, he has donated large areas of park land to New York State and to the federal government.

Although the fund has specifically avoided the formulation of a fixed set of program objectives, a review of its grant pattern suggests that in geographical terms there is a roughly equal division of interest between the problems of New York, those of national

significance, and those of international character. Roughly half of
its outlays go to hospitals, child welfare organizations, and church
groups. It has made substantial "brick and mortar" grants, notably
a commitment of $2.5 million to help establish the Lincoln Center
for the Performing Arts in New York City. It has also made a succession of large gifts for the preservation of historical monuments,
especially for the restoration of Colonial Williamsburg and for the
development of its educational programs.

In parallel with such traditional charitable activities, the fund—
in contrast to the Rockefeller Foundation—has also shown a sensitive interest in emerging social problems. In the field of race relations and civil rights, for example, it has made a succession of
grants to the Southern Regional Council for voter education and
registration. It has given continuing support and encouragement to
the National Urban League for its varied programs in behalf of
economic and social equality for blacks. The fund has repeatedly
been able—not only by the use of its own resources but also by
calling on the help of members of the family and their friends—to
provide a number of civil rights leaders, including the late Martin
Luther King Jr., with emergency help when crises have arisen.

Because of their prominence, the Rockefeller brothers are especially vulnerable to criticism in their philanthropic activities, but
this does not seem to have restrained them from sponsoring a number of controversial projects. One, launched in 1956, was a series of
studies on American foreign and domestic policy. The several reports, prepared by panels composed of eminent figures in various
fields, dealt with military security, foreign economic policy, domestic economic and social policy, and the status of the performing
arts. In some cases, they stirred sharp political debate because of
their recommendations. (The 1959 report on foreign policy, for example, took issue with a number of positions then supported by the
State Department, such as the prohibition against travel by American newsmen and scholars to Communist China.)

In 1960 the wave of political independence in Africa was beginning to crest. Anticipating the intensified problems of economic
development that would follow, the fund undertook to spur the
flow of capital into Nigeria and Ghana by commissioning a series

of studies on opportunities for private investment. Few new ventures were actually launched as a result, but the willingness of the fund to expose itself to the possible criticism of indirectly serving the ramified financial interests of the brothers by such a program was impressive.

In all, the fund has come to represent a creditable combination of somewhat incompatible qualities: traditionalism yet innovation, flexibility yet focus. How it has been able to do this within the framework of a family philanthropy is instructive to examine.

One factor has undoubtedly been the deliberate open-endedness of program. Unlike the Rockefeller Foundation, the Rockefeller Brothers Fund does not carry the heavy freight of a long institutional history or the inhibitions that can grow out of an organization's traditions and sense of self-importance. It retains its flexibility by operating essentially as a grant-making institution and not acquiring a large and specialized technical staff. In addition, there is the wholesome respect that has developed between the professional staff and the family members.

The size and diversity of Rockefeller philanthropic assets also contribute to the quality of both program and staff. The resources of the fund itself are substantial, and the numerous smaller family foundations provide staff members with a variety of alternatives for financing unusual projects, even when they are of interest only to one or two members of the family.

But fundamentally the effectiveness of the fund's program derives directly from the caliber of the family members who dominate its board, as well as the Rockefeller family respect for "philanthropy as an art and as an obligation for personal involvement." In describing the brothers' participation in the fund's work, Laurance Rockefeller has said, "My grandfather gave like a forward pass— he threw the ball out and it was up to the others to make a go of it. We feel you must give with the heart as well as the head. There must be a deep personal commitment along with an intellectual understanding of the project." [5]

In connection with the 1969 Tax Reform Act, the Treasury Department proposed that family membership be limited to one quarter of the board after a foundation had been in existence twenty-five years. Commenting on this recommendation to discourage "family domination," Dana Creel commented at the hearings: "This strikes me as ridiculous. It is immensely helpful to have trustees intensely interested in a project. Their leadership and their cooperation with the staff in searching for new ideas has made this a dynamic shop." Creel's comments, although true of the situation in the Rockefeller Brothers Fund, are unfortunately true of only a few other family foundations in the United States.

As time passes, the fund continues to evolve both in program and in structure. The size of the board has been progressively increased and in 1970 numbered thirteen. Nonfamily members have been added, along with members from the younger generation of Rockefellers. Just as the special interest of each of the founding brothers has shaped the fund's activities in the past, so the field of its work continues to widen as new family members are brought in. With the addition of their sister, Mrs. Abbie Rockefeller Mauzé, in 1954, for example, its program expanded noticeably into the field of higher education for women. And as the fourth generation, the great-grandchildren of John D. Rockefeller Sr., become active, their interest in civil rights and urban and rural poverty is gradually being reflected.

The Rockefeller family philanthropic tradition is without equal in the United States and probably in the world in terms of duration, scale, and achievement. If the holding of vast wealth by a single family generation after generation can be justified by devotion to charitable work, then even critics would have to concede that the Rockefeller family, more than any other American plutocratic dynasty, has done so.

5.

Coming of Age in the Ford Foundation

EVERY FOUNDATION is in some sense *sui generis:* the Ford Foundation is that in almost every sense. This prodigal young giant of philanthropy—now in full operation only twenty years—has resources about four times as great as those of Rockefeller and twelve times those of Carnegie. Its assets, which totaled $3.7 billion at the end of 1968, were equal to one-third of the assets of the top thirty-three foundations and one-sixth of those of all 25,000 American foundations.

In its brief career, it has had triumphs as well as conspicuous failures. It has careened from bold attack to indecisive floundering, from conservatism to activism. It is an adolescent that has had great trouble growing up.

The foundation was born out of the ruins of family and corporate disaster. By 1945 old Henry Ford seemed to have gone from eccentricity to the brink of madness. In the view of close associates, he had by his harassment destroyed his son Edsel, who had died two years earlier; and by his paranoia and arbitrariness he had virtually destroyed his great company. It was losing money at a record rate, and management had fallen into the hands of a gang of hired thugs under director Harry Bennett, long-time head of Ford's private NKVD. At that dismal point, the hopes of arresting the plunge into bankruptcy depended on a quiet and gracious widow, Mrs. Edsel Ford, and the eldest of her three sons, Henry 2d, a rather plumpish Yale dropout then in his twenties. But Mrs. Ford and young Henry proved to have toughness as well as vision, and a transformation was effected. They forced the aged founder to relinquish his formal hold over the company in 1945 and, with the help of a group of well-chosen advisers, including New York public relations counsel Earl Newsom, they attacked the more difficult and even dangerous problem of removing Bennett and his group from power. There were days when Henry 2d had to carry a gun to the office.[1]

By 1947—with the company losing $10 million a month—young Henry and his family supporters finally were able to take over. They brought in a new management team, headed by Ernest R. Breech, which within twelve months brought the deficits under control. Within two years profits had begun a spectacular climb. While this revolution was going on, the elder Ford died. His death confronted the surviving members of the family with a task of major proportions, namely, activating the foundation that he and Edsel had established a decade earlier. It had been conceived as a device to administer gifts to the family's favorite charities, mainly the Henry Ford Hospital in Detroit and the Edison Institute, but also to avoid the necessity of selling control of the company in order to pay estate taxes after the death of the donors. By the terms of the wills, the foundation acquired some 90 percent of the shares of the company, shares that within a short period were to be worth billions.

The future level of the income of the foundation, however, was uncertain. The family was preoccupied with the rejuvenation of the company, and the principal donor had left his foundation and his descendants a minimal philanthropic tradition. But again Mrs. Edsel Ford and young Henry achieved the improbable. On the advice of a leading nonfamily member of the five-member board of trustees, Dr. Karl Compton, president of the Massachusetts Institute of Technology, a study committee was appointed to develop plans and recommendations for the foundation's program. The committee, set up in 1948, was under the chairmanship of a San Francisco lawyer, H. Rowan Gaither, who had been Compton's assistant at MIT's Radiation Laboratory during World War II. For the next two years the group Gaither gathered from the social sciences, public administration, economics, and medicine talked with hundreds of persons throughout the United States and abroad about how the foundation should be organized and the fields in which it should concentrate its activities.

Their report was presented in 1950, and with only slight modification it was adopted by the trustees as the foundation's initial plan of action. The board, while the study committee had been at work, had been enlarged from five to twelve by the addition of a number of New York businessmen and financiers, a Midwestern publisher, and a federal judge. In making the new selections, young Henry Ford felt strongly that the board should not be overloaded with persons primarily affiliated with academic institutions and that Wall Streeters and men from other automobile companies should be excluded.

The report, the finest statement of the case for modern creative philanthropy yet produced, aroused great excitement when it was distributed. It began with the premise that the most important problems of contemporary life lay in man's relation to man, not his relation to nature. The foundation would therefore not concentrate on science or technology but would give priority to five areas:

1) the problem of world peace—including the strengthening of the United Nations and its associated international agencies;

2) the problems of democracy—including the elimination of restrictions on freedom of thought and other civil rights; the maintenance of democratic control over concentrations of public and private power; and the improvement of the political processes through which public officers are chosen and policies determined;

3) problems of the economy—including the achievement of high and stable employment levels; greater equality of economic opportunity for all citizens; more satisfactory labor-management relations; and the attainment "of that balance between freedom and control in our economic life which will most effectively serve the well-being of our entire society";

4) the problems of education—including the clarification of educational goals and the evaluation of current educational practices; the reduction of economic, religious, and racial barriers to equality of educational opportunity; and the more effective use of the mass media for nonacademic education of citizens of all ages;

5) the scientific study of man—including his values, motivations, and maladjustments; and the greater use of such knowledge in every aspect of democratic life.

It was an idealistic document. Its unanimous endorsement by trustees of generally conservative business orientation was in part a reflection of the generally hopeful spirit in America then prevailing.To carry it out the trustees named Paul G. Hoffman as president. He was a successful businessman who from 1948 until his appointment in 1951 had gained worldwide recognition for his inspired leadership of the Marshall Plan. Before accepting the assignment, he had long conversations with the trustees, especially Henry Ford 2d, to make certain they understood that he proposed to take the goals laid down in the 1950 report with full seriousness and that he would bring in a team of activists, including the abrasive Robert M. Hutchins, then chancellor of the University of Chicago, to help him. He predicted clashes and controversies as a result, but he was reassured that the trustees were prepared to stand firm even if the winds of public criticism should blow. On this basis Hoffman took command of the foundation's new headquarters, which were established in his home town of Pasadena, California. In addition to Hutchins, he brought in Milton Katz, a lawyer who had been on the faculty of the Harvard Law School before serving as a Marshall Plan ambassador in Europe, and Chester A. Davis, a long-term administrator of government programs in the field of agriculture. Rowan Gaither was also named as a part-time member of the executive group.

Under them, the foundation broke fast from the gate. In the field of education two major quasi-independent agencies were created with their own boards and staffs—the Fund for the Advancement of Education and the Fund for Adult Education. They were suggested by Dr. Hutchins, who believed that as a matter of principle the foundation should operate by broad delegation, and that as a matter of tactics such agencies, to be effective, had to be insulated from interference by the Ford trustees, in whom he had less than unqualified confidence. In the two-year period 1951 to 1953 the foundation gave more than $100 million in grants to these new organizations, which then proceeded vigorously and against considerable opposition to impose a number of Hutchins' reformist ideas upon the American educational establishment.

In the area of international affairs—a primary interest of Hoffman's—the foundation launched an economic development program, the main recipient of which was India; a program of grants in Western Europe; and, reflecting the intensity of Cold War concerns after 1950, a new subsidiary to concentrate on East European problems. In the domestic economics program, an important new agency, the now well-known Resources for the Future, was established; and the so-called "behavioral sciences" program, under the leadership of Dr. Bernard Berelson, began a Center for Advanced Study in the Behavioral Sciences at Palo Alto. A Radio and Television Workshop was set up which, through its program "Omnibus," was to exert a significant influence for a while upon the cultural programing of the commercial networks.

But within two years of Hoffman's arrival the foundation was in a turmoil. Hoffman was often absent from the foundation offices working in the presidential campaign of General Dwight D. Eisenhower. Without his unifying personality, frictions developed among some of the men he had brought in, and over time these escalated into systematic internecine warfare. Relations between the staff and the board rapidly worsened, primarily because of Hutchins' high-handed, almost contemptuous attitude toward the trustees.

But still more serious troubles were developing outside. After the outbreak of the Korean War in 1950, the national mood perceptibly shifted from one of confidence to fear and from progressivism to reaction. The rise of Senator Joseph McCarthy to prominence symbolized the change. The Ford Foundation and its various subsidiaries quickly became one of the favorite targets of the militant anti-Communists. The conservative press began to lay down a barrage of accusations against it, and the House of Representatives, mirroring the new mood, authorized a special committee under the chairmanship of Representative Eugene Cox to investigate "subversion and Communist penetration" among the philanthropic foundations.

The Ford family in Detroit and top officials of the Ford Motor Company, whose automobile sales for the first time in many years had begun to challenge the preeminence of General Motors in the low-cost field, were infuriated by the controversies and by the spasmodic boycotts of Ford products then being organized by extremist groups, especially in the South, the Midwest, and the Far West. The telephone lines from company headquarters in Dearborn, Michigan, to Pasadena and to the individual offices of the trustees began to crackle with complaints about Hoffman and Hutchins, his alleged Rasputin. Within a relatively short time, a sense of bewildered panic developed.

During Christmas week of 1952, Henry Ford, who had become aware of the foundation's internal tensions during his tenure in the preceding months as acting president while Hoffman was campaigning, decided to remove Hoffman and to clean house. In effecting the change, he chose as his trouble-shooter Donald K. David, a member of the boards of both the company and the foundation—and an outspoken critic of Hutchins' educational and social ideas.° In reversing his original position toward Hoffman, Henry Ford 2d displayed the tough decision-making ability which was later to become his trademark in handling business or philanthropic problems; and Donald David's intervention as the agent for both the family and the company in the foundation's affairs also established a pattern.

Announcement of Hoffman's "resignation" was made on February 4, 1953. Rowan Gaither was named to succeed him, and the foundation's headquarters were transferred to New York City.† The controversial Hutchins was left behind in Pasadena, in charge of the manorial house with its swimming pool and rose garden which

° Mr. David in his varied career had been both a prominent corporation executive and an educator; he was at the time dean of the Harvard Business School.

† This was a move welcomed not only by the trustees, who by then wanted to get the foundation out from under Hoffman's influence, but also by those staff members who had discovered the impossibility of running a major intellectual institution from a California retreat. They found it necessary to make so many transcontinental flights to get their work done that the foundation became known to insiders as "the Fund for the Advancement of Aviation."

had served as the foundation's headquarters, almost totally cut off from contact with the new offices. Milton Katz moved east and after a decent interval went back to Harvard with a $10 million grant to establish a new Center of International Legal Studies. Chester Davis also moved to New York, where he sulked on the foundation payroll without a function until he was retired several months later.

Gaither, a mild and reflective man, was chosen as president partly because he was known to be a good problem-solver and partly because the trustees were confident, given his unforceful personality, that he would carry out instructions and not plunge the institution into new difficulties. The tasks he was given were several: to bring in a new group of officers; to "recapture foundation control" over the two major educational funds which Hoffman and Hutchins had put into orbit; to keep at bay the officers of the Ford Motor Company, who were then aggressively attempting to intervene in foundation affairs; and to calm and reunify the board, which was in a state of great agitation and division.

Gaither's problems were not made easier when the trustees in February 1953 granted $15 million to the Fund for the Republic, a new body established to concentrate on problems of civil liberties in the United States. Its creation had been approved in principle eighteen months before, but grant action had been delayed out of "public relations considerations" until after the presidential election of November 1952. This fateful stroke, taken at the height of the McCarthy mania, infuriated the senator's supporters. Westbrook Pegler and George Sokolsky, in their widely syndicated columns, blasted the fund several times a week as "a Communist front," and Fulton Lewis Jr. harped on the same theme in his nightly radio broadcasts to the nation. The virulence of this sustained attack was somewhat surprising in view of the extremely cautious approach taken by the man initially chosen to head it— Clifford Case, a former Republican congressman from New Jersey with a reputation as a moderate liberal. Anti-McCarthy commentators at the time called his leadership limp and fumbling. One of them, Frank J. Donner, later wrote, "He cast the fund in the passive role of a sort of Prince Charming whose tender kiss would awaken the innate good sense of the American people." When Case resigned within a few months to run for the Senate in his home state, the Ford trustees were stunned to learn that the fund board, then headed by Paul Hoffman, had proceeded, without consulting them, to name Hutchins as his successor.° Hutchins promptly turned the fund head-on into the gale with a series of highly controversial actions and statements. Then in mid-1953, seeking to ride the wave of anti-Communism, Representative B. Carroll Reece mounted a second congressional investigation of the foundations, centering on Ford.

For the next three years, until his health failed, Gaither worked assiduously to carry out his assignments. He named as officers several men who had worked with him on the study committee, including Thomas Carroll, Don K. Price, and William McPeak. After much bureaucratic strife and painful negotiation, settlements were reached in 1954 with both the Fund for the Advancement of Education and the Fund for Adult Education, the former receiving a farewell grant of $25 million and the latter one of $7.5 million. The Fund for Advancement was eventually absorbed into the foundation; the Fund for Adult Education, once its resources were exhausted, expired.

But the main energies of the foundation in 1953 and 1954 were consumed in defending itself against public and congressional criticism. It was still a young, wobbly, almost invertebrate institution under pressure, and it did not distinguish itself by its response.

One critical weakness was the fact that the board itself was unseasoned and many of its members were not well equipped, intellectually or otherwise, to cope with the complex philanthropic and political issues that confronted them. Gaither's approach was to search everywhere for possible compromises—between the foundation's new officers and the company, between the company and

° Word of the action reached key foundation officers and trustees at a mid-Manhattan motion picture studio where, as it happened, they were being filmed for a public relations documentary. Despite their heavy makeup, the klieg lights revealed their flushed faces in reactions that went from disbelief to indignation. The fact that the cameras were not turning at that point is a permanent loss to historiography of one of philanthropy's more vivid moments.

the board, and between factions of the board itself. Floundering about, the foundation was saved from utter disaster only by the integrity of a few trustees, the courage and loyalty of a few members of the staff, and the sober good sense of its legal counsel, plus the unexpected boon of the ineptly conducted Reece investigation.

By late 1954, as the anti-Communist storm began to subside, the trustees began to turn their attention to new problems, one of which had to do with diversification of investments. The board recognized that even though the profits of the company were then growing splendidly, linking the foundation's income exclusively to the fortunes of a single company in a historically cyclical industry was inherently unsafe. They also recognized that as long as its holdings were undiversified the foundation would be confronted with allegations about company control over the foundation, or vice-versa. Diversification also began to seem desirable to the company: the foundation was not necessarily an asset to its sales efforts, and the fact that most of the profits were flowing into philanthropy had, in the opinion of some of its executives, created a dangerous vulnerability in their efforts to resist union wage demands in contract negotiations. For these and other reasons, the trustees in late 1954 directed the finance committee of the board to begin planning for the first public sale of the foundation's shares in the company.

Another problem was that of "unreasonable accumulation of income" as prohibited by tax legislation. Profits of the company had increased at such a rate (from large deficits in the late 1940s to $195.6 million of income in 1954) that foundation expenditures had difficulty keeping up. Not unexpectedly it was perceived that the foundation at one stroke might dispose of its backlog of income and also appease some of its political attackers by making a large distribution of string-free general support grants to established, uncontroversial institutions throughout the country. To what extent worry about the foundation's bad public relations was more important in the minds of the trustees than concern about legal difficulties arising from undistributed income is impossible to say. In any event, in March 1955 they announced a package of $50 million in grants to private colleges throughout the country; and a month later, an advisory committee of prominent businessmen and educators was created to plan the outlay of a still larger amount. In these actions the trustees had been spurred on and guided by Donald David in his triple capacity as foundation trustee, company director, and Ford family confidant.

At the same time the board became increasingly concerned over the indecisive direction of Gaither. The situation came to a head in September 1955, when the board asked David to set up a full-time office in the foundation to see to it that action was completed on the stock sale, the general grants program, and other matters. Once David started to work, results came quickly.

In late 1955, the foundation announced that it would market to the public the first block of its auto company shares. After complex negotiations with the family, it had been agreed that the foundation's nonvoting stock, upon sale, would acquire voting rights, thereby eliminating the earlier division of the shares into voting and nonvoting classes.°

Later a stock split was also decided upon in order to make possible a lower unit offering price and thereby achieve wider public distribution. On January 26, 1956, the foundation sold 10.2 million of the new shares for $642.6 million.†

In anticipation of the proceeds of the sale, the foundation had announced in December 1955 the most massive single unloading of philanthropic resources ever known—grants totaling $550 million. More than 600 private accredited four-year colleges and universities throughout the United States were given $260 million for the

° More precisely, the shares of the company were reclassified into three categories: a new Class A nonvoting stock owned by the Ford Foundation; a Class B voting stock held by the Ford family and their associates, which was assigned 40 percent of the total voting rights; and a new common stock to which 60 percent of the voting rights was assigned, a share of the new common stock to come into being whenever a share of the new Class A stock was sold to the public or otherwise disposed of by the foundation. The three categories were assigned equal participation in dividends. By this carefully formulated plan the control of the family over the company was effectively preserved, the lack of voting power by the foundation over the affairs of the company was perpetuated, and a type of voting share was created that could be offered to the public.

† Prior to the sale the foundation owned 88 percent of the shares of the company. As of 1972, after further sales, it had disposed of most of its original holdings, but it still owned about 16 percent of the shares outstanding.

purpose of increasing faculty salaries. The sum of $198 million was
distributed to 3,500 voluntary nonprofit hospitals to improve and
extend their services. Over $90 million was given to the forty-five
privately supported medical schools. The impatience of the trustees
to announce this vast distribution—which amounted to more than
150 percent of the foundation's total outlays over its prior eighteen
years of existence—was astonishing. It was only through the determined efforts of staff member William McPeak that any selectivity
was attached to the college and university grants. The hospital
awards were made without the benefit of recommendations by an
advisory committee, and the medical school grants were almost an
afterthought. (At the meeting at which these latter were approved,
and which the author attended, Henry Ford 2d remarked ironically, "Let's make the total an uneven number—perhaps $91 mil-
lion point something—so it will look like we have considered the
matter carefully.") To ensure that the grants would have maximum
impact on press and congressional opinion, the foundation widely
distributed a series of special booklets listing, by state and congressional district, the hundreds of institutions that had been assisted.

In its first six years the foundation's relationship with the Ford
Motor Company had gone through fundamental change. For several years members of the company in Dearborn had not hesitated
to blast specific foundation plans and actions in the most direct
fashion and even to demand the removal of certain foundation personnel. They may not have transgressed the bounds of legality in
so doing, but they repeatedly skirted close. By 1956, however, they
had developed more restraint; and the foundation, having regained
a degree of self-confidence and composure as political attacks sub-
sided, developed a greater degree of resistance.°

° Even as late as 1964 the problem of Ford Motor Company intrusion had
not been totally eliminated. The specific incident involved relations with the
Portuguese government. African nationalist movements at the time were carrying on both guerrilla and political activities in opposition to Portuguese control in its African colonies, Angola, Mozambique, and Portuguese Guinea. In
the late 1950s the Ford Foundation had begun supporting various projects
and programs in Africa, one of which was a training school in Tanzania for African political refugees from areas to the south, including the Portuguese terri-

By 1956, Rowan Gaither had become too ill to perform his functions and the trustees were faced with the necessity of making a third choice of president. On September 30 they named Dr. Henry T. Heald, then head of New York University, to succeed Gaither, who was at the same time promoted to chairman of the board to succeed Henry Ford 2d. Heald was to hold his new position for nine years.

He came to the foundation at the age of fifty-one. Trained as a civil engineer, he had taught at the Armour Institute of Technology, then a small struggling college in the slums of Chicago's South Side, and became its head at the age of thirty-two. For the next fourteen years he built up both its income and its enrollment. He also became involved in Chicago's troubled and sometimes sordid civic affairs, heading various committees to clean up the city's politics-ridden school system and to plan the redevelopment of the decayed central core. As his reputation spread he was offered highly paid positions in business as well as the opportunity to run for mayor of Chicago on the Republican ticket. But he preferred to stay in the field of education, and in 1952 he moved to New York University, where he took on the complicated task of its reorganization and refinancing.

As soon as Heald took office he hung his favorite lithograph of the dark, brooding, unbearded Lincoln, whom he resembles slightly, on the otherwise bare walls of his office and then proceeded to make himself master of the house. He quickly put the

tories. Advertisements financed by the motor company's competitors began to appear in various newspapers in the Portuguese colonies attacking Ford dealers and Ford products because they were helping to finance the "revolutionaries who are killing our Portuguese brothers." In September 1964 the Portuguese foreign minister publicly attacked the Ford Foundation for its alleged support of one of the revolutionary organizations. On December 19, 1964, the New York *Times* carried the following report datelined Lisbon under the headline "Ford Fund Seeking to Placate Lisbon":

"The Ford Foundation is reported to have assured the government of Premier Antonio de Oliveira Salazar that it would be consulted before any future grants were given to African areas of particular interest to Portugal.

"The Foundation's concession was made public today in a communiqué from Ford-Lusitania, a subsidiary of the Ford Motor Company. At the same time Ford-Lusitania denied any connection with the Ford Foundation, which it stressed was a 'completely independent institution.'"

foundation's affairs in order and put the trustees back in their place. He made decisions on operational matters promptly and systematically, and within a few weeks the frozen executive machinery of the foundation again began to whir. He then put his stamp—unfortunately an intellectually narrow and desiccated stamp—on the programs of the foundation. He had no interest or experience in international matters; he actively disliked "reformers," including such black spokesmen as Roy Wilkins and Martin Luther King Jr., whom he considered "propagandistic politicians"; and he had no natural sympathy for "impractical men of ideas," including social scientists in general. Against the advice of many prominent scientists and educators, he promptly closed down both the behavioral sciences and mental health programs. International programs were deemphasized and all staff recommendations of a controversial nature encountered Heald's flat opposition.

On the other hand, he had a strong interest in improving the management and financing of educational institutions. In his first public statements he stressed emphatically that "the Ford Foundation is essentially an educational foundation." Massive allocations were subsequently made to provide fellowships for students wishing to become teachers, to help some sixty colleges and universities to improve teacher education, and to upgrade the nation's engineering schools. Substantial funds were also given to encourage the development of educational television.

In addition, by 1961, three essentially new programs had begun to develop, if not under Heald's leadership at least with his acceptance. Under the dedicated direction of W. McNeil Lowry the foundation's small and tentative program in the fine arts and humanities had begun to win wide public and professional acceptance and with the support of a few key trustees was accorded an increasing proportion of the foundation's budget. Paul Ylvisaker began to transform the foundation's staid public affairs program into a lively attack on the problems of youth, the aged, and the urban ghettos. And, as a result of staff proposals and the persuasive initiative of the Rockefeller Foundation and John D. Rockefeller 3d, the foundation began to give increasing attention to the interrelated problems of world population growth and chronic food shortages.

It can fairly be said that during his first five years in office Heald delivered to the trustees what they wanted of him. He made the foundation run; he extricated it from many of its earlier controversial involvements, regaining for it the respect of many of its former conservative critics, including even Representative Reece; and though the projects of his own initiative were more massive than brilliant, he permitted pockets of innovation to exist in the foundation's huge and diverse program.

But most of the trustees by 1961 had become dissatisfied with him and his style. In large part the difficulty stemmed from Heald's unbending insistence on his executive prerogatives and his aloof, uncommunicative manner in dealing with the board. His practice was to inform the trustees about major program and policy decisions only in the final phase and, in the opinion of board members, after many of the preliminary decisions had already been made. In addition there was a widespread feeling that although the foundation's program had not stagnated under Heald, it was hamstrung by his negative attitude toward new ideas. In September 1961 the trustees, over Heald's strenuous objection, set up a committee to conduct "a general review of the programs and procedures of the foundation." Ostensibly it was to help define policies and programs for the coming decade but, to a number of its proponents, the study had at least two additional purposes: first, to redress the imbalance of authority which, in their opinion, had developed between the trustees and the president and to make the board more influential, particularly in relation to program development; second, to force Heald to open the foundation's program to a number of new areas of activity. At least a few members of the board also entertained the hope that the study might precipitate Heald's ouster.

Completed in mid-1962, the committee's report laid down a number of stringent directives about the mode of the foundation's future operation. The president was instructed to develop a closer relationship with the trustees "through formal and informal means" on all policy and program questions. New procedures were instituted for periodic review of ongoing programs by the trustees and their direct participation in the planning of new programs. On a point of special sensitivity he was instructed to extend the work of the foundation in the field of civil rights, "including support for projects to promote full exercise of voting rights" and to extend equal educational, employment, housing, recreational, social, and political opportunities to persons of all races. He was also required, almost insultingly, to transmit periodically a "general identification of all major projects and proposals which have been rejected by the president and his staff, together with the principal reasons for rejection."

The public version of the report, distributed in July 1962, tactfully obscured, of course, the power struggle that had taken place. Heald accepted the outcome realistically, and positive results followed. Tension between him and the board was lessened by the new operating procedures, which secured his position for an additional three years. During that period significant program developments occurred: expanded support was given to individual artists as well as to cultural institutions; a major integrated attack was launched on the problems of several large metropolitan areas throughout the United States; and activities in the field of race relations and international affairs were accelerated. But the largest set of grants (totaling $252 million) was made to twelve universities and fifty-seven colleges to further "their overall development as regional and national centers of excellence." They reflected Heald's concept of the Ford Foundation as a kind of banking partner to higher education. The grants required that the recipients raise matching funds, and Heald later claimed with pride that the program had generated some $900 million in university gifts.

But by 1965 strains between Heald and the board were again evident. Many of the trustees still found him a stiff and uninspiring man, inadequate both intellectually and in social outlook to lead the world's largest private foundation. By the summer of 1965 the hunt was on once again for a new president.

Businesslike Philanthropy

Henry T. Heald presided over the Ford Foundation for nine years, nearly half of the institution's active life to date. In the fashion of a good corporation executive, he had managed it responsibly, efficiently, and prudently. Some of the major projects financed with his active support, such as the International Rice Research Institute (in cooperation with the Rockefeller Foundation) and the Educational Facilities Laboratory for experimentation in the design of school facilities and equipment, had been highly successful; but ironically, the two most distinguished achievements of his term —the program dealing with urban poverty and racial discrimination and the program in the arts—were philosophically in conflict with his natural sympathies and outlook.

As he was leaving office in January 1966 Heald speculated that in the coming years the foundation would probably change considerably and unpredictably: "A foundation inevitably reflects in some measure the people involved in it, and a lot depends simply on what happens, on the temper of the times." His words were prophetic.

At that moment, McGeorge Bundy, who had been tapped by the trustees to become Ford's fourth president, was concluding his duties in Washington as White House national security adviser. In many ways Bundy was the antithesis of his predecessor. Heald was a son of plain Midwestern parents, Bundy a scion of wealthy Boston Brahmins. Heald's concerns and experience were essentially domestic; Bundy was an authority on international affairs and, according to his friends, aspired to become secretary of state. Heald was a lonely and austere man; Bundy was outgoing and companionable, at least among his close friends of the political and academic elite. Heald was a thoroughgoing conservative; Bundy, though not necessarily liberal in his own convictions, enjoyed some of the reflected liberal luster of John F. Kennedy's New Frontier.

Jet Take-Off

Bundy's installation on March 1, 1966, was accompanied by the simultaneous resignation of John J. McCloy after six years as chairman of the board and the succession of Dr. Julius Stratton, retired president of the Massachusetts Institute of Technology, a quiet man whose influence on the foundation over the years has been unobtrusive but important. This new directing team prompted one long-time member of the board to say: "The foundation began with a roar fifteen years ago, then sank to a whisper. It's about time it began to roar again."

Bundy's opportunity was to give the foundation new leadership and direction at a time when ominous crises were developing internationally and domestically, when powerful new social forces had begun to impose their demands on the nation, and when the expansion of federal programs urgently required restructuring of the relationship between private philanthropy and government. The news of his appointment gave the foundation an immediate lift, and he moved into his new responsibilities with ease and assurance. To the board he conveyed an impression of supreme self-confidence, and he immediately won the support of the staff by the quickness of his mind as well as his receptivity to fresh ideas. Their fears that he might begin by conducting a purge and by sharply restricting their authority were quickly dissipated. Although he took a direct hand in a number of important new program decisions, on the whole he drove with a loose and light rein, leaving the several directors as free as they had ever been. They concluded that Bundy had brought to the foundation his administrative habits from Harvard—supervisory permissiveness and scrupulous respect for the judgment of his colleagues. Within a few weeks the foundation achieved the highest level of morale that it had seen in more than a decade. This was further boosted when David E. Bell, who had acquired a fine reputation first as President Kennedy's budget director and later as head of the foreign aid program, took charge of all the foundation's international activities.

Surprisingly, the major changes introduced during Bundy's first year as president were in financial policy, not program. Under Heald the outlays of the foundation had risen rapidly from a level of $162 million in 1957 to $365 million in 1966. But shortly after Bundy's appointment the board decided to cut them back roughly to the level of the foundation's annual income at the time, about $200 million a year.*

＊ The trustees' new sense of thriftiness about grant levels was not evident, however, in their attitude toward administrative expenses. Their decision to

In September 1968 a second major change in financial policy was announced, a decision to take social criteria into account in making some of the foundation's future investments. It hoped thereby to advance its program objectives not only by the traditional mode of outright grants to nonprofit organizations but also by loans and temporary transfers of funds. Some of the most promising work in certain fields of high foundation priority—minority entrepreneurship, for example, and low income housing—it claimed was being carried out by organizations which were ineligible for grants but which could be helped through the foundation's investment account. A policy breakthrough had been made, but great difficulties were later encountered in identifying and in carrying out such quasi-investment, quasi-philanthropic projects.

The same year significant actions were taken to diversify the foundation's board. The traditional line-up of white Establishment figures was broken with the addition of the first black, Dr. Vivian Henderson of Clark College in Atlanta. Two of Bundy's former Washington colleagues were also elected: Kermit Gordon, former director of the Bureau of the U.S. Budget under President Johnson and now head of the Brookings Institution, and Robert McNamara, formerly secretary of defense and now head of the World Bank.

But there was little change made after Bundy's takeover, initially at least, in most of the foundation's programs. Those in the arts and humanities, for example, and in population studies and control were under strong professional direction and had developed their own momentum which he did not choose to interfere with. In the

---

erect a dramatic new headquarter building in 1967 at a cost of $17.5 million resulted in a sixfold increase in office costs at one stroke. Before moving to the new structure the foundation paid a not inconsiderable annual rent of $550,000 for its offices on New York's elegant Madison Avenue. But thereafter office costs jumped to more than $3 million a year, counting housekeeping expenses, a $1 million annual payment to New York City in lieu of taxes, and the forgone income on the huge capital investment in the building.

Foundation officials have never contended that the cost of the building was necessary for the efficient functioning of the organization, although some have expressed the hope that with the passage of time and the progress of inflation the foundation would eventually come out ahead. Whether its lavish expense could be defended as an esthetic contribution to the quality of life in New York City is a matter on which architectural critics are in sharp disagreement.

work in education Bundy fostered a gradual turning away from bulk grants to private colleges and universities toward diversified experiments to encourage innovation and improvement at all levels of the educational system. The new approach was less arm-twisting than it had been under Hutchins, but more activist than it had been under Heald.

The most noticeable change he introduced was in the program called "national affairs." Bundy replaced Paul Ylvisaker, who had led it during the Heald period, with a man of his own choice, Mitchell Sviridoff, a former trade union leader and New York City official. Very quickly the percentage of the foundation's outlays allocated to it doubled, many of the new grants being sharp, reformist interventions into sensitive social areas. The foundation's international programs, which some had thought might be Bundy's primary interest, were simultaneously given a lower priority than the domestic programs. The European segment, under a rapid succession of chiefs, almost disintegrated; but work in the poorer areas of the world, under David Bell's conscientious direction,

Table 2

Ford Foundation Grant Breakdown by Program Divisions,
1966 and 1969 (in millions)

	1966		1969	
	$	% of total	$	% of total
National affairs	29.0	8.3	42.	20.6
Education	72.6	20.8	46.	22.5
Humanities and arts	88.0°	25.2	20.	9.8
Noncommercial TV	15.9	4.5	16.5	8.1
International	118.4	34.0	51.5†	25.2
Population	21.3	6.1	8.	3.9
Nonprogram	2.7	.7	20.	9.8
Total	347.9	100.0	204.0	100.0
		(99.6) ‡		(99.9) ‡

° This figure was unusually high for the year because of $80 million of special grants to symphony orchestras.

† The reduction is largely due to the elimination of the international training and research program, which had supported extensive fellowships and grants to United States institutions dealing with international affairs.

‡ Figures supplied by the Office of Reports of the Ford Foundations. Because of rounding, figures do not add to 100 percent.

achieved greater focus and a higher level of professionalization. Table 2 summarizes in dollar terms the major changes in program scale and emphasis between 1966, Heald's last year, and 1969, by which time Bundy's new directions were fully evident.

In the broadest sense, Bundy's selection signified a decision by the trustees to return to the spirit of their 1950 report on policy and program, which had declared a strong concern for the human problems of a democratic society. It reflected a determination to make the Ford Foundation a relevant philanthropic force in a time of controversial social and political change. As the instrument of their purpose, Bundy was an appropriate choice and he has sought to carry out their intent energetically and imaginatively, even if not always judiciously.

Crash-Landing

By 1969 the foundation had once again aroused deep public apprehension, mainly in conservative circles but elsewhere too, as starkly confirmed by the congressional events leading to passage of the Tax Reform Act. By 1970 it was expected by many that Ford had been so lacerated by adverse publicity that it might shift back to a more cautious program. But only its tone of voice seemed to change, becoming more subdued. The actual character of its subsequent grants showed that Ford remained essentially undeterred in using a portion of its huge resources to help solve explosive social problems.° How long it could hold to that course was a moot question. But there seemed to be a good possibility at least that the foundation had achieved a sufficient degree of independence and maturity to be able to withstand the attacks that such a course would inevitably arouse. Progressive diversification of its investments had freed it from undue influence by the Ford Motor Com-

° Ford, however, is an "activist" foundation only in relation to the general conservatism of the large foundations. As will be documented in chapter 21, well under 10 percent of its outlays to date can be called experimental or activist. The comparable figure for most of the large foundations would be nearer 1 percent. In contrast, there are several medium-sized and smaller foundations that devote most of their outlays to grants of this kind.

pany; the board, tempered in the fires of successive congressional investigations and other public disputes, had become a more able and strong-minded group; and the influence of Henry Ford 2d was increasingly constructive. Although no longer young, he seemed more youthful in his ideas. In fact, he had become one of the most militant of the major industrialists in urging the need for national reforms.

That the foundation has not chosen to seek maximum safety and minimum controversy has undoubtedly given courage to other smaller foundations. But Ford also creates serious problems for them: it looms so high it always draws lightning. As the heads of some of the *avant-garde* foundations are inclined to say, "Ford gets into more trouble dollar for dollar in any controversial thing it does than any other foundation, by far. And when it gets into trouble, we are all in trouble." Ford's sheer mass also introduces an unnecessary and unhelpful factor of fear into public consideration of philanthropic issues—fear of undue influence, of intimidation of grantees, of thought control.

Nor does an examination of its grant record provide evidence that it has to be as large as it is to do its best work and play its most useful role. On the contrary, its scale seems to have contributed to a characteristic sloppiness in grant-making and to have impaired, not strengthened, its leadership capacity. Its bulk excites more resentment than admiration, and its example, even when good, is often felt to be inapplicable to their circumstances by smaller foundations.

Quite probably, the best thing Ford's trustees could do for the foundation itself, and philanthropy in general, would be to put aside the vanity of being "the world's largest" and now break it up into three or four Rockefeller-sized separate institutions. But *la folie de la grandeur*, as General de Gaulle demonstrated, is an almost incurable disease.

6.

Danforth and Kellogg:
Fine But Flawed

DANFORTH AND KELLOGG, two of the best of the large foundations, present a paradox. Each has business ties so close that a question arises whether their devotion to the public welfare is not also allied with service to private economic interests. Both of them demonstrate that such linkage is not necessarily incompatible with effective—even superb—philanthropic performance. Moreover, there is no evidence of detriment to the economic performance of the associated companies as a result of the foundation—business relationship. Does this mean, then, that in terms of public policy and the ethics of philanthropy such relationships should simply be accepted?

Both foundations were outgrowths of the phenomenal rise of mass merchandising in American economic development. Since both are based on large Midwestern fortunes, they also symbolize the beginning of a westward shift of the geographical center in American finance. The donors were among the first to realize the great profit-making possibilities in the emergence of mass consumption and standardized products, and both William Danforth and Will Kellogg possessed transcendent ability in devising new techniques to capitalize on them. In their private lives, both were strongly motivated by religious principles and had active interest in civic and charitable affairs. But there the similarity ends. In personality, Danforth was exuberant and outgoing, while Kellogg was withdrawn and desperately unhappy.

The Danforth Foundation

William H. Danforth was a promotional genius in business and an indefatigable do-gooder in his community. He was, in fact, such a stereotype of the Victorian virtues of hard work, clean living, and positive thinking that he would have been a comic figure had he not been so obviously sincere—and so successful.

He was born in 1870 in a small town in southeast Missouri, and in the closing years of the nineteenth century began a small feed and grain business in St. Louis, which he eventually developed into a giant international enterprise. He advertised the products of his company by a distinctive trademark (the familiar Purina red checkerboard), slogans ("If Chicken Chowder won't make your hens lay, they must be roosters"), and prize contests (an annual competition for the best answer to why the Purina mule, another trademark of the company, had a kettle hung on its outstretched tail). He sometimes wore a red checkerboard jacket and matching socks to the office.

He made the workers in his company begin each day with a prayer and subjected them to calisthenics every morning and afternoon in lieu of coffee breaks. A believer in the power of inspiration, he wrote them a message of uplift every week for thirty-five years, a copy of which was placed on each employee's desk first thing Monday morning. A typical example: [1]

PRESIDENT'S PERSONAL MONDAY MORNING MESSAGE

August 7, 1929

"I like a Good Haircut"

Hans Koener, the *first-class* barber on the steamer *Reliance*, gave me a good haircut. When he had finished he looked me over and said, "I like a good haircut." He knew the secret of life—loving your job and doing it well.

When you have surveyed this week's work, I wonder if you

will have the same feeling of joy and consciousness of work
well done as did Hans when he said, "I like a good haircut."

William H. Danforth
President

In his civic and home life Danforth's energies and enthusiasms
were boundless. Daily exercise was an obligation for each member
of his family. He took his son on frequent hunting trips; he show-
ered his daughter with handwritten notes of advice and affection;
and he and his wife traveled systematically to all parts of the
world. Devoutly religious, he always carried a pocket Bible with
him, well thumbed and underlined. For most of his working life he
taught Sunday school at his local church and built up attendance
by the same kind of promotional methods he used in his business.
On one occasion he gave out live baby alligators as prizes for new
members.

In 1932, the fortunes of his company having reached a low ebb,
Danforth, after nearly forty years in command, suddenly turned
over control to his son, Donald. Thereafter, freed from company responsibilities, he devoted himself to the foundation which he and
his wife had established in 1927. Through it he gave a great many
loans to young men and women for their college education—
sending them letters of advice and inspiration with their monthly
checks. He made grants to help construct "meditation chapels" on
a number of college campuses and gave scholarships to the American Youth Foundation for its summer leadership camp. He personally attended the camping sessions, challenging the boys to live the
"Four-Square Life," to "Stand tall, Think tall, Smile tall, and Live
tall." His own library at the camp featured such works as *The
Charm of the Impossible* and *The Quest of the Best.* He also
widely distributed a book he had written in 1930, *I Dare You;*
some 750,000 copies were sold or given away, a good many by
Danforth himself, who passed them out to airline hostesses, wait-
ers, and others whom he encountered on his constant travels. Until
1940 his foundation was little more than a lavish hobby. But in
that year he named a friend, Dr. William J. Hutchins (whose son

Robert was then chancellor of the University of Chicago), former president of Berea College in Kentucky, as an adviser. Under Hutchins' influence the foundation developed a program to strengthen college teaching and improve faculty-student relationships.

Through the 1940s the foundation slowly expanded these activities, but because of the rapid growth which began to take place in company profits the level of its grants fell further and further behind its income. In 1950 a new federal revenue act had added a rule against the "unreasonable accumulation" of income by foundations—a provision that eventually got the Danforth Foundation into trouble. In 1958 the Internal Revenue Service revoked Danforth's tax exemption for the years 1951 and 1952 on the ground that the foundation's accumulation for that biennium as well as for prior years was "grossly unreasonable." The government alleged that up until 1951 the foundation had received income of more than $5.7 million but had distributed only $1.06 million, or 19 percent, in grants. For 1951 and 1952 it had received more than $2.5 million but had granted only $304,000, or 12 percent. The foundation was obliged to pay $557,000 in tax deficiencies—which it did under protest.

In its defense the foundation said that in January 1951 it had hired its first full-time director, Dr. Kenneth I. Brown, former head of Denison University in Ohio, and that it had not had sufficient time to expand its grant-making program. But the judge who ruled against the foundation said that no evidence had been submitted of a serious attempt by the foundation "to relate its program to anticipated income." In any event, the foundation's outlays rose steeply thereafter, increasing to $937,000 in 1953 and $3.7 million by 1960. In fact, Danforth grants have exceeded income every year since 1953; in 1968 they reached the extraordinary total of $11.4 million, roughly $7 million more than income for that year.

During Brown's ten-year tenure, the foundation moved progressively further away from family-style, donor-directed charity. Its grants emphasized higher education, not infrequently with a religious overtone. The Danforth graduate fellowships were established in 1952 as a foundation-operated project to attract able younger people to college teaching.° In 1955 a teacher grants program was inaugurated to enable faculty members at accredited colleges to complete their doctoral programs. In 1956 the foundation began an internship project to prepare theological students for the profession of "the campus ministry." A year later it introduced a program to provide graduate study for college chaplains and directors of campus religious activities, and an annual workshop was started for college and university faculty members to study ways and means of strengthening undergraduate liberal arts education. In 1959, in a random leap overseas, the foundation began its first foreign program by offering graduate fellowships in the United States to young teachers in thirty private colleges in India.†

The most creative phase of the foundation's evolution began with the appointment of its second executive director, Merrimon Cuninggim, in 1961. He had been a Rhodes scholar, an intercollegiate tennis champion, chaplain of the battleship *Tennessee* in World War II, and a popular dean of the Perkins School of Theology at Southern Methodist University in Texas. A sharp increase in the size and professional competence of the staff immediately took place, and in early 1962 the foundation moved its offices from the premises of the Ralston Purina Company to a separate location in St. Louis. That same year Cuninggim published the first formal statement of the foundation's aims: to give aid and encouragement to persons rather than provide capital funds for the impersonal aspects of education; to emphasize the humane values of the Hebrew-Christian tradition and of a free democratic society; and to strengthen the essential quality of education.

In the same document, notice was given that the foundation thereafter intended to be somewhat more entrepreneurial in its approach: "By virtue of its aims . . . the foundation comes to be something more than a reservoir of resources for the support of

° That same year William Danforth died. He had helped form the Christian Carolers Association in St. Louis in 1911 and had served as its president for forty years; he died on Christmas Eve while waiting for the singers to arrive at his home.
† The program was terminated in 1965 after some difficulties with the local educational authorities. In 1969, however, the Indian government approved the foundation's request to resume certain educational activities.

other institutions. Rather, the foundation itself is a specialized educational institution, a working agency. Its self-confessed purposes point toward the necessity of its trying to help solve the chief educational problems of the day."

In 1963–64 the foundation accentuated its interest in the education of blacks. Earlier it had given some twenty-eight black colleges in the South direct budgetary support to help them to achieve full accreditation. It then financed a pace-setting program in collaboration with the Southern Association of Colleges and Schools and the College Entrance Examination Board to widen opportunities for black students in the South to get a college education. In the next year it extended its work in the field of black education to secondary schools and began to be actively concerned with the problems of student unrest on American campuses, the special needs of urban universities, and schooling problems in Appalachia. As Danforth moved more directly into these urgent secular problems it apparently felt it necessary to reaffirm its commitment to the religious aspects of education, which it did in a rather labored and equivocal manner. In its report for 1964–65, it said: "It should not need to be said that this interest has nothing to do with proselytizing for a particular faith or propagandizing for a peculiar creed." It went on to say, "Because the foundation has gladly confessed this interest through the years, some observers have sometimes thought that it represented its central, even its sole, purpose as a philanthropy. Such an opinion is mistaken. Because the foundation has changed its expression of this interest from time to time, other observers have occasionally thought that it was being weakened or even discontinued. Such a notion is equally erroneous. It is the foundation's view that neither piety nor impiety is a substitute for education's giving proper place for the consideration of nonsectarian religious values." *

Between 1956 and 1966 the foundation's board was progressively

---

° A few months later, however, the foundation redefined the terms of its Kent fellowship program—one of its principal activities related to the moral and religious aspects of education—by eliminating specific reference to religious commitment as a qualification for candidates. Despite the protestations of the annual report, secularization seemed to be under way.

expanded from seven to twelve, of whom a majority after 1960 were non-family. In 1966 the foundation committed $5 million to support a seven-year program by the Council of Southern Universities to upgrade the faculties of predominantly black schools. It also joined with the Carnegie Corporation to support a newly formed Education Commission of the States to bring educators and politicians into closer working relationships and to foster competent research into educational problems at the state level.

In the late 1960s Danforth enlarged its program to include the problem of the urban crisis, appropriating an initial sum of $1.5 million to be used for projects in the St. Louis metropolitan area. It decided not to concentrate on those aspects of the urban problem that are primarily technological in nature, such as transportation or pollution, but rather on housing, employment, education, and "community reconciliation." It also established a special postgraduate fellowship program to help qualified teachers prepare for university black studies programs.

Although it had come late and cautiously into the turbulent fields of urban and racial problems, Danforth was quickly subjected to backlash pressures opposed to such a course. The crisis was precipitated in 1970 by the scholarship program it financed under its 1968 appropriation for young persons from poor neighborhoods. One of the first awards went to a young black, Percy Green, a militant ghetto leader. This caused acute resentment in some white conservative circles that considered him "a troublemaker." Final selection of awards had been made not by the foundation itself but by a committee of prominent private citizens. Despite such insulation, however, Danforth felt the heat. And under it, a good portion of the board wilted. Several members urged that the selection committee be overruled and Green's scholarship canceled. A panicky few were even inclined to cancel the entire program. It required a special all-day meeting of the board before it was decided not to withdraw the disputed scholarship. But the decision was not without its price.

This became apparent in June 1970 when, in a wide departure from the general pattern of its grants, the foundation announced a $15 million general support gift to Washington University (of which William H. Danforth, grandson of the founder and chairman of the foundation's board, was vice-chancellor for Medical Affairs and has since been made chancellor) and one of $1.5 million to St. Louis University. The foundation disingenuously explained its action simply as a response to the financial stringency being faced by those two institutions as well as by many private universities throughout the country. It carefully avoided reference to the privately expressed view of some of the trustees that the foundation had been forced to "atone" to its critics in the St. Louis area for having given educational assistance to a black radical.*

Whatever the true reasons for the grants, the order of events constitutes an interesting example of the consequences for a large foundation, given present conditions, of trying to work in fields of social tension, even in a limited and moderate way; and it suggests that the public relations penalty can be a considerable multiple of the original offending outlay.

Judged strictly on its philanthropic performance, Danforth compares well with the other major foundations. During the past decade it has initiated creative, socially pertinent, and professionally competent programs. In formulating its priorities it has taken a broad view and has carefully considered the relationship of its activities to the work of other foundations and to expanding federal and state programs. In its attitude toward outside agencies, public and private, it has been neither excessively individualistic nor carelessly collaborative. Danforth continuously exposes itself to internal and external program evaluation perhaps more than any other major foundation in the United States. The staff actively participates in forming policy and programs and shares a mutual responsibility with the trustees in governing the institution. As a result, most if its grants have been intelligently crafted and conscientiously executed. Its work has gained respect in academic circles, in the government, and among other foundations.

The principal flaw in this picture is the relationship of the foundation to the Ralston Purina Company, which is controlled by the donor family. The Danforth family has shown a genuine and con-

---

* For a polished example of evasiveness in foundation reporting, see the account of these grants in the foundation's *News and Notes* for September 1970.

tinuing interest in philanthropy. It is reported that William Danforth's two children, Donald Danforth and Mrs. Randolph Compton, asked their father, several years before his death, to rewrite his will to give his entire estate to the foundation instead of dividing it between them and the foundation as he had proposed to do. In 1960 they voluntarily agreed to an expansion of the board which then put family members in the minority.

At the same time, the family has remained dominant in matters of financial policy, insisting that stockholdings in the company not be diluted. As a result, forty years after its establishment, the foundation has not yet taken a significant step toward investment diversification.*

Whatever indirect benefits this policy may have brought to the family and the company, it has not been financially injurious to the foundation. An analysis of the company's performance and of the value of its shares indicates that since the depression, the company's earnings and the growth in the market value of its shares has been better than the market average (see Appendix). Had Danforth reinvested its holdings in a diversified list of reputable common stocks and bonds, or in one of the major mutual funds, it would not have done better in terms of income or growth of capital than it has done by holding Ralston Purina shares.

The Kellogg Foundation

The W. K. Kellogg Foundation of Battle Creek, Michigan, has compiled a record of philanthropic achievement fully as distinguished as that of Danforth, but it presents a problem of economic interlinkage of an even more complicated kind.

Will Kellogg, the "King of Cornflakes," in the course of his ninety-one years lived three distinctly different lives. Born in 1860, he was until middle age a frustrated and discouraged bookkeeper in a health sanatorium at Battle Creek. From his forties until his seven-

* Its $15 million grant to Washington University in 1970, however, was in Ralston Purina stock, and the board reportedly has now begun to plan for some future diversification.

ties, by a combination of fierce energy and unexpected merchandising genius, he built a worldwide and highly profitable breakfast food company. And in the last third of his life he created the major philanthropic foundation now bearing his name.

His father was an impoverished Seventh-Day Adventist preacher who also ran a small broom factory to support his family. Will later recalled that "as a boy I never learned to play." He had little formal education; his only academic degree was from the Parsons' Business College in Kalamazoo, Michigan. The Seventh-Day Adventists in the latter part of the nineteenth century had established a sanatorium at Battle Creek based on their beliefs in the simple restorative methods of nature, the use of hydrotherapy, and vegetarianism. Will's dynamic elder brother, Dr. John Harvey Kellogg, became physician-in-chief at the sanatorium in 1880. As it flourished, Battle Creek became a health mecca for thousands of Americans, including many of the wealthy and celebrated, and Dr. Kellogg became nationally famous. His rules were strict: "I don't take patients at my sanatorium unless they agree to abstain from eating flesh and from smoking and drinking." He wrote more than fifty books and established dozens of companies to manufacture health foods, alcoholism cures, and other products. Some of his ideas were far in advance of their time. In the first years of the twentieth century, for example, he went to the expense of having a film made about the harmful effects of tobacco, particularly its relationship to lung cancer.

Will was employed at the sanatorium for twenty-five years after John Harvey took charge, working long hours for little pay in a back room as clerk, business manager, and jack-of-all-trades, lost from view in the shadow of his renowned brother. Busy every day and most evenings, he neglected his unhappy wife and their three children. He was a slender, intense little man, lacking self-confidence and resentful of his situation. But then his fortunes began dramatically to change.

His brother conducted constant experiments to devise vegetarian foods that would be more attractive and digestible than those then available, and in these efforts Will was his general helper. Together they invented a number of new foods, including peanut butter (a product whose sale they did not promote because its taste was judged unlikely to gain public acceptance) and, in 1894, the first precooked flaked cereal. They had no idea they were inventing a breakfast food, the phrase itself being unknown at the time. But sales of the new product, primarily to former patients at the sanatorium, began to grow encouragingly. Will sensed the possibility of enormous profits if the marketing could be developed on a nationwide basis.

At this point another of the many conflicts between the two brothers broke out. Dr. Kellogg was firmly opposed to an active promotional effort to sell health foods, feeling that it might damage his medical reputation and the prestige of the sanatorium. Will determined to break free of his brother's control and acquired the dominant interest in the cornflakes company. Suddenly the former backroom bookkeeper displayed an amazing talent for inventing new concepts of mass merchandising, utilizing the then infant medium of advertising. Will Kellogg drove himself and his colleagues with almost uncontrollable energy. By day he handled the problems of organizing, financing, and increasing the production capabilities of his company with consummate skill; by night, a poor sleeper, he scribbled an endless flow of new promotional ideas for his product.°

Within a few years the little company, with sales skyrocketing and profits pouring in, became a major enterprise. As time went on Will Kellogg became one of the great business successes of the twentieth century, and with his new wealth and power new facets of his complex personality manifested themselves. In politics he was a conservative, voting a straight Republican ticket; his hero in public life was President Herbert Hoover. His economic philosophy was Hamiltonian; during the New Deal he became outspokenly critical of the growing role of the federal government and its tendency to encroach upon the freedom of private enterprise. Part

° He introduced door-to-door distribution of new food samples and also new point-of-sale techniques. In New York City in 1911 an intensive advertising campaign daringly invited housewives to "wink at their local storekeeper to see what would happen." What happened was that they got a free sample package of Kellogg Cornflakes. As a result, sales of the product leapt from 200 cases a week in the city to 200,000 in six weeks.

of his social outlook was the belief that the vast majority of people needed leadership from men of superior qualities and that some were born to lead just as others were born to follow.

At the same time, in his own company he was generously paternalistic, sponsoring a great variety of recreational and social activities for the benefit of the workers. Early in the depression he instituted a six-hour working day at the Battle Creek plant for employees on continuous production processes, and in 1935 he made the practice permanent. He also hired men and women on the basis of the number of their dependents, giving priority to breadwinners of large families. Although he was not a churchgoing man, he had been indelibly marked by the injunctions of the Seventh-Day Adventist Church in his youth and had a lifelong aversion to alcohol and tobacco, as well as a severe, puritanical attitude on questions of morals and mores.

But his most conspicuous trait was a profound shyness and an inability to relate to others, even to those members of his own family for whom he had strong sentimental attachment. He had hoped to create a family dynasty in the company, but in the process of trying to groom his son, John L. Kellogg, to take over, he broke his spirit and the young man fled the organization. He then focused his attention on John L. Kellogg Jr., his fourteen-year-old grandson. As the boy grew to young manhood, Kellogg put increasing burdens of responsibility upon him, but in trying to push him too fast he drove him out of the company. Later the young man committed suicide. In later years Kellogg never completely overcame his sorrow that he had no descendant to run the business.

As he grew richer and older, Kellogg strove to develop new hobbies and interests and to enjoy himself. He spent months traveling about the world. After the death of his first wife he remarried, but the new relationship seemingly added no pleasure to his life. He built several lavish homes in California and started a ranch for breeding Arabian horses near Pomona, where he began to spend several months each year. But after more than fifteen years there he remarked to a visitor, "I have only three friends in the whole valley." Finally, well into his sixties, Will Kellogg's interests began to turn increasingly toward philanthropy as an outlet for his energies and as a means of personal fulfillment.°

His interest in charity was not new. Many years before, when his company was just beginning to show promise of financial success, he had written a close friend, "It is my hope that anything I accumulate can be used for the benefit of mankind." From his personal records it is apparent that as soon as he was in a position to do so he made hundreds of small gifts to relatives and friends to help them send their children to school, to pay hospital and funeral expenses, and for other emergency needs. But it was in 1925, when Kellogg was sixty-five years old, that he made his first move to put his donations on a systematic basis. In that year he established The Fellowship Corporation to distribute his gifts anonymously. In the following five years the projects financed by the corporation included an agricultural school, a bird sanctuary, an experimental farm, a reforestation demonstration, a civic auditorium for Battle Creek, a day nursery, a city market for farmers, a Boy Scout camp, and many student scholarships. Almost as soon as the corporation began to function, Kellogg discussed with the other members of the board his desire "to get a child welfare foundation established and set in operation during my lifetime." This he did in 1930, in a manner which again displayed the extraordinary capacity of the man. His approach and methods could profitably be studied by other philanthropists.†

First, he gave the foundation a general direction and philosophy based on his own convictions and personal experience. It was to concern itself initially with the welfare of children, particularly

° He had a strong distaste, incidentally, for the words "philanthropy" and "philanthropist." He once wrote, "A philanthropist is one who would do good for the love of his fellowman. I love to do things for children because I get a kick out of it. Therefore, I am a selfish person and no philanthropist."

† But not necessarily his method of selecting an executive head. He chose Dr. A. C. Selman to be the first president of the Kellogg Foundation as an act of gratitude. Selman had at one time been on the staff of the Battle Creek Sanatorium and later served an an Adventist medical missionary in China. When Kellogg, in the course of one of his world tours, was hospitalized in Hong Kong, he cabled Selman in the interior of China to hurry to his bedside. The doctor did, and Kellogg never forgot the kindness.

children of poor parents and in rural areas. His own strong interest
in their problems derived partly from his remembrance of a tragedy in his own family. One of his grandchildren as an infant had
fallen from an upstairs window and suffered permanent injury. In
discussing his motivation in establishing the foundation Kellogg
later wrote that it "was due in part to the fact that although I was
happily able to pay the medical and surgical bills for Kenneth [the
injured grandson], I found it almost impossible to obtain adequate
treatment for him during the first ten or twelve years of his life.
This caused me to wonder what difficulties were in the path of
needy parents who seek help for their children when catastrophes
strike, and I resolved to lend what aid I could." In time, the donor
himself broadened the scope of his foundation from child welfare
to "the welfare of mankind." But the spirit of concern for the needs
of individual, ordinary people persisted and has become the foundation's distinguishing characteristic.

Second, he believed that a foundation's role was not to serve
merely as a vehicle to channel funds into ongoing charitable institutions. He encouraged his trustees to put the Kellogg Foundation's resources behind pioneering ventures and new initiatives.

Third, he established from the start the principle that the foundation should operate as an independent and professionalized
institution. He delegated broad responsibility to his trustees and
encouraged them to use their own judgment in directing the foundation's affairs. To reinforce their sense of freedom he refused to
accept membership on the board for the first five years, and thereafter he adhered strictly to a "no dictation" policy, speaking little
and staying only briefly at board meetings. He studiously avoided
any publicity for himself as a result of his charities and desired
none for the foundation.

Fourth, he encouraged the trustees to make a systematic study of
the operations of other foundations as a basis for their own planning. During the first two years, this in fact was the foundation's
principal activity. On the basis of their findings, the trustees decided that its initial project should be to assist selected nearby
communities to become "a laboratory in applied social welfare."
They felt that the foundation in that way could begin on a small

and practical basis and then guide the subsequent evolution of its program by the results of that experience.

Fifth, until the foundation had proved itself, Kellogg made only annual gifts to support the programs that the trustees proposed. But in 1935, satisfied with the institution's performance, he made substantial resources available to it on a permanent basis.

Compared to the egocentricity and the narrow perspective of many foundation donors, Will Kellogg's approach was one of rare breadth and wisdom. And the results achieved by the foundation he created have been impressive. Launched in the depth of the great depression, the foundation for a time gave a considerable portion of its funds to direct relief. This program was discontinued by the end of the 1930s, partly because of the expansion of federal welfare efforts and partly because the foundation had been able to move forward with its own "social laboratory" program.*

This began with a careful survey of the needs of the seven counties surrounding Battle Creek, particularly in the fields of health services and education. Subsequently, county health departments were strengthened; rural hospitals were reorganized; new diagnostic centers were created; the teaching of health and hygiene in public schools was introduced; adult education programs in nutrition and home accident prevention were conducted; and the results of each project were carefully evaluated. After more than a decade of concentrated effort, the foundation then extended the experiment to other parts of the nation.

With the advent of World War II, the Kellogg Foundation temporarily redirected its outlays to projects that made a direct contribution to the war effort; it also extended its activities outside the borders of the United States by financing a series of pilot nutrition projects in Central and South America. After the war the foundation laid painstaking plans for the long-range development of its program, appointing committees of outside advisers for each gen-

---

* In 1932 Kellogg gave his California ranch and his purebred Arabian horses, together with a trust fund for maintenance, to the University of California. In turning over the ranch, the publicity-shy man was subjected to a ceremony before 25,000 people. Music was provided by bands of the 116th National Guard and the University of California, and Will Rogers arrived in an antique stagecoach to perform as the master of ceremonies.

eral field of its interest. By the 1950s its new programs had taken definite form. The earlier concentration on child health and welfare was replaced by the general field of medicine and health, followed by education, particularly continuing education for adults. In 1951 after Kellogg's death, a third program area—agriculture— was added.

The annual reports of the foundation, which began to appear regularly after 1955, reflect the flexibility of its program, the practicality of its general approach, and the widening scope of its interests. In all its work it has concentrated on those grass-roots problems and institutions that most other major foundations working in medicine and education have ignored. Kellogg thus gave important assistance to dentistry and dental education. Its program for hospital improvement has been directed to the needs of rural institutions, improving their administration and reducing their operating costs. It has addressed itself to the nursing shortage in different areas of the country and the training of medical auxiliaries, including practical nurses, dental hygienists, and occupational therapists. In education Kellogg has concerned itself with the needs of the public schools, including the improvement of educational administration, the reorganization of school districts and school consolidation, the improvement of school libraries, and the financing of public education. It has now become the principal foundation concerned with the development of community colleges, and has fostered the establishment of university centers offering continuing education for adults, regardless of their formal educational preparation.

The decade of the 1960s was on the whole a period of continuity for the foundation. More than half of its grants were devoted to medicine and health, about 30 percent to education, and much of the remainder to agriculture. Internationally the program was extended to additional countries in the Western Hemisphere, including Canada, and to Western Europe and Australia, but 80 percent of the grants were still made within the United States. Nevertheless, some limited change in program emphasis began to appear. The foundation began to note urgent new needs arising in the field of "public affairs." In 1962 it made grants to study improvements in the Michigan judicial system and to assist in the drafting of a new constitution for the state. It financed a study of black education to develop programs "for a changing biracial society," and by 1965 it began to provide help to thirty-four black colleges and universities to strengthen their faculties and expand their curricula. In 1968 the president of the foundation, Philip E. Blackerby, wrote an essay entitled "A Better Answer than Extremism" for the annual report, which implied a growing interest in the problems of black education and the urban crisis. This however has not developed.

The foundation still remains heavily committed to its established concerns with health care, rural development, and education, although with some added nuances. In health it is giving greater priority to population control, environmental quality, and the availability and delivery of health services, including the possibility of national health insurance. In rural development it has set up farmers' study programs at several universities to train young rural leaders.

Under the catchall category of public affairs, which was intended to embrace its interests in "the disadvantaged" and in nonrural social issues, the foundation has given a few lump-sum grants to such groups as The Urban Coalition and the United Negro College Fund. More innovative has been its support of the National College of State Trial Judges at the University of Nevada, which helps new judges to learn their job. But Kellogg's enthusiasm for activism, never great, has begun to decline and the public affairs program has now lost its momentum.

Kellogg has, nonetheless, compiled a record of unusual effectiveness in the course of its forty years. It has been influential in extending the teaching of health and hygiene in public schools throughout the country. Its program to improve educational administration has influenced the practices of most state departments of education; its program to improve hospital administration has had worldwide impact and has led to the creation of an international network of specialized training centers in the field. Its staff (including eight program professionals) is highly qualified and keeps unusually well informed on community and institutional needs. It has shown good strategic sense by placing funds in ways

that multiply their effect—for example, upon the practices of publicly supported health and educational systems. By its approach
and the nature of its programs it has performed an important com-
plementary role in relation to the work of the older and larger
Eastern foundations. Not burdened by the "elegance imperative"
from which many of them suffer, it has provided an admirable example of a shirt-sleeve Midwestern fund working effectively on a
range of problems overlooked by most foundations.

Whether Kellogg—given its traditions, the Battle Creek environment, and the nature of its board—will ever be able, or will even
seriously try, to relate itself as closely to the needs of urbanized
and industrialized America as it has to rural America is problematical. So far, the grants it has made to help solve the urban crisis
and the race problem show little of the initiative and willingness
to take risks that characterized its early work in southwestern
Michigan, for example, and its subsequent health programs.

The most serious question that arises with respect to Kellogg involves the intimate financial and other links between it, the Kellogg Company, and the W. K. Kellogg Foundation Trust. The trust
owns 51 percent of the voting shares of the breakfast food company, the dividends of which provide most of the foundation's
income. The company officers, in return for the insulation from
general stockholder interference that trust and foundation control
provides, have allowed the foundation to operate independently in
philanthropic matters. It has not been required to serve the public
relations interests of the company, nor is there any evidence of the
cruder forms of corruption that close foundation-company ties have
sometimes produced. (It is noteworthy, however, that the chairman
of the foundation's board, Emory W. Morris, who also holds a position of key influence in the company by his position as a co-trustee
of the trust, receives $130,000 a year for his part-time services. This
is the highest individual salary of any officer or trustee of a major
American foundation and more than twice the salary of the full-
time president of the Kellogg Foundation.)

Kellogg created the foundation trust in 1931 and subsequently
transferred a majority of the shares of his company to it. His original intention, it seems, was to give it the central and dominant role

in the company–foundation–trust triangle. Its responsibility was to determine periodically whether the financial performance of the Kellogg Company justified continued retention of its stock by the trust and to examine and certify whether the foundation was performing in accordance with its charter and bylaws. The trust was to be managed by a corporate trustee, the Harris Trust and Savings Bank of Chicago, plus three individual "co-trustees." Further evidence of his original intention was the donor's expressed desire that no "co-trustee" should be related by blood, marriage, adoption, or employment to him or be associated with any corporation directly or indirectly controlled by him. He also seemed willing to grant the trustees the discretion to sell shares in the Kellogg Company and reinvest in other securities.

In time, however—judging from the successive amendments he made to his original trust indenture—he changed his mind and made it more difficult for the foundation to dispose of shares of the Kellogg Company. (They now can be sold only if the corporate trustee and a majority of the individual co-trustees agree.) He also provided that the co-trustees could be officers or directors of the company and the foundation, and thus cleared the way for the fusion of trust, foundation, and company. This in fact is what has happened. Voting control of the company is in the hands of the trust and the foundation; five of the nine members of the foundation's board (composed largely of active or retired foundation and company officers and local businessmen) sit on the company's board; and the co-trustees of the trust are the board chairman of the foundation, the board chairman of the company, and a Battle Creek businessman long associated with both the company and the foundation.

During the 1969 tax hearings the Kellogg Foundation—in the most dubious single episode in its generally creditable history—lobbied actively for special exemption from the divestiture provisions of the law. It succeeded in getting the approval of the House but the move was killed by the Senate. In presenting its case, the foundation cited a long array of arguments: that it had not engaged in self-dealing or other improper financial transactions; that it was not donor-family controlled in any degree; that from the be-

ginning it had fully expended its income; and that its philanthropic performance had been exemplary. With the support of
comprehensive financial data, it showed that foundation control of
the company had not produced any deficiencies of competitive
vigor, profitability, or dividend pay-out. Moreover, it demonstrated
that the foundation would have lost both substantial income and
capital growth if it had divested itself of Kellogg shares and diversified its portfolio.

In effect, the foundation proved that it had gambled on Kellogg
stock and had come out ahead, and it sought the right to continue
the gamble. But Kellogg's real motivation in seeking the exemption
was in all likelihood not the desire to gamble, but the desire to
keep the ownership of the company in "safe hands," beyond the
reach of outside shareholders, especially conglomerate builders.
The foundation's strenuous effort to perpetuate the position of present management naturally raises the suspicion that some important private interests were being protected.

Both the Danforth and Kellogg Foundations are of special interest because they pose in a clear and ultimate form questions of the
proper relationship between philanthropic institutions and the corporate interests from which their resources derive.

7.

Surdna, Bush, Pew, and Irvine:
Underachievers and Delinquents

PHILANTHROPIC INSTITUTIONS, like other organisms, are vulnerable to major diseases and disabilities. Among the big foundations that have been stricken, four provide illustrative case histories. The Surdna Foundation of Yonkers, New York, exemplifies arrested development. The Bush Foundation of St. Paul, Minnesota, has been paralyzed since birth by a bitter conflict within itself. The Pew Memorial of Philadelphia is a furtive creature with an antisocial psychosis. The Irvine Foundation of California displays all the symptoms of a fundamental lack of character and honorable purpose, which it tries to camouflage with slick public relations.

The Surdna Foundation

The Surdna Foundation bears the name of its donor, John Andrus, spelled backward. It was established on November 26, 1917, and of the big foundations over fifty years old it has made the least institutional progress of any.

The donor was a great bull of a man who, in the course of his ninety-three years, built a great fortune in pharmaceuticals, real estate, gold mining, and lumber. He was also active in politics, serving for a period as mayor of Yonkers and four terms in Congress. The son of an impoverished Methodist minister, he was a God-fearing and simple man. He proudly claimed that no one had ever shined his shoes or shaved his face, and from his practice of travel-ing to work every day by subway he came to be known as "the millionaire straphanger." His wife, who was an Irish orphan, bore him nine children and died at an early age. He created his founda-tion eight years after her death in 1909. Its principal activity has been the support of the Julia Dyckman Andrus Memorial, which was built in 1923 in her honor. It consists of a facility for children from broken homes and another for infirm and destitute old peo-ple, built on the family estate overlooking the Hudson River. As an arcadian amenity, a small farm has been maintained on the place, including four sheep tended by an elderly shepherdess.

During Andrus' life, the foundation made a few miscellaneous gifts to his alma mater, Wesleyan University, and other educa-tional and charitable institutions. When he died in 1934 he left part of his estate to the foundation (valued in 1968 at $105 million) and put the remainder in three family trusts which have assets to-taling nearly $400 million, of which the foundation is a 45 percent income beneficiary.

After 1934, one of his daughters, Mrs. Helen A. Benedict, as-sumed the presidency of the foundation. A strong-willed woman, fiercely loyal to her father's memory, she single-handedly ran the foundation from her home on the family estate, guiding its grants according to what she felt would have been his wishes. During her thirty-year tenure, the foundation used about half of its income to support the memorial and gave away the rest in the form of capital and general support grants to local institutions near Yonkers and to various colleges and universities, generally for medical research and physical facilities. Since her death in 1969 no member of the small family-dominated board has shown much interest in the foundation and it has idled along in its habitual grooves.

In response to public and congressional criticism of foundations in 1969—and to fulfill the minimum pay-out provisions of the new Tax Reform Act—the board recently hired a retired executive of the bank that handles the investments of the foundation and the various family trusts as a part-time program consultant. Nonethe-less, the Surdna Foundation remains an inert institution whose cre-ative period, if it ever has one, still lies in the future.

The Bush Foundation

In 1909, energetic Archibald Bush, at the age of twenty-one, joined the Minnesota Mining and Manufacturing Company as an assistant bookkeeper. When he died in 1966, he was one of the two dominant figures in the company and had amassed a major fortune from its extraordinary growth.

He created his foundation in 1953, but it remained largely inactive until his death since neither he nor his wife had strong charitable inclinations. In fact, in so far as Bush ever showed any interest in civic or public affairs it was usually to deplore the "dangers of liberalism" and to support antilabor and anti-international schemes of various kinds. Having no children, he left virtually all of his estate to the foundation. His will provided that, if for tax or other reasons the foundation should be disqualified to receive his bequest, the assets should go to another nonprofit entity he had created—the A. G. Bush Institute. He named his wife and a small group of individuals closely connected with the 3M Company as the board of the foundation.

From the day of his funeral until late 1969, when a Minnesota court enlarged and thoroughly reorganized the board, the story of the Bush Foundation was one of conflict interlaced with chicanery. The first flare-up between the widow and the company officers occurred in mid-1966 over the basic issue of control of the foundation. It was so serious that Mrs. Bush threatened to contest her husband's will and reclaim her share of the estate which she had earlier renounced, whereupon a deal was made—which the other directors later said was accepted "under duress and coercion"—putting a number of dubious arrangements into effect. Mrs. Bush was paid $2.1 million for maintenance of her Florida home and for lawyers fees; Cecil C. March, an officer of the company and a board member of the foundation, was given exclusive authority to vote the 1.6 million shares of 3M stock that the foundation owned; and the board was broken into a bicameral body of four "Class A" directors, all executives of the 3M company, and three "Class B" directors, consisting of Mrs. Bush and her supporters—each group having a veto over any action of the other.

The agreement did nothing to reduce the bitterness between the two factions, and by mid-1967 it appeared that the Class A, or company, directors were seeking some new way of dislodging the Class B group. One method they considered was to disqualify the foundation from receiving the donor's estate, thereby making possible the transfer of its assets to the A. G. Bush Institute, whose board was controlled by the Class A directors of the foundation. In another tactic, the Class A directors petitioned a Minnesota court in December 1967 to abolish the two classes of board membership. Mrs. Bush's attorneys filed a countersuit, charging the Class A directors with "delaying distribution of the bequest until they could gain control of the foundation." The attorney-general of Minnesota was also included as a defendant on the grounds that he had not taken proper action to protect the interest of the people of the state. In March 1968 the court broke the impasse by ruling the foundation eligible to receive Archibald Bush's estate, and a first major portion of the assets was transferred to it.

The state attorney-general then filed suit in December asking a state court for complete reorganization of the foundation's board. In a trial in late 1969 the judge forced the two groups of directors into a new agreement. By its terms, the board was expanded from seven to sixteen, the nine new members to be named with the approval of the state attorney-general. Upon Mrs. Bush's death, the board would maintain a membership of fifteen. Cecil March was removed as president, and his personal authority to vote the foundation's 3M shares was canceled. Mrs. Bush and two of her supporters were renamed to the enlarged board but their veto power over the foundation's actions was eliminated, as was the division of the board into separate classes. One concession made to the "Bush family-member directors" was that they could choose their own successors. Thus, through the intervention of public authority, the protracted squabble was finally brought to an end.

Through the years of dispute, the foundation disposed of most of its income—more than $4 million—in various lump-sum grants. Among the largest grants were one of $790,000 to the Greater St.

Paul United Fund, and another to Rollins College of Winter Park, Florida, for retirement of a mortgage on its science building. The Minnesota Orchestral Association received $250,000 for a principal trumpet chair, and an equal amount was given to the University of Minnesota for an arboretum.

The new board, which cannot include individuals with more than a 5 percent ownership of any profit-making corporation, is a diverse group of businessmen, educators, and former public officials. It has now chosen a full-time director, Dr. Humphrey Doermann, formerly a financial officer on the staff at Harvard, but it has not yet formulated a program. With its new board the Bush Foundation will undoubtedly become a more active and useful institution. But no credit for that development can be given to the donor family or the officials of the 3M Company.

The Pew Memorial Trust

The Pew family of Philadelphia—a highly successful business dynasty for three-quarters of a century—controls Sun Oil, one of the nation's largest oil companies, as well as other industrial and mineral enterprises. Its principal side interest has been politics. The Pews have long been major financial supporters of the Republican party, identified with its most conservative wing. In the 1956 presidential election campaign, for example, twelve members of the Pew family gave $216,800 to the party; by contrast fourteen Rockefellers the same year reported giving $152,000. As a result the Pews' political influence has been considerable. In its obituary for Joseph N. Pew, who headed the family until his death on April 10, 1963, the New York *Times* wrote: "He operated behind the scenes but frequently dictated party policies that were announced by others or incorporated into national platforms at election time." His successor as senior member of the family was his brother, J. Howard Pew, who died on November 27, 1971. He was a militant rugged individualist opposed to all forms of governmental intervention. His personal philanthropy, the J. Howard Pew Freedom Trust, directed its grants almost exclusively to anti-Communist organizations, some religious and others military in orientation, and to groups advocating *laissez-faire* economics.

The main family philanthropy is now the Pew Memorial Trust, incorporated in January 1948 for "general religious, charitable, scientific, literary, and educational purposes" by a group of seven persons, of whom six were family members. Subsequently they became the board of directors. Within a few years, however, they apparently felt that the foundation was too exposed to public view, and in 1956 the Glenmede Trust Company was organized by four members of the family. The new company apparently was founded primarily to handle family trusts, not to enter the banking business. A year later the original foundation was liquidated and replaced by the Pew Memorial Trust, whose affairs have since been conducted behind the screen of the Glenmede Trust, which has been able to claim the privacy of the bank-customer relationship.

The assets of the Pew Memorial totaled $541 million in 1968, a leap of $100 million over its resources a year earlier. But in 1969 they had dropped almost $175 million to $367 million—a dramatic instance of the volatility of an undiversified portfolio. Its principal holdings are in the stock of two companies: Sun Oil and Minerals Development. It owns 5.5 million of the 25 million voting shares of the former and all of the 124,000 voting shares of the latter. Allyn R. Bell, head of Glenmede Trust, is also vice-president of Minerals Development.

On its federal tax return the Memorial groups its grants by broad categories: religious, educational, medical-hospital, medical-research, and charitable. The following are a sample of items for the year 1969:

RELIGIOUS

Billy Graham Evangelistic Association, Minneap-
olis $ 85,000
Christian Anti-Communism Crusade, Long Beach,
Calif.°   30,000

° The Crusade, under the leadership of Dr. Fred Charles Schwartz, a former psychiatrist from Australia, conducts schools of anti-Communism around the country and sells books and pamphlets ("How to Spot a Communist Trap") as well as anti-Communist folk songs ("Poor Left-Winger").

Evangelical Foundation, Inc., Philadelphia (Bible Study House)	15,000
National Association of Evangelicals World Relief Commission Inc., Long Island, N.Y. (Biafra Relief Program)	75,000

EDUCATIONAL

Americans for the Competitive Enterprise System, Philadelphia	$ 5,000
Gordon College, Wenham, Mass. (Gordon-Conwall Theological Seminary)	254,110
Freedoms Foundation at Valley Forge, Pa.	10,000
Rudolf Steiner School, New York City (Development Fund)	100,000
American Educational League, Buena Park, Calif.	2,500
Pepperdine College, Los Angeles (California Freedom Forum Program)	3,000

MEDICAL-HOSPITAL

Presbyterian University of Pennsylvania Medical Center, Philadelphia (Eye Institute)	$600,000
The People-to-People Health Foundation, Inc., Washington, D.C.	25,000

MEDICAL-RESEARCH

The Institute for Cancer Research, Philadelphia	$ 50,000

CHARITABLE

American Red Cross, Philadelphia	$ 35,000
Citizens for Decent Literature, Inc., Philadelphia	5,000
Crime Prevention Association of Philadelphia	5,000
Philadelphia Lyric Opera	85,000
United Fund of Philadelphia	225,000
Morality in Media, Inc., New York City	5,000

With the exception of a few grants to black institutions, the grant pattern heavily favors ideological and evangelical causes. The memorial employs no professional staff and has never made formal announcements of its program or its grant-making policies.

Allyn Bell, when questioned about the activities of the memorial, has consistently refused to comment. Until 1970 the memorial had never issued any annual or other report to the public. When asked about this at a business luncheon a few years ago, J. Howard Pew shouted, "I'm not telling anybody anything. It's my money, isn't it?"[1] Because of the death of J. Howard Pew, changes in the family leadership are now taking place and it is rumored that some of the more influential younger members have a more modern social outlook than their forebears. But any concrete evidence of a change in the foundation's philosophy remains to be seen.

The Irvine Foundation

The saga of the Irvine Foundation begins with land—land that rolls southward for twenty-two miles from the Riverside County line just outside Los Angeles to San Diego. These 88,000 acres are known as the Irvine Ranch and are controlled by the foundation. The tract—three times the size of San Francisco and five times as large as Manhattan—constitutes probably the single most valuable piece of undeveloped real estate in the United States.

The ranch was put together in substantially its present form nearly a hundred years ago by an Irish immigrant, James Irvine, who made his fortune in groceries and gold mining. Until the mid-1960s, much of the land remained as it had been when the first Spanish explorers—members of the Portolá expedition—passed through in the eighteenth century. The more fertile portions were devoted to agricultural uses; on its undulating hills sheep grazed, orange groves blossomed, and field workers bent over endless rows of beans, lettuce, and sugar beets. Spurred and booted cowboys still herded cattle in some places, and they slept in a bunkhouse that had stood since 1879.

In 1961, the directors, after much prodding by a disaffected family stockholder, finally formulated a limited plan for the development of the property. In more recent years, they have enlarged and accelerated it. Their earlier reluctance to exploit the financial possibilities of the land aroused considerable criticism; their new eagerness has aroused even more. For more than twenty years the interlinked ranch company and foundation have gained a particularly unsavory reputation for financial misconduct. And the foundation's philanthropic program is widely regarded as one of the poorest in the country.

James Irvine died in 1886. His son, James Irvine 2d, inherited the ranch and gradually transformed its use from livestock grazing to field crops and eventually to citrus production. In 1937 he established the James Irvine Foundation, transferring to it 459 shares (53.7 percent) of the 855 voting shares of the company. At the same time he admonished his trustees that "no other security could afford the James Irvine Foundation a more stable and safe investment than the capital of the Irvine Company" and specifically forbade them to sell any of its shares except by unanimous vote. The donor's motives in creating the foundation are singularly indistinct. During his long life he was known as a notoriously uncharitable man. President McLaren of the foundation, who was also one of his associates, has said of him; "While Mr. Irvine had a reputation for being pretty hard-boiled, he regularly made substantial contributions to charity because he realized, as a rich man, he had an obligation to help others. However, he had a horror of getting on anyone's sucker list so he always made his donations anonymously." [2]

In the opinion of Congressman Wright Patman, who studied the case in great detail, Irvine "had no charitable thoughts in mind when he created the foundation. It was nothing more than a device for the purpose of escaping federal and state income taxes and California inheritance taxes upon his death." Patman also pointed out that according to the minutes of the foundation the donor did not attend a single meeting of its board during the first ten years of operation and that he was interested only in the running of the ranch company.

According to the donor's trust, the foundation was to exist "solely for charitable purposes, namely public welfare, health, education, comfort, happiness and general well-being, particularly for the citizens and residents of the state of California or any part thereof and does not contemplate pecuniary gain or profit to the members." But at the same time he left his company and his foundation affairs completely entangled. By owning a majority of voting stock of the company, the foundation controls four of the seven seats on the ranch's board of directors, and from the beginning there has been considerable cross-membership among the officers and directors of the two organizations. Myford Irvine, the son of the donor, was the first president of the foundation and, following his father's death in 1947, he also became the president of the Ranch Company. He held both positions for the next twelve years until he took his own life in 1959. The peculiar circumstances of his death have been described by crime-reporter Ed Reid:

We can, however, piece together some of the story. Irvine apparently had made commitments to a gambling group in Las Vegas. The result was that the sixty-year-old protagonist in one of Las Vegas' oldest and most repeated plays got deeply involved and had to produce a fantastic sum of cash in a hurry. Irvine could have done it, given time. He was president of a vast trust left to him by his father, and a brother who could have shared it with him had died of tuberculosis in 1939. However, at first he tried to buck the pressures placed upon him. Then, it seems, he suddenly decided to go ahead and provide the money. . . .

But by then it was too late. He asked the men who helped him administer his trust to give him the money he needed—reportedly about a million dollars—and for some incredible reason insisted he had to have it almost instantly: on Saturday, January 11, 1959. It was not possible, and Myford cried, "Too late, too late!" when he learned that his trustees would not be able to meet until the following Monday to vote the funds. His niece, Joan, tried to speed the loan but failed.

According to the Orange County police files, on Saturday, January 11, Irvine went into the den of his home on the estate and fired a shotgun blast into his body. Then he is supposed to have secured a .22-caliber pistol and finished the job with a shot in the temple. Why?

Part of the answer to the Irvine mystery may have come in a disclosure made by U.S. Judge Thurmond Clarke and his wife, a former sister-in-law of the dead man, whose death was finally listed by law officials as a suicide. Judge Clarke recounted that "Irvine approached Mrs. Clarke and her daughter [Joan Irvine Burt] and said he needed $5 million right away. He said he had to have $400,000 of it by Monday morning.

"He said he was 'sitting on a keg of dynamite' and had been trying to sell some stock to friends," Judge Clarke continued. "One was interested but decided he couldn't set up a company to take the stock in time for Irvine's needs."

Judge Clarke said he asked Irvine why he didn't go to a bank for the loan, and the man replied: "I've never had to borrow from a bank before and I don't want to start now."

"We never did find out what the keg of dynamite was," Judge Clarke concluded.[3]

Since then the president of the foundation has been N. Loyall McLaren, a San Francisco accountant and businessman, who also serves on the board of the company. When asked about foundation–company relationships, he solemnly affirms that the foundation does not exercise control of the Irvine Company "*per se.*" According to McLaren, it "has never taken any position on the general conduct of the business of the ranch itself." But one foundation director has admitted that "occasionally when there is a particularly sticky problem they [the officers of the company] may make a telephone canvass of the foundation directors as a guide to their own stand, but that's about all."[4] These ambiguous interlocks have led to more than a decade of feuding and growing public suspicion.

Since 1957 Mrs. Joan Irvine Smith, a member of the donor family and a principal stockholder of the Irvine Company, has carried on a running battle with the foundation. Her interest has not been to improve its philanthropy but to obtain more dividend income from her stockholdings in the ranch. In a succession of lawsuits she has charged the trustees with mismanagement and "failure to give leadership and direction to the company." She has accused McLaren of ruling the foundation and the company "with the ruthless tactics and strong-arm methods of a dictator." She has also charged him and the other trustees of the foundation with "self-dealing" and "self-aggrandizement." *

---

* She has even alleged foul play by one of the company's directors. On February 21, 1969, the New York *Times* carried the following report:

"A tale of high finance, violent death, and corporate wheeling and dealing told by a blonde enlivened the tax reform hearings by the House Ways and Means Committee today.

"Mrs. Joan Irvine Smith, heiress of the California landowner, held the committee in rapt attention as she described her prolonged running feud with a private foundation that controls the family land holdings south of Los Angeles. . . .

"She also challenged the legality of the foundation's take-over of the company which followed the death of her grandfather in 1947 while on a fishing trip in Montana with a company director. 'He was found floating in a stream where he was supposed to be fishing,' she said, making it clear she viewed the circumstances suspiciously."

Unsuccessful in her prior efforts, Mrs. Smith brought suit in the federal courts in 1966 to overturn the terms of her grandfather's trust and to return the stock in the ranch to members of the family. The case was terminated in 1969 when the United States Supreme Court refused to hear an appeal from two lower court rulings against her.

The foundation trustees, whose position has been upheld by the courts, have given vivid accounts of their efforts to fend off Mrs. Smith's charges. McLaren testified that she regularly followed the practice "of surreptitiously recording, by the hiding of recording devices in the living room of her home and by concealing recording devices on her own person, private conversations with directors of the company and directors of the foundation."

In 1967 the attorney-general of California, after conducting an investigation, ordered the foundation to expand and broaden its board or face public reorganization. (The board was enlarged from nine to eleven, ten of whom are now California businessmen and one, Mrs. Charles S. Wheeler, a member of the donor family.) Simultaneously, the Patman subcommittee published extensive data about the foundation and its links with the company—all of it derogatory.[5]

More recently, the foundation has been accused of intervening in county, state, and national politics. In Orange County, taxpayers' groups claim the foundation and the company have meddled in elections for the board of supervisors, which has zoning authority and the power to approve land development plans. As a result of Irvine influence over local officials, they say, the holdings of the ranch are underassessed, leaving other taxpayers with a disproportionate share of the tax burden. State Democrats assert that the foundation and the ranch company constitute a financial bastion of Republican conservative forces that has been responsible for the election of Governor Ronald Reagan and other high state officials. And according to Democratic Senator John Tunney, who defeated incumbent Republican George Murphy in the 1970 elections, four of Murphy's principal campaign contributors were "prominent in the Irvine interests": McLaren, J. V. Newman and Edward W. Carter, foundation trustees, and Charles S. Thomas, former president of the ranch company. In turn, according to Tunney, Murphy sponsored a "special interest" amendment to the 1969 Tax Reform Act to exempt the foundation from some of its provisions. If it had passed, the ranch would have profited by an estimated $100 million.*

For the last ten years the foundation and the ranch company have also had an intricate relationship with the University of California and its board of regents. This has produced a multitude of charges alleging the manipulation of the university for the profit of a private company as well as political indiscretions.†

The relationship began in 1960 when the ranch company gave the university a thousand acres of its land for a new campus. The

---

* Murphy, in reply, claimed the original bill included a "discriminatory amendment" that applied only to the Irvine Foundation and which by requiring it to dissolve within a two-year period would have produced "chaos" and a precipitous breakup of the Irvine properties.

† The regents have long operated according to unusual rules of procedure. It has not been an uncommon practice for the university to join with members of the board in "carve-out" deals in oil exploration, which have brought modest gifts to the university and millions of dollars to the promoters. The most recent of these, exposed in October 1970, involved Regent Edwin W. Pauley, a Los Angeles oil operator, and five other top university officials, including President Charles J. Hitch. According to a report of the California state auditor, transactions totaling $10.7 million were involved, from which the university may have received no net financial benefit while Pauley may have made tax savings of about $2 million. When asked whether any regent had questioned "the ethics involved" when the board approved the transaction, the treasurer of the university replied, "To my knowledge, that did not come up, sir." (Los Angeles *Times*, October 29, 1970)

President Hitch defended the deal on grounds that it was merely to put UC "on an equal footing with many other universities throughout the country in receiving gifts from oil and other extractive industry companies." (Los Angeles *Times*, November 5, 1970) At the same time the Pauley deal was investigated, the auditor general also looked into a curious transaction between the university and Regent Edward W. Carter, who is also on the Irvine Foundation board. Carter first made the university a $200,000 gift of stock in his company, presumably taking a tax deduction for his contribution. The university and Carter then jointly purchased two acres of land in Los Angeles containing a private residence and a Japanese-style garden. The total price was $253,000, of which the university paid $178,000 and Carter $75,000. The university received title to the garden together with maintenance responsibilities and title to the house after Carter's death. Carter received the house and land and the virtually exclusive use of the garden during his lifetime.

agreement specified a land-use plan for the development of a "university community" of about 100,000 people on 10,000 adjacent acres, stipulating that "there shall be no significant departure without mutual consent of the parties." But by 1970 the company had developed more ambitious ideas. It asked urgent approval by the regents of a change to permit a population of 430,000 in the "university community," a change which press reports estimated would profit the land company by about $400 million. Some of the regents, led by the multimillionaire industrialist Norton Simon, objected to the haste of the proceedings and to the fact that the university would not share in the increased company profits.°

They also pointed to a possible conflict of interest between the chairman of the board of regents, William French Smith, a lawyer who was also representing the Irvine Ranch Company, and Regent Carter. The sensitivity of Governor Reagan to the Irvine issue is indicated by the following item from the Los Angeles *Times* of October 17, 1970:

SAN FRANCISCO—A UC Board of Regents meeting erupted Friday into an angry, shoving, name-calling confrontation between Gov. Reagan and regents Frederick Dutton and Norton Simon.

Reagan called Dutton a "lying son of a bitch."

The incident took place just after the meeting adjourned, minutes after Dutton accused the board majority of postponing discussion of a controversial Irvine Co. land development plan for political reasons.

° Following is an explanatory excerpt from the transcript of the meeting of the board of regents, September 18, 1970 (p. 9):

"Regent [Frederick P.] Dutton: . . . 'I question very much the university lending its authority and prestige to a step that will result in millions of dollars in additional profits for this particular tract developer. But, if we are going to enter into such agreement, if that is what the desire of the majority of the board is, then I think we should negotiate to share in a reasonable portion of the additional profits and benefits that are going to come from increasing the size of the city. . . .

'Irvine already is made richer by millions of dollars by our locating a campus there, millions of dollars beyond the value of the particular campus property which they gave to us. The proposed changes in the size of the city, under the terms agreed to with the university ten years ago, are being done to meet the new foundation tax law passed by the Congress in 1969. We are lending ourselves to what Irvine needs to do to beat a particular tax law. I don't object to that, but I say when it makes a profit, then we should get that benefit.' "

Reagan quickly rose from his seat at the long, rectangular meeting table in the UC Extension Center auditorium. He moved toward Dutton, wagging his finger, his face red with anger.

"You're a lying son of a bitch," the governor told Dutton, a prominent Democrat who managed former Gov. Pat Brown's losing race against Reagan in 1966.

"I hope the press heard that," Dutton said.

Dutton asked Reagan to discuss the Irvine plan, but the governor replied, "I'm not going to talk to you because you know you're lying."

At that point regent Simon, who had been baiting Reagan about the Irvine plan, moved into the discussion, but Reagan turned and shoved him away with a light push on the shoulder.

"Don't push that man!" Dutton said.

Simon said to Reagan, "You've been using it (the university) for political purposes for 3½ years and you finally got caught at it . . . You got caught with your pants down this time."

Before anything more was said, the governor was hurried away by Press Secretary Paul Beck and several bodyguards.

Such has been the lively and unusual atmosphere in which the philanthropic operations of the Irvine Foundation have been conducted.

The foundation now has two full-time administrative employees, although until 1966 it had no paid staff. (The Irvine Ranch Company has 380 employees, including 228 in its agriculture work, 113 in land development, and 48 in general administration.) According to Miss Claire F. Denahy, secretary of the foundation, the trustees are directly responsible for its grant-making and "the process of deciding who gets how much is virtually a year-long task" for them. During its first thirteen years—from 1937 to 1950—the foundation reported a gross income of $812,000, of which only $306,000 was distributed in grants. Since 1950 the annual income of the foundation has grown steadily, reaching $1.9 million in 1970.°

Recently—except for a two-and-a-half-year suspension of grant-

---

° In 1969 the recorded price of a share of the company's stock was $250,-000. On that basis the foundation's holdings are worth $114.7 million. However, ranch property has recently been sold for more than $13,000 an acre—which would make the ranch as a whole worth over one billion dollars and the foundation's share well over half a billion. According to Mrs. Smith, foundation and company mismanagement has prevented a value of $2 billion being realized from the land. She has also complained about the penurious dividend policy, which pays $1,500 a year per share, a return of only 0.6 percent.

making while in litigation—the foundation's grants have been in line with income. To date, Orange County has received approximately 60 percent of all donations. According to Irvine's federal tax returns, its recipients are essentially local educational and welfare institutions. For example, the foundation has helped to build and expand Boy Scout and YMCA camps and has established small scholarship funds at several universities for Orange County students. In 1969 it gave $500,000 to endow the A. J. McFadden Library at the Claremont Colleges in California (which simultaneously produced an honorary degree for McFadden, one of the foundation's board members). It has also given support to the Santa Ana Community Hospital in South Laguna. As of 1970, the grants, while increasing in size, remained of the same general character, the largest single gift being one of $400,000 to Stanford University for the construction of a school of business.

It is noteworthy that the medical facilities that the foundation has supported have an obvious economic value to the Irvine Ranch Company, which is currently selling and leasing land to home owners and companies in the same areas.

These four sterile foundations are not representative of large philanthropy. They are rather the warts on the institution's nose. But they must be painted in if a true portrait is to be rendered.

8.
The Ducal Du Ponts

FOR GENERATIONS, no family in the United States has had greater wealth or more industrial power than the du Ponts of Delaware. But while their global chemical combine has been dynamic and innovative, their philanthropies have been antiquated, provincial, and decidedly second-rate.

Pierre Samuel du Pont, founder of the dynasty, was a well-born Huguenot who emigrated to the United States with his two sons after the French Revolution to escape Jacobin persecution. The small company they established on Brandywine Creek in Delaware to manufacture gunpowder prospered during the War of 1812 and became still more prosperous during the Civil War. By the late nineteenth century the du Ponts were sufficiently powerful to organize other explosives manufacturers into the Powder Trust, which controlled production and prices of hunting and blasting powder in the American market into the early years of the twentieth century. By then, the du Ponts themselves controlled almost three-quarters of the total output of several basic types of explosives and all of the privately produced smokeless military powder. During World War I, some 40 percent of the shells from Allied cannon were fired by du Pont explosives and the company's fortunes, which had ebbed in the period after the Spanish-American War, improved again.

With its wartime profits, the company branched out into the general chemical field—German interests having been driven out —by taking over various smaller chemical producers. It also bought a substantial interest in the General Motors Corporation. Because of these timely moves, the family's wealth continued to grow even in the great depression. World War II brought more profits, and in the years since the company has continued its vigorous expansion, largely in new synthetic products, particularly cellophane and nylon, which were invented in its research laboratories.

As a family, the du Ponts have mainly concentrated their energies on their business affairs. At times they have attempted to wield their power in national politics, but generally with little success. Traditionally their support went to the Democrats; later it shifted to the Republicans, but in both parties they consistently backed conservative factions.*

In the 1920s a number of prominent du Ponts joined in efforts to repeal the Eighteenth Amendment, in the hope that government revenue from liquor sales would make it possible to reduce income taxes. Later, they gave their endorsement to Al Smith, the Democratic presidential candidate in 1928. But after the election of Franklin D. Roosevelt in 1932, the du Ponts came to regard him and the Democrats as both distasteful and dangerous. Enlisting some of their old conservative allies in the drive to repeal Prohibition, the du Ponts then organized a bipartisan movement to "protect property rights and basic Constitutional principles," to oppose the New Deal, and to defeat Roosevelt for reelection. But the Liberty League, as the organization was called, quickly degenerated from a half-comical Blimpish operation into an extremist splinter group tinged with fascism and racism.

Recalling the "merchants of death" label pinned on them in the 1920s, the Liberty League excursion in the 1930s, and the revelations in the 1940s of their cartel arrangements with the Germans and the Japanese, the family since World War II has generally avoided any visible engagement in national politics. (In November, 1970, however, one younger member, Pierre S. du Pont 4th, was elected to Congress from the only district of Delaware.) They have retreated to their private principality in Delaware, tending their lavish estates and their investments with shrewd unobtrusiveness.

* One rare exception to this family bias was Miss Zara du Pont, who marched in a Boston picket line in the 1930s protesting police use of tear gas against strikers.

The family now consists of some 250 "major" and 1,200 "minor" du Ponts, some bearing the du Pont name, others the names of men who have married into the family. In financial and business affairs, they operate as a snugly organized group through a network of family holding companies and trust funds. Their combined wealth cannot be calculated precisely but in the opinion of a number of analysts it is on the order of $10 billion.

Because of their far-flung profit-making activities, they have repeatedly been dragged into the limelight, despite their distaste for publicity. One of their major attackers has been the federal government, which has repeatedly accused the du Ponts of monopolistic practices. In the most recent of the several court rulings against the company, the United States Supreme Court in 1964 ordered du Pont to divest itself of its General Motors shares, finding it in violation of Section VII of the Clayton Act, which forbids any stock acquisition whose effect "may be substantially to lessen competition or tend to create a monopoly." At the time, the holdings of the company and the family in General Motors had a market value of $6.2 billion of which the Christiana Securities Company, the largest of the several family holding companies, owned more than 18 million shares worth $1.8 billion. Even after divestiture by the company, individual members of the du Pont family were able to retain their holdings and they still constitute the largest identifiable block of General Motors shareholders. The government contended that the du Ponts were a "cohesive group of at least seventy-five persons," and went on to name 184 members of the family in its complaint.

The most recent and most sweeping attack on the family's operations was made by a group of young investigators working under Ralph Nader. Their two-volume report, "The Company State," was issued on November 30, 1971. In it they alleged that the du Ponts by their domination of Delaware are able to win favorable tax treatment for their companies, pollute the air and water of the area with impunity, control state welfare and education policy, and shape urban planning and public transportation to their advantage. The Nader group also charged that by their control of the state's two largest newspapers, the *Morning News* and the *Evening Journal* in Wilmington, the du Ponts maintain "a virtual monopoly" over the news.*

To understand the du Pont philanthropies, one must first comprehend the antiquated view of life and social responsibility that prevails among the members of this unique clan. In their civic and cultural interests, they have retained unchanged the attitudes of their own eighteenth-century origins. For generations, they have lived in a dreamlike world of formal elegance modeled on the *ancien régime* of prerevolutionary France. They have built an array of sumptuous chateaux complete with formal gardens, aviaries, and romantic statuary. With a strong sense of family tradition, verging on ancestor worship, they have carefully preserved the artifacts, records, and memorabilia of their past. To the extent that they have performed charitable works, they have done so in a self-conscious manner of *noblesse oblige*.†

At first the du Ponts distributed their gifts personally and directly. But once important tax advantages could be gained, they began to establish foundations. Of these there are now more than twenty, bearing such names as Bredin, Carpenter, Christiana, Copeland, Andelot, Lesesne, Rencourt, Theano, and Winterthur. The two largest are the Longwood Foundation, established in 1937 by Pierre S. du Pont, and the Nemours Foundation, established in 1936 in accordance with the will of Alfred I. du Pont.‡ These two

* In a seven-page rejoinder, Charles B. McCoy, president and chairman of the company, said, "The report espouses a political philosophy that is alien to the essential directions of American public policy and proposes to alter drastically our economic system, which is based on free enterprise." (New York *Times,* November 30, 1971) He also charged that the 800-page report contained "many inaccuracies." But when questioned by reporters, he could think of only three relatively minor examples. (*Wall Street Journal,* November 30, 1971)

† Speaking of the Rockefellers' sober approach to life and philanthropy, one of the du Ponts has said, "They are too Protestant. They take themselves too seriously. They are not frivolous enough. Wealth is something to luxuriate in, but not a one of the Rockefellers, even among the younger ones, knows how to enjoy it." (Interview with family member unwilling to be identified.)

‡ Since 1970, Longwood has been subdivided (to escape restrictions of the 1969 Tax Reform Act) into Longwood Gardens, Inc. and the Longwood Foundation, Inc. Technically, the great resources of the Nemours Foundation are owned and controlled by the Alfred I. du Pont Estate, not by the foundation itself. But as will be explained later, the foundation is now the sole beneficiary of the estate's income and the two reportedly plan to merge.

institutions deserve special study not only for their size but because they illustrate so clearly the eccentric du Pont conception of
philanthropy. In addition, the interlock between the Alfred I. du
Pont Estate and the Nemours Foundation poses a special problem
of the exploitation of philanthropic privilege for competitive corporate advantage.

At the end of 1968 Longwood had assets of $217 million; the
Alfred I. du Pont Estate, from which the Nemours Foundation
draws its income, had assets conservatively estimated at $400 mil-
lion. They are the creations of the two principal members of the
family, Pierre S. du Pont and Alfred I. du Pont, whose leadership
was largely responsible for bringing the du Pont Company to its
present preeminence. In the early years of the twentieth century
they rescued it from economic disaster; but later, for nearly thirty
years, they were embroiled in an unrelenting and bitter conflict
that extended to all family, financial, political, and philanthropic
matters.

Alfred I. du Pont was regarded by most of the du Ponts as the
savior of the company but the saboteur of the family. By 1902 the
elder generation of du Ponts had died and the company, lacking
leadership, faced serious difficulties. To prevent its sale to a com-
petitor, Alfred, then thirty-eight years old, brought in two of his
cousins, Pierre S. and T. Coleman, to purchase control. Their vigorous management—and the advent of World War I—brought
new success. But frictions among the three soon developed and
Alfred was forced out by the others. Then in 1915, Pierre, with his
two brothers, Lammot and Irenée, purchased T. Coleman's shares
and gained complete control of the company. In fury, Alfred sued
Pierre, charging that he had used the credit standing of the company to borrow money from J. P. Morgan for the purchase. (A
lower court judge, although ruling against Alfred, assailed Pierre
for "trickery and double-dealing" in displacing the other members
of the family.) The breach between the two men was never closed.

At root, however, their differences involved family more than
finances. Even as a young man, Alfred—handsome, aggressive, and
impulsive—had annoyed the older du Ponts, and later his three
marriages made him a virtual outcast. In 1892 he married his
brother's sweetheart, after which the brother killed himself. By this

marriage Alfred had four children. But blighted from the beginning, it ended in divorce and the estrangement of the children
from their father. In 1907 he married the former wife of a du Pont
executive who had mysteriously disappeared after reportedly being
paid a million dollars by Alfred to "go away quietly." [1] It was for
this second wife that he built his spacious estate, Nemours, near
Wilmington. The high wall surrounding it had broken glass
embedded along the top "to keep out intruders," according to
Alfred, "mainly of the name of du Pont." [2] The next few years were
especially difficult for him. He lost the sight of one eye in a shotgun accident, his second wife died, and he became stone deaf. In
1921 he married Jessie Ball, the daughter of a Confederate captain
from Virginia. Thereafter, until his death in 1935, his life became
more subdued.

In almost total contrast to Alfred, Pierre was calm, gracious in
manner, and a paragon of respectability. After World War I, it was
he who overhauled the management of the company and initiated
its productive research into new products. It was also he who
made the major du Pont investment in the new General Motors
Corporation, surely one of the most monumentally rewarding speculations in the history of American high finance. But though his
business life was a consummate success, Pierre's personal life was
not. When well beyond his youth he married a deaf cousin, and
they were childless. In later years, he withdrew progressively from
company affairs, devoting himself to his vast gardens—his passion-
ate interest—and to the maintenance of the du Pont genealogical
tables.

By the 1920s, the clashes between the two men extended to local
Delaware politics and then to philanthropy. After he was driven
out of the company, Alfred acquired ownership of several newspapers in the state, whose influence he then used to help defeat two
other du Ponts—T. Coleman and Henry Algernon—for election to
the United States Senate. He and Pierre at the same time carried
on an intermittent civic competition at the state level. In 1929
Alfred was appointed Old Age and Welfare Commissioner for the
state. As a challenge to the Delaware legislature, he gave $350,000
of his own money to be used for payments to the needy until a

state pension plan should be adopted, an action which the legislature, in fact, took two years later. Pierre made his cause that of better schools. Immediately after the war, the Rockefeller-financed General Education Board had conducted a survey of the needs of secondary education in Delaware. As a result of its recommendations, interest in the problems of public schools markedly increased. Pierre, who was then a member of the state board of education—in a remarkable spurt of philanthropic generosity which was not sustained and never repeated—made a gift of $2.5 million to be used to build schoolhouses; and of this sum, nearly $1 million was spent to build schools for blacks.

So great was the animosity between these two men that when Alfred died in 1935, Pierre, still the dominant figure in the company and the spokesman for the great majority of du Ponts, refused to attend the funeral.

The Longwood Foundation

The Longwood Foundation was established in 1937 by Pierre S. du Pont, seventeen years before his death at the age of eighty-four. The primary obligation of the foundation, according to his will, is "the support, operation, and development of the Longwood gardens near Kennett Square, Pennsylvania." Any income beyond the needs of the gardens is given to local educational, scientific, and medical institutions.

The Longwood gardens are the most extensive horticultural gardens in the United States, covering a thousand acres and containing a conservatory (equipped with an enormous pipe-organ), an arboretum, flower gardens, Italian gardens, a vast planting of sculptured boxwood, an open air theater, scores of greenhouses, a sunken garden with more than thirty fountains, and a reception center. According to a description from the Milton (Pa.) *Standard*, "Longwood has no closed season. The greenhouses, largest in the world, outwit winter cold and summer heat at will. Bloom goes on throughout the year; though snow may blanket the rolling countryside outdoors, the display rooms inside show a garden in the full bloom of late spring—primroses, tulips, and narcissuses edging a lawn of perfect turf." The gardens are open to the public and there are organ concerts, horticultural lectures, and displays of the illuminated fountains.

Apart from maintenance of the gardens, the foundation has made a limited number of grants each year to charitable institutions in the locality, ranging from the Boy Scouts, the YMCA, and the Delaware Federation of Garden Clubs to various hospitals and universities. In 1958 Swarthmore College was given $1.8 million for a new science building, and in 1968 Lincoln University, a predominantly black institution near Philadelphia, was given $1 million. The foundation has also established a program of fellowships in ornamental horticulture. "This program is of vital importance," its coordinator, Dr. Richard W. Lighty, told the Dover (Del.) *State News*, in reporting fellowship grants to five students on March 26, 1969. "The need for skilled horticulturists has never been greater."

The 1968 market value of the securities of the foundation was $217.2 million; its income for the year was nearly $7 million. Apart from employees working at the gardens, the foundation has no full-time professional staff. It is governed by a seven-member board of trustees, all of them du Ponts by blood or marriage. The major investments are in du Pont Company stock and in the Christiana Securities holding company. In structure and policy, the Longwood Foundation is typical of many of the du Pont philanthropies, whose basic characteristics include: full family control of the small governing boards; close coordination of investments among the foundations and members of the family; little or no use of professional staff; local focus of activities; and issuance of minimal information to the public about their activities. Most of the du Pont foundations, like Longwood, provide for conversion to public use of the mansions, gardens, and various du Pont collections, which include military implements, antique automobiles, period furniture, old machinery, and family records.

The Eleutherian Mills–Hagley Foundation, for example, was established in 1952. Its immediate purpose is "to preserve and interpret the original site of E. I. du Pont's powder manufactory and to relate this regional development to the broader story of the nation's industrial progress." The Eleutherian Mills Historical Library, operated by the foundation, contains the archives of the du Pont Company from 1802 to 1902, as well as various family papers; it has a small publications program and makes grants-in-aid to encourage scholars to use its materials. In July 1959 the foundation acquired its first executive employee, Philip J. Kimball, who for forty years had been the manager of the company's explosives department.

Another of the larger du Pont philanthropies is the Winterthur Museum, Inc., formerly known as the Winterthur Foundation. It owns and operates the Winterthur Museum, the adjoining Winterthur Gardens, and the Corbit-Sharp House in Delaware. The museum includes materials from the original thirteen colonies which illustrate the major style periods and regional characteristics of American interior decoration. It is housed in the former home of Henry Francis du Pont, the donor. In its small grants program, the foundation contributes to the local fire department and to the Junior League (which conducts the May tours at the museum). It also maintains a small fellowship program in early American culture at the University of Delaware.

The grandiosity of the du Pont estates and collections reflect the family's aristocratic pretensions, but their taste has been essentially bourgeois. Over the years members of the family have bought vast quantities of paintings, sculpture, and *objets d'art;* but with the exception of the antiques at Winterthur, the collections are mediocre. Their educational, health, and scientific endeavors have been equally unimpressive. Similarly, although they have made numerous gifts to hospitals and universities in the area, they have not created one significant center of scientific or humanistic studies or of medical research or treatment.

At best, most of the family's philanthropies are a means of preserving for the American public a glimpse of the aristocratic life style of prerevolutionary Europe. In an increasingly industrialized society this may provide a therapeutic contrast to the bleakness of modern mass culture. By this view, the du Ponts may not practice creative modern philanthropy, but they at least make a contribution to the recreational life of one vicinity.

The Nemours Foundation

A less benign judgment, however, has to be rendered on the largest single du Pont philanthropy, the interconnected Nemours Foundation and the Alfred I. du Pont Estate. The stormy and unhappy life of the family rebel, Alfred I. du Pont, came to an end in 1935 in Florida, where he had located his business interests after his ostracism by the family. The event clearly did not take him by surprise: in 1932 he drafted a will that provided carefully for the use of his wealth after his death. In the du Pont manner, his first concern was to ensure full and perpetual family control; his second was to ensure a munificent income for his widow "against all contingencies" during her lifetime. He then authorized his trustees to create the Nemours Foundation to receive the income of his estate, but only after his wife's death. The philanthropic objectives were, again, in the du Pont manner: monumental, sentimental, and provincial.

To make certain that the foundation at no point interfered with the management of his properties he subordinated it absolutely to the estate. The latter was placed in the hands of three personal trustees and one corporate trustee "to have and to hold . . . forever." Until the death of his widow in 1970, the trustees were Mrs. Jessie Ball du Pont, her elderly brother, Edward Ball, and a son-in-law. The corporate trustee is the Florida National Bank of Jacksonville, which is controlled by the estate and whose board chairman is Edward Ball. The trustees are granted sweeping powers to carry on business enterprises, make investments, and to "do every and all things that they may deem best for the conservation, protection, and betterment of my Estate, as fully and completely as I might do, personally, were I alive and able to act for myself." The trustees are self-perpetuating. When one of them dies or ceases to act, the surviving trustees are directed to select a new one at once. The personal trustees may also change the corporate trustee at their discretion. By the terms of the will, the trustees of the estate "shall have full charge of the management and policy" of the Ne-

mours Foundation. It is they who appoint the five-member board of
managers of the foundation, and they may at any time remove any
member of the board "and shall not be required to specify the
cause for such removal." The trustees of the estate also have "full
power to employ and discharge any employees of the Foundation."

The primary purpose of the foundation is the maintenance of the
Nemours estate "as a memorial to my great, great grandfather,
Pierre Samuel du Pont de Nemours and to my father, Eleuthere Irenée du Pont de Nemours, and a proper tablet shall be erected in
the present Mansion to so indicate. . . . My Trustees are specifically instructed that it shall be their duty, first, to care for the
Mansion and grounds and gardens surrounding Nemours in order
that they may be maintained for the pleasure and benefit of the
public in their present condition and the grounds improved from
time to time, as their funds warrant; it being my particular desire
that this memorial to my great, great grandfather . . . and to my
father . . . be not permitted to deteriorate, but that it shall constantly become more beautiful and attractive to those who view it
as time passes. Only after faithfully carrying out the above instructions shall my Trustees be warranted in using any portion of the
capital or income of my estate for additional charitable purposes."
Such other charitable purposes were also specified, namely, "the
care and treatment of crippled children, but not incurables, and
old men and women, particularly old couples, first consideration
being given to residents of Delaware." In accordance with the
terms of the will, the trustees of the estate incorporated the foundation on February 25, 1936. They transferred to it $1 million of
the capital of the estate, which at that time was appraised at $39
million. Mrs. du Pont subsequently made an irrevocable assignment of 12 percent of her income from the estate to the foundation.
In 1939, the foundation built in Delaware the Alfred I. du Pont Institute, a children's hospital.

Over the years, the annual income of the estate has steadily increased: in 1951 it totaled $4.1 million; in 1957, $7.3 million; and in
1968, $10.5 million. Of this, 88 percent was taken annually by Mrs.
du Pont until her death. In addition she received a $200,000 fixed
annuity, plus a $5,000 annual fee as a trustee of the estate, a $1,000

fee as a member of the board of managers of the foundation, and miscellaneous expenses. In 1968 she received a total of $9.5 million from the estate. That same year the Nemours Foundation received $1.1 million. From its income, the foundation spends some $400,000 annually for the maintenance of the Nemours mansion and grounds; most of the remainder is used for the expenses of the Alfred I. du Pont Institute.*

A standard guidebook to Delaware describes Nemours: "On the 300-acre property there are the Chateau of Nemours itself, a carillon tower, and the several hospital buildings of the Nemours Foundation. . . . The residence of Nemours, built in 1908, is of formal French style throughout, the exterior finished in Indiana limestone. . . . The colonnade, grand basin, fountains and statuary, pool and water courses, urns and lawns, all suggest the Gardens of Versailles. . . . The front terrace is flanked by two white marble sphinxes formerly at the Chateau de Sceaux (in France). . . . Behind the sunken Gardens, on an eminence, stands a classic 'Temple of Love.'" [3]

The children's hospital has its own medical staff and treats some 2,000 patients annually. In the view of leading pediatricians and orthopedists, it is a worthwhile local institution, affluent in its facilities but having no particular significance as a center of research or experimentation. The institute publishes a thoroughly confusing annual report of its activities, which also gives a partial account of the work of the Nemours Foundation. According to it, the foundation distributes the small remainder of its funds to other organizations working with crippled children and sponsors a small program of conferences and research fellowships. In 1964, it announced that

* By the time of her death in 1970, Mrs. du Pont had received well over $100 million in income from the estate. During her life she made various gifts to such magnolia-scented institutions as Mary Washington College of the University of Virginia, the University of the South, Washington and Lee University, and Hollins College. In 1942, in her most innovative action, she established in memory of her husband an annual award program—similar to the Pulitzer Prizes in Journalism—for radio stations and commentators. Her large estate has now been bequeathed to the Jessie Ball du Pont Religious, Educational and Charitable Fund.

it was preparing a general program for the aging and that after consultation with the governors of the fifty states, it would determine what action could be taken to aid state programs for the elderly. But as of 1971 no further action had been reported.

The main concern posed by the Nemours Foundation arises from the financial and political dealings of the Alfred I. du Pont Estate from which it derives its income. Although the foundation has remained relatively undeveloped in the course of the thirty years since its donor's death, his estate has flourished. In 1936 it was appraised at $39.4 million. Since then, guided primarily by one man, Edward Ball, it has been built into a formidable economic and political power in Florida. The New York *Times* (June 17, 1965) reported its worth at more than $1 billion.

Its largest single holding is 764,280 shares of du Pont stock with a market value of nearly $100 million. It also owns 444,618 shares of General Motors common stock with a market value of about $30 million. In Florida, where the du Pont Estate is known as "the Empire" and Ed Ball as "the Emperor," the estate controls the Florida National group of banks and the St. Joe Paper Company of Jacksonville. At the time of du Pont's death, it controlled eight banks; it now has thirty, owning from 44 to 87 percent of each bank's capital stock. Another bank, the Jacksonville National, is controlled indirectly by the estate through the St. Joe Paper Company, which owns 82 percent of the bank's shares. The total assets of the chain are in excess of $700 million. The estate not only controls these resources but also exercises considerable influence over the investment funds managed by the banks. Seven in the group have trust departments; one of them, the Jacksonville National Bank, has the state's largest trust department, with a portfolio of more than $1 billion. The St. Joe Paper Company, controlled by the estate, is a major producer of pulp and paper products, serves all parts of the United States east of the Rocky Mountains, and owns more than a million acres of woodland in northwest Florida and southwest Georgia. The estate also controls the Appalachicola Northern Railroad, the St. Joseph Telephone and Telegraph Company, and the Florida East Coast Railway. The St. Joe Paper Company owns 52 percent of the common stock of the latter; and in addition the estate owns shares in the railroad directly and holds several millions of dollars of its mortgage bonds.

The economic influence of the estate and the special privileges it enjoys, partly because of its legal linkage with the Nemours Foundation, have repeatedly come under criticism in the Florida legislature and in Congress. There are many who believe that its extraordinary growth results in no small part from its exemption from regulation under the Bank Holding Company Act of 1956, which specifically forbids a bank holding company from owning other types of businesses. In addition, the act imposes regulation by the Federal Reserve Board on various activities of bank holding companies, including the acquisition of new banking properties. The du Pont estate was exempted from these provisions under an amendment sponsored by former Democratic Senator George A. Smathers of Florida and written into the bill on the Senate floor. Members of the House and Senate, then and since, have denounced the Smathers amendment as a flagrant example of the purchase of special legislative favor by a powerful economic interest. William McChesney Martin, former chairman of the board of governors of the Federal Reserve System, has called the argument used to justify the Smathers amendment—that the estate merited special exemption because its income would flow into philanthropic activities—a bald misrepresentation.

Since 1956, doughty Ed Ball—now in his eighties—has fought vigorously to stave off a succession of attempts to regulate the estate's banking and other activities. In 1965, when the House Banking Committee was considering a bill to lift the estate's exemption and force a partial breakup of its business interests, Ball denounced the proceedings as a punitive action with dangerous implications for the future of the republic. In his testimony to the committee he stated: "If it is the decision of this Congress to force the du Pont Estate to summarily dispose of a portion of its holdings, it is one more step, you must realize, toward total government control and one more step away from the individual's constitutional guarantee to acquire and hold private property. I am an old man and whatever action you take will not affect me personally. My meal ticket is in pretty good repair and will last me out until I meet my Maker. But . . . the right to work and acquire your own property, and to keep it, is our greatest birthright. If we lose this, or if it becomes meaningless, truly we will have then been destroyed from within."

Ignoring Ball's warning, the Congress acted in 1966 to require the estate to get rid of all its banks but one; or alternatively to keep the banks but dispose of its railway, paper company, and other nonbanking holdings. The deadline for compliance was set at July 1, 1971. For the next five years Ball actively lobbied the Florida legislature to obtain passage of a branch banking bill which would have enabled the estate in effect to escape the federal deadline and preserve its special privileges. He also worked the congressional corridors in Washington trying to head off new legislation to regulate bank holding companies. But by mid-1971, these moves having failed, he finally gave up and announced plans to sell enough of the estate's shares in the Florida National banking chain to enable it to declare itself no longer a bank holding company within the terms of the law.[4]

The du Pont family, with its undeviating preoccupation with material aggrandizement and self-indulgence, has nevertheless created a number of foundations. But they are of a characteristically unproductive, and in at least one instance unedifying, kind. Nor is there much indication that they will get any better. On the contrary, it appears that the more influential members of the family would rather see them liquidated than modernized. As one of their advisers who reflects their thinking has put it: "On balance, I am in favor of a forty-year limit on the life of foundations. The danger is that after that they fall into the hands of the damned sociologists."[5]

9.

Texas: Rich Land, Poor Land Moody, Houston, Richardson, and Brown

TEXAS IS A STATE with a unique political and economic history, a special ethos, and its own mythology. It also claims a separate chapter in the story of American philanthropy.

Until the turn of the century, Texas had been little more than a vast, impoverished rural expanse. But after 1901, when the Spindletop oil gusher blew in at Beaumont, it began a spectacular economic development. For the next forty years its economy was centered on raw materials—principally cotton and beef and oil and natural gas—which it exported to other more advanced states for final processing. After World War II, Texas began to develop industrially, first in petrochemicals and later in electronics and aerospace technology. This in turn led to accelerated urbanization, particularly along the Gulf Coast, and to a huge, sustained real estate boom.

Despite its reputation for riches and the legend of the "Texas millionaire," however, it has long been a poor state. The income of the average family until recently was well below the national average. Texas also continues to be dominated politically by rural interests, and culturally by that form of the frontier spirit in which personal goals are material rather than civic, and the acquisition of wealth and power takes precedence over esthetics and social reform. That spirit is steadily being eroded. But its memory has not vanished, particularly in the field of business.

In the brutality of the economic struggle in Texas, those who had the courage, the competence, or the luck to win, won heavily; and their fortunes, in many cases, have now been bequeathed to foundations. The four created thus far that have more than $100 million in assets each are the Moody Foundation of Galveston, the Houston Endowment and the Brown Foundation of Houston, and the Sid W. Richardson Foundation of Fort Worth.

The Moody Foundation

William L. Moody Jr., donor of the Moody Foundation, inherited from his father, Colonel William L. Moody, a successful cotton-trading firm, which by compulsive dedication to hard work he built into a diversified empire. When he died in 1954, at the age of eighty-nine, it was valued at more than $400 million. Among his holdings were the American National Insurance Company, the Moody National Bank of Galveston, three newspapers, a chain of hotels, extensive ranchland, and numerous oil and mineral properties.

He was a tall, slender man, taciturn in manner. With his small gray mustache and neat appearance, he resembled an elderly bookkeeper, and it always amused him to be mistaken for one. In business circles, though, he was known to be "tighter than the paper on the wall" and "meaner than a bullwhip." To his employees, he was a tireless and tyrannical taskmaster. He labored at his desk seven days a week, often sixteen hours a day. Appropriately, he was working in his insurance company office the day he died.

Apart from making money, almost his only other interest was duck hunting. His civic impulses were minimal. There are many in Galveston who believe that his steadfast opposition to any bond issues or expenditures for the improvement of the city largely explains why its development lagged badly behind that of neighboring Houston. Some also believe that Galveston's reputation as a "sin city" derives in good part from Moody's encouragement of gambling and other unpuritanical activities on grounds that they were good for his hotel business.

William Moody created his foundation in August 1942, twelve

years before his death. The terms of his trust indenture make obvious that his primary concerns at the time were the maintenance of family control over his properties and the avoidance of taxes. His trustees were instructed to administer his gifts strictly in accordance with conditions he set forth. The corpus of the trust was to be kept intact and the income was to be applied to religious, charitable, scientific, and educational purposes within the state of Texas.*

When Mrs. Moody died in 1943 the assets of the foundation were substantially increased. Various members of the family were given a life interest in the income of her Libbie Shearn Moody Trust, but three-quarters of its assets were earmarked to revert eventually to the foundation. The remainder was designated for the Methodist Church, of which she was a devout member. The assets of the trust in 1968 were valued at $157 million, by which time the foundation had purchased more than half of the income interests of the family members with lump-sum payments from capital.

When Moody died, he left the bulk of his wealth, consisting of his numerous business enterprises, to the foundation. But most of them, because of his monarchical methods of management, lacked an effective executive structure and their profits quickly sagged. (As of 1968, the foundation's assets were valued at $191 million, a dramatic decrease from their reported worth a decade earlier. Their value has since dropped still further.) In addition, a succession of bitter legal disputes among members of the Moody family, who were also trustees of the foundation, immediately erupted. Mr. and Mrs. Moody had two sons and two daughters, and family strife was not unknown to them. The older son, W. L. Moody 3d, had worked with his father in running the family businesses, but broke

---

* At the time, Texas law (Article 7112, Ch. V, Revised Civil Statutes of 1925) provided that inheritance tax would not be applied to property passing to or for the use of "any religious, educational, or charitable organization, when such bequests were to be used within the state of Texas." If such property were transferred outside of Texas, an inheritance tax rate of up to 20 percent was to be applied depending upon the size of the estate. Since 1965, the Texas legislature has removed bequests to tax-exempt foundations from taxation even if they are located outside Texas and the funds are used outside the state.

with him in the 1920s. They came together again in the 1940s, but frictions again developed and they separated definitely in 1950. In his will, the father left William one dollar, which now hangs framed in his office in San Antonio, Texas.°

Shearn, the second son, died in 1936. His two sons, Shearn Jr. and Robert, after their grandfather's death, sought to break his will by court action, charging that he had robbed them of their proper share of the family fortune. The suit outraged their aunt, Mary Moody Northen (Moody's elder daughter), and split the family trustees of the foundation into two warring groups. In her lifelong devotion to her father and his memory, the childless Aunt Mary resembles a character out of a nineteenth-century novel. After her mother's death, she spent every night in her father's thirty-room house, staying awake in his chair on the ground floor until he arose at daybreak, when she would return to her own house to sleep. After he died she moved into the big house and simultaneously assumed his place as head of the family companies and the foundation.

The rupture produced by the lawsuit of the two grandsons paralyzed the foundation for four years. The trustees in that period could not even agree on a date for a board meeting.† Finally, in 1958, the Texas attorney-general, Will Wilson, felt obliged to intervene. Filing suit in the 122d District Court of Texas, he argued that under the prevailing circumstances the foundation "could not operate for the benefit of the people of Texas" and asked the court to increase the number of trustees from the four relatives then composing it to "nine or such other odd number as the court may

° In reply to a note from his father in 1950 suggesting he resign from the company, William wrote: "I have hoped that I came into this world happily for you, but whether or not, my heart beats with your blood. . . . I had hoped with all my heart, as we both grew older and you much more successful, that small but honest differences would appear as trivial as they are, and that the years and better understanding would . . . strengthen the ties of affection and loyalty which should exist between father and son and son and father." The father was unmoved and fired him. (*Fortune*, March 1971, p. 112)

† During this time a close associate of the family and the foundation became so troubled by possible tax problems and legal violations that he visited the Ford Foundation in New York to ask whether it would be willing to take over the tangled affairs of the Moody Foundation. The offer was declined.

deem proper." He requested that the new trustees not be members of the family or related to any of the Moody enterprises.[1]

The threat of being ousted from control of their companies and the foundation caused the quarreling relatives to compose their differences, at least temporarily, and to work out a compromise settlement with the state. Mary Moody Northen agreed to step down as president of the various businesses, cash settlements were agreed upon with the two grandsons, and three new independent trustees were named to the foundation's board. Because the family proposed three individuals of high standing—Sales Leach, a retired executive of the Texaco Company; Marcus Greer, a Houston banker; and James M. Lykes Jr., head of a large Texas shipping company—the attorney-general did not insist on his own appointees. It was further agreed that no trustee of the foundation could be a paid officer of any company owned by it or the family and that the controlled companies would institute dividend policies sufficient to enable the foundation to carry out a program of "normal" size.

Final agreement with the Texas authorities was reached in April 1959, and for the next few years some progress was made. Leach became chairman of the board and worked diligently to halt the deterioration of the Moody companies and to activate the foundation. But he died in 1964 and the foundation once again became stagnant. Paul R. Haas, a wealthy San Antonio investor who was named to succeed Leach, found his difficulties sharply increased when the two grandsons attempted to raid the assets of the foundation in the spring of 1968—this time by legislative rather than judicial proceedings.* They arranged to have a special bill introduced into the Texas legislature that would have changed Texas law to permit stock dividends of any company to be considered as income for beneficiaries of a trust rather than as accretions to the corpus.

This technical change, given the relationship of the Moody

---

* At the time Shearn Jr. issued a press release describing himself in the third person as "a world traveler, art patron, and a well-rounded individual of many interests. His palm-studded ranch home on Galveston Island is a show place—filled with tapestries, paintings, imported rugs, and other *objets d'art*. He has contributed generously, for many years, to the civic opera companies of San Antonio, Houston, and Dallas, to name just a few."

Foundation to the associated Libbie Shearn Moody Trust, would have resulted in the transfer of as much as $50 million of the assets of the trust to the two grandsons and would have put the foundation at a disadvantage in the event of future stock dividends by the foundation-controlled American National Insurance Company. To fulfill their obligations to the foundation, the nonfamily trustees fought the so-called "Moody bill," and it was defeated.

A few months later, fresh disputes and scandal erupted. Witnesses before a committee of the Texas House of Representatives investigating foundations accused the Moody Foundation and some of its associated companies of corruption, conflict of interest, and self-dealing. On October 11, 1970, Roy Cohn, one-time counsel to the late Senator Joseph R. McCarthy, charged the foundation with making an "inside deal" with Carey Mayfield, head of the foundation-controlled Moody National Bank, to buy a chain of hotels owned by the foundation at a giveaway price. Cohn's client, New York investor Laurence Hurwitz, had reportedly made a bid substantially higher than Mayfield's, but it was rejected. The foundation's claim of innocence was not strengthened when, six days after the storm broke, it announced that the proposed sale to Mayfield had been canceled and that bidding was being reopened.

Subsequently, a former general agent of the American National Insurance Company, Norman Revie, claimed that the foundation had been bilked out of income by the company's practice of keeping a huge noninterest-bearing cash deposit in the First City National Bank of Houston, headed by Moody Foundation trustee S. Marcus Greer. He also charged that the insurance company directly supported by mortgage loans at least half of all the gambling casinos in Las Vegas and the Bahamas. He stated that two former officers of the insurance company had richly profited from these mortgage and lending transactions, many of which were arranged through a Morris Shenker of St. Louis, described by *Life* magazine as "the foremost lawyer for the mob in the United States." [2]

In the same period, Shearn Moody Jr., undaunted by his earlier defeats in the courts and legislature, made still another attack on the foundation. He filed suit to block a proposed increase in the size of its board from seven to nine and challenged the legality of the membership of the three nonfamily trustees. With Roy Cohn and young Shearn Moody simultaneously on the attack, the foundation was caught between the malodorous and the disreputable and was beginning to look rather soiled itself from the dirt being thrown.[3]

ONWARD AND UPWARD, SLIGHTLY

The Moody Foundation has now existed nearly thirty years, and its performance for at least two-thirds of that period has been miserable. Its only significant grant until the 1950s was one of $246,-000 to a school for cerebral-palsied children. From 1954 to 1960, while it was enmeshed in family quarrels and litigation, it received little income from its controlled companies and dispensed almost nothing in grants. From 1960, when nonfamily members were added to the board, until 1965 the foundation went through its first period of real philanthropic activity. Until 1960 it had dispensed less than $400,000 in total grants, but between then and 1965 it gave $25 million, largely in the form of lump-sum contributions to colleges, hospitals, and welfare organizations. By 1965 it had acquired its first full-time professional staff member and had issued its first public report.

According to its annual report for 1969, outlays to that point had reached a total of $34.2 million, broken down as follows:

	Percent
Education	53.6
Health	13.6
Welfare	12.0
Humanities	10.6
Religion	8.6
Scientific research	1.6
Total	100.0

In each category the grants were almost entirely for buildings, equipment, or general support. But in the 1969 list, there were some indications of a slightly changing approach: $160,800 to the

Moody Scholars Program for high-school seniors to help finance their college education; $30,000 to the Mission Information on Drugs and Narcotics Project for the printing and distribution of pamphlets to high-school students; and $37,500 to the Corpus Christi Symphony Orchestra. As of 1970 the Moody Foundation had eliminated an earlier accumulation-of-income problem by a series of lump-sum grants and had reached a significant level of current income on investments and of annual grant distributions. It had succeeded also in defining some program objectives and in beginning a planning process for the future. Public reports were being issued, and the trustees had taken initial action to sell some of the companies controlled by the foundation and to diversify its portfolio. But four-fifths of the assets were still in American National Insurance Company stock and an even higher proportion of those of the Libbie Shearn Moody Trust were in shares of the same company.

That the Moody Foundation has made any progress at all is a tribute to the initiative of the Texas attorney-general, the courts of the state, and the willingness of the nonfamily members of the board to undertake the difficult task of extricating the institution from a morass of legal, financial, and managerial problems in the face of unremitting personal antagonism from family members.

The Houston Endowment

Jesse H. Jones, the donor of the Houston Endowment, lived in the same economic era as William Moody but was a much bigger person in every sense. A self-made man of imposing physical stature, he was the indisputable "Mr. Houston." More than any other individual in its history, he led the city's growth and shaped its development.

Born in Tennessee, he settled in Houston early in the century and began his career as a builder and real estate operator. By 1910 he owned more than a dozen hotels and office buildings and was buying others. Although he was not primarily an oilman, he

speculated in oil leases and was one of the founders of Humble Oil
and Refining Company. By the time of his death in 1956, at the age
of eighty-two, his interests had spread into life insurance and
banking and he had also acquired a vast acreage of west Texas
ranchland and extensive urban real estate in Texas and New
York. His estate was valued at more than $200 million.

In parallel with his business activities Jones also played a large
role on the national political scene. During the Woodrow Wilson
administration he served as director-general of military relief, and
in the 1920s President Herbert Hoover appointed him as director
of the Reconstruction Finance Corporation. Under Franklin D.
Roosevelt, Jones became secretary of commerce, serving for thirteen years as the leading conservative member of the New Deal
cabinet. His long period of national service came to an end in
1945, after a spectacular feud with former Vice-President Henry A.
Wallace over postwar economic policy.

During Jones's years with the New Deal, he and his wife, who
were childless, laid the plans for their foundation. It was incorporated in 1937 and given broad goals, namely, "to support any charitable, educational, or religious undertaking." The six-member
board of trustees has since been made up predominantly of family
members and the donor's close business associates. During his lifetime, Jones and his wife supported the endowment's activities with
annual gifts.

After his death in 1956 the foundation inherited what are known
in Houston as the "Jones interests," which consisted of controlling
shares in twenty-six separate corporations. Because of the nature of
its assets the foundation's board has necessarily had to devote a
large portion of its energies to direct business management. For example, over a six-year period, $6.5 million was spent to modernize
the major Jones hotel, the Rice in Houston; late in 1963, the National Bank of Commerce, then 53 percent owned by the endowment and members of the Jones family, merged with another major
Houston bank to become one of the two leading financial institutions of the city; and the Houston *Chronicle*, owned by the
endowment, bought out its ailing afternoon rival, the Houston
Press, in 1964 and moved slightly ahead in the circulation race

with Mrs. Oveta Culp Hobby's morning Houston *Post*. In 1969 the foundation sold a downtown block of buildings to a local public utility company for a new office building; it also realized $10 million in cash from the sale of its wholly owned Commercial and Industrial Life Insurance Company to Houston's American General Life Insurance Company, in which the foundation already had a strong minority position.

The operating heads of all the properties and companies controlled by the endowment report directly to its board, and several of the board's members are officers of endowment-controlled enterprises. Trustee and President J. Howard Creekmore, who worked his way up through the Jones organization while the donor was alive, has been the decisive force in the foundation. An unsocial and remarkably little-known person in Houston, he is directly responsible for managing the endowment's properties and business affairs.

In 1968, it had $214 million worth of assets, most of them concentrated in Houston and constituting, therefore, a powerful economic nexus on the local scene. The board has stated that its general investment policy is to upgrade the endowment's property holdings to ensure their profitability and then carefully to shift its investments over time into a diversified portfolio of government and corporate securities. Some diversification has been accomplished, but it is unclear whether the endowment is yet prepared to relinquish its major properties.

In its philanthropic operations, the board retains full authority and close control. Members of the board also serve as officers of the foundation: the president-treasurer and the secretary are employed full time, the two vice-presidents part time. The only direct contact with the public is through a "grants coordinator" who prepares the agenda of proposals for decision by the board, which meets monthly. The endowment published its first report in 1959 after twenty-two years of operation. During that period, it granted a total of $13.5 million, of which $10 million was given to educational institutions, $3 million to charitable organizations, and $500,000 to religious bodies. On the whole the grants went to reputable institutions in the Houston area, principally for the construction of facilities. Beginning in 1958 it made grants of less orthodox character, one of which was an experimental scholarship program in the Houston area for graduating high-school seniors. The awards permitted the winners, chosen by committees of local citizens, to attend any accredited American university. Over the years several thousand of these scholarships have been granted. Possibly reflecting the interest of the donor, who took active part in the development of higher education for blacks for many years, the endowment has made a number of grants to such institutions, including one of $127,000 to build a men's dormitory at Texas Southern University.

Since 1963 the endowment has given increased help to organizations in Houston dealing with the problems of ghetto residents. But its most striking program has been its support for the fine arts. Beginning in the mid-1950s, it made a series of gifts eventually totaling $7.4 million for the construction of a performing arts center for the city. This handsome marble structure won high commendation from the American Institute of Architects in 1967 for its design. In 1963, the endowment granted a half-block of valuable downtown real estate to the nationally known, experimental Alley Theatre.

Although it is slowly becoming a more productive philanthropy, it is still heavily involved in business activities that distract from, if not conflict with, its philanthropic responsibilities. A conspicuous example is its ownership of the Houston *Chronicle*, now the only afternoon paper in a big, prosperous, and growing market. Although the newspaper is "independent," it consistently supported conservative political candidates and the right-wing position on most local and national issues from 1940 to 1960. In 1960, however, after the election of John F. Kennedy and reportedly because of the influence of trustee John T. Jones Jr., a nephew of the donor, a new editor was named, William T. Steven, formerly of the Minneapolis *Star and Tribune*. He shifted the paper to a moderate, even mildly liberal, line.

Thereafter friction between Steven and the trustees steadily increased. In August 1965 Jones resigned from the board, reportedly because of political disagreements with his fellow trustees and also because he planned to buy the radio and television stations owned by the endowment and wanted to avoid charges of conflict of interest. Within a month, Steven and other key editorial employees were dismissed. Calling his removal an "act of political assassination," Steven said: "We've had a good battle for five years. The conservatives won but I am proud of the reason I was fired. As General Custer said, 'I've been scalped right through the neck.' " [4]

Three months later it was announced that John W. Mecom, one of the few independent oilmen in Texas still active on a grand scale, had bought the *Chronicle* as well as control of Houston's Texas National Bank of Commerce, the city's largest downtown hotel, and a garage and laundry from the endowment for a total of $84 million. In June 1966, Mecom's name was carried as president and publisher of the *Chronicle;* and because he was known as a moderate Democrat, a strong financial supporter of President Johnson, and a progressive on questions of civil rights, there was much speculation in Houston at the time concerning the editorial direction the newspaper would take under his ownership. In the end, the multimillion-dollar deal collapsed, leaving many observers wondering whether it was because Mecom, in a tightening money market, had been unable to raise the necessary funds to complete his purchase, or whether political factors had persuaded Creekmore to suspend negotiations.*

The case highlighted some of the unrecognized complexities in restricting political activity by foundations. More than a few major publications throughout the country, as well as radio and television stations and networks, are now owned by foundations. Many of them, particularly the newspapers, take partisan positions on candidates, pending legislation, and various public issues. Foundations are forbidden to engage in political or propaganda activity through their grant-making or direct operations. But under established rulings and procedures of the Internal Revenue Service a foundation is apparently freed from these prohibitions if its political, legislative, or propagandistic activity is carried out by a separate profit-making corporation that it controls.

The Houston Endowment is not in the same class as the best of

* Mecom's problems have worsened since, and in 1970 he had to ask a Federal Court to reorganize his oil empire under the Federal Bankruptcy Act.

the big foundations, but it is far from the worst. Conservatives on the board who are the former associates of the donor are now elderly and before long must cede their power. If they are succeeded by less archaic individuals, the endowment may yet achieve a record worthy of its founder.

The Richardson Foundation

Sid W. Richardson, donor of the Richardson Foundation of Fort Worth, was one of the high-flying wheeler-dealers who made their fortunes gambling in the oil boom of the American Southwest after the 1930s. The uneducated son of a hard-scrabble Texas farmer, Richardson by 1939 had made and lost two fortunes and begun the accumulation of his third, which, by the time of his death, was reputed to be worth several hundreds of millions of dollars. His close friend and associate in many of his deals was another rich wildcatter, Clint Murchison. Of the two, a friend once said, "They are both nice guys. They have the simplest, most innocent desire in the world—to make money. All they want is more." The style and scale of their transactions is suggested by the story of their purchase of $20 million in New York Central stock in 1954 to help their friend and fellow Texan, Robert R. Young, gain control of that railroad. A half-hour after agreeing to the deal Richardson asked an associate, "What the hell's the name of that railroad again?" Richardson shared his fellow Texas millionaires' dislike for publicity and rarely talked to newsmen. One of his favorite maxims was, "You don't learn nothin' when you're talkin'."

Richardson owned a private island in the Gulf of Mexico that was his retreat. Presidents Roosevelt and Eisenhower visited him at its lodge, where he kept a large collection of Western paintings by Frederic Remington and Charles Russell. He died there in October 1959 at the age of sixty-eight. Billy Graham was flown in Richardson's private plane to officiate at the funeral.

For all his financial success, Richardson seems to have been a limited and lonely man. Stocky, with a great barrel-shaped body and a lined, homely face, he was a lifelong bachelor. His home for his last twenty-one years was a two-room suite at the Fort Worth Club. The pattern of his days and nights fitted the stereotype of the rough and tough oil millionaire: bourbon, branchwater, and an endless game of poker. His abstinence from ordinary social life may have stemmed from sensitivity about one of his legs being shorter than the other, a result of an early oil-field accident. Speaking once of the rolling gait which he had perfected, he said, "I practiced me a walk that wouldn't make me limp. It took me a year."

Richardson, once his fortune swelled, began to make a number of gifts to local charities and for student scholarships. In 1947, after being repeatedly pressed by an old friend, oilman and civic leader Amon Carter, to widen his philanthropic horizon, he set up his foundation. During the remaining years of his life he made gifts to various Texas institutions through it.

After his death the foundation received the bulk of his properties, which included land, oil leases, and operating companies as well as a portfolio of stocks and bonds. In 1961 the executors of the estate, after two years of trying to pay off the tax liabilities of the complicated Richardson holdings, decided to turn the entire corpus and its debts over to the foundation.*

---

* In February 1971, John B. Connally, former governor of Texas, was nominated by President Nixon for the post of secretary of the treasury. During the Senate hearings on his appointment, two matters came to light involving the Richardson Foundation and its donor. Connally had been a business partner of Richardson in a number of oil deals and other transactions, and he was named one of three executors of Richardson's estate. For his fifteen months of service he received a fee of $750,000 from the foundation, paid over a ten-year period to lessen the tax bite. During his term as governor he received not less than $575,000 of this sum in secret payments, which he admitted to the Senate committee in 1971. At the same time it became known that another of the executors, Richardson's nephew, Perry Bass, who is also chairman of the foundation's board of trustees, received not less than $960,000 in fees.

The second matter involved an intricate scheme for diverting the profits of a racetrack, the Del Mar Turf Club in California, to a nonprofit organization, Boys, Inc., which had been set up in 1954 by Richardson and Clint Murchison, with Connally serving as one of the directors. In 1959 the state of California investigated charges that the arrangement was a means of giving the Texas oilmen control of the track without payment of taxes. One of its investigators called it a "sweetheart" contract. The state then began taxing the receipts of Boys, Inc., and in 1962 the Internal Revenue Service followed suit.

The foundation then took out loans to settle the tax claims at once. Most of its income over the next two years was used to pay off the loans. Thus its grants totaled only $7,000 in 1961, $14,500 in 1962, and $52,000 in 1963. Thereafter, the total rose rapidly, reaching $2.4 million in 1965, but by 1968 it had dropped to $1.6 million.

Because of the nature of its assets the principal activity of the foundation to date, according to reports filed with the Internal Revenue Service, has been the management of its properties, collecting revenues, and settling obligations and claims. A review of its recent tax returns still reveals a rat's nest of miscellaneous properties, loans to related companies, and unpaid debts.

The philanthropic record of the Richardson Foundation is a Texas-style exaggeration of the faults of others in its asset group. It has no defined program, no formulated plans for the future, and has not voluntarily issued any public reports. It had no professional staff until 1971, when it appointed one full-time employee, Elizabeth Ledyard. The board of five trustees consists of the donor's nephew, the nephew's wife, two executives of other Richardson enterprises, and the chairman of the board of the Fort Worth National Bank. The nephew, Perry Bass, is also head of Insurance Securities, Inc., 8.5 percent of whose stock the foundation owns, and he is a director of Allegheny Airlines, 8 percent of whose stock is in the foundation's portfolio. In 1966 he purchased from the foundation its control of a chain of television stations in Texas, Oklahoma, New Mexico, and California. All the nonfamily trustees are financially involved with enterprises in which the foundation's assets are held.*

Most of the foundation's grants are given for physical facilities and general support of Texas hospitals, colleges, libraries, medical laboratories, churches, and civic organizations. The largest com-

---

Later, a federal district court in Dallas ruled that Boys, Inc., was entitled to a tax exemption and ordered the taxes that had been paid refunded. By 1971 the organization had still done little to instill virtue into homeless boys because of the heavy payments it had to make to the owners of the racetrack.

* For example, trustee H. B. Fuqua is chairman of the directors of the Fort Worth National Bank, which owns 24.9 percent of the Tarrant State Bank, which in turn is 20 percent owned by the Richardson Foundation.

mitments have been $3.4 million for a science building at Texas Christian University in 1967 and $2 million to the University of Texas for a library collection on the history of science in 1969. One million dollars was given for a physical fitness center at Texas Wesleyan University in Fort Worth, and an equal amount to the Fort Worth Country Day School. The Sid W. Richardson Memorial Fund, which distributes scholarships to children of employees in companies the donor organized or was associated with, has received more than $2 million. The cemetery in which he is buried in Athens, Texas, was given $100,000. The Sid W. Richardson Boy Scout Wilderness Camp has also received several large grants. Among its smaller grants the foundation has been providing $25,-000 a year to the Billy Graham Evangelical Association and $500 a year to the United Negro College Fund.

The Brown Foundation

Herman Brown, founder of the Brown Foundation, built a worldwide engineering and construction firm, Brown and Root, on the basis of his mastery of maneuver in the twilight zone where contracting meets politics. Born in a small town in the hill country of central Texas, he had one year at the state university and then went to work in 1914 as a foreman for a road builder. He got into contracting almost by necessity when he had to accept from his failing employer eighteen tired and mortgaged mules and some well-worn equipment in lieu of a year's back wages. In an early display of the shrewdness that was to make him his fortune, his first visit thereafter was to the county commissioner's office. He left with a small road-building contract. As the nation shifted from the horse and buggy to the automobile, the company Brown formed with his brother-in-law prospered. They built roads and bridges all over the Southwest. In those days, road builders lived in camps with a mule corral, a cook tent, and sleeping tents for the workmen. It was to such a camp that Brown brought his bride, the former Margaret Root, in 1919.

Through the 1920s he traveled 75,000 miles a year inspecting jobs. He would spend most of a day on one job, then get a night's sleep on the back seat of the car while his chauffeur took him to the next. When the depression came, the company survived by making the most of the pump-priming projects offered by the New Deal. In 1936 it got its first big contract, the construction of Marshall Ford Dam on the Colorado River. During World War II the company built vast military installations, airfields, and a shipyard. After the war it built dams, petrochemical plants, pipelines, and hydroelectric installations throughout the world, as well as United States military facilities in Europe, Africa, and Asia.

Brown was a man of warmth and humor, of salty talk and directness. His tastes were simple and thrifty, and he scrupulously avoided exposing his private life or business affairs to public gaze. At the same time, he and his brother George, who was his longtime partner in the company, were among the most astute behind-the-scenes political operators the state of Texas has ever known. Every Texas governor for thirty years sought their counsel and support. Their influence ranged from the selection of local school boards to the nomination of senators and governors. They actively backed conservative candidates in the South and were strong supporters of Lyndon Johnson, who was staying at Herman Brown's home in Virginia in 1956 when he suffered his first heart attack. In 1962 Vice-President Johnson was among the 1,500 prominent figures who attended Brown's funeral.

The single political issue that most aroused the Brown brothers was unionism. Herman Brown had early laid down the dictum that "any man who works for me won't have to go through a middleman to get or keep his job," and of the tens of thousands of Brown and Root employees who have worked on construction sites all over the world, none has ever worked under a union contract. The Brown brothers were high on the union list of people to fight, and they in turn gave their full financial and political support to anti-union forces. In Texas they spearheaded the passage of the so-called antiviolence bill, the right-to-work laws, and statutes to limit picketing. Nationally, the passage of the Taft-Hartley Act was attributed in significant part to their powerful backing.

Herman Brown was essentially a hard-driving businessman, not a do-gooder. But in his later years, perhaps at his wife's instigation, he served on several civic boards, including the Texas Children's Hospital in Houston and Southwestern University in Georgetown. In 1951 he set up his foundation and through it made substantial unpublicized gifts until his death in 1962, when he left it the bulk of his estate. His wife, who had become interested in art, ballet, literature, and music, served on the boards of the Houston Museum of Fine Arts, the Foundation for Ballet, and the Symphony Society. When she died two months after her husband, she left the residue of her estate to the foundation, further increasing its resources. By the end of their lives, this childless couple had come a very long way in wealth, position, and interests from the road-builder's camp where their marriage began.

The Brown foundation, true to its donor's passion for anonymity, has since its establishment quietly disbursed a total of nearly $30 million in grants—more than half of it for land, buildings, and endowment to Texas colleges, hospitals, and museums. The Herman Brown Library at the University of St. Thomas and Herman Brown Hall and the Herman Brown Space Science and Technology Building at Rice University are among the monuments to its generosity.

Until 1970 the foundation had its offices in the Brown and Root Company and operated with no full-time professional staff. It issued no reports, and its grantees have been permitted to release information about its actions only when necessary, as in 1963 when Southwestern University announced a $1.4 million grant from Brown in order to publicize the need for matching grants.

The five-member board is headed by the donor's brother, George Brown. The others are Mrs. George Brown; Alfred W. Negley, their son-in-law; James Root Paden, a nephew of Mrs. Herman Brown; and Herbert J. Frensley, president of Brown and Root. After the donor's death in 1962, the foundation's holdings in Brown and Root were sold to the Halliburton Company, on which George Brown and Frensley are board members. As of 1968, its assets had a value of $108 million.

Since the passage of the 1969 Tax Reform Act, the foundation has opened small separate offices and transferred a financial officer of Brown and Root to serve as executive head. But there is little

prospect so long as the present members of the board are in control that its program will greatly change. Nor does it appear that
any younger members of the family are being groomed to take over
responsibility for the foundation or that they have any noticeable
interest in philanthropy.

The Texas Tradition

The economic boom in Texas in recent decades has already produced several major foundations, and within the next decade the
number may double. In fact, as many as half of the large American
foundations expected to appear by the end of the century may derive from Texas wealth. Thus far, the story of the big Texas foundations is the story of first-generation money, of eminently practical fortune-builders who wanted to see something tangible for their
charity. Some of the donors were men of primitive intellectual and
social outlook, but even the more enlightened ones have been little
more than sentimental givers and civic boosters with a predilection
for personal monuments. Often their wives have guided their gifts
toward cultural activities, usually for building a museum or an
opera house. As a result, the big Texas foundations have had relatively little intellectual impact on the life of the state and have
made little contribution to the solution of its many grave social
problems.

The showiness of Texas philanthropy is oddly combined with a
common donor posture of "the strong silent man," a highly developed sense of privacy about money—even in giving it away. The
stout aversion of wealthy families to publicity may be attrib-
utable to a prudent desire not to excite envy or criticism—or, given
the frequency with which Texas foundations have engaged in questionable business practices, to a simple preference for keeping in
the shade. In the context of Texas culture there may even be a reverse snobbishness in seeming to do good without fanfare.

The fundamental limitation on the quality of big philanthropy in
Texas is the quality of the wealthy class and the forms taken by its
competition for status. In addition, the donors typically acquired

their wealth by the accumulation of many smaller properties and operating businesses in which they were predominant owner and whose securities were not listed and traded on the major stock exchanges. Mediocre philanthropic programs have been the typical outcome, combined with complex and distracting financial ties.

10.

Lilly, Hartford, and Duke: Birds in Gilded Cages

MOST OF THE LARGE American foundations have been built back-to-back with the corporate holdings of the donor family. In the Lilly Endowment, the Hartford Foundation, and the Duke Endowment the effects of this Siamese relationship for philanthropy have been unmistakably negative. Nor has it been uniformly beneficial for the associated companies. In the case of Hartford and Duke, the companies have lagged in growth and profitability; Lilly, however, remains vigorously competitive and profitable. These company–foundation links illustrate some of the most serious structural weaknesses of modern American philanthropy.

The Lilly Endowment

This Indianapolis-based foundation, the second largest in the United States as of 1970, was established in 1937 by the Lilly family, which also controls Eli Lilly & Company, a large pharmaceutical manufacturer with headquarters in the same city.* Its organizers were J. K. Lilly Sr., who built a small drug company founded by his father in 1876 into a giant corporation, and his two sons, J. K. Lilly 2d and Eli Lilly. The latter, now in his eighties, is the only survivor of the founding group. The endowment's assets—entirely

* As noted in chapter 2, it was displaced in ranking the following year by the Robert Wood Johnson Foundation of New Jersey.

in shares of Eli Lilly & Company—had a market value of $579 million in 1968. These holdings constitute slightly more than 20 percent of the outstanding voting shares and ensure, when combined with those of the family, the latter's control of the company. The Lilly Endowment is distinctive among the large foundations for its keen interest in Indiana and in religion. It is also a unique example of retrogression in development: after a steadily productive period of more than twenty years, it has more recently become highly ideological and as a result has now lost much of its good reputation in the swamps of the far Right.

The foundation began without professional staff or formulated program. J. K. Lilly 2d was chairman of the board and his brother, Eli, assumed executive responsibility as part-time secretary-treasurer. For the next several years he operated the foundation "out of the left-hand drawer of his desk." Its first board of five was a bouquet of four Lillys and an in-law. It now consists of seven trustees, with one exception all members of the family or officers of the company. Grants during the initial years were confined to the family's favorite charities.

In 1949 J. K. Lilly 3d became the first full-time director, and a separate office for the foundation was opened. During the five years of his capable administration, an earnest effort was made to define a program and recruit a staff. In 1951 the first annual report was published. But by 1954, in a repetition of a familiar story, friction between father and son had caused the younger Lilly to resign his position; he left Indianapolis and has never since been involved with the foundation. He was succeeded by his assistant, Harold Duling, the first nonfamily member to be given significant responsibility in the endowment. During the next fifteen years under Duling, it reached its highest development. In 1957, when it published a twenty-year review of its grants, it showed the following geographical pattern: of a total of $18.5 million, $6.3 million had been given to organizations in Indianapolis, $6.7 million to grantees in Indiana outside the city of Indianapolis, and $5.2 million outside Indiana but within the United States; less than $500,000 had been given abroad. By fields, $8.8 million had been given for education; $3.9 million for religion, the social sciences, and humanities; $2.6

million for community services; and $1.6 million to public health. The remainder went to cultural and research projects.

In education, which received roughly half the total grants, the endowment explained its concentration on Indiana by the fact that few other foundations operate there. It expressed the belief that a regional foundation "can develop and maintain particularly close and fruitful and continuing relationships with educational institutions in its own vicinity." The grants emphasized the improvement of higher education, particularly in private colleges, although some help was given to Indiana University. A few grants went to black institutions, mostly via the United Negro College Fund.

Religion was the second distinctive field of activity. The endowment asserted that it was "constantly in search of ideas which had strong overtones of religious and spiritual purpose," and by the 1950s it had become the largest single source of U.S. philanthropic assistance in the specific field of religion. It favored middle-of-the-road Protestantism and played a particularly influential role in improving theological education.*

The third field of concentration was community services, a catchall category covering the various charities of the Lilly family and miscellaneous local institutions. Almost any Indianapolis organization whose goals fell within the terms of the endowment's charter got some help.

Although most of the grants were $500 or less, in a few cases they were considerably larger. In 1961, for example, the Indianapolis Day Nursery Association (of which Mrs. Donald C. Duck was then president) received a grant of $62,000. On the whole, the endowment pursued a passive policy in its community grants, avoiding primary responsibility for the financing of new or existing institutions. Occasionally it made equal gifts to competing fund-raising drives to emphasize its neutrality. A noteworthy exception was its initiative in 1952 in creating Community Surveys, Inc., which made a general study of the social and welfare needs of Indianapo-

* The two other major foundations working in this field were the Sealantic Fund, supported by the Rockefellers, and the Pew Memorial. Sealantic grants tended to reflect a liberal Protestant orientation, while those of the Pew Memorial were directed primarily to fundamentalist and evangelical sects.

lis. The subsequent report led to a useful reorganization of private voluntary activities in the city.

By 1959, it appeared that the endowment might be on the verge of a commitment to social change. Its report for that year contained this tortured passage: "A long time ago, charity may have been confined to the relief of the poor . . . but today it has become a part of the very fabric of our social system and our economy. Charitable organizations and agencies such as those supported by the Lilly Endowment and other foundations are now prime movers in the constant re-examination and development of man's abilities and responsibilities which lead the way to great advances in social, economic, and scientific horizons and accomplishments."

But within a few months Harold Duling was replaced by Richard R. McGinnis, a retired lawyer from Evansville, Indiana, whose local reputation was based largely on his extremist political activities. Within two years McGinnis was succeeded by John S. Lynn, a former assistant director of corporate development for the Lilly Company. Lynn was also known primarily for his affiliation with the far Right. He was considered to be on particularly close terms with leaders of the John Birch Society (which was started in Marion County, where Indianapolis is located) and identified himself in his *Who's Who* entry as chairman of the Indianapolis chapter of the Christian Anti-Communism Crusade. Why the endowment took such a sharp political turn at that time can only be surmised. Some believe that it simply succumbed to the political environment of Indiana, a state that has long been a center of strength of the Ku Klux Klan, militant anticommunism, and superpatriotism. Others lay the change to the impact of two specific developments on the Lilly family: the Kefauver investigation of the drug industry in the late 1950s, which produced acute resentment and fear of federal "intervention"; and the "radicalization" of American Protestantism, symbolized at that time by the National Council of Churches declaring its support for the recognition of Communist China and its admission to the United Nations.

J. K. Lilly 2d, who was the dominant influence in the endowment until he died in 1966, was a reserved, enigmatic man. In his later years he developed a serious heart condition and his life became almost totally cloistered. He spent his lonely days in his private museum, working on his various collections of rare books, stamps, jewels, gold coins, maritime objects, and toy soldiers. The curator of the Smithsonian Institution in Washington has called his collection of 6,113 gold coins, dating from the early Mesopotamian empires to modern times, one that "surpasses in scope any other collected by one man." He also devoted hours to reading the Encyclopaedia Britannica, and according to newspaper reports had reached the letter G at the time of his death.[1]

His brother, Eli, who is now the leading family trustee, has been an active churchman and also a student of history and archeology. Both he and his wife, also a long-time member of the endowment's board, have played an especially influential role in its evolution. From the early 1940s through most of the 1950s Eli Lilly was regarded as a force for moderation in guiding the endowment's community activities and also its broader programs in education and religion. He was consistently anti-Ku Klux Klan and during the height of the McCarthy period stanchly defended the foundation against pressures by McCarthy's Indiana adherents. But in the late 1950s he and his wife apparently joined the forces he had long opposed.

The change in their views was quickly reflected in the pattern of the foundation's grants. Funds were given to the Hoover Institute of War and Peace at Stanford for a study of the nature of communism; to Radio Free Europe for broadcasting behind the Iron Curtain; to the Inter-Collegiate Society of Individualists "to put in the hands of college students publications explaining the free market and limited government concepts"; to the American Economic Foundation for a Hall of Free Enterprise at the New York World's Fair; to the American Bar Association for a program of public education in anticommunism; and to Vanderbilt University for a summer course on communism for high-school teachers. Although the number of such grants was considerable, they represented in total only a minor portion of the endowment's outlays. But its annual reports began to suggest that the foundation's major purpose had become its crusade in defense of "human freedom." The report of 1962 declared that the endowment—through its community services, education, and religion grants—intended to "contribute to a better understanding of the anticommunist free enterprise limited government concept." *

The ideological fever persisted through 1964. In that year, the Communists, according to its annual report, were infiltrating Formosa, an "outpost of the Free World," by deluging the underprivileged tribespeople with written propaganda. A grant was made through a California organization called Mustard Seed, Inc., for a program to translate and distribute books to "strategically placed reading rooms by which the Christian message and the Free World heritage can be shared with these people."

By 1965 some of the better staff members had either resigned or been forced out, and anxiety about its political coloration began to spread among many of the local colleges and other institutions dependent upon the endowment for special assistance. Some public protest even developed. (One group of Indiana doctors, for example, threatened to boycott products of the Lilly Company.) Possibly because of these developments, the shrill note that had been evident in the endowment's reports was muted after 1967. Unadorned financial data took over the featured position formerly reserved for politics and preachments. But as of 1970 John Lynn was still executive director and a number of ideological grants were still being made (for further details see chapter 21).

There are some good things to be said about the policies and grants of the Lilly Endowment. By its concern for educational institutions in its locality and by its special interest in religious education, it has helped fill certain gaps in the spectrum of activity of the big foundations. Also, the endowment in recent years has fastidiously avoided any appearance of serving the interests of the pharmaceutical company by staying out of the field of medicine and medical research. The Lilly family, conscious of its potentially dominating influence on the life of Indianapolis, has consistently tried to avoid undermining the community's sense of responsibility for the support of its principal voluntary agencies and institutions.

* In the same document it was soberly noted that because "Christianity is the great unifying force" in international affairs, it thereafter would receive the endowment's increased support.

To many, however, it appears that this self-restraint has been
carried to the point of an unwillingness to accept leadership responsibilities in the city and the area. Overall, the endowment
has never realized its potential and is now in a process of deterioration. The active family members are now elderly, and the younger
generation has no interest. The staff, which once seemed to be
developing in size and quality, has become third-rate. Its education
program has lost much of its earlier vigor and quality. Its religious
projects have drifted toward fundamentalism and lost the respect
of most theological educators, and its community services program has dissipated its energies in quixotic political adventures.
To the great loss of the troubled city of Indianapolis and the surrounding region the endowment remains a mediocre and incoherent philanthropy—major only in its resources.

The John A. Hartford Foundation

The Hartford Foundation of New York is based on wealth produced by the Great Atlantic and Pacific Tea Company. The foundation holds effective control of the company, and at the same time
the foundation's board and management are dominated by a group
of present and retired company executives.

A & P is one of the oldest, largest, and most successful examples
of mass consumer merchandising in the United States, an industry
that has given rise to four of the nation's major foundations—
Kresge, Danforth, Kellogg, and Hartford. Organized in the mid-
nineteenth century by George Huntington Hartford, the company
was developed into the leader of its field by his two sons, John and
George.°

Mr. John and Mr. George, as they were known in the company
where they spent their entire working lives, were dissimilar in per-

---

° In 1968 the annual sales of A & P were $5.4 billion, by far the largest of
any of the retail food chains. In 1912 it operated 480 stores with $23.6 million
in sales; by 1920 it operated 4,544 stores with sales of $235 million; by 1925
it operated 14,000 stores with sales of $440 million. During that period of
rapid expansion, the A & P often opened new stores at the rate of 200 to 300
a week. (*The Progressive Grocer*, February 1970, p. 60)

sonality, but made a balanced team. George, the older, was a quiet man with a passion for efficiency and financial analysis; John was elegant and outgoing, at ease with people and ideas. The company's financial policy was very conservative: growth was financed strictly out of earnings, not borrowing, and it continuously maintained a large cash position. Publicity-shy, it did not hire its first public relations adviser until the mid-1930s, when forced to do so by a series of congressional investigations into chain store practices.* In their personnel policy, the Hartfords adhered firmly to "promotion from within," which meant that the small group of executives who rose to the top had spent their lives within the company and felt an unusual loyalty to it.

At the founder's death in 1917 the shares in the company were distributed to his five children and their descendants. John and George were to retain full managerial authority until their deaths. In turn, these two sons did their best to perpetuate the intimacy of the original arrangements. When John set up the Hartford Foundation in 1929 he did so partly as a device to prevent any dispersion of ownership or breakup in the company's leadership. He told a meeting of store managers a few months before his death that after he and his brother died their shares would go to the foundation and that this pooling of stock plus "some other friendly interests" would ensure continuity in the control of the company "as we know it today." [2] Since he and his wife were childless, the foundation received his estate when he died in 1951 at the age of seventy-nine. In 1957, George Hartford died at ninety-three and left his entire estate also to the foundation, his only child having died early in life.

By the terms of Mr. John's will the guardian of continuity in A & P was to be Ralph W. Burger, who had begun his career with the food chain in 1911, starting as a store clerk and rising eventually to chief executive officer in 1951. For the next twelve years he served as president of both the company and the foundation.

After the two brothers died, a reorganization of A & P became

---

* Wright Patman from Texas led the attack on chain stores and was co-author of the 1936 Robinson-Patman Act, passed to prevent unfair competition and unlawful combinations from developing in the field of food distribution.

necessary. Under a plan approved by the family in 1958, the company became a publicly held corporation, the foundation owning 34 percent of its voting shares and the family owning a large portion of the remainder. In subsequent years, the sales and profits of the company sagged and some Hartfords began to demand a much stronger voice in its management. But Burger and his associates, who were in a strategic position because of their power over the foundation and its holdings, refused to give way, provoking a long and at times noisy controversy. Huntington Hartford, a grandson of the founder of the company and a large stockholder, repeatedly charged Burger with mismanagement and personal domination of the company. Partly as a result, Burger was forced to retire from A & P in 1963; but because he remained head of the foundation and also because of his close association with senior executives of the company, he continued to wield a controlling influence over its affairs until his death in 1969. On that occasion, Huntington Hartford repeated his charge that Burger had run the company and the foundation "100 percent," adding, "Now, however, I think the A & P management will have a much freer hand. It will be much more progressive and we will see an entire change for the better." [3]

Although some improvement in management has taken place, A & P still has not achieved a rate of growth or profits in recent years comparable to the other large food chains. No sale of the foundation's huge holdings of A & P stock has yet taken place. It continues therefore to be a buttress to traditionalism and fraternalism in the company's direction. While many of the smaller stockholders joined the members of the Hartford family in complaining that the foundation–company links had gravely injured their interests, there has been relatively little criticism about the ways in which the close relationship may have injured the foundation.

John Hartford described the purposes of his foundation in broad terms, leaving the trustees free to adjust its course to changing public needs. Neither he nor his brother laid down any requirement as to how the funds they provided should be used; in fact, John stressed that he did not want "a dead man's hand on the wheel." [4]

But Burger assembled a few friends as trustees from among the only circle he knew, the executives of A & P. Despite the flexibility permitted by the donors, the board imposed on the foundation a fixed program focus from the start—medical research. In their report for 1961 they defined its purposes even more narrowly: "The foundation has not been content merely to initiate and sponsor research in the critical disease problems confronting mankind. . . . If the foundation can be said to have an obsession, it has been with the problem of supporting as quickly and as widely as possible the clinical application of laboratory discovery that gives new promise of relieving misery and saving lives." Throughout his eighteen years as president, Burger took personal responsibility for the foundation's management. He believed that in making grants it should react to proposals made to it, to serve a market. He kept overhead expenditures in its small and spartan headquarters to a minimum, and he operated until 1960 with only two full-time assistants; since then there have been three, none trained in the medical field. But to obtain technical evaluation of applications, a nationwide panel of medical specialists was gradually developed.

Even so, Hartford has remained an obscure institution to most medical scientists and administrators, and suffers a poor reputation. Nor have its public reports greatly assisted understanding of its activities. They have had the virtue of omitting the trumpet-blowing and self-congratulation common to philanthropic publications, but they have had a catalogue format that conveys an image of almost random activity. Grants are given brief, one-sentence descriptions and are listed alphabetically, not by type or purpose.

Partly because of this, Hartford's grants are commonly criticized for lack of pattern, faddishness, and poor technical quality. To each of these charges, some defense of Hartford can be made. Although it has never defined its program goals or priorities and has responded to a wide variety of research proposals, its grants over the years clearly reflect two major concerns—clinical research and biomedical engineering. The former has accounted for roughly two-thirds of its outlays, the latter for the remainder.°

° Between 1959 and 1966, the foundation, in a mystifying departure, made a series of grants totaling $2 million to the Lincoln Center for the Performing Arts in New York City. These grants were reported to be a concession to a trustee and member of the family, Josephine Hartford Brice, whose cooperation in the voting of her personal shares in A & P was necessary to ensure absolute control by the foundation. (*Show* magazine, October 1967)

The charge of faddishness probably derives from the foundation's heavy investment in engineering innovations. Many members of the medical profession object to the emphasis on such instrumentation, thinking it demeans professional skills and judgment. Others object that the instruments developed tend to be expensive to purchase and maintain and that they contribute to the maldistribution of medical services in the country. At least one authority, however, Dr. Joseph Hinsey, dean emeritus of the Cornell medical school and a former director of New York-Cornell Medical Center, strongly praises such outlays. Speaking of similar Rockefeller Foundation grants, which led to the development of the electron microscope, the oscilloscope, and the ultracentrifuge, he has said: "Each time a new piece of equipment is developed, new vistas open for investigation and treatment. These instrumental developments are often costly and without foundation support, they would not have been developed or would have been delayed." [5]

The technical quality of Hartford grants is difficult to appraise without thorough examination of the literature produced by the investigators—a task made more difficult by the foundation's general failure to list the published works of its grantees. (Only its annual report for 1961 does so.) However, its grants are made only to technically qualified persons connected with recognized medical or scientific institutions, all of which have their own internal systems for the review and supervision of research projects. The list of grant recipients, in fact, includes most of the major medical schools, the major research hospitals, and the biology departments of many leading universities.

Though the practice has been questioned in the case of Hartford, it is not unprecedented for an institution making grants in the field of medicine to do so on the basis of lay judgment. The Markel Foundation, during its years of concentration on the problems of medical education, operated on this basis, as do the National Institutes of Health in their project-screening procedures. There are obvious disadvantages in building up a highly specialized medical staff, which can develop its own bureaucratic tendencies and rigidified interests. On the other hand, making wide use of part-time consultants, as Hartford does, can provide both flexibility and expert technical judgment.

In testimony to the effectiveness of its own work, Hartford points to a number of pioneering developments it has financed, particularly in biomedical engineering: a blood flow meter, artificial heart valves, the heart pacemaker, the laser knife, the cryogenic probe, and the kidney dialysis machine. Most of these are no longer esoteric gadgets but are in regular clinical use. It has also made several grants in the field of computer diagnosis and the computerization of research data. It has helped bring into being a new kind of clinical research center consisting of six to twelve beds set aside in various teaching hospitals for long-term studies of patients with certain diseases. Seventy such centers, according to the foundation, have now been funded by the National Institutes of Health, based on a concept originally developed with its assistance. Some of its grants might even be said to have made some contribution to the reduction of medical care costs, such as its help for the development of mass screening procedures for glaucoma, for simple tests to determine hypersensitivity to drugs, and for the preparation of manuals for care of accident victims by paramedical groups such as volunteer rescue squads and the police.

By its method of operation, the Hartford Foundation performs a service function in its chosen field: it provides a place where medical investigators and inventors can go for help in doing something they want to do. This is not unworthy. The history of medical research shows repeated instances where assistance given to an unknown researcher or improbable project has led to a major discovery. Nevertheless, judged by even the most generous standards, the achievements of Hartford have been at best fragmentary. The level of its concerns has not risen above the peripheral and the piecemeal. Its accomplishments are not to be compared with those of several Rockefeller philanthropies which, through pursuit of carefully developed long-term research objectives, have been monumental. The critical difference is not so much that Hartford has lacked technical staff as that it has never equipped itself with any intellectual competence. It has therefore never generated an input of ideas comparable to its money, nor has it developed programmatic criteria that would indicate an awareness of the larger scientific, social, and structural problems of the American medical system. In turn, these shortcomings lead directly back to the foundation's entanglements with the A & P, and they are not being corrected.

On May 14, 1969, following the death of Burger, Harry B. George, a vice-president of the foundation for the preceding several years and a former executive of A & P, was elected to succeed him. At the same time, John Ehrgott was elected vice-president of the foundation; he, too, was a retired executive of the company. It is difficult to imagine that a foundation such as Hartford can perform a significant role in serving the rapidly changing needs of American society when it routinely continues to recruit its leadership on a basis utterly unrelated to philanthropic considerations.

The Duke Endowment

By their family and company ties, the Lilly and Hartford foundations are burdened with incestuous and now elderly leadership. The Duke Endowment is also linked to one company, but suffers from a different kind of handicap: it lives in a strait jacket, namely, the terms of the donor's indenture. Its story is the struggle of an institution to remain vital and relevant while governed largely by officers of the company and obliged to operate in accordance with detailed and unchanging specifications laid down nearly a half-century ago.

The donor, James Buchanan (Buck) Duke, the son of an impoverished North Carolina tobacco farmer, acquired extraordinary wealth by a fanatical devotion to work and an unusual talent for merchandising and monopoly-building. At fourteen he was a factory manager in his father's tobacco business. At eighteen, by threatening to go into business for himself, he was accepted as a partner in the family enterprise. At twenty-seven he opened the Dukes' New York factory. Within six years the company had become the largest cigarette and smoking tobacco producer in the world. Of his own dedication to business he once commented: "I had confidence in myself. I said to myself, 'If John D. Rockefeller can do what he is doing in oil, why should I not do it in tobacco?' I resolved from the time I was a mere boy to do a big business. I loved business better than anything else. I worked from early morning until late at night. I was sorry to have to leave off at night and glad when morning came so I could get at it again." [6]

In an era of savage competition in the tobacco business—largely fought among five major companies at the time—Duke outsold, outbid, and outworked them all. By 1890 he had formed the American Tobacco Company, absorbing the others and establishing a monopoly. After the turn of the century he extended his reach abroad, eventually dividing the world's tobacco trade between his own forces and the British-American Tobacco Company, Ltd. It took the federal government twenty-one years and a series of bitter legal fights to break his stranglehold on the American market. Finally, in 1910, his American Tobacco Company was proved to have violated the Sherman Anti-Trust Act and was ordered to dissolve. Thereafter, several smaller companies were formed, all managed by men that he had trained.

Looking for new worlds to conquer, Duke turned to hydroelectric power. In 1905 he organized the Southern Power Company to serve the developing textile industry in the Carolinas. Successful in that undertaking, he became a major investor in hydroelectric development in other areas, including Canada.

Once his wealth had burgeoned, he began protracted discussions with his lawyers about how some of it might be devoted to philanthropic purposes, particularly for the benefit of the Carolinas. He was not inclined, however, to relinquish control of his money prematurely. In a much quoted statement he once said, "I am going to give a good part of what I make to the Lord, but I can make better interest for Him by keeping it while I live." [7]

In December 1924 he established the Duke Endowment by means of a lengthy and complex trust indenture and at the same time conveyed to it shares of stock in various corporations valued at approximately $40 million. Duke described his general objective thus:

For many years I have been engaged in the development of water power in certain sections of the States of North Carolina and South Carolina. In my study of this subject I have observed how such utilization of a natural resource, which would otherwise run in waste to the sea and not re-

main and increase as a forest, both gives importance to industrial life and
provides a safe and enduring investment for capital. My ambition is that
the revenues of such developments shall administer to the social welfare,
as the operation of such developments is administering to the economic
welfare, of the communities which they serve.

Having fixed the geographical scope of its programs, he then
specified—in order to emphasize the perpetual existence of the
endowment—that 20 percent of its income had to be accumulated
annually and added to the corpus until his initial gift of $40 mil-
lion had been doubled. He linked the endowment to the Duke
Power Company by stipulating in the indenture that no loans were
to be made except to Duke Power and added, "I recommend the
securities of the Southern Power System (the Duke Power Company and its subsidiary companies) as the prime investment for the
funds of this trust; and I advise the trustees that they do not
change any such investments except in response to the most urgent
and extraordinary necessity." As a result, as of 1968, $482 million
of the endowment's total assets of $629 million were still in Duke
Power Company stock, constituting about 55 percent of the shares
of that company. The company is also heavily represented on the
endowment's board. (In 1963, the trustees of the endowment
sought before the Supreme Court of North Carolina to be allowed
to revise the investment provisions of the indenture so as to be
able to diversify but their application was denied.)

Duke was equally specific about the board of trustees. He directed that the endowment should be administered by a self-perpetuating group of fifteen and that a majority should be natives or
residents of North or South Carolina. They had to meet at least ten
times in each calendar year and each trustee was to be given a
specified fraction of the trust's income, which in 1970 amounted to
more than $47,000 a year each. He then required that the endow-
ment's income be divided precisely as follows:

	Percent
To Duke University °	32
For hospitals in North and South Carolina	32

° The creation of Duke University was provided for in the will by the stipulation
that if Trinity College at Durham, North Carolina, would change its name to

To Davidson College, Davidson, N.C.	5
To Furman University, Greenville, S.C.	5
To Johnson C. Smith University, Charlotte, N.C.	4
To orphanages in North and South Carolina	10
For superannuated preachers and widows and orphans of preachers who have served in the Conference of the Methodist Church in North Carolina	2
For building rural Methodist churches in North Carolina	6
For maintaining and operating rural Methodist churches in North Carolina	4
	100

This fixed formula was eased slightly by provisions giving the trustees latitude to withhold the recommended distributions and to use the funds withheld either for the same purpose at a later time or for related purposes.

Less than a year after executing his indenture, Duke died. By the terms of his will, the funds of the endowment were substantially augmented and additional highly specific requirements were imposed upon the trustees in expending the proceeds of the estate. By 1968, in obedience to all these requirements, the endowment had given more than $282 million, distributed as follows:

Duke University	$151,000,000
Hospitals	78,000,000
Davidson College	11,000,000
Furman University	11,000,000
Johnson C. Smith University	8,000,000
Orphanages	11,000,000
Superannuated preachers	2,000,000
Building rural churches	5,500,000
Operating rural churches	4,500,000

Duke University as a memorial to the donor's father, it would receive a gift of $6 million for its expansion. The offer was irresistible to the college, which then became Duke University.

Such a crude breakdown, however, tells little about the nature and the evolution of the endowment's program over the years. Its first published report, covering the period 1924–28, contained essays for each grant area, outlining needs in North and South Carolina and summarizing the results of gifts already made. Duke University, for example, had constructed a number of new buildings with endowment money and planned to open a number of graduate schools in law, religion, forestry, and medicine. The hospital section of the report, by far the most extensive, restated the stipulations of the indenture with regard to aid to hospitals: first, those operated for private gain were excluded because of the belief that medical care is a community problem and should therefore be handled by community hospitals; second, financial assistance would be limited on the basis of the charity work done by the recipient hospital; third, assistance would be limited to one dollar per day per charity patient.

The analysis of the inadequacy and maldistribution of hospital services in the Carolinas was impressive, but the reasoning behind the dollar-a-day policy was rather odd:

If no one suffered, if no one was in distress, there would be no one with whom to sympathize. . . . Sympathy, born in the travail of suffering, is perhaps the finest quality in human character. It gives the individual the capacity to feel with and the feeling of being identified with others. . . . brings about the development of another constituent of the character closely akin to sympathy, namely, love. Love in its turn generates service. Service, in its turn, results in sacrifice, not symbolically but literally, since all work, manual and mental, is accomplished through cellular activity and cellular activity is effected through the actual consumption and wearing out, in short, the sacrifice of the cells of the body. . . . And so it is of suffering that sympathy is born; of sympathy, love is born; of love, service is born; and of service, sacrifice is born; and thus it is that out of trial and tribulation the finer elements of human character develop.

This Tertullianesque reasoning seemed to say that if suffering were eliminated in North and South Carolina, character development would stop and moral deterioration of the society would follow. One dollar a day presumably would ensure that sufferers would always be available.

The subsequent reports for the years up to World War II describe a pattern of service by the endowment to its region that was of more than ordinary scope and benefit. In its higher education program, a black institution was included. In its hospitals and orphanages programs, help to poor black patients and to black children was included. The aid to "superannuated Methodist preachers" was in effect a specialized program of welfare assistance to the elderly.

In the postwar period, various developments ranging from the region's industrialization to the advent of massive federal hospital assistance under the Hill-Burton Act have forced changes on the endowment's program. Within the confines of the indenture, it has made an effort to respond. The quality of its staff (which now numbers thirteen professionals) has enabled the endowment to become an operating foundation in some ways. It now renders research and consultative assistance to many of the region's religious, health, and welfare institutions. Before granting church building funds, for example, it encourages preliminary studies of community needs, stressing the potential constituency, relationship to other churches, and local economic patterns.

It also appears that the staff tries to find legitimate justification within the terms of the indenture for taking on new problems. Orphanages, for example, are now subsumed under child care programs, which have a broader focus. Similarly, it has updated the criteria for allocating money for maintenance and operation of Methodist churches in accordance with new concepts of what a ministry should do in modern society. Since the indenture empowers the trustees to cut off funds to inefficiently operated hospitals, the endowment staff can reinterpret this to mean that its mission is to provide, as it has done, statistical comparisons by which a hospital can gauge the efficiency of its operations and plan its self-improvement.

Because the endowment is committed to the continuing support of designated colleges and universities and has become a major element in their financing, special problems of grantor-grantee relationship arise. It is theoretically possible for such a grantor to become so dominant an influence as to affect the integrity of the

recipient institutions. In the case of Furman, Davidson, and Johnson C. Smith universities, this does not seem to have taken place,
even though the endowment on occasion has become directly involved in their internal problems. For example, it made large special grants in 1968 to stimulate the development of a new
curriculum—and also to raise faculty salaries—at Davidson. It
promoted and funded an "in house" examination to reorganize and
improve Johnson C. Smith University in 1966. But the trustees, administration, and faculties of these institutions do not feel that the
endowment's actions have involved undue pressure or interference.

In the case of Duke University, relationships have been particularly close because of the large scale of financial assistance that has
been provided. Most of the physical development of the university
has been funded by the endowment as well as a significant portion
of its annual operating budget. Beginning in 1924 and continuing
over the next thirty years, the endowment also came to play an influential, sometimes decisive role, in the management of the university.

In the 1950s the university undertook a basic revaluation of its
future course. Out of this process clear differences of opinion developed among faculty, administration, and trustees, some feeling
that the university should continue to be a regional institution emphasizing undergraduate training, others believing that it should
seek to become an institution of national standing, which would require, among other things, strong emphasis on graduate study and
research. Through the early 1960s the university was preoccupied
by this conflict. The passions that were aroused involved allegations that the endowment, which favored the regional emphasis,
had made the university its "captive" and was arbitrarily determining its future. But a number of those who were deeply involved in
the struggles, including key members of the university faculty
today, state that the endowment used its influence constructively
and with restraint.[8]

In any event, its once dominant position on the university's executive committee has now been ended. At present only two of the
ten members are also endowment trustees and of the thirty-six
members of the board itself, only four sit on the endowment's

board. Both institutions now take pains to state in their publications that "neither exercises any degree of control over the other." The complex relationship between the Duke Endowment and Duke University cannot be explained in simple terms of control or noncontrol. The strains that have developed can be traced to the inherent conflict between the foundation's limited geographical focus and the necessarily larger concerns of the university, which almost inevitably must expand its perspectives and seek help from diversified sources if it is to realize its full potential.

The Duke Endowment has rendered important services to the people of the Carolinas. Its trustees and staff are intimately knowledgeable about the area, and its programs have been carried out competently and responsibly. Despite the program changes that have been introduced over the years, however, its outlook remains conservative, even somewhat old-fashioned. In regard to blacks, for example, it has given its help on a nondiscriminatory basis from the beginning, but it has never taken active leadership in attempting to advance desegregation. Its board is mostly composed of very southern Southerners. Even though many of the endowment's avowed concerns relate directly to the needs of the large black population of the Carolinas, no black has ever served as a trustee. Nor is it likely that one will be elected to it in the foreseeable future.

By comparison with other foundations in the area, such as Z. Smith Reynolds and Mary Reynolds Babcock, the endowment is less than a dynamic and creative force. The restrictiveness of Duke's indenture has hurt it financially, has condemned it to a degree of provincialism, and has generally handicapped the normal evolution of its program. By tying the foundation so closely to Duke Power it has caused a considerable loss of benefit to charity since the company has lagged in both growth and profits in recent years and has paid dividends substantially less than the endowment would have earned from a diversified portfolio. (For details, see Appendix.) Close financial linkage with the power company also has helped perpetuate other kinds of ties. The company has from the beginning been heavily represented on the endowment's board (at present, seven of the fifteen trustees, including the chairman of the board, are active or retired executives). This group not only has been deeply loyal to the memory of the founder, but has felt committed to the letter of his trust. One of its annual rituals is a reading of the entire indenture, a procedure that is taken very seriously. Moreover, the restrictions of the indenture have forced the endowment and its staff to resort to ingenious reinterpretations in order to undertake new programs. This game of rule-stretching has modernized the program to a degree, but does not permit the introduction of changes in its fundamental priorities or in the philosophical base of its approach.

But changes will have to come. Time, if nothing else, will alter the composition of the board, for all but two of its members are over sixty at present; several are in their seventies, approaching mandatory retirement at seventy-five. The professional staff can also be considered an internal force for change. In addition, the Tax Reform Act of 1969 will gradually require the endowment to diversify some of its holdings in Duke Power. Old Buck Duke's attempt to defy time by encasing his foundation in the rigid framework of a detailed set of operating instructions has worked for fifty years, but it cannot work forever.

11.

Sloan, Kettering, and Mott: GM's Philanthropic Offspring

THE AUTOMOBILE INDUSTRY led the transition from the era of primitive industrialization in American economic development to full-fledged mass production. Its spectacular growth was characterized by rapid technological change in the vehicle itself, pioneering developments in the techniques of production and marketing, and new concepts of business organization. It was an industry that required—and produced—men who could operate on an unprecedented plane of complexity.

The giant company that came to dominate the industry was the General Motors Corporation, formed out of the fusion of twenty-one smaller companies in 1908. As a by-product of its dramatic rise a number of great fortunes were built. Three of those have now produced major foundations, of which one is becoming excellent, one is promising, and one is a snarl of paradoxes. Alfred P. Sloan, Charles F. Kettering, and Charles Stewart Mott were all associated with GM during its years of expansion, and their approach to philanthropy has been strongly affected by their involvement with that vast and dynamic company. Though all three were preeminent members of the American corporate elite in the 1920s and 1930s, they were markedly different in temperament, talents, and interests.

The Sloan Foundation

Alfred P. Sloan, who headed the company for nearly thirty-five years, was the major architect of its success. A slender six-footer

with hawklike, angular features, he was a functional man, austere
and intense. He did not smoke, rarely drank, read little for pleasure, and rarely engaged in golf or any other sport. He dressed like
a dapper *boulevardier,* but he took little part in the social scene.
General Motors was his occupation, his avocation, and his recrea-
tion. For many years, he spent half of each month in New York
and the other half at his office in Detroit, which he seldom left
even to go to his hotel. In New York he generally dined alone with
his wife in their Fifth Avenue apartment (the couple was childless), and after dinner he would work on the papers he had taken
home. At the office he worked his way through a daily schedule of
conferences with metronomic precision. Although he drove himself
and others relentlessly, his method of executive leadership was quietly persuasive, not bombastic. He had many close friends among
the top echelon of American business and finance, and in the late
1920s and through the 1930s this capable and highly successful
man enjoyed a unique prestige among them.

The origins of the Sloan Foundation have to be sought in the
well of the donor's emotions. During the New Deal, Sloan, in the
militantly open-shop tradition of the automobile industry, became
an implacable foe of its labor policies. In 1937, when the workers
of General Motors struck and conducted sit-ins, Sloan haughtily refused to deal with them "so long as they continue to hold our
plants unlawfully"—and drew a public rebuke from President Roosevelt. Subsequently, as public opinion turned against him and the
company, Sloan had to retreat from his position. In that same year
he suffered a more personal embarrassment when Treasury experts
reported to a congressional committee that he and his wife had
avoided payment of $1.9 million in federal income taxes over a
three-year period by the device of personal holding companies.
The story made headlines throughout the country. Even though
there was no charge of illegal conduct, the implications of the allegation were so unpleasant that Sloan went to great lengths to re-
fute them.

Perhaps by coincidence or, as some skeptics have suggested, because of the injury to his pride and reputation, Sloan at the end of
that difficult year, 1937, made a gift of $10 million to activate the

foundation that he and his wife had created three years before. Over the next twenty-eight years, until his death at the age of ninety, he and his foundation passed through a succession of changes that constitute one of the more instructive transformations in the story of American philanthropy. Sloan was a man with definite ideas about almost everything, including philanthropy. In announcing his $10 million gift, he said, "Having been connected with industry during my entire life, it seems eminently proper that I should turn back, in part, the proceeds of that activity with the hope of promoting a broader as well as a better understanding of the economic principles and national policies which have characterized American enterprise down through the years." He then went on to say, "This particular foundation proposes to concentrate to an important degree on a single objective, i.e., the promotion of a wider knowledge of basic economic truths." Decoded, this meant he intended to use it primarily to oppose the economic philosophy of the New Deal.

The foundation's board consisted of Sloan, his wife, his brother Harold, and two close business associates. His brother was named as executive director, immediately resigning his position as associate professor of economics at the state teachers college in Montclair, New Jersey. He brought unstinted enthusiasm, if not much else, to his new position. A year later he reported major gains in the battle against "American economic illiteracy." Knowledge of elementary economic principles, he said, "is being hammered into American minds to strengthen one of the weak spots in our industrial system. We are going places. There is no doubt about it." For seven years the foundation poured its grants into a variety of projects utilizing films, pamphlets, and audiovisual aids to carry the doctrines of free enterprise into every American home and high school. But by 1945 it was clear the foundation was not going places. Harold Sloan was fired from the staff, and the foundation took off on a different course. Grants for cancer research (largely through the Sloan-Kettering Institute, which the foundation established) and to Sloan's alma mater, MIT, were emphasized and continued to be until the early 1960s.

In 1956 Sloan resigned as chairman of the board of GM and devoted himself thereafter to the affairs of his foundation, serving both as chairman of its board and chief executive officer.° From the beginning he had ruled his foundation autocratically. The small staff was used merely to carry out his instructions. The original board was composed of three elements: family (Sloan, his wife, and his brother), long-time business associates (the *Who Was Who* of American industry and finance), and representatives of two major built-in grantees (Sloan-Kettering and MIT). According to members at the time, the only real "debates" at meetings were between MIT and Sloan-Kettering representatives over their share of the spoils; the other trustees simply took their cue from Sloan, interpreting their responsibility to be to help him give away his money as he saw fit.

To clinch his control, Sloan appointed a small executive committee composed of his closest friends, which operated as a screening device for proposals presented to the entire board. Some trustees who served for as long as a decade cannot remember any instance in which the board overruled or even modified an executive committee recommendation.† But by 1962 Sloan himself was becoming dissatisfied with the routine character of the institution he had created. In the mid-1950s, he began to write fervent little sermons in the foundation's annual reports on behalf of "risk taking" and philanthropy's capacity to stimulate social change. Perhaps it was the

° Nightly during that period he worked on his autobiography, *My Years with General Motors* (Garden City, N.Y., Doubleday, 1964), which became a best-seller.

† Warren Weaver, who joined the Sloan Foundation after his retirement from the Rockefeller Foundation, has described its procedures in his autobiography:
"There were at that time no staff meetings and no general staff discussions; each officer worked directly with Sloan. At trustee meetings Sloan, as the presiding officer, gave extraordinarily clear and complete reports of all financial aspects of the foundation's business, and he himself described—with no notes, in a meticulously accurate way and often with a touch here and there of penetrating humor—the proposals on which the board was to act. The meetings were never long. Sloan always commenced by thanking the trustees for their interest and their presence; and when the business had been briskly concluded—extended discussion was of course handicapped by his deafness—the meetings were promptly terminated." (*Scene of Change* [New York, Scribner's, 1970] p. 125)

contrast between those ideals and his own foundation's uninspired grants that impelled him to act.°

In any event, in 1962 he appointed Dr. Everett Case, a distinguished educator, to head his foundation. During his tenure, Case made a conscientious effort to free the foundation from its past and to relate it to contemporary social problems. Sloan was both a help and a hindrance to Case in these efforts. Although he understood the need to strengthen and broaden the foundation's program, he at the same time found it impossible to break his deeply ingrained habit of absolute rule, and he rarely surrendered his personal control over final decisions. He remained an autocrat to the end.

Ironically, just as the Sloan Foundation was beginning to move in a more liberal direction, the ghost of one of its earlier follies came back to haunt it. In September 1964, the Anti-Defamation League of B'nai B'rith in New York made public its study of the major financial supporters of right-wing propaganda in the United States, naming in its charges fourteen individuals and organizations, one of which was the Sloan Foundation. The ADL alleged that the foundation had aided extremist assaults on American democratic processes by a succession of major grants to the National Education Program, headed by Dr. George Benson, president of Harding College at Searcy, Arkansas, which the ADL called "the largest producer of radical Right propaganda in the country." The foundation, in a half-embarrassed reply, said that the films and other materials produced through its grants were purely "economic" in content, but the league pointed out that the Sloan-sup-

---

° In Weaver's opinion he himself had some influence on changes in Sloan's thinking. In his autobiography, Weaver writes: "Thus a great deal of my effort, especially over the first two or three years was devoted to getting Mr. Sloan to recognize that it was essential that some less personalized organization be planned and staffed. I told him bluntly that as things then were, his knowledge, his insights, his experience, his vision, and his ideals would end abruptly on that inevitable morning when he failed to show up. . . . I suppose I was the only person around the office in a position to urge him to resign as president and bring in someone who could work with him and could thus be able to carry on the fine tradition he had established. After I had brought this up several times . . . in a long talk he said that he had decided to make the move." (*Ibid.*, pp. 125–26)

ported materials had been based largely on the writings of Robert Welch, founder of the John Birch Society. The grants to Harding College had been made in the late 1940s, when Sloan's enthusiasm for instructing Americans in the "basic principles of the American enterprise system" was still a significant part of its program.

At the time of Sloan's death in February 1966, definite changes had become evident in his foundation, but encrusted old habits had not totally been dissolved. Although several members of the board had come to share Sloan's new ideas, others were still firmly committed to the programs of the past. The staff was neither strong nor highly developed. But at least one able younger member, Robert Kreidler, was prepared with well-formulated program and organizational ideas to facilitate the impending transformation.

After the donor's death, the habitually passive board began to play a more active role in determining foundation policies. The staff was increased and improved (including the appointment of a black senior program officer), and in early 1969 it presented its first comprehensive set of program recommendations to the board. It was proposed that the foundation commit itself to three broad and interrelated areas: science and technology, education, and "the range of problems posed by the pressing needs of our current society." Two of them were, of course, fields of traditional interest, but new wine was poured into the old bottles. In science and technology there would be a new emphasis on the biological sciences and neurosciences; in education more emphasis would be placed on the training of blacks and other minority groups for the professions, including medicine and engineering. The foundation had long given support to schools of business management; now it proposed to support management training for urban leadership and government service. In its recognition of "pressing social needs," the foundation proposed to concentrate principally on those areas that related to its established interests in science, technology, and education rather than make a complete break with its own past.

Still, a distinctly new note was being struck. When the foundation announced a set of new urban affairs grants in March 1969, Dr. Nils Y. Wessel, who had by then succeeded Case as president, took pains to emphasize that foundations "must show some imagi-

nation in the way they spend their money," and the chairman of
the board, Frederick Donner, a long-time General Motors executive, agreed: "You have to take some risks—if you take no risks
and run a bland foundation, you are running an ineffective foundation." Thirty-two years after its activation, the Sloan Foundation
had at last begun to make a strong move away from one-man, eccentric philanthropy. By 1971 the shift was already beginning to
show impressive results. The Commission on Cable Communications, which had been set up by the foundation in June 1970, re-
leased its recommendations on the problems and potentialities of
that new medium in December 1971.[1] In the resounding impact of
the Sloan Commission Report could be heard the sound of another
first-class large foundation moving onto the national scene.

The Kettering Foundation

Charles F. Kettering was one of the great "monkey-wrench scientists" in the automobile industry. He invented the self-starter in
1912, which not only greatly added to the convenience of the new
horseless carriages but, by making it possible for women to drive
them, opened major new marketing possibilities. For twenty-seven
years he headed the research laboratory of General Motors, one of
the first of its kind financed by a major corporation. Under his
direction it produced a steady flow of innovations and discoveries
from antiknock gasoline to better automobile finishes to a practical
diesel engine. He had a penchant for speaking on complex subjects
in earthy aphorisms and became known throughout the country for
his articles and off-the-cuff speeches.*

Kettering's foundation had its roots in the convictions of a one-

* Some of his phrases were widely quoted: "Look to the future, for that is
where you will spend the rest of your life"; "You can send a message around
the world in a seventh of a second, yet it may take years to force a simple
idea through a quarter inch of human skull"; "You can't have a better tomorrow if you are thinking about yesterday all the time"; "Research is a high-hat
word that scares a lot of people. It needn't. Research is nothing but a state of
mind—a friendly welcoming attitude toward change."

time farmboy and country schoolteacher about the importance of
education and in the curiosity of a scientist and inventor about
such problems as the earth's magnetism and, in his words, "what
makes the grass grow green." He created it in 1927, when he was
fifty-one years old, and for three decades thereafter managed its affairs. "Boss Ket" was no less the autocrat than Sloan, his lifelong
friend. The small board was made up of close friends he could
count on to be pliant to his wishes. During his lifetime the foundation distributed $16 million in grants in three areas: in education,
nearly $6 million was given for scholarships, the construction of
college buildings, especially science facilities, and the support of
institutions that encouraged practical work combined with academic study, typified by Antioch College in Ohio; nearly $5 mil-
lion was put into medical research, largely relating to cancer; and
an equal amount was distributed for other scientific research, most
of it to the Charles F. Kettering Research Laboratory in Yellow
Springs, Ohio, for work on photosynthesis. The foundation's
achievements in this period, though not brilliant, were somewhat
superior to those of most donor-dominated foundations because of
Kettering's superior talents and creativity.

After Kettering's death in 1958, his son Eugene assumed leadership of the foundation and made the fundamental decision that it
should become an independent rather than a family-controlled institution. In early 1959 a special meeting of the board was called to
formulate future objectives. By 1962 the clear beginnings of a
changeover could be discerned. In its report for that year the foundation stated that its "fields of interest will certainly change with
the passage of time" and that "the category almost certain to retain
a permanent appeal to the foundation is education"—implying a
decline of interest, relatively at least, in scientific and medical research.

The board was gradually strengthened by the addition of men of
diverse backgrounds, and by 1964 the foundation claimed it had
completed its effort "to identify the most significant problems facing
the American people during the next decade." It decided to concentrate its efforts in "assisting the nation's schools in meeting the
needs of a changing society." This aim was formulated into a costly

new internal project called IDEA (Institute for Development of Educational Activities), described as "a vehicle expressly designed to reduce the gap between what is known about superior educational practice and what actually takes place in most elementary and secondary school classrooms." The donor's grandson, who was then on the foundation's staff, was the originator of the scheme.

With the creation of IDEA, a program pattern was beginning to emerge: a sizable portion of the foundation's funds had long been given to support the Charles F. Kettering Research Laboratory; now a second internally controlled project would take another considerable slice of the foundation's resources. In its 1967 report it formulated a rationale for the new program approach: "The most serious contemporary problem confronting foundations," it confidently asserted, "is whether to diffuse resources into external channels or to concentrate them into a variety of carefully chosen internal functions . . . the trustees have directed that the foundation's major resources be concentrated in support of its internally developed institutions. . . . Some examples of these possible areas [of foundation interest] are: social ills in society, including the difficulties encountered by the socially deprived; technological problems associated with environmental pollution, including conservation of air and water resources; and social applications of genetic control, life creation, and intelligence development as biological knowledge advances."

A New Ventures staff was established to seek a new program that might become, like IDEA, a major new project within the foundation, and the skills of a specialized outside institution, the Institute for the Future, were used to solicit promising ideas from authorities in various fields.

In 1968 Eugene Kettering was succeeded as president by Richard Lombard, a New York financier married to a member of the Kettering family. In his preface to the foundation's report for that year Lombard declared that the challenge to all foundations today "is relevance—how to insure that their efforts are, in fact, directed to defining and solving problems of importance to the society of today and tomorrow. . . . To keep pace with the changing needs of society . . . the Kettering Foundation has relinquished most of

its conventional grant-giving functions and has replaced this passive participation with a more meaningful activity: institution-
building. As a consequence, the primary purpose of the foundation
has become the development of new enterprises charged with examining the compelling needs of society. . . . The very nature of
grantmanship forces foundations to react passively, through funding, to external interpretations of needs, rather than to act aggressively on problems as seen by the foundations themselves. . . .
Having wrestled with these limitations on conventional philanthropy, the trustees chose to set a totally different course for the
foundation: The deliberate building of new, viable institutions.
Their decision represents, on the part of trustees and staff alike, an
eagerness to experiment, to undertake organizational risks, to gamble on new solutions for tough problems."

The program interests of the donor—science, medical research,
and work-study education—were left well behind as the foundation set a new course of social concern. By 1968 the board had
been developed into one of the most prestigious and diverse of any
foundation in the United States. Only two of its eighteen members
were related to the donor family, the rest being scientists, educators, and intellectuals of national and international reputation. But
the staff, although it had been enlarged and somewhat improved,
still lagged well behind the caliber of the board. It remains to be
seen whether a first-class professional group can be recruited to
live in Dayton, Ohio and whether such a staff could function effectively in that provincial atmosphere. It also remains to be seen
whether the foundation can develop the actual capacity to achieve
its stated objective of creating significant new (and self-sustaining)
institutions. Its research laboratories have not been outstanding
nor have they shown an ability to survive without Kettering's continuing financial support. And IDEA, for all its fanfare, still has
few real innovations that it can point to.

Kettering is not the first foundation to project its rhetoric beyond
its capability. But despite its lack of great achievements to date, it
has now set great goals for itself. It has taken some preparatory
steps to make itself one of the better of the big foundations; its
task now is to become one.

The Charles Stewart Mott Foundation

Charles Stewart Mott, the third of the trio of large GM philanthropists, represents the entrepreneurial tradition in the industry.
His connection with the company preceded that of Sloan and Kettering, and he has outlived both of them. He acquired a substantial
equity interest in General Motors in 1909 when he sold it a wheel
manufacturing firm founded by his father. He has been a director
since 1913 and is now probably its largest single stockholder.*

Mott calls himself a conservative Republican and is a regular
contributor to organizations of the extreme Right. A glimpse of his
social outlook is provided by Studs Terkel's interview with him reprinted in the national best-seller, *Hard Times*.[2]

Speaking of Frank Murphy, a Michigan politician in the 1930s
and later a Supreme Court justice, Mott told Terkel: "He was governor during the sit-down strikes, and he didn't do his job. He
didn't enforce the law. He kept his hands off. He didn't protect our
property."

* On October 7, 1969, at the age of ninety-four, Charles Mott appeared before the Senate Finance Committee in Washington to testify on behalf of private foundations. One of the news stories about his appearance gives a picture
of the style of this durable citizen of Flint, Michigan:
"The old man spoke in a firm sure voice and read from notes without using
glasses. The opinions he expressed were brief and to the point. But the Senators seemed more interested in the man than in his testimony.
" 'Where are your glasses?' inquired Senator Carl D. Curtis, Republican of
Nebraska. 'We are amazed you can read without them.'
" 'They are in my pocket,' snapped Mr. Mott.
" 'How do you keep your youth?' asked Senator Paul J. Fannin, Republican
of Arizona.
" 'I am absolutely dedicated to what we are trying to do in the Foundation.
I don't have time to think about my age,' Mr. Mott replied. 'I feel I was born
today. I am looking to the future. I am going ahead full steam.'
"His duty done, Mr. Mott rose from the witness chair, to his full six-foot
height. The diamond stickpin in his mod wide gray tie flashed in the light. He
remarked that it had been nice to testify, but no, the Senators hadn't bothered
him. But he would have a martini for lunch nonetheless, very dry with an
olive." (*Washington Daily News*, Oct. 8, 1969)

Terkel: You feel the National Guard should have evicted the sit-down-
         ers?

Mott: They have no right to sit down there. They were illegally oc-
         cupying it. The owners had the right to demand from the
         governor to get those people out. It wasn't done. The same as
         today.

         Communities allow all this hoodlum stuff. It's an outrage. When
         you have people breaking into stores, and you have police and
         the National Guard with things loaded, and they don't stop
         those people—it's terrible. They should have said, "Stop that
         thing. Move on, or we'll shoot." And if they didn't, they should
         have been shot. They'd have killed a certain number of people,
         but it would have been a lot less than would have been killed
         afterwards. It's an absolute duplicate of the Thirties, with the sit
         down strikes.

Terkel: What are your memories of Franklin D. Roosevelt?

Mott: Someone said to me: "Did you see the picture on those new
         dimes?" It's our new destroyer. It was a picture of Roosevelt.
         He was the great destroyer. He was the beginner of our down-
         hill slide. Boy, what he did to this country. I don't think we'll
         ever get over it. Terrible. °

   The Mott Foundation of Flint, Michigan, stands in almost
black-and-white contrast to the typical large foundation in its
objectives, program, and operating methods. Whereas most of them
have only a vague notion of their philosophic purpose, Mott has
formulated a highly specific concept of the economic, social, and
individual values it intends to support. It has a conspicuously active rather than reactive program, giving its grants almost entirely
to projects of its own formulation. And it concentrates on one locality, carefully selecting its priorities.

   Most foundations have been reluctant to deal with the urban crisis; Mott centers its efforts on that very problem in all its aspects.
And whereas most foundations operate in an informal, quasi-aca-

° In contrast to the conservatism of most of the Mott family, his son Stewart, one of six children born of Mr. Mott's four marriages, spends his inherited
family money to support such causes as the presidential campaign of Senator
Eugene McCarthy, birth control, research on human sexual response, and ex-
trasensory perception. He has also given generously to campaigns against the
Vietnam War. He operates through his own foundation, Spectemur Agendo
("Let us be known by our deeds").

demic way, Mott has applied the techniques of modern industrial management—production planning, product promotion, statistical control, and follow-up—to its philanthropies. The foundation says it pursues a double strategy: it seeks out new solutions to social problems and tests them in experimental demonstration projects. Because a single foundation cannot support such efforts for the whole country, Mott's approach is "to learn how to do this in Flint—help make Flint the laboratory and proving grounds, and let other communities observe and hopefully adopt these programs." * The foundation invites experts and leaders from all over the world to see what has been accomplished in Flint. It also trains selected individuals to manage its kind of programs elsewhere; if other communities wish to adopt similar programs, Mott provides financial help to get them started.

The centerpiece of the foundation's program since its inception in 1926 has been a special working partnership with the Flint Board of Education in behalf of what is known as "the community school concept." The traditional role of the neighborhood school has been expanded, according to the foundation, from that of a "formal learning center for the young, operating six hours a day, five days a week, thirty-nine weeks a year, to a total community center for young and old operating virtually around the clock, around the year." A community school director is assigned to each of the city's fifty-five schools. At the end of the school day, other activities begin. There are consumer education courses, nursing programs, basketball games, sewing lessons, bridge games, civic meetings and discussions, music lessons, and potluck suppers for senior citizens. The foundation keeps careful statistics on the results of its efforts. It claims that its adult education activities are the largest in the country after New York, Chicago, and Los Angeles, involving 92,000 people every week, or almost half the total population of Flint.

It has also created a large children's health center, which pro-

---

* *Mott Projects Report, 1967–68*, p. 1. The language is reminiscent of that which another Michigan foundation, Kellogg, had used years before in launching its initial program in seven rural counties of the state to improve child health and welfare services.

vides coordinated services for the total physical and mental health of the community's children; its staff of more than a hundred treats some 60,000 young patients annually. In 1967, the foundation made a $6.5 million capital grant for the building of a children's hospital at the University of Michigan, and in 1970 it gave $4.5 million for the construction of a research center on human reproduction and birth defects at Wayne State University in Detroit.

In the field of social welfare, the foundation supports a program for fatherless boys through the Big Brother movement; a "farm experience program" to provide urban children with an opportunity to visit and work on a farm; a summer camp and club program for girls; and a program in cooperation with the Flint Police Department to prevent crime and delinquency. Among its more unorthodox projects, the foundation helped to create a mayor's committee that conducted a successful search for new jobs for young people, particularly those from low-income families. It has employed a consultant in consumer education to work with groups in low-income areas throughout the city. It has also instituted a "personalized curriculum program" in the city's high schools as a preventive approach to the dropout problem. To extend and reinforce its programs, it has funded seven colleges in Michigan, Indiana, and Florida to serve as regional demonstration centers for the concept of community school education, and it has created a special institute at Michigan State University to improve the preparation of teachers for disadvantaged children.

In every aspect of its structure and operation, the Mott Foundation is a disciplined instrument of the donor's will. He dominates the small board of six, which includes three members of the Mott family. He tolerates no interference in his handling of the foundation's investments and the staff of sixteen operates through an almost military system of administration.

But apart from a crisp and purposeful style, what in the end hath Mott wrought? There have been several positive achievements. In child health, the foundation's clinic in Flint and the facilities it has funded at Ann Arbor and in Detroit are valuable community additions. In Flint, some reduction of the school dropout problem apparently has been achieved as a result of the foundation's efforts, as well as an increase in the employment of ghetto youths, and crime rates allegedly have been reduced. The city was the first of its size in the United States to pass an open occupancy ordinance for housing, a precedent that can be credited, indirectly at least, to Mott's support. And the people of Flint have consistently supported tax increases in recent years to improve their schools—a reflection perhaps of the civic interest engendered by the community school system.

These are not inconsequential results. But the quality of education for children in Flint schools, despite the heavy outlays of the foundation, is not superior to that of other cities in the state; in fact, some recent surveys suggest that it may be inferior. Nor is the community schools program for adults impressively "educational": in 1970, the most popular evening course in thirty-five of the city's fifty-five schools was lingerie-making.

If the purpose of the Mott program is to "increase the strength and stature of character in individuals," as the foundation declares, and to produce citizens "each of whom accepts his full responsibility as a citizen," there appears to be a grating discord between ends and means. The Mott method is one of aggressive evangelism and rigidly organized civic uplift, arbitrarily imposed from the top. One local black leader says, "Self help is not built into the program. The participation of the poor in the design of their own programs is lacking," and the Flint chapter of the NAACP has repeatedly made proposals—which have been ignored—to correct this lack. A labor leader says: "The people here have received great benefit from old man Mott. But his purpose and the result of his generosity have been to make Flint a new and highly sophisticated kind of company town. Because I believe in people being responsible for themselves in their own communities, and in trade unions, I am opposed to this kind of paternalism."

By the leverage of its money and its methods of operation, the foundation may also have undermined control by the citizens of Flint over their own government and public officials. For example, the foundation gives its funds to the Mott programs of the Board of Education as seed money for three years. After that, a project is either dropped or it has to be taken over by the regular school budget. The practical result, in the opinion of a number of educators, is to give the foundation's annual contribution (about $5 million) decisive influence on a large part of the city's annual school budget ($45 million). Also the Mott program staff is housed in the same building as the general superintendent of schools, creating an ambiguous situation in which one whole segment of his organization —the "Associate Superintendent for Mott Programs," the "Regional Community School Directors," and the individual "Community School Directors"—is dually responsible to the Mott Foundation and to him. As one of the city's senior educators says: "If you agree with Mott's ideas and are prepared to accept the lead of the foundation, the generosity is wonderful. But God help you if you disagree. Then the juggernaut will roll over you and you disappear without a trace."

12.

The Middling Mellons

THE MELLON FAMILY constitutes one of the three great dynasties of wealth in the United States, the others being the Rockefellers and the du Ponts. Since the late nineteenth century, its holdings have steadily increased in both size and diversity, and now extend to banking, petroleum, aluminum, chemicals, insurance, and real estate. Although not as wealthy as the du Ponts, they are probably wealthier than the Rockefellers; but given the intricacies and inponderables of wealth on such a scale, not even the Internal Revenue Service knows for sure.

In philanthropy, though, the ranking can be established unequivocally: the Rockefellers are in a class by themselves, comparable on a historical scale with the Florentine Medicis. The du Ponts, at the other extreme, range from niggling to deplorable. The Mellons of Pennsylvania are in between: in their charities they have never approached the sweep and sophistication of the Rockefellers, but they far outrank the du Ponts. In recent times they have created four major foundations—the Avalon, Old Dominion, Sarah Mellon Scaife, and the Richard King Mellon. Except for Scaife, all have improved slowly and steadily since their founding. But the deaths of three of the four founders have now brought the major Mellon philanthropies to a time of decision. They are likely to lose the limited momentum they have so far achieved unless a strong new thrust of family or executive leadership is generated—and whether this will be forthcoming is problematical.

The history of the Mellon philanthropies provides a fascinating look at the evolution of a lordly family's concepts of social responsibility. It begins before the Civil War with old Judge Thomas

Mellon. The son of a destitute farmer, he grew up in the small town of Poverty Point, Pennsylvania. In 1839, at the age of twenty-five and after a grim struggle for an education, he hung out his shingle as a lawyer. Within five years, by methodical effort, he had acquired the beginnings of a fortune. At that point he applied his business methods to the search for a wife. He made a list of the eligible young women in the city and catalogued their virtues and faults. But, according to his diary, "some were too gay and frivolous or self-conceited; others too slovenly and ungainly; and others again too coarse or stupid. It was rather a more difficult task than I had expected, and I was impatient of spending much time on it." [1]

Eventually, arrangements were made with the Negley family for him to marry their daughter, Sarah Jane. Reflecting on his courtship in later years, the judge wrote, "All in all, I saw no one that pleased me better or that I thought would wear better roughing it through life. . . . There was no love-making or no love beforehand so far as I was concerned. . . . When I proposed, if I had been rejected, I would have left neither sad nor depressed nor greatly disappointed, only annoyed at the loss of time." [2]

His pragmatic approach to females extended to his own daughters, two of whom died in early childhood. He thought it was probably just as well: "Females may be brought up in all the comfort and enjoyment which tender care and wealth can confer, to be launched on a hard and unfeeling world. Whilst celibacy is the safest, it has its drawbacks; and marriage is a fearful risk. Apart from the pains and anxious cares of maternity, the chances are so great of obtaining a husband who may turn out to be heartless and cruel, or a drunkard and spendthrift, and the consequences so tremendous, that daughters who die young need not be greatly lamented." [3]

Of his eight children, his son Andrew most closely reflected those qualities which the father had found and admired in his own ancestors—"Solid, steady, careful men who appear to have no nonsense in their composition." The judge, who by 1860 had left law for banking and real estate, took full advantage of Civil War prosperity in Pittsburgh and amassed a considerable fortune. Andrew, in the late years of the nineteenth century, built on this base a huge financial and industrial complex. He was among the first to see the limitations of small-scale, competitive production and to learn the techniques of merger and corporate combination to achieve the vastly greater returns of large-scale production and monopoly. He was also quick to sense the possibilities in a time of national economic surge and rapid technological change of backing a hustling young entrepreneur or inventor, taking a good share of his company in return. He organized the United States Shipbuilding Company and the Standard Steel Car Company out of various smaller companies. He sensed the possibilities of the emerging petroleum industry and with his brothers Richard and William organized what is now the Gulf Oil Company. But his masterstroke was the Aluminum Company of America, which he began by taking over a small Pittsburgh company that had the rights to a new electrical process for refining aluminum. The company's control over aluminum production and prices was so tight for nearly half a century that even during the depression, its price did not vary by even a fraction of a cent.

Largely due to Andrew Mellon's financial genius, the family today has major holdings in perhaps a hundred large American corporations, including Alcoa, Gulf Oil, Koppers, Carborundum, General Reinsurance, the First Boston Corporation, and the Mellon National Bank. They hold these interests directly and through various holding, insurance, and investment companies, as well as their several foundations.

In his private life, however, Andrew was less than brilliantly successful. He did not marry until he was in his forties when, with unusual impetuosity, he took Nora McMullen, the vivacious daughter of a Dublin distiller, for his bride. Before they separated nine years later, they had two children, Paul and Ailsa. In 1910 Mellon filed suit for divorce, the proceedings of which provided a glimpse of their bizarre marriage. Nora, in her deposition, said: "I had arrived in a strange land with strange people, strangers in the strange land. . . . There were women and children, too, all toilers in my husband's vineyard; but none of them given the laborer's recognition, toiling and working on the estate and adding to its wealth but not recognized as part of it. The whole community spirit was as cold and hard as the steel it made, and chilled my heart to the core. . . . Nights that I spent in my baby boy's bedroom nursing these thoughts of his future, my husband, locked in his study, nursed his dollars, millions of dollars. . . . Always new plans, bigger plans for new dollars, bigger dollars, dollars that robbed him and his family of the time, he could have devoted far more profitably to a mere 'Thank God we are living.' " * After much publicity, which distressed Mellon and which he tried to suppress, a divorce was granted in 1912.⁴ The children had a difficult childhood, shunted back and forth between hostile parents and suffering the competing demands of the cold banker and the warm-hearted Irishwoman. Andrew devoted himself with new fervor to business during the years before and after World War I. And since war has characteristically been a boon to Pittsburgh, he was able to expand the family's wealth to undreamed-of proportions. Then, in 1920, at the pinnacle of financial success, Andrew turned to a new career.

The Mellons, though they had never taken direct part in political life, had been active in the Republican party behind the scenes for many years. The Mellon Bank had underwritten the party's campaign deficit in the 1920 presidential election, and partly as a result, Warren G. Harding chose Andrew Mellon as his secretary of the treasury, thereby launching a most unpublic figure into public life. Mellon, despite the fact that he was the second or third richest man in the country at the time, was almost unknown outside Pittsburgh and the inner circles of finance and industry. His name had never even appeared in the New York *Times*. But this wraith-like man with an instinctive distaste for publicity soon came to be regarded as the *eminence grise* behind Harding's economic policies, winning lavish praise from the conservative press and arousing the hostility of the trade unions and the farmers, who called him the spokesman of the trusts and the war profiteers.⁵

In 1923 the Mellon Plan for tax reduction was introduced, cut-

---

* In the Allegheny County Courthouse, the curious can still inspect Andrew Mellon's charges against his wife. But her replies are not to be found, having mysteriously been withdrawn years ago from the records "for examination" and never returned.

ting the federal income surtax from 50 percent to 25 percent and inheritance taxes from 40 percent to 20 percent. It was cut to ribbons in the Senate by a Democratic-Progressive coalition, but its defeat did not reduce Mellon's influence in the cabinet to any perceptible degree. After President Harding died and Coolidge took over, Mellon's position was further strengthened. The new president found the secretary his own kind of man, laconic and severe. It was said they got on so well because they conversed mainly in pauses.

In 1926 Mellon's tax plan was finally passed, cutting taxes for the wealthy and providing large postwar tax rebates to a number of leading corporations. One check issued to the United States Steel Corporation, in which the Mellons were important shareholders, totaled $27 million. In 1927 the lean gray secretary achieved further prominence as the leading administration spokesman for protectionism in the debates that led to the Smoot-Hawley tariff.° When Herbert Hoover became president in 1928, he reappointed Mellon to the Treasury post. But the onset of the depression quickly dimmed his reputation; by 1929 he had become a political liability to Hoover.† Hoover finally appointed him ambassador to Britain, an action which Mellon regarded as a capitulation to demagogic politicians. Mellon's performance in his new post was not impressive. He tried in vain to persuade British audiences of the soundness of the American economy. Of his efforts, one English editor wrote: "In an almost inaudible voice, he carefully read platitudes to the assembled company." Another commented: "It was like trying to catch the whisperings of a ghost. And when you'd caught what he had said, he had said nothing in particular." [6]

The political conservatism of Andrew Mellon was a reflection of

° During those same years Secretary Mellon also had a decisive voice in both the financing and the architecture of the $190 million public building program of the federal government in the District of Columbia. The huge neoclassical structures built at the time along Constitution and Pennsylvania avenues bear a strong resemblance to the façade of the Mellon National Bank and Trust Company in Pittsburgh.

† Wright Patman, then a young maverick congressman from Texas, made his first headlines in 1932 with a broadside attack on Mellon, whom he tried to have impeached on a variety of charges ranging from malfeasance to conflict of interest.

the harsh *laissez-faire* philosophy he inherited from his father and practiced in his business dealings. The Mellon companies from the beginning had had a reputation for being ruthless—even by the standards of the time—in the treatment of the laborers in their mines and mills. The family's critical biographer, Harvey O'Connor, has written, "If native labor was too expensive, the Mellons and their fellows used thousands of southern and eastern European workers imported to do the Nation's dirty work. If these in turn rebelled, the Mellons imported hordes of Negroes from the South." In 1915 a savage labor outbreak took place in a mill of the Mellon-controlled Aluminum Company of America in Massena, New York, and was broken by the employment of an army of Pinkerton gunmen and industrial spies. Later, that same company's labor policies were judged by a congressional committee to have been responsible for the bloody race riots that occurred in East St. Louis in 1917.[7]

Through the depression years, the Mellon companies were militantly antiunion and did even less than most to shield their discharged employees from destitution. They provided no unemployment insurance and refused all responsibility for those who were cast off. As the economic crisis worsened, various joint efforts were organized by some of the leading companies in Pittsburgh to provide relief and prevent starvation. But the Mellons made a minimal contribution. To Andrew Mellon, the depression was a passing thing, and he repeatedly said that its victims would come through the storm better disciplined by its rigors, better qualified for survival.

In recognizing their civic responsibilities for the accumulating environmental and social problems of Pittsburgh and the surrounding area, Andrew and his brothers were equally backward. As early as the turn of the century, by which time Pittsburgh had become preeminent in iron and steel production, it already symbolized rampant industrialization and its social by-products—a contaminated atmosphere, poverty, class friction, and dehumanizing ugliness. But they gave no leadership and took little part in the belated and inadequate efforts of the Pittsburgh business community to do something about such problems as smoke abatement, public health, housing, and physical planning of the region. Not until the third generation of Mellons—the sons of Andrew and Richard— did the family join actively in the rehabilitation of the city.

Andrew Mellon was a nineteenth-century American capitalist of the most rapacious kind in his business affairs. But he was also attracted to the "gospel of wealth" preached by his fellow Pittsburgh millionaire, Andrew Carnegie. In 1908 he and his brother founded the Mellon Institute in memory of their father, who had died shortly before at the age of ninety-five. The new center was devoted to applied research and industrial technology, which possibly served the interests of the Mellon companies as much as the general welfare, but it still represented a departure from the hard Knoxian ideology of the man it honored, who made no benefactions except to certain old friends who had fallen into adversity.

Two years later Andrew turned his attention to his father's alma mater, the neglected and rundown University of Pittsburgh, and helped to finance its physical rehabilitation. But he did little to improve its intellectual or scientific standing. There is evidence that a condition of the university's continued enjoyment of Mellon benefactions was its compliance in suppressing the teachings of doctrines considered antithetical to Mellon interests. That charge was investigated in 1926 by a committee of the American Association of University Professors, which concluded: "It is generally agreed by all members of the Pittsburgh faculty with whom we have conversed that there exists in the faculty of that institution a widespread feeling of insecurity and timidity. . . . They state that over a period of several years there has existed a conviction that a teacher must be extremely cautious in taking part in public discussions, especially if his convictions are enlisted on the side of unpopular causes. . . . This feeling applies to the public discussion of controversial social and economic questions such as the relations of labor and capital, governmental regulation of industry, and the domination of government by financial and industrial interests."

From the early 1920s, with the encouragement and assistance of Joseph Duveen, the internationally known dealer,[8] Mellon began to invest in works of art, acquiring a collection of paintings of first-rank importance.* And it was through the collection of fine art that Andrew's principal philanthropic contributions were eventually made.

In 1930, while still at the Treasury, he established the A. W. Mellon Educational and Charitable Trust; when Roosevelt became president, he offered his entire collection to the government and agreed to pay the costs of a gallery for it to be constructed in Washington. With a modesty not characteristic of many philanthropists, he stipulated that the institution, if created, should not bear his name. The offer was accepted.

Whether Andrew Mellon's establishment of the National Gallery was purely an act of patriotism and philanthropy is a matter on which opinions differ. According to S. N. Behrman, Duveen planted and nurtured the idea of a national gallery in Mellon's mind, although a court action in 1934 against Mellon for income tax evasion may have forced Mellon finally to go through with the plan. "The nub of Mellon's defense—a nub that the Government apparently had not anticipated—was that in 1931 Mellon, without talking about it, without even bothering to mention it to the Government, had given more than $3 million worth of pictures to the Mellon Trust, a foundation he had set up the year before for charitable purposes. The Government answered that the foundation itself was a tax dodge, that the pictures were hanging in his apartment and were inaccessible to the public." But to prove that Mellon had intended to create a gallery even before 1931, the year the government charged he had evaded several millions of dollars in income tax, Mellon's counsel called Duveen to the stand, who was able, in Behrman's words, "to slant a shaft of benevolent, lateral light on Mellon: here was the Government insisting that Mellon was trying to cheat it out of over $3 million; Duveen was pres-

* The story is told that Duveen made his largest single sale to Mellon by renting the apartment on the floor below him in Washington and filling it with forty-two masterpieces. He gave Mellon the key and encouraged him to look at them at his leisure—which the silent potentate, in dressing gown and carpet slippers, frequently did. After six months, he bought the entire collection with a check for $21 million. (Behrman, pp. 270–73)

ent to prove that Mellon had spent vastly more than that on a project he had long been preparing to hand over to the Government he was supposed to be defrauding." As Mellon's attorney, Frank J. Hogan, put it, "God doesn't place in the hearts and minds of men such diverse and opposite traits as these; it is impossible to conceive of a man planning such benefactions as these and at the same time plotting and scheming to defraud his government."

In the end, the Board of Tax Appeals exonerated Mellon of the government's charges. But the conclusion of the tax hearings in Washington "left Duveen in a handsome position; the idea of a National Gallery was out in the open, and Mellon could not very gracefully change his mind about it." [9]

From 1930 until his death in 1937 Mellon gave the trust some $50 million in cash and works of art and he made it the residuary legatee of his estate: in all, his gifts and bequests totaled more than $100 million.[10] Its main preoccupation over the next five years, under the leadership of his two children, Paul and Ailsa, who were trustees, was the construction of the National Gallery, a project on which it eventually spent more than $71 million.

After World War II, with the gallery completed and the assets of the trust substantially reduced, the trustees decided to concentrate its future grants on "projects of significance to the well-being of an urban industrial community, that is, Pittsburgh." Its principal single project in the subsequent phase of its existence, under the capable leadership of Thomas W. Parran, former surgeon-general of the United States, was the establishment of a graduate school of public health at the University of Pittsburgh, to which it gave more than $13 million. This admirable move to train doctors for positions in public service, in industrial medicine, and in research on the health problems of an industrial area required particular courage, as it was actively opposed by the American Medical Association in the Pittsburgh region. At the dedication of the school in 1951, Paul Mellon delicately referred to this controversy by saying, "the medical status quo in Pittsburgh would never be the same." After 1959, the trustees decided to stabilize the assets of the trust at a level of $20 million for a continuing attack on the problems of

the city, especially its health problems, "using the city as a laboratory typical of the predicament of other highly urbanized and industrialized centers."

Although the trust has now reached a somewhat attenuated existence, it has displayed a certain boldness over the years and a
penchant for large undertakings. The institutions it has created in
Washington and in Pittsburgh stand as creditable monuments to a
man who might otherwise have passed into history as a singularly
arid, unhappy, and unloved figure.

The Third Generation

The third generation of Mellons has been the philanthropic generation. The four principal figures have been the son and daughter
of Richard B. Mellon and the son and daughter of Andrew, all of
whom have established foundations. The dominant one among
them has been Richard King Mellon, who became president of the
Mellon National Bank in 1934 and thereby head of the family and
of its financial empire. He had been groomed for the position since
childhood. Ten years after he left Princeton he held directorships
in thirty-four major corporations and had convincingly demonstrated his skill in the management of large financial undertakings.

In his personal manner and habits the husky and gregarious six-
footer was a far cry from his austere grandfather and his uncle Andrew. As a young man, he spent all his free time at Rolling Rock, a
hunt club developed by his father in the hills outside Pittsburgh.
In his attitude toward the needs of Pittsburgh he also departed
from the Mellon tradition. By the outbreak of World War II the
city's problems piled up to the point of disaster, and in 1943 he
made a personal decision to take the lead in rebuilding it. He
helped to form the Allegheny Conference on Community Development, through which the subsequent renaissance was directed, and
he recruited the corporate elite of the area to participate in its
work, giving it extraordinary power and influence. (A fuller analysis of the motives, objectives, and methods of this instructive exam-

ple of business leadership in urban redevelopment is presented in
chapter 18.)

In a statement that might have choked his grandfather and his
uncle, Richard King Mellon declared in 1962, "We businessmen
must participate in the formulation of public policy even though
the particular issues may not have an immediate influence upon
our individual businesses. This necessitates unselfish leadership
and personal participation. However important the daily conduct
of our business is to all of us, however demanding of our time and
energy, it is clear that we cannot isolate ourselves from the universal public service demands and the social problems which sur-
round us. We cannot get away from the fact that the very basis of
our industrial society rests upon the environment in which we
live."

THE RICHARD KING MELLON FOUNDATION

His deepening interest in Pittsburgh's redevelopment apparently
led him to establish his Richard King Mellon Foundation in November 1947. To run it, he set up a small board of four individual
trustees and one corporate trustee, the Mellon Bank. The four
trustees consisted of his wife as chairman and three other close associates, one of them General Joseph D. Hughes, the paid head of
its small staff. Its initial assets of $50 million were in the form of
shares in Mellon-controlled companies, and its program was centered primarily on the needs of the Pittsburgh area and western
Pennsylvania. Over the following fifteen years, the foundation was
used largely to plan and launch strategic projects which were subsequently executed through far larger corporate and public funds.
About 80 percent of its grants during this period were spent in
Pittsburgh, largely in support of its redevelopment program. The
most favored single recipient was the Mellon Institute, which was
granted $7.7 million. The Medical School of the University of Pitts-
burgh was given $2.5 million; Mellon Square Park was created in
the downtown Golden Triangle area with a donation of $1 million.
In these undertakings, Mellon was usually able to persuade the
other Mellon foundations to join in providing equivalent gifts.

But by the mid-1960s, as the redevelopment program encountered resistance from citizens of threatened ghetto neighborhoods, his foundation acknowledged the inner-city's social problems of race and poverty. In its report for 1966–68, it explained that although it had been primarily interested in helping the physical improvement of Pittsburgh, the poor and the blacks had nevertheless benefited, even if only indirectly, from its grants. The report then added that "it is now possible to direct further attention towards parts of the community where the force of the renaissance has not yet fully penetrated. . . . Therefore, the foundation is making a number of additional grants for the specific purpose of aiding disadvantaged members of the community. The programs range from remedial tutoring to training of hard-core unemployed; from recreational and cultural programs in the inner-city to a mobile library that tours the slum areas with books, records, and films." To carry out these more complex social programs the foundation strengthened its full-time professional staff and by 1968 had in addition retained several specialized consultants in the fields of medicine and urban affairs.

Richard King Mellon died at the age of seventy in 1970, leaving behind a steadily improving record as a philanthropist. His foundation had disbursed more than $40 million in recorded grants, and its assets at the time of his death, before any distributions from his huge estate, totaled more than $160 million. His close associates believe that he gave many additional millions in anonymous personal gifts to hospitals, local universities, and other charities. He was a thorough-going economic and political conservative; he also was a tough pragmatist, never loosening his tight control over the board of his foundation, its program priorities, or its investments. But at the same time, he made a strong personal commitment to the improvement of his city, vigorously using his philanthropy to fulfill that commitment, and was willing, when faced with the necessity, to expand his concept of his own social responsibility.

THE SARAH MELLON SCAIFE FOUNDATION

The ladylike companion to the foundation of Richard King Mellon was that of his sister, Sarah Mellon Scaife. Established in

December 1941, it was inactive during the war years. But when her brother created his foundation, hers also became active. Largely because of his influence, her foundation concentrated on the Pittsburgh area, emphasizing urban renewal and the support of institutions bearing the Mellon name. This well-bred gentlewoman had more than a trace of the practical Mellon in her. Once when asked what constituted her favorite reading, she replied, "A financial report." Personally shy and modest, her one moment in the limelight was her marriage in 1927 to Alan M. Scaife, son of another wealthy Pittsburgh family. The ceremony was performed in flower-bedecked East Liberty Presbyterian Church. That evening, a thousand guests, the elite of the Iron City as well as contingents from Philadelphia and New York, were entertained on the grounds of her father's estate under a marquee especially built for the feast, reportedly at a cost of $100,000. It resembled a medieval castle with rich tapestry decorations and silver and crystal birds swinging in cages hung as lights. A Pittsburgh newspaper rhapsodized: "In providing a scene rivaling the beauty of fairyland, the Mellons last night challenged the elements. Although there was no moon, there was synthetic moonlight, serene and mellow from all four sides of the pavillion. Looking from the windows the guests gazed out on classic gardens where the synthetic moonlight illuminated marble images of Venus, Psyche, and Diana."

But in the same edition of the paper, other stories involving the Mellons were reminders of the real Pittsburgh—the eviction of a score of miners and their families from their Mellon company-owned houses because they had struck for union recognition, and a description of the hardships of the widows and children of fourteen workers in a Mellon company, who had been burned to death in an explosion while repairing a fuel tank.

Once the great occasion was over, the social princess of Pittsburgh, now Sarah Mellon Scaife, withdrew permanently from public view. In the Mellon manner, her foundation was structured so as to ensure family control over both program and investments. It began with a board of five including her husband, her brother, and officials of three institutions heavily dependent on Mellon financial support. It operated without professional staff, and its assets were

entirely in securities of Mellon companies, largely Gulf Oil. Over
time, the resources of the foundation were enlarged considerably.
Mrs. Scaife made a succession of large gifts; in 1948 the foundation
received a major share of a trust which her parents had established; and after her death, in 1965, it received an additional $65
million from her estate. As of 1968, its assets totaled $145 million.
The largest holdings were still in Gulf Oil, although it also controlled 43 percent of the shares of the First Boston Corporation, a
leading investment banking house.

By the time of her death, the foundation's program had taken
definite form. A portion of its grants were an expression of her personal civic and cultural interests: for parks and tree-planting in
Pittsburgh, for a light opera company, and for the construction of
an underground children's zoo. A major collection of paintings was
donated to the city museum and various grants were given for the
preservation and reconstruction of historic sites. A second and
larger portion consisted of contributions, in concert with other
Mellon foundations, to educational, medical, and research institutions in and near Pittsburgh that were associated with the Mellon
name. The third portion went to conservation and urban redevelopment, fields in which Mrs. Scaife's husband and brother played
leading roles. Since her death, there has been little change in the
general character of the foundation's program, except a somewhat
greater emphasis—in step with the evolving interest of her brother's foundation—on educational and other activities for the city's
ghettos. Its largest individual grants in recent years have gone to
the medical school at the University of Pittsburgh and for the construction of the new Sarah M. Scaife Art Gallery. Its board has
been enlarged by stages to eight trustees, two of whom are Mellons. The others are mostly persons closely connected with organizations and institutions dependent upon or controlled by the family. Its staff consists of one full-time administrative officer and a
few part-time employees.

As of 1972, the Richard King Mellon and the Sarah Mellon
Scaife foundations could look back on more than thirty years of
contribution to the improvement of institutions and the quality of
life in the Pittsburgh region. But what they could look forward to

is less certain, for the man who had given them their direction and
strength had died, as had his sister, and without them the philanthropies they left behind were little more than rudderless ships
freighted with money.

Richard King Mellon and Sarah Mellon Scaife were the branch
of the Mellon clan in the third generation that remained true to
Pittsburgh. But when Andrew left Pittsburgh for Washington in
1921, his interests were never again to be limited essentially to that
city; and his two young children, Paul and Ailsa, with their mother
in Europe and their father in the capital, developed a worldliness
and a range of cultivated tastes quite different from those of their
more provincial relatives in their western Pennsylvania fiefdom.

Paul and Ailsa later also established major foundations which
have not been indifferent to traditional family responsibilities in
Pittsburgh, but have reflected the wider horizons and, in a curious
way, the complex personalities of their donors. Ailsa, while her father was secretary of the treasury, served as his official hostess and
inspired her share of Washington society gossip. In the winter of
1925–26, David K. E. Bruce, the handsome son of a Maryland senator and a newly appointed foreign service officer, won the fancy
of the somewhat imperious young heiress. Their wedding the following spring was described by the New York *Times* as "the most
notable Washington has ever seen. . . . equalled in interest only
by the marriage twenty years ago of Miss Alice Lee Roosevelt."
Ailsa's father reportedly gave his new son-in-law a huge sum (some
said $10 million) "so that he could feel financially independent."
The couple had one child, a daughter, but after a few years their
marriage failed. Bruce remarried and went on to a long career of
distinguished government service. Ailsa retired from public view,
and the last years of her life were shattered with tragedy when her
daughter and son-in-law died in an airplane accident in 1967.

Her brother, Paul, even as a young man, had shown little interest in money-making and preferred scholarly pursuits. In his freshman year at Yale he was awarded the top prize for excellence in
English literature and the next year became editor of the *Yale Literary Magazine*. Later, while at Cambridge University in England,
he decided to enter publishing instead of banking or industry. But

his father had other plans, announcing publicly that the boy would enter the Mellon National Bank after his graduation. Eventually some kind of a compromise was struck. Paul spent a brief period of apprenticeship at the bank in Pittsburgh and then moved to a country estate which his father bought for him in the heart of the horse and hunt club region of Virginia. In the years since he has played only a minor role in the family's business affairs, devoting most of his time to his cultural interests and enjoying the life of a country squire and horsebreeder.

After their father's death in 1937, Paul and Ailsa became increasingly active in philanthropy, at first as trustees of his A. W. Mellon Educational and Charitable Trust. Then in 1940, Ailsa established her Avalon Foundation and a year later Paul created his Old Dominion Foundation. In many respects these two foundations, during the years of their separate existence until 1969, closely resembled each other in objectives and philanthropic approach. At the end of 1968, Avalon had assets of $156.5 million, Old Dominion of $116.5 million.[11] They collaborated in joint financing on a number of major projects, and there was cross-membership on the two boards by almost half the members.

THE AVALON FOUNDATION

Until it was absorbed into the new A. W. Mellon Foundation in 1969, the Avalon Foundation operated with a small board of trustees consisting of Mrs. Bruce and her brother, Paul, and up to five others. In the subdued and genteel atmosphere of a New York townhouse, the foundation operated with a small staff of four. During its twenty-nine years of operation it made grants of more than $67 million, including $25 million for medicine and health, $17 million for education, $15 million for the fine arts and conservation, and $10 million for civic and youth programs. Its program reflected the interests of a cultivated and civic-minded woman of fundamentally conservative tendencies.

In the area of health, its grants were largely to universities and hospitals for construction and general improvement, including the training of nurses. It avoided advanced scientific research, nor did it become involved in the social or economic aspects of medical care. The limits of its daring were gifts of $300,000 in 1964 to Hampton Institute, a black school in Virginia, and another of $100,000 to the Planned Parenthood Federation in 1965. Its grants in education were essentially to well-known institutions for physical facilities, library development, and the endowment of professorial chairs. General support was given to two black colleges, Hampton and Morehouse, but the foundation refrained from educational experimentation. In the cultural areas, its major grants were to the Metropolitan Opera, the New York Philharmonic, and the Bronx Zoo. Its community service grants were for the blind, conservation organizations, and the Regional Planning Association of New York. Starting in the 1960s, a number of smaller grants were made to assist organizations working with black and other poor children. Occasionally, in order not to become "a captive of the applicants," the staff reshaped proposals by adding what it considered to be innovative features. But fundamentally, the foundation operated on the principle that it could best serve social needs by helping to sustain and improve the work of reputable existing institutions, not by breaking new ground.

THE OLD DOMINION FOUNDATION

Even more than Avalon, the Old Dominion Foundation, because of the donor's interests, had a strong cultural and humanistic orientation. At first, the foundation devoted itself to war relief. But after the war its areas of concern became the humanities and liberal education and, in lesser degree, the fine arts, mental health, conservation, and special projects in Virginia, where Paul Mellon makes his home.

In its major grants to a selected group of schools the foundation's intention was "to help remedy the imbalance of support" in higher education between technical and professional education on the one hand and the humanities and liberal arts on the other. A large portion of these grants went to three private institutions in the East: $20 million to Yale; $7 million to St. John's College; and $5 million to Harvard. The more unusual items in the foundation's grant list have been its support for research and publication in the fine arts and its training fellowships for museum curators.* It has made significant gifts for the acquisition of national parkland and the rehabilitation of public parks. It has helped a number of black educational and cultural institutions, including the United Negro College Fund, Hampton Institute, Tuskegee Institute, and various museums of African and black American art.

The six-member board of the foundation, until its consolidation into the A. W. Mellon Foundation in 1969, consisted of Paul Mellon; Adolph W. Schmidt, also related to the family; Stoddard M. Stevens, a New York lawyer who served on the Avalon board; and William O. Baker, vice-president of Bell Laboratories, who also served on both boards. During its twenty-eight years, the Old Dominion Foundation operated with a small professional staff. Under the competent presidency of Ernest Brooks Jr., its grants were of better technical quality than those of most family-style foundations. This was also partly due to Mellon, a man of unusual scholarly and intellectual qualifications, who devoted a considerable portion of his time to his foundation.

Because of the close relationship between Ailsa Mellon Bruce and her brother, the similarity of their two foundations, and their frequent collaboration in grant-making, it was not surprising that the two foundations were merged in June 1969 into the Andrew W. Mellon Foundation. The action may have been precipitated by the illness of Mrs. Bruce, who died less than two months later. The consolidated assets of the two foundations, at the end of 1968, were $273 million at market value, and after the settlement of the estate of Mrs. Bruce (reported to be the richest woman in the United States at the time of her death with a fortune estimated at more than $500 million), it was anticipated that the new foundation's resources would be substantially increased.[12]

The merger aroused many hopes that the new organization would become a more active and creative force than either of its

* Paul Mellon in 1945 also established the Bollingen Foundation, whose principal objective is "the advancement and preservation of learning in the humanities." It sponsors a program of publication under the name of the Bollingen Series and gives annual prizes in poetry and poetry translation. The 1967 market value of its assets was $1.9 million.

component foundations had been. But these rather quickly faded when it was announced in late 1970 that Dr. Nathan Pusey had been named as the new president. His record until his retirement as head of Harvard University had been staunchly uninspired, and it seemed most unlikely that the Mellon atmosphere would excite him to any outburst of adventuresomeness.

The Mellon Trademark

The major Mellon foundations all bear a strong family resemblance. They are closely interlinked with one another and with the family and its sense of dynasty. They have collaborated with one another extensively in their grant-making to favored institutions, and through their small and intimate boards their investment policies have been harmonized with the interests of the total Mellon banking and industrial complex.

They have paid out substantial sums to charity over the years, and they have regularly reported to the public on their operations. In their financial dealings they have been honorable, not engaging in any of the lower forms of self-dealing or other abuse. Some diversification of holdings has also begun to occur, especially by the Avalon and Old Dominion foundations which even before their merger had already disposed of a substantial part of their Gulf Oil shares.

In the style of their giving, the Mellons typify the responsible American Establishment—not at its finest, perhaps, but certainly not at its narrowest and most reactionary.° In philanthropic terms, their trademark has been respectability.

° Not all the shirts of the Mellons have been quite so stuffed as those of the "major" members of the family. Among the "lesser" ones, there was Matthew, son of William, who devoted himself to mountain climbing, photography, and lecturing on American literature at European universities. His brother, Larimer, while a gentleman rancher in Arizona, became so inspired in his forties by a book on Albert Schweitzer that he enrolled in the Tulane Medical School, took his medical degree, and later specialized in tropical diseases. His wife became a medical technician, and at Schweitzer's suggestion they established a hospital in the most impoverished part of Haiti. For more than a decade the two of them have worked there in tropical isolation, serving the

It was not until the third generation of their wealth and power that the Mellons developed a sense of civic and charitable responsibility. But three of the four members of that generation who established large foundations have now died, and the foundations they left behind have little institutional strength or momentum. The immediate question is, where does Mellon philanthropy go from here? Much of the answer depends on slight, scholarly Paul Mellon, the last remaining member of the founding foursome. A very heavy responsibility rests therefore on frail shoulders.

---

needs of the local population. Perhaps the greatest exception of all to Mellon conservatism was Audrey, the only child of Ailsa Mellon Bruce, who, with her husband, Stephen R. Currier, established the spectacularly brave and controversial Taconic Foundation, which in the 1950s and 1960s played a leading role in the advancement of black rights and racial justice in the United States. Their untimely death in an airplane accident was a particularly severe loss to philanthropy.

13.

Astor, Woodruff, Kresge, Waterman, and Kaiser: Philanthropy Family Style

THE TERM "BIG PHILANTHROPY" usually brings to mind the Rockefeller, Carnegie, and Ford foundations—the leading professionalized institutions. But in many respects, "family-style" foundations—characterized by either donor or donor-family control, close financial linkage with the donor's company, and a personal approach to grant-making—are more typical of the group.

Of the many big foundations still operating family-style, some are disreputable, such as Nemours, and others torpid, such as Surdna. But there are five creditable examples: Astor, Woodruff, Kresge, Waterman, and Kaiser. If large-scale private philanthropy can be defended as an institution productively serving the needs of American society, it has to be largely on the basis of the purposes, operating methods, and results of foundations like these.

The Vincent Astor Foundation

The donor of the Vincent Astor Foundation was a great-great-grandson of John Jacob Astor, a poor butcher who came to America from Germany in 1784, made a fortune in the fur trade, and then multiplied it by investing heavily in Manhattan real estate. Ever since, the family has been involved in the city's history. Some of its most famous landmarks—the Waldorf Astoria Hotel and the old Hotel Astor—have carried its name; Vincent Astor's grandmother was *the* Mrs. Astor, whose ballroom at Fifth Avenue and

Thirty-fourth Street could accommodate four hundred persons and gave the name "Four Hundred" to New York's social elite.

When he was twenty-one, Vincent Astor inherited $70 million from his father, John Jacob Astor 4th, who went down with the *Titanic* in 1912. Vincent promptly left Harvard to manage his inheritance, then largely in real estate. Over the years he extended his holdings into shipping and petroleum; at the time of his death in 1959, he was also board chairman and principal stockholder of *Newsweek* magazine. Many of his associates considered him to be the best businessman in the family since John Jacob. He was also serious about the responsibilities of wealth, giving generously to charity and working through his real estate interests to rid Manhattan of its slums. A moody and complex man, Astor had little interest in fashionable social life. His principal extravagance and pleasure was sailing; in its day his racing sloop *Nourmahal* was one of the best-known of its class.

Astor developed a close friendship with his Dutchess County neighbor, Franklin Delano Roosevelt, after the president-to-be contracted polio in 1921. FDR used the swimming pool on the Astor estate during his convalescence and was a frequent guest on the *Nourmahal*. Astor worked for Roosevelt's election in 1932, but later he cooled toward the New Deal and resumed his contributions to the Republican party.

He died at the age of sixty-seven. Childless after three marriages, he left a large part of his estate to his foundation, which he had established in 1948 "for the alleviation of human misery." The trustees were some of his close friends. During his lifetime he made many contributions to charity through the foundation; the principal beneficiaries were the Astor Home for Children in Rhinebeck, New York, founded in 1917 in honor of his father, and the Society of the New York Hospital. Since his death, the foundation has not become a professionalized philanthropy, but it has to its credit an original and useful program in urban affairs.

It started with several advantages: the donor's habit of generosity; the diversity of its investment portfolio—which in 1968 had a market value of $103 million; and above all the active interest in philanthropy of his widow, Brooke Astor. Over the last decade, she as president and Allen W. Betts as vice-president have run the foundation's affairs, personally screening grant applications and interviewing prospective grantees. Membership of the board has changed somewhat, but it still consists largely of socially prominent New York financiers, lawyers, and corporate executives. They meet only three times a year and have little direct involvement with project decisions. The foundation focuses mainly on New York City, particularly on the needs of the ghettos and of ghetto youth. It has made substantial grants to community centers in Harlem, boys' clubs in slum areas, low-income housing, and recreational activities in the Bedford-Stuyvesant area of Brooklyn.

According to Mrs. Astor, the foundation selects its projects from formal applications or from proposals suggested by friends, often at dinner parties. This admittedly haphazard approach has nonetheless produced grants that show individuality and innovativeness. Although some professional social workers regard her as a whimsical Lady Bountiful, she has won high praise from others. In recent years the foundation has become known for the financing of experimental park-and-playground complexes where children play by day and families gather in the evening. These projects, which Mrs. Astor refers to as "outdoor living rooms," are largely the result of her initiative. In praise of her efforts, Thomas P. F. Hoving, director of the Metropolitan Museum of Art and former city parks commissioner, has said, "She is a genius. It's as simple as that."

The foundation's board is generally free of conflicts of interest, its investments are productive, and it distributes its income fully and promptly. Since 1964 it has issued public reports that are informative, brief, and uncommonly modest. On the other hand, the foundation has experienced some internal tension over the direction of its future policy and programs. Although it is concerned primarily with the problems of the poor and the blacks, its all-white board of trustees in terms of personal background and position is almost totally removed from such problems. The trustees are unanimous in believing that the foundation's commitment should be to New York City, its youth, and its poor, but some of them are opposed to an exclusive concentration in these areas and to an overly activist approach. Mrs. Astor herself prefers to avoid projects that are controversial, fearing entanglement in power struggles and factional confrontations, but Betts and some other trustees feel the foundation should undertake "gut projects" in the ghettos, eliminating conventional grants such as its $5 million pledge in 1970 to the Bronx Zoo.

The future of the Vincent Astor foundation is uncertain. It may become a more professionalized institution, but it is equally likely that it may dissolve itself and distribute its assets to institutions in the New York City area.

The (Emily and Ernest) Woodruff Foundation

The Woodruff Foundation of Atlanta is a distinctive example of productive paternalism. It also illustrates the interrelationship between philanthropy and power—economic, social, political—in a local situation. Because large foundations, particularly of the family type, frequently concentrate their influence upon a given locality, the Woodruff case has broad implications.

The donor, Ernest Woodruff, who headed the Trust Company of Georgia in the early decades of the century, was largely responsible for the initial development of Atlanta as a regional commercial and business center; he also formed the syndicate which, in 1919, bought control of the Coca-Cola Company. His and his wife's bequests provided the main resources of the foundation, but his son, Robert, now in his eighties and childless, has been the dominant figure in the foundation for many years.

Robert had little formal education, but even as a young man he displayed a natural talent for business. Starting out on his own, he progressed rapidly from machinist to salesman to purchasing agent in various companies and, after service in World War I, became vice-president and general manager of the White Motor Company in Cleveland, Ohio. Having proved himself, he returned to his father's domain, becoming president and a director of Coca-Cola in 1923. Since then he has been chiefly responsible for the growth of that company. Apart from business, his great enthusiasm has been philanthropy. He has focused the activities of his parents' foundation and other foundations with which he is connected upon Atlanta and the surrounding region.

The assets of the Woodruff Foundation are almost entirely in voting stock of the International Coca-Cola Company, its holdings representing about 15 percent of the shares outstanding, with a market value of $158.2 million at the end of 1968. The board consists of a small group of men all directly related to the economic interests of the Woodruff family and accustomed to following Robert Woodruff's leadership. They are his brother George; Arthur Acklin, a retired president of the Coca-Cola Company; John A. Sibley, a long-time business associate and chairman emeritus of the Trust Company of Georgia; and Paul Austin, the current president of the Coca-Cola Company. Of this group, Austin is the youngest at 58, and several are in their eighties. The two "alternate trustees" are Joseph Jones, Woodruff's personal secretary, and James Sibley, John Sibley's son, whose firm handles legal matters for the family and the foundation. Until 1953 the foundation operated with only a parttime bookkeeper and no professional staff. But in that year Dr. Philip Weltner, former president of Oglethorpe University, was employed as a consultant. In July 1964 the foundation named its first full-time professional head, Boisfeuillet Jones, a former administrative officer of Emory University who served as a special assistant to the secretary of health, education, and welfare during the Kennedy administration.

The major program interest of the foundation has been capital projects in the Atlanta area, particularly those serving a regional purpose. It avoids gifts for operating expenses and rarely provides assistance to tax-supported institutions or to individuals. It has made many grants to established local institutions such as private schools, hospitals, the Boy Scouts, and the Traffic and Safety Council. But the chief recipient of Woodruff's philanthropy over the years has been the medical school and health facilities at Emory University in Atlanta. His first important gift was in 1937 for a tumor clinic. After World War II he helped to strengthen and enlarge the medical school and for several years thereafter provided its major financial support. In the early 1950s he encouraged the drafting of a plan for a complete health services center at the university and subsequently gave $5 million to implement it. More recently, he has made a succession of additional gifts for a medical research building, a school of nursing, and an out-patient clinic. In all, it is estimated that his personal gifts and those of the foundation to the university have totaled $60 million.[1]

In 1961, Emory challenged a Georgia law financially penalizing racially integrated institutions and succeeded in having it declared unconstitutional. The university and its health complex have since operated on a desegregated basis. With its general growth and improvement the health complex has attracted a number of other medical facilities—the Egleston Hospital for Children, the Elks Hospital for Crippled Children, the Yerkes Regional Primate Research Center, a new communicable disease center of the U.S. Public Health Service, and a large Veterans Administration hospital. As a result, it has become the leading medical center in the Southeast.

Another major project initiated by Woodruff is the Atlanta Arts Alliance, which has received some $8 million from the foundation and an additional $6 million from Woodruff's friends and other foundations. More recently, he has taken the lead in raising funds for the Metropolitan Foundation of Atlanta, which has built a new science center, including a planetarium and natural history museum. In financing these undertakings, Woodruff is not limited to the funds of his parents' foundation. He is also the principal figure in four others, which share its offices: the Joseph B. Whitehead Foundation ($46 million in assets); the Lettie Tate Evans Foundation ($13.6 million); the Lettie Tate Whitehead Foundation— Whitehead had the original bottling rights for Coca-Cola in the Atlanta area, Lettie Tate was his wife ($17 million); and his own Trebor Foundation—Trebor is Robert spelled backward ($12 million). Although Trebor's assets are limited, Woodruff uses it as a vehicle for a part of his substantial current giving. In addition, he occasionally makes large personal gifts directly to favored institutions. In 1969 he reportedly gave $8 million to Emory University in this way. Because of his central financial role and his own generosity Woodruff is an almost irresistible force in Atlanta in obtaining matching gifts from his friends and their foundations for civic projects in which he takes an active interest.

In the middle 1960s, after the appointment of Jones as director, the Woodruff Foundation began for the first time to concern itself with problems of crime, delinquency, job training, and welfare services in Atlanta's inner city. While this aspect of its program does not yet claim a large portion of the foundation's outlays, it represents a significant new direction. It has also required greater initiative on the part of the foundation in developing new grantee organizations and in seeking government funds to expand successful demonstration projects. These grants, together with a series of capital gifts totaling more than $1 million to the various black colleges forming the Atlanta University complex, have begun to give the Woodruff Foundation an unprecedented degree of local visibility, particularly to the black community. For despite its huge outlays, the Woodruff Foundation for many years remained almost unknown to the average citizen of Atlanta. Woodruff in all his civic and charitable activities preferred to operate anonymously; the foundation carefully avoided publicity and never published an annual report until after 1969, when the law required it. (One leading Atlantan who has worked with Woodruff on philanthropic matters for a long time has said, "He feels that operating quietly gets more done, avoids a lot of unnecessary trouble and, in any event, the people who really count know about the grants anyway.")

In regard to Atlanta's racial problems, Woodruff's philosophy has been one of responsible conservatism—or as a black leader in Atlanta has described it, of "progressive paternalism." [2] In his business, political, and civic activities he has been neither a crusading reformer nor a hard-shelled reactionary. As black demands and social tensions have grown, the Coca-Cola Company and the Woodruff Foundation have responded constructively. In city politics Woodruff has usually put his influence behind moderates such as Mayor Ivan Allen Jr., who steered Atlanta through its many desegregation crises in the 1960s without the violence that scarred Birmingham and other cities.

Robert Woodruff's pervasive influence in the Southeast makes the Woodruff Foundation a particularly clear-cut example of the interconnection between philanthropy and power, including political power. As Floyd Hunter pointed out in his highly regarded study on the leadership structure of the city of Atlanta:

It is true that there is no formal tie between the economic interests and government, but the structure of policy-determining committees and their tie-ins with the other powerful institutions and organizations of the community make government subservient to the interests of these combined groups. Governmental departments and their personnel are acutely aware of the power of key individuals, . . . the same groups and cliques, and the same interests dominate each sphere of property and politics . . . the structure is that of a dominant policy-making group, using the machinery of government as a bureaucracy for the attainment of certain goals coordinate with the interests of the policy-forming group.[3]

Power is an undeniable fact of life in communities, even though there are widely divergent theories as to how such power should be legitimized and exercised. Any close connection between philanthropic, economic, and political power can be regarded as evil and dangerous, but it can also be regarded as in the interest of a dynamic and democratic society. But whichever moral or ideological position is taken, a lack of awareness of the interrelationship between foundations and the general structure of power in a number of localities in the United States can only lead to an incomplete understanding of the institution of private philanthropy.

Power, however, even of the decisive kind of Robert Woodruff's, is ultimately a passing thing. With advancing age, his is declining. In the Coca-Cola Company, it is generally said that "as long as he lives, his word will be law," but the senior executives of the company are already talking of the time when his grip will be loosened. In his foundations, Woodruff remains in full control; but most of the board members are elderly, and a new generation of trustees will take over before long. The change in program direction of the Woodruff Foundation since it acquired professional leadership is a clear indication of things to come.

In Atlanta politics, Woodruff's era is already over. The old coalition of big business, middle-class whites, and well-organized blacks, which gave Atlanta its progressive Southern image and which he generally supported, has begun to crack between the jaws of black militancy and white resistance to accelerated change. These new forces promise rougher political and social times in the future. They will also undoubtedly smite all the works of Robert Woodruff—including his important philanthropic creations.

The Kresge Foundation

The Kresge Foundation of Detroit, with assets in 1968 in excess of $350 million (approaching $450 million as of 1970), has an explicit philosophy of noninnovation in its grant-making. Its characteristic simplicity and honorable, old-fashioned purpose mirror the qualities of Sebastian S. Kresge, its founder, who personally guided its affairs from its start in 1924 until his death at ninety-nine in 1966.

The story of S. S. Kresge's life was the fulfillment of the American Dream of an earlier day. Born to a poor farm family in the heart of the Pennsylvania Dutch country just after the Civil War, he eventually became head of one of the sixty wealthiest families in America.[4] He began his business career as a bookkeeper and then became a traveling salesman for a hardware company, when he made the acquaintance of some of the early pioneers in chain store cash-and-carry merchandising, including Frank W. Woolworth and John G. McCrory. He quickly saw the huge opportunity for profits in that field and acquired a part interest in a small variety store in Memphis, Tennessee, in 1897. By 1912, he owned eighty-five stores; by 1922, more than 200; and by 1932, more than 700.

He had a lifelong ambition to make money and an obsession to keep it. Stories of his parsimony abound. Married three times, his first two wives divorced him, each citing his stinginess as a major complaint. He would wear a pair of shoes until they literally fell apart; when the soles got too thin, he would line them with newspaper. He gave up golf because he could not stand to lose the balls. Of his own career he once said: "I was a worker—and I didn't work only eight hours a day but sometimes eighteen hours. When one starts at the bottom and learns to scrape, then everything becomes easy." He explained his hobby of bee-keeping: "My bees always remind me that hard work, thrift, sobriety, and an earnest struggle to live an upright Christian life are the first rungs of the ladder of success."[5] A zealous advocate of his Puritanical beliefs, he helped to organize the National Vigilance Committee for

Prohibition Enforcement and spent an estimated $1 million of his fortune to oppose the use of cigarettes and alcohol.

He was generous to the employees of his company, and because of his religious convictions about the obligations of wealth, he made large contributions to charity throughout his life. Without fanfare or ceremony he established his foundation in 1924, at a time of relatively low taxes, with an initial gift of $1.3 million. Its board consisted of himself and three close friends. The first president was Paul W. Voorhies, his lawyer, whose legal pen seems to have phrased the statement of the new foundation's purpose, "the maintenance, establishment and perpetuation of those many deserving objects of charity and benefaction to assist which no organized effort has been extended and for which no support has been provided."

For the next forty years under Kresge's guidance the foundation operated with its small board and a staff of one, an executive secretary. The donor's son, Stanley, joined the board in 1930 and succeeded Voorhies as president in 1952; he remains chairman today, devoting much of his time to the foundation and drawing a limited salary. The donor retained the position of treasurer, keeping his personal hand on all matters relating to finance. His donations to the foundation were almost entirely in the form of stock in his company, and he permitted no investment diversification to take place as long as he lived. After his death the board was reorganized. William H. Baldwin, a successful practicing attorney in Detroit, was elected president and the administrative staff was expanded to three persons. Baldwin devotes less than full time to its affairs. All grant decisions are made by the board in a two-month period, April and May, of each year.

In its first report, covering the three-year period 1954–56, the foundation described its operating philosophy: "Our Board of Trustees is relatively small and we do not have many investigators or a large clerical personnel. We may in the future, of necessity, adopt the professional approach. Thus far, every trustee, from the founder down, is in a real sense a full-time trustee, familiar with many phases of the applications submitted, granted and denied."

Regarding its program philosophy, the foundation stated: "While all applications for grants are judged on their own merits, it is one of the present broad policies of the Kresge Foundation to favor grants providing for the maintenance, expansion, or perpetuation of deserving existing organizations over grants which look to the establishment or initiating of new organizations or experimental projects. The policy does not preclude consideration of new projects nor is it meant as an attempt to value the relevant merits of the existing as against the proposed. It does, however, indicate a main direction of support and is based in part at least on the fact that other capable and well-advised philanthropic organizations have made and will make considerable funds available for exploratory and experimental projects."

Geographically, nearly half the foundation's grants have been made to institutions in Michigan; much of the remainder has gone to states in the Northeast. Kresge acquired his fortune through retail merchandising in this region and felt that benefactions from that wealth properly should flow back to it. But since his death, other areas have also benefited. The fields of primary interest have generally reflected his own philanthropic interests—education, religion, health, children, youth, and the aged. Colleges and universities have received the largest support, hospitals and medical institutions somewhat less. Institutions for religious training and leadership have been given substantial but diminishing assistance, and in its recent reports, Kresge has explained that "it is no part of foundation policy to foster sectarian interests." In the late 1950s the foundation began to assist cultural institutions, first with a grant of $1.5 million for the construction of an art center at Michigan State University. But except for this departure, the foundation's program remained essentially in the same groove for more than forty years.*

* The only important exception to the foundation's general policy of helping existing organizations was its creation in 1948 of the Kresge Eye Institute, a center for research and experimental surgery. After providing $200,000 a year in sustaining support for seventeen years, the foundation transferred this institution in 1965 to Wayne State University, which is now responsible for its operation.

After Kresge's death in 1966, however, the foundation began to move in some new directions. In 1968, the first large step toward investment diversification was taken when 500,000 shares of Kresge stock, worth $46 million, were sold.* In program, some limited evolution beyond traditional policy also occurred. In the 1967 annual report reference was made for the first time to world population growth, the urban crisis, racial strife, and educational reform. Striking a restrained but new note, President Baldwin in his introduction said: "As much as any institution, and more than most, foundations have a duty not to neglect the world even though they may have doubts about the proposals for changing it. In fulfillment of that duty, the Kresge Foundation will do what it feels it knows best. In so doing we are much aware that we have no special knowledge which enables us to perform our assigned tasks better than others. It will try to relate its gifts of facilities and equipment to the major problems of the time in the hope that creative minds can use the given facilities and equipment as instruments to the advantage of mankind."

The words were still conservative in spirit, but they revealed at least a recognition that social changes were taking place. The foundation followed up by announcing grants of $235,000 in the field of urban affairs for legal aid, job training, community organization, and inner-city schooling in Detroit. Cautiously, its 1967 report explained: "Some of such grants constitute exceptions to established foundation policy and for the present, such exceptions will not be extended beyond the metropolitan Detroit area." In 1968, it went a bit further, approving a $500,000 grant to the New Detroit Committee as well as a few smaller grants for legal aid and job retraining programs. Since then the total has fallen to $367,000 in 1969 and $314,000 in 1970. Kresge, having begun halfheartedly to modernize, seems to have become easily discouraged.†

  * As of the end of 1969 $330 million of the foundation's assets of $430 million were still in S. S. Kresge shares, representing 17 percent of the company's ownership.
  † In 1970 the foundation moved its headquarters from the strife-torn central section of Detroit to the posh white suburb of Birmingham.

The Phoebe Waterman Foundation

The Waterman Foundation of Philadelphia differs from the usual family-controlled philanthropy mainly in its departure from traditional patterns of charitable giving and in its strong and growing interest in the social and racial issues of a large metropolitan area. Its founder, Otto Haas, was the son of impoverished parents, and from the time of his boyhood in Germany he was driven by an insatiable hunger for wealth. It began, he told an intimate friend, when as a boy he walked in the hills outside Stuttgart and "saw all those roofs and realized that not one belonged to me." [6] He came to the United States in 1909. Over the next fifty years, he built up the Rohm and Haas industrial chemicals company from an operation with two assistants and himself in a ramshackle building to a richly profitable organization of 11,000 employees. He rarely missed a day at his office, working in a black silk coat in a room furnished with only a simple wooden table and four straight chairs. He kept the reins of management firmly in his own hands until days before his death of cancer in 1960 at the age of eighty-eight, when he designated a long-time associate, Ralph Connor, as chairman of the board of the company. At the same time he made one of his sons, F. Otto Haas, president and the other, John Haas, executive vice-president. Like their father, the sons have remained deeply absorbed in the family business. Only a few years ago, one of the company's executives said: "They are the first to arrive in the morning, the last to go at night, and they know every employee in the plant. They represent paternalism of the very best kind." [7]

Their father's interest in philanthropy derived, initially at least, from a simple desire to save estate taxes and protect family control of the company. Once these objectives were secured, he became more interested in his foundation's work. His own impulse was reinforced by his wife's strong interest in social welfare activities; she was an army colonel's daughter who grew up on an Indian reservation and later gained her Ph.D. in astronomy. The foundation, named in her honor, was established in 1945. For the first ten years it operated with limited resources and no staff. In 1955, however, it came to life with the appointment of a consultant, Richard K. Bennett, who was asked on a one-day-a-week basis to study the problems of the Philadelphia area and to write "think pieces" for the guidance of the board in the development of the foundation's program. He had come to the attention of the Haas family in connection with his work in race relations and, incidentally, as an outspoken critic of their company's employment practices with respect to blacks. Bennett, who has since become the foundation's executive director, is a Quaker and was interned during World War II as a conscientious objector. He later headed the community division of the American Friends Service Committee, which was concerned with interracial affairs and the problems of minority groups.

Since the death of Mrs. Haas in 1967 the board now consists of the donor's sons as chairman and vice-chairman; their two wives; William Kohler, lawyer to the family as well as a staff member of the foundation; Ralph Connor, board chairman of the company; Duncan Merriwether, a retired executive of the company; and Bennett. John C. Haas also holds the title of president and devotes a substantial part of his time to foundation affairs. The assets of the foundation, which in 1968 had a market value of $114.8 million, consist essentially of Rohm and Haas voting stock and comprise about 19 percent of the total outstanding. Paralleling the resources of the Waterman Foundation are those of three charitable trusts, also controlled by the Haas family, which roughly equal those of the foundation. These are the Otto Haas Charitable Trust No. 1 (assets of $9 million); the Otto Haas Charitable Trust No. 2 ($64 million); and the Phoebe W. Haas Charitable Trust ($24 million). The charitable grants of the trusts resemble and are coordinated with those of the foundation.° For the year 1969, Trust No. 1 made

° A spokesman for the Phoebe Waterman Foundation, Albert E. Arent, told the Senate Finance Committee during its hearings on the 1969 tax reform bill that the foundation had been created in 1945 "to establish a major philanthropy and to enable the family to satisfy their desire for such philanthropy without jeopardizing their control of the family business. . . . The company is a prime target for raiders and is protected only by the fact that as much as 49 percent of the stock can be considered in friendly hands." Since the foundation itself owns 19 percent of the company shares outstanding, the holdings of the individual members of the family plus the three family trusts presumably constitute an additional 30 percent.

grants of $180,000 to social welfare projects in Philadelphia, Trust No. 2 distributed $2.7 million to various local cultural and educational institutions, and the Phoebe W. Haas Trust gave over $300,000, largely for social welfare and cultural projects. The management of the financial affairs of the trusts and of the foundation is in the hands of John C. Haas.

The program policies of the trusts are set by committees of five members. In each case three members are chosen from the community at large for six-year terms, which are not renewable. In the future these public members will also be elected to the board of the foundation for the period of their terms, an interesting way of achieving a degree of both diversity and rotation. The 1969 annual report of the Waterman Foundation—in an extraordinary step in the direction of full disclosure—embraced the activities not only of the foundation itself but of the associated trusts, the group being informally designated as the Haas Community Funds.*

The program of the foundation in its earlier years consisted largely of grants to existing hospitals, centers of medical research, and educational institutions in the Philadelphia area. But more recently increasing emphasis has been given to social welfare projects, housing, and scholarship assistance to underprivileged children. In 1969, nearly one-third of its outlays were for child and youth activities, vocational training, and other social welfare needs. Grants to universities and hospitals for buildings, equipment, and general support received another third. The remainder went to research and housing projects and to various cultural institutions. The foundation's reports, though brief, describe its grants in terms which clearly indicate their nature and purpose. The following examples are from the 1969 report:

EDUCATION: *Medical Schools*

Hahnemann Medical College and Hospital, Philadelphia $ 26,603

    General support of a neighborhood health center operated by the college's Department of

---

* The name of the Phoebe Waterman Foundation was formally changed at the end of 1970 to the Haas Community Fund.

Community Medicine at the Spring Garden
Community Service Center, Philadelphia.

HEALTH CARE: *Intensive Cardiac Care*

In recent years there has been an encouraging
rise in the survival rate of heart-attack victims
hospitalized in institutions equipped with intensive cardiac care units. A significant portion of the foundation's support of health care
has been devoted to the establishment of such
units. Grants totaling $413,503 were made for
this purpose during the 1967–68–69 period.

HOUSING

The Maple Corporation, Philadelphia $200,000
The Foundation has been interested for sev-
eral years in methods of making good housing
available to people of low and moderate incomes. Grants totaling $570,000 have been
made in the past three years to establish and
expand the operations of the Maple Corporation, a nonprofit sponsor of such housing. The
corporation seeks to create home ownership
and rental units on an open occupancy basis,
for families of limited means in Philadelphia
and its suburbs.

RESEARCH

Academy of Natural Sciences, Philadelphia $ 95,583
The study of the interrelationship of plant life
and management of wild areas is fundamental
to the understanding and solution of many
problems. Grants were made to the Academy's
Department of Ecology and Land Management and to its Waterloo Mills Research Station in support of such ecological research.

SOCIAL WELFARE: *Child and Youth Activities*

Fellowship House and Farm, Philadelphia $ 25,000
An annual summertime problem is that of get-

ting underprivileged children out of the heat
of the city and into the countryside for a
change of scenery and interests. In "Operation Greengrass," thousands of Philadelphia
children were taken on trips to the open country and suburban recreational areas. The program was supported by a foundation grant and
by gifts from individuals, groups and other
foundations.

Philadelphia Council for Community Advance-
ment $ 20,000

Established in 1968 with the aid of a foundation grant, the Council's Project "IN" (for Interested Negroes) helps Negro children ex-
plore possible career areas. Under the program, operated in close cooperation with the
Philadelphia school system, children spend full
days with Negro adults engaged in various
professional and skilled occupations. At the
end of 1969 the project involved more than
1,400 students and 1,000 adult volunteers."

Although it shows no sign yet of severing its economic links with
the donor-family's enterprise, the Waterman Foundation has been
moving vigorously in the direction of greater social concern. Its
programs, though local in scope, are knowledgeable and forward-
looking. When necessary, it has freed itself from dependence on established community welfare institutions by creating new grantee
organizations to carry on innovative programs. The board, including members of the Haas family, takes its responsibilities seriously.
The staff has now grown to six full-time professionals, one of whom
is a black. If and when its board is broadened and diversified and
the financial ties between the foundation, the family, and the company are reduced, Waterman could move into the front ranks of
creative and independent American philanthropy.

The Henry J. Kaiser Family Foundation

This new California foundation (not to be confused with the Kaiser Foundation Health Plan and other foundations bearing the Kaiser name) is still in the process of being organized. Given the family context out of which it arises, it may be an institution of great promise. The donor, a man of prodigious energy and ingenuity, was one of the great builders and entrepreneurs in modern history. A high-school dropout from upstate New York, he began his business career as an errand boy in a dry goods store in Utica. By the time he died at the age of eighty-five he had built a multibillion dollar group of companies which operated 180 plants in thirty-two states and forty-four countries and employed more than 900,000 workers. In 1906 at the age of twenty-four, having decided to stake his future with the West, he moved to Spokane, Washington, and shortly thereafter entered the construction field. He developed a reputation as a road builder by using new production methods and by doing jobs better and faster than his competitors. In the late 1920s he completed a 200-mile, 500-bridge highway project in Cuba; and in the 1930s, the era of the big dams, he headed a consortium of companies that built the Hoover Dam in four years (two years ahead of schedule) and then Bonneville and Grand Coulee. By World War II, his construction company was building roads, bridges, dams, and pipelines all over America and had also set up a large cement-producing subsidiary. When the Allies desperately needed ships, Kaiser applied his innovative methods to ship-building, and by 1945 his company had built some 1,490 cargo vessels, roughly 30 percent of the American wartime production of merchant shipping, plus fifty small aircraft carriers.

After the war, Kaiser entered the aluminum business by leasing surplus plants from the War Assets Administration. The company today is the world's fourth-largest aluminum producer and also has extensive operations in chemicals, refractories, and agricultural fertilizers. In the same period he mobilized hundreds of millions of dollars of private capital to create the first fully integrated iron-

and-steel complex in the American West. It has now reached a capacity of three million ingot tons a year.

The array of companies he established reached well beyond basic industry. The Kaiser Jeep Corporation had achieved vehicle sales of more than $300 million annually when it was sold to American Motors Corporation in 1970. The Kaiser Broadcasting Corporation owns UHF television stations and FM radio stations throughout the United States. The Kaiser Aerospace and Electronics Corporation has become an important manufacturer of aircraft and missile components. In addition, Kaiser set up large and successful companies in building materials, prefabricated homes, engineering services, and real estate development. When he died in 1967, he was busy building the new community of Hawaii Kai in Honolulu for 60,000 residents.

Henry J. Kaiser was single-minded in his devotion to business; he had little time for politics or philanthropy. Yet some of the major projects he undertook for farsighted but practical business reasons had important social side effects. To increase productivity at his Kaiser Steel plants, for example, the company and the United Steel Workers of America joined in organizing a plan for sharing cost savings that has so far paid participating employees more than $20 million in cash bonuses and in benefit reserves. The plan also protects employees against technological displacement. (Because of Kaiser's decent treatment of his workers, the AFL-CIO in his later years awarded him a special medal stating that his lifelong theme was "the worker as a human being.")

His most important social contribution was his "Kaiser Foundation Medical Care Program"—a classic demonstration of Adam Smith's contention that the best things businessmen do for human well-being are done out of motives of profit, not charity. Kaiser became aware of the relationship between health care and worker productivity in the 1930s, when he was building pipelines and dams in locations far away from hospitals and doctors. Later, one of the greatest problems faced by his shipyards in meeting their war production goals was absenteeism due to illness. In order to keep his men healthy, Kaiser built health clinics at a number of his production sites. The financing of these clinics was provided out of government contracts, since their cost was accepted by the authorities as a bona fide operating expense. After the war the clinics and their equipment were declared surplus war property. The Kaiser Hospital Foundation was established by Kaiser and his wife, Bess, to buy them at 1 percent of cost.

With an initial contribution of $200,000, the Kaiser medical plan was born. It was based on five fundamental principles: voluntary membership open to the public; prepayment for services; group medical practice; emphasis on preventive services; and interrelated hospitals and medical offices. To ensure that the plan would be self-supporting, Kaiser created three separate cooperating entities —the Health Plan itself, which enrolls subscribers and collects their payments; the Hospital Foundation, which finances and operates the hospitals and medical clinics; and the Group Medical Organization, consisting now of some 1,500 doctors organized into their own partnerships. By this ingenious combination of industrial management concepts and financial planning in the field of health services, the objective of self-support without dependence on governmental or charitable subsidies has been achieved and the plan has become the world's largest private system of hospitals and prepaid medical care. Its facilities now include eighteen hospitals with 3,200 beds and more than forty medical clinics in three Western states. More than two million persons are now enrolled in the plan and the number is growing at the rate of 10 percent a year.

The plan's great success has not been achieved without opposition and some criticism. The California Medical Association fought it for years because of its group practice aspect, and it has been criticized by liberals on the ground that it does nothing for the very poor who are unable to pay the subscription fees. The National Advisory Commission on Health Manpower, however, published a special report on the plan in November 1967 and gave this evaluation:

The Kaiser Foundation Medical Care Program provides comprehensive services to more than a million and a half members [as of 1967] drawn primarily from the working population. These services are provided at significant savings by comparison with the cost for equivalent services purchased in the surrounding communities and the country at large.

The quality of care provided by Kaiser is equivalent, if not superior to that available in most communities. . . .

The program has achieved real economies, while maintaining high quality of care, through a delicate interplay of managerial and professional interest. This has resulted from structuring economic arrangements so that both professional and managerial partners have a direct economic stake in the successful and efficient operation of the overall program. As a result there has been created a cost consciousness among the professionals and a health care consciousness among the administrators which enables them to work toward a common goal without either sacrificing or overemphasizing their own points of view.

In setting up his major philanthropy in 1948, the Henry J. Kaiser Family Foundation, he seemed more interested in providing a vehicle for tax planning and estate management than in the execution of a charitable program. When Mrs. Kaiser died in 1951 she bequeathed her shares in the Kaiser companies to the foundation. Next, the younger of the two sons of Mr. and Mrs. Kaiser, Henry J., died in 1961 of multiple sclerosis and most of his stock holdings in the company were received by the foundation. The same was true after the death of his father in 1967. As of 1968, the combined assets of the foundation were valued at $106 million, and when all the shares from the three bequests have been received, it is anticipated that its assets will reach some $200 million. Initially the board was composed entirely of officers and directors of Kaiser Industries Corporation. (Members of the Kaiser family were prohibited from serving as trustees by the terms of the original trust.) E. E. Trefethen Jr., who had been Henry Kaiser's right-hand man in the company, was named the first president.

For a number of years the foundation received little or no dividend income from its Kaiser stock and its grants were minuscule. In 1969, Edgar Kaiser, the sole surviving son and head of the Kaiser companies, asked George D. Woods upon his retirement as head of the World Bank to become chairman and chief executive officer. Woods, an eminent investment banker, had been associated with the Kaiser family and companies for many years prior to his service in Washington. His first action was to have the board change the rule barring family members as trustees so that Edgar Kaiser could be elected. Next he formulated a statement of purposes, policies, and procedures for the foundation. According to this proposal, completed in May of 1970, the foundation would focus its activities in three major areas: the improvement of health and medical care, particularly in the state of California; community problems in the San Francisco–Oakland bay area; and general education, including schools, colleges, and universities.

Specifically, the foundation would continue to provide capital to the Kaiser Foundation Medical Care program to assist its expansion in California and into new regions of the United States. It would also continue its support of health and medical activities not related to the program, with preference given to requests from California. In the field of education the foundation's support might include assistance for the construction of facilities, grants for scholarships, fellowships or student loan programs, unrestricted grants to meet operating expenses, and grants for innovative or experimental educational projects. Woods's statement observed that the trustees of the foundation "are aware of the critical problems facing society today, problems which were little recognized several years ago. . . . The cities and the counties of the Bay Area are currently facing the same problems which are present in urban environments throughout the country—e.g., poverty, unemployment, inadequate schools, discrimination of all kinds, a high crime rate, inadequate housing and many more. Therefore the foundation intends to accelerate its active support of various public agencies and community improvement projects . . . particularly those dealing with the problems of the poor and disadvantaged."

Woods emphasized that the foundation would make no grants to any church or religious groups and would operate as a grant-making, not an operating, foundation. As to its investment policy, the foundation would not dispose of blocks of Kaiser Industries Corporation common stock "merely to diversify the investment portfolio or for the purpose of increasing current income."

The Kaiser Family Foundation is now activated and on its way.* If it can approximate the contributions to the public welfare

* In July 1972, Dr. Robert Glazer, who had been an outstanding medical dean at Stanford University and later vice-president of the Commonwealth Fund, became the new president.

through its philanthropic activities which the founder accomplished as a by-product of his business activities, it will compile a distinguished record indeed.

Conclusions

These, then, are among the best of the family-style foundations. The general level of their performance is greatly affected by the caliber and degree of dedication of the donor and his family. Characterized by small boards tied to the family and the family company, they typically operate with little professional staff. Their programs are concentrated on a locality or a region, and their grants are mostly of a traditional charitable kind.

But these are exceptions. When the donor has been a man of strength and of ambitious purpose, his foundation has been capable of innovations and large undertakings. In at least two of these five foundations, Astor and Waterman, the active interest and involvement of family members has given them a courage and warm-heartedness seldom found among the highly professionalized institutions and in most of them, along with much conservatism, there is some indication of change in the form of a growing interest in newer social issues. In their financial and investment policies, however, an equal degree of change is not evident. They are mostly interlinked with the donor's company, and he or his descendants are not inclined to diversify and weaken their control.

But predominant family influence over a foundation, whether good or bad, declines with time. Of these five, the family line will be broken in two cases with the death of the donor or the donor's widow. In the others, the family involvement is at present active and influential, but whether it will continue with the same intensity even through one more generation is doubtful.

14.

Fleischmann and Commonwealth: Two Intriguing Aberrations Land: A Gleam of Hope

IT MAY BE USEFUL to conclude these institutional portraits with two oddities and a ray of hope—a foundation that by most standard criteria ought to be one of the poorest, but is not; a foundation that should be one of the finest, but is not; and a new and unproven foundation that has unusual prospects.

The Max C. Fleischmann Foundation

This foundation's small, plain offices are located over a bank in Reno, Nevada. It has no professional staff. Its trustees draw substantial fees for their part-time services, and for many years they issued no reports to the public. Available information about its grants during its first decade of operation suggested a program of sheer banality relieved occasionally by ideological digression. But despite this background the Max C. Fleischmann Foundation must now be taken seriously. In terms of both program fields and operating procedure it contributes an important form of diversity to big philanthropy.

Max C. Fleischmann, the donor, was a son of the founder of the well-known Cincinnati yeast and gin company. After an undistinguished record at the Ohio Military Institute he entered the family firm at eighteen and predictably advanced rapidly in its hierarchy. In 1929, he sold his financial interest to the J. P. Morgan banking house for $20 million worth of stock in Standard Brands, Inc., of which he then became a director and eventually chairman of the board. Completing his active business career at a relatively early age, he retired to the pleasures of Santa Barbara and Lake Tahoe, devoting himself to various amusements—amorous, athletic, and civic. He became an enthusiastic yachtsman, polo player, duck hunter, and fisherman. He was for a time owner of the Cincinnati Reds baseball team and also an ardent explorer and big-game hunter. Known to his friends as Major—a title he acquired during World War I in the Balloon Corps—he never lost his boyish sense of adventure. At Lake Tahoe he added a certain color to the local scene through his activities as an honorary state policeman. Habitually attired in unmatching coat and trousers and a plaid shirt, with a .38-caliber pistol or two strapped to his belt, he relieved the tedium by quelling local disturbances and chasing down speeders along the highway.

He felt that his fortune was his own, to do with as he pleased. It pleased him to use some of it for charity, which he dispensed in his characteristically egocentric way. "I pick my own charities," he once declared. "It doesn't do anybody a damn bit of good to write to me." In Santa Barbara he made gifts to help build a breakwater for the yacht harbor, a beach playground, and three polo fields. In Nevada, he helped convert the old United States Mint in Carson City into a museum, and he was a generous contributor to the Boy Scouts. Among the various matters that engaged Fleischmann's active interest were not to be found the larger problems of the nation or the world. In so far as he could be said to have had a political or social philosophy, it was vaguely pro-business.

Presumably in the spirit of the founder's ideas, the chairman of the foundation's board of trustees declared in 1960 that its program "is built around a strong belief in the Free Enterprise System and the American Way of Life. Its program is to assist organizations and institutions which foster such a tradition." Fleischmann signed the trust agreement creating his foundation on March 23, 1951, in Douglas County, Nevada. A few months later, on learning he was suffering from incurable cancer, he committed suicide in his Santa Barbara home. His estate was appraised at $37 million at the time.

By the terms of his will the foundation was to dispose of its capital and be liquidated within twenty years after the death of his wife, Sara Hamilton Fleischmann, who died in 1960. The assets of the foundation were further increased by $10 million from her estate. By 1968 its holdings had a market value of just over $100 million.

To run the affairs of his foundation, Fleischmann designated six trustees—his widow, his private secretary, and four close friends. The trustees were given wide powers, but because of his dislike of administrative bureaucracy, the donor specified that they were personally to handle both the investments and the grants of his foundation. To make it worth their while, he provided for them to be compensated at "rates prescribed by law in the State of Nevada for a sole testamentary executor," which in 1968 meant that each of the six was receiving $30,000 a year for his services. In his original trust Fleischmann specified that the funds of the foundation were to be expended exclusively in the United States and only to organizations listed as tax exempt by the government. There were to be no grants to individuals. Shortly after its activation the trustees added that "the foundation's primary interest lay in the State of Nevada. Almost all of the grants from income are made to institutions and projects which were contributed to by Major Fleischmann in his lifetime."

When the foundation issued its first public report in 1963, the list of grants was found to be more interesting than had been anticipated. Mingled with the many small gifts to churches and the Camp Fire Girls were a series of substantial grants to improve the facilities and increase the quality of teaching of the then weak University of Nevada, especially in agricultural subjects; funds had also been given to help the university establish a Desert Research Institute. In an unusual departure the trustees had designed and funded a forward-looking antipollution program for the Lake Tahoe area. A survey had also been made of the needs of Nevada hospitals, followed by a series of grants for modern medical equipment which the scattered local communities could not themselves afford.

In recent years new program areas of special relevance to the West have been added: rural library development; educational opportunities for American Indians, Mexican-Americans, and other minority groups; wildlife protection; the conservation of natural resources; ecology and the environment; and atmospheric research. Since 1964, on a national level, the foundation has concerned itself with the administration of justice, particularly the training of state trial judges and the functioning of juvenile courts. Its work in this field has already won high praise from leading jurists, sociologists, and criminologists.

The Fleischmann Foundation's evolution is perhaps unexpected, but not entirely strange. The Fleischmanns had no children, so there has been no problem of donor-family domination; because of the nature of its assets the foundation has not been diverted by problems of corporate control or of property management. But primarily, the foundation's performance is a tribute to the special qualities and remarkable devotion of its trustees. Credit for their selection must be given to the donor, who evidently was a man of greater perception and seriousness than his behavior indicated.

One trustee, Sessions S. Wheeler, otherwise known as Buck, who now plays a leading part in the foundation's work in conservation and Indian affairs, served as Major Fleischmann's guide on hunting and fishing trips. A man of singular dedication to the West, he was at the time a teacher of biology in a Reno high school. The two men packed into wilderness areas together, explored Indian country, rode the high mesas, and became close friends. Fleischmann named Wheeler to the initial board of the foundation and his commitment to it has since become total. He has given up all other gainful employment to avoid any possible conflict of interest.

Some of the board members gather daily for conferences. A meeting of a majority of the trustees usually occurs at least once a week. They avoid any publicity that tends to honor them individually or collectively. In program planning, each trustee takes an active responsibility in his own field of special interest and competence. Requests for help have to be submitted in writing and there is no face-to-face contact with an applicant unless a grant is made. After that, frequent communication is maintained. The trustees seldom consult or cross-check with other foundations, preferring to judge applicants by their individual qualities rather than by their academic credentials. They "bet on the man more than his institution." [1]

As of 1970, the Fleischmann Foundation had begun to demonstrate a competence and creativity in its grant-making that compared with the best of the big foundations. To its credit, it has focused on a series of neglected problems that need foundation support. It provides a source of funds for a region of the United States that has few large-scale foundations, and it also provides a place where able mavericks—who are usually ignored by the big foundations—can receive a sympathetic hearing. In this respect, it makes a distinctive contribution to the pluralism of philanthropy itself.

One experienced observer evaluates Fleischmann in these terms: "I have great respect for all of the foundations with which I have been involved. But if I had to choose between professionalism and the Fleischmann kind of amateurism as a mode of foundation operation, I would choose the latter. It is an amateurism based on deep personal involvement and guided by great idealism and commitment. With all of the hazards and weaknesses it presents, I think on balance it renders a particularly valuable service to the public interest by providing some of genuine variety in our national life." [2]

In accordance with the donor's original wishes, the foundation is scheduled to go out of existence by 1980.

The Commonwealth Fund

In almost total contrast to the Fleischmann Foundation, the Commonwealth Fund of New York derives from an aristocratic family of humanitarian traditions, the Harknesses; it has long been professionalized; and until recent changes were introduced it had become the quintessence of orthodoxy.

The wealth of the donor family originated with the large fortune amassed by Stephen V. Harkness, an Ohio businessman who was one of John D. Rockefeller's original partners in the Standard Oil Company. After he died his wife moved her family to New York, where she became prominent as a generous supporter of various cultural projects and civic organizations. In 1918, she and her only surviving son, Edward S. Harkness, created the Commonwealth

Fund. He devoted his life to the administration of his family's financial and philanthropic interests. Those who knew him remember a slight, reticent man who acutely felt the burden and responsibility of great wealth. He administered the fund as he ran his life—earnestly, methodically, and ethically.

The board of trustees was drawn from a rather narrow sector of upper-class Easterners, usually fellow graduates of Yale, but it also included individuals of some diversity of viewpoint. To capitalize on this diversity, Harkness encouraged the active discussion of program matters at board meetings. Beginning with the appointment of Max Farrand, a professor of history from Yale, as general director, Harkness gradually built a small but highly competent staff, which he encouraged to act on its own and to participate in policy deliberations.

The program of the fund was systematically constructed. In its first annual report, issued in 1919, Farrand wrote: "The responsibility which rests upon the Directors to use to the best advantage the funds which have been placed in their trust is a heavy one, and the General Director recommends that they should not be in haste to reach a conclusion in determining lines of policy." He further remarked that "the staff is seeking light from every quarter, and is giving its best time and attention to a study of the whole subject of philanthropic and charitable work" to identify the field or fields in which the fund should concentrate. Out of this process emerged a varied program which reflected both the breadth of Harkness' interests and a courageous concern in the repressive atmosphere of the early 1920s for the problems of the urban and rural poor.

Barry C. Smith succeeded Farrand in mid-1921 and started a series of innovative programs, many in the field of medicine and health services. An educational research committee was established which, over the next seven years, made a large number of grants for studies on such problems as the financing of public schools, improvement of their curricula, and the reorganization of public educational systems. The welfare of children was also a strong initial interest, and the fund actively participated in the development of the new professional disciplines of child psychology, child psychiatry, and psychiatric social work. Demonstration child guidance clinics were established in a number of major cities. Visiting teachers trained in child guidance work were placed in thirty communities in different parts of the United States, and with fund assistance a number of major research studies on the prevention of juvenile delinquency were completed.

In addition, the fund in 1922 launched a child health demonstration program that also introduced new educational methods. In two small cities (Fargo, North Dakota and Athens, Georgia) and in two rural areas (Rutherford County, Tennessee and Marion County, Oregon) it installed temporary staff to give pediatric and nursing services for children and mothers in local clinics and to develop health education programs in the schools. These demonstration projects, particularly the one in Rutherford County, dramatized the great need for better pediatric and maternal care in rural areas and for better facilities and standards of patient care in all community hospitals. In 1926 the fund established its division of rural hospitals, which assisted a number of communities to build and maintain small hospitals, all directed by representative lay boards. During that period when the American Medical Association was falling increasingly under the control of rural and racist practitioners, it was noteworthy that the new hospitals created with the help of the fund had medical staffs open to all reputable physicians; and they offered care without restriction as to the race, color, creed, or economic status of the patients.

In another sphere, Edward Harkness, through the fund, sought to realize one of his most cherished personal dreams. Proud of his own Scottish heritage, he had a special admiration for the British people which was further increased by their courageous recovery after World War I. To strengthen the ties of Anglo-American friendship, a fellowship program was established by which a number of British graduate students were brought to the United States each year for advanced training. In time, this program, which achieved a high reputation for the excellence of its selections, was extended to other countries of the Commonwealth and to Western Europe.

Through the 1930s, Harkness' personal interest in the fields of medicine and public health grew and the fund acquired an increasingly strong medical orientation. This tendency was given a major thrust in 1937 when he made a large personal gift designated specifically for medical research and medical education; in that same year a program of advanced medical fellowships was initiated.

In 1940, after twenty-two years of personal direction of the fund, Harkness died. His death marked the close of its brilliant first period and the beginning of its second, which proved less brilliant. Malcolm P. Aldrich, who then assumed leadership, was to be its dominant figure for almost thirty years. He was a man of modest origins who achieved an outstanding record at Yale, especially in athletics. After graduation, he went to work for Edward Harkness, one of Yale's most loyal as well as most wealthy alumni. Able and ambitious, Aldrich soon solidified his position in his patron's favor and, at the same time, through his management of the Harkness family's large investments, built a circle of influential friends among the well-placed Elis on Wall Street. Edward Harkness' only brother, with whom he had been close, had died a few years earlier and that, as well as his childlessness, left him a rather lonely man. He and Aldrich developed a relationship that was like that of father and son. Upon Harkness' death, Aldrich was named executor of his estate as well as his successor as chairman of the board of the Commonwealth Fund.

At the time the foundation was vigorous and effective, and Aldrich introduced no abrupt changes. But little by little the influence of his more limited outlook took effect. The board became heavily weighted with his Yale friends from the financial community. The program continued for a time to include some unusual projects that reflected the fund's earlier spirit. But it gradually lost its experimental quality and sense of social concern and, apart from the international fellowships program, came to center almost exclusively on medical research and education. This shift accorded with what Aldrich asserted to be the direction of Harkness' desires, and it clearly fitted his own preferences for professional elegance and respectability.

After World War II, the rural hospital program was closed down when Congress passed the Hill-Burton Act, which made large-scale federal funds available for local hospital construction. Slightly later, and for reasons much less clear, the division of public health was discontinued after achieving an outstanding record in strengthening public and preventive health services in many parts of the nation. The fund's reasons were stated in these words: "By the late 1940s it was evident that public health as a professional field had become well established and was receiving strong support from local, state and federal sources. The need for the pioneering kind of assistance that the Fund had given it in its earlier years had greatly diminished." [3] Then the fund's activities in mental health were sharply cut back on similar grounds.

In 1946 Barry Smith helped bring into being the Rochester (New York) Regional Hospital Council, an early and successful model of areawide planning and institutional cooperation in the more efficient use of hospital facilities, and the Hunterdon Medical Center in New Jersey, an equally fruitful experiment in the local delivery of medical care. A year later, after a quarter-century of service, Smith retired, and after a decent interval Aldrich assumed the title of general director in addition to that of chairman of the board. Thereafter the withdrawal from other fields and concentration of the fund's work solely in medical education was accelerated. The transformation of the fund from an initiative-taking, idea-generating institution into a service facility at the disposition of the leading members of the academic medical establishment within a few years became almost complete. This evolution was signaled and reinforced by the addition to the fund's board of David P. Barr, chairman of Cornell's department of medicine, in 1946, and especially of George P. Berry, dean of Harvard's medical school, who was elected to the board in 1950.

Its new program displayed both the virtues and weaknesses of a foundation responsive essentially to technocratic rather than social needs. It continued to give numerous fellowships for advanced training to members of medical school faculties. It also made major grants to improve the teaching approach at existing medical schools. Several were assisted in conducting experiments in tutorial education and in integrating the basic and clinical sciences in the study of physiological systems and disease processes. The fund helped Barr's New York Hospital–Cornell Medical Center to experiment with what was called "comprehensive medical care," that is, concern not only with the patient's specific disease but also with its effects on his personal well-being and that of his family. And to help medical schools break away from the tradition of rigidly prescribed courses of study and much rote learning, it helped a few medical schools, notably Western Reserve University, to reformulate their curricula and teaching methods. The boldest aspect of the fund's program during these years was its assistance for the creation of a number of new medical schools.

By the early 1960s, Aldrich had made the fund into a trim and tidy ship set on a safe and careful course. Like the Hartford Foundation, it had adopted a servicing approach, but it dealt with a higher level of problems—essentially the institutional needs of medical schools rather than the projects of individual researchers. Its program earned the respect of the most reputable figures of the medical and academic establishments. The elderly staff performed its habitual functions capably, and the board was a congenial and untroublesome circle of friends, responsive to Aldrich's wishes. But by the 1960s, the inequities and inadequacy of the nation's system of health services, which had been growing worse for many years, reached catastrophic proportions. Principal responsibility for the situation could be attributed to the greed and social indifference of the medical profession itself. But the fund, which had conceded the direction of its program to the academic leadership of that profession, had to accept some of the discredit itself.

At about the same time Aldrich began the painful process of relinquishing control of the fund to someone else, not because of any apparent awareness of the swelling social disaster in the health field but inexorably because his retirement date was approaching. His first concern was to find a proper successor as executive head, and he found a younger man at hand who eminently fulfilled his criteria of familiarity and continuity. The man was J. Quigg Newton, a Yale man and an old friend of Aldrich (they had first come to know one another as naval officers in World War II in Washington). He was thoroughly familiar with the fund, having served as a member of its board from 1958 until 1962, and he was well tai-

lored, well mannered, and socially presentable. In addition, he had
other qualities and experience to make him acceptable to that minority of the board who were not totally satisfied with the
orthodoxy of the Aldrich regime and who were ready, even eager,
for some decided changes in the fund's program. Newton had had
experience in practical politics as the mayor of Denver; he had a
philanthropic background, having served in the Ford Foundation
as a vice-president for public relations for a period after 1962; and
he had credentials as an academic administrator, having been
president of the University of Colorado between 1956 and 1963
where he acquired a mildly progressive reputation by his opposition to unethical recruiting practices for football players and his
defense of the freedom of the school's newspaper to criticize such
public figures as Senator Barry Goldwater and former President
Eisenhower. Newton was named executive head of the fund in
1963.

But Aldrich continued to maintain an office in the magnificent
old Harkness mansion where the fund has its headquarters, and as
his mandatory retirement as a member of the board approached,
his fellow trustees made special provision for him as an "honorary
director" to attend board meetings. His brother Hulbert, who had
been elected a director in 1963, was simultaneously moved forward
as heir-apparent for the chairmanship of the board. With the
groundwork well laid, it astonished few observers when Malcolm
stepped down as active chairman in 1968 that his brother was
named to succeed him.

In retrospect, Aldrich is an inviting figure to caricature: a real-
life Frank Merriwell who, by ambitious determination cloaked in
charm, eventually captured the great Harkness wealth. But he is a
far more honorable and substantial person than appearances would
suggest. He exemplifies concepts of personal responsibility to a
donor and a philosophy of trusteeship which in times past have been
considered wholly acceptable if not admirable and which, because
they are still not uncommon in the big foundations, require
thoughtful examination. Aldrich, in taking over after Edward
Harkness, believed he was inheriting a mantle, a rigorous obligation to maintain the spirit and tradition of the donor. He believed

that the donor's trust could best be executed by assembling as board members a group of intimate friends, each of whom had been demonstrably "successful" in life. As a financial man himself, Aldrich naturally measured success in financial terms.

But however sincere Aldrich's intentions, the result of his approach was to put a dead hand on the tiller of Edward Harkness' foundation for nearly thirty years, to subordinate it to the guild interests of institutionalized academic medicine, and to make it indifferent to the economic, social, and moral deformities of the American health system, defects which have been public knowledge at least since the reports of the Ray Lyman Wilbur Commission in the early 1930s.

Quigg Newton, although he is Aldrich's choice as successor, manifestly intends to redefine the Harkness legacy and its obligations in his own terms. Newton was selected largely for reasons of continuity, and he took over his post in that spirit. Since then— slowly at first but at increasing tempo more recently—he has begun to alter the direction of the fund's program as well as its implicit governing social values. In a general review and analysis which he submitted to the board shortly after becoming president, he urged that the fund remain primarily in the medical field and that it build upon, rather than abandon, its extensive experience and network of associations with the leadership of the American medical profession. Despite the tremendous growth of governmental activity in the health field, he felt there was an important role and opportunity for a competent private agency. But he suggested that the fund interpret its commitment to medicine more broadly to include the social and economic inadequacies of the entire American medical system.

Later, in his 1969 annual report, Newton struck a note that, in comparison with the bland pronouncements of his predecessor, smacked almost of radicalism:

American medicine and medical education have entered a crisis of the most sobering dimension. Medical services are fragmented, maldistributed, costly, and to a substantial number of people—especially the rural and urban poor—exceedingly difficult to obtain.

That these deficiencies prevail within medical care structures built on high standards of scientific and professional excellence underscores the inability of our existing health arrangements to translate the vital store of medical knowledge and skill into an attainable benefit for society as a whole. . . . A chief task ahead therefore is to improve the institutional, organizational, managerial, and financial framework governing the delivery of medical care; in short to develop effective, economical systems of health care.

Thus, as the Commonwealth Fund entered its second half-century, it began to describe its goals and priorities in a new vocabulary—or perhaps more accurately, in the old vocabulary of social concern which was its trademark in the early 1920s when Edward Harkness was at the helm. To implement these reformulated objectives, Newton has begun, with the guiding and helping hand of the Carnegie Corporation in several instances, to search more actively for promising projects relating to the health needs of the ghettos, the problems of violence and drug addiction, and the complex questions of environmental health and the mental health of society in general. As part of his effort to rebuild the staff he brought in as vice-president Dr. Robert Glazer, formerly of the Stanford medical school, a man with a reputation as an innovator and reformer. In an unusual move, Glazer was also named a trustee, reflecting a feeling of several on the board that the time had come to break up the old clique and broaden the membership.° The third chapter of the fund's career has now opened; there is definite promise of renovation and reinvigoration.

The Edwin H. and Helen Land Foundation of Cambridge

To the naked eye, the Land Foundation gives the appearance of a commonplace philanthropy oddly joined to a man and a company (Polaroid) of surpassing innovativeness. But beneath the surface are some hitherto obscured developments that give grounds

° Dr. Glazer left the fund to become president of the newly activated Kaiser Foundation in mid-1972.

for the belief it could shortly burst forth as a highly creative institution.

The visible facts are quickly told and are unimpressive. This newest of the large foundations was founded by Mr. and Mrs. Land in 1961 and was supported in its first years at a modest level by annual gifts from them. In 1967 Mrs. Land transferred to it one million shares of Polaroid common stock that by 1968 had a market value of $107 million. Its board is made up of four family members, the donors and their two daughters. Until 1971 it had no formulated program or professional staff. Its scattered grants to various universities, museums, and civic organizations were decided by the family and administered by the secretary, Julius Silver, a New York attorney and a lifelong friend and business associate of Edwin Land. For 1968 they totaled only $154,000 and for 1969 $342,000—0.1 percent and 0.2 percent of the foundation's asset value in those respective years. Until passage of the 1969 Tax Reform Act requiring public reports, the Land Foundation had issued none.

Its mediocre record during its first decade may be radically changed in the future, however, because its founder and dominant personality, Dr. Edwin H. Land, has only recently begun to take a serious interest in it. This is of more than ordinary significance because he is very probably the most remarkable individual to create a large foundation since Andrew Carnegie, John D. Rockefeller Sr., and Julius Rosenwald, the giants of the early twentieth century.

Now a young-looking sixty-one years of age, Land has been most widely recognized as a scientific genius. But in his shy, reflective way he is also a social visionary, preaching a gospel of human self-realization through scientific progress, industrial democracy, and educational reform. And he has sought systematically to put his ideas into action through the instruments at his disposal, namely his laboratory (where he still spends a large proportion of his time), his company (which he fully controls as chief executive officer and principal shareholder), and his swelling personal fortune (an increasing part of which is now being committed to philanthropy).

Out of his laboratory has come a spectacular succession of research achievements in the fields of polarized light, photography, and color vision. Based on these discoveries, he has provided Polaroid with a flow of highly marketable inventions which have now made it one of the most rapidly growing and profitable corporations in the United States.

Land's ideas about the organization and leadership of the company have been as unorthodox as his efforts in the laboratory. He first stated them in a speech in 1944, when Polaroid had only begun its dazzling development:

The business of the future will be a scientific, social, and economic unit. It will be vigorously creative in pure science, where its contributions will compare with those of the universities. . . .

Internally this business will be a new type of social unit. There will be a different kind of boundary between management and labor. All will regard themselves as *labor* in the sense of having as their common purpose learning new things and applying that knowledge for public welfare. . . .

Economically such small scientific manufacturing companies can, I believe, carry us quickly into the next and best phase of the industrial revolution. . . .

Each individual will be a member of a group small enough so that he feels a full participant in the purpose and activity of the group. His voice will be heard and his individuality recognized. He will not feel the bitter need, now felt by countless thousands, for becoming a member of a great mystic mass movement that will protect him and give him a sense of importance.[4]

In the years since he has not deviated from this philosophy. In 1958 he told the annual meeting of the shareholders:

The dream of Polaroid for a generation has been to arrive at a one-class society, a society in which we are all scientist, inventor, manager, builder. A society in which there is no hierarchy, such as we now inherit from the older industries; no groups and strata, and little difference between jobs, between the foremen and the supervisors, and the general managers, the assistant general managers, and the people to be rated and the raters. . . .

We have brought into industry from feudal times, a feudal structure. Industry still has an aristocracy. In a country like America, where we left behind the social strata of England and France, where we left behind the nobility, there is a hidden appetite to create a new nobility and a new aristocracy. . . .

What we would like to build at Polaroid is a nonfeudal society. We would like to build a society that carries . . . a genuine feeling that when you walk into your company, you are not walking out of your neighborhood; that when you walk into your company you are not walking into a social niche from which you have to fight your way upward, or from which you look down at somebody else working for you.[5]

The same year, at the Christmas party for his employees, he remarked: "My fantasy is this: that we can now use the industrial system at the same time we are making cameras; that we can use this system for another thing, and that is to find out what's inside each of your heads and hearts, to find out how to make each one of you an individual and find a channel . . . for the fulfillment for your personal growth." [6]

The evangelistic, egalitarian tone of these statements by a man whose fortune is now in the hundreds of millions might readily be discounted as the naïveté of the scientist who ventures too far from his laboratory into unfamiliar social and economic realms, or as a slick new brand of paternalism, or even as hypocrisy. But the persistence with which he has attempted to put his ideas into effect testifies at least to the genuineness of his motivation.

In 1959 he launched a "Pathfinder Program" whereby workers on the production line at Polaroid could spend half their time in research, in the library, or in other branches of the company. It eventually foundered on unanticipated operational difficulties. Undiscouraged, he then set the goal in 1960 of an hour a day in class for all employees, an effort which met with greater success. As of 1970, the company was making available on a cost-free basis various kinds of educational opportunities to all its 8,000 employees, of whom some 2,700 were actually enrolled in various training programs within the company or in nearby universities.

In reacting to demands during the 1960s to increase employment opportunities for blacks, Polaroid under Land's leadership showed far more initiative than most major companies. He explained the company's approach to the problem to a special meeting of the company's employees on May 3, 1968:

We will seek out together those ways of bringing into the company people who need to work here; bringing into the company black people at the proper level of competence for each one of them. And then when they are here, depending on what their need is, we will provide that need. If they are people, as many of them are, who have every bit of competence and distinction that anyone of us has, then we need to do nothing about them except enjoy them. If they are people who have never worked; who have never seen work; whose father was unable to get work; who have never had the experience of knowing what it is to get to a job on time—they have never seen a job—then each department has to be tender and creative and help that person to be productive and effective.

Some of you may find in yourselves—a very few of you—those latent instincts of the clan, the tribal instincts, that make it impossible for you to accept in your immediate company people who seem different to you simply because they look different. . . .

Let us take these people who have been isolated in a cul-de-sac of history; who through no fault of their own have been stranded and left abandoned—a portion of America that no proud American can dare let exist. I hear the majority of the people in the company, the *great* majority, saying, "Let us all work together on this; let's work together on taking them in, on training them, on making them a happy part of our community." [7]

On the basis of this policy, over 20 percent of the newly hired employees since have been black. And partly as a result, Polaroid was soon confronted with a new pressure. In 1970 some of its growing number of black employees at that time organized demonstrations protesting the company's business activities in South Africa. The group demanded that it end its business ties and turn over the profits it had earned to groups fighting that government's policy of racial segregation and discrimination.

In response, the company set up a biracial group of employees to study the problem, including the moral issue of whether it was right or wrong to do business in South Africa. After weeks of interviews and discussion, including a visit to South Africa itself, the group made its recommendations, which the company then adopted and announced in newspaper advertisements throughout the United States and in South Africa itself: Polaroid would "for the time being" continue its business relationships in South Africa but on a new, experimental basis. It would attempt to improve dramatically the salaries and other benefits of the nonwhite South African employees. It would initiate a program to train them for higher positions. It would commit a portion of its profits in South Africa to various educational projects for blacks. It would make no further sales to the South African government itself. And after twelve months of operation on the new basis it would take a careful look to see what effects its actions had had in order to determine whether to continue further or whether to pull out of that racially troubled region of Africa entirely. Polaroid's actions went considerably further than those of any other major American corporation which has been faced with a similar challenge, particularly its explicit commitment to the moral and political principle of human equality.*

Just as Land has had his own strong conceptions about transforming the work experience of his employees, so he has had his distinctive notions about the reform of education. As a young student at Harvard more than forty years ago, he left after one year to carry out his own program of research in connection with the polarization of light. Two years later he returned to the university, having already achieved a number of patentable research discoveries. But a year later he left again, this time for good, to pursue his own independent scientific work.

His personal experience as a student is reflected in the educational credo he first expressed in a lecture at the Massachusetts Institute of Technology on May 22, 1957. In this period he was the holder of a special lectureship at the university, and he said of the undergraduates with whom he had come in contact that he believed "each of them felt secretly—it was his very special secret and his deepest secret—that he could be great. . . . But not many undergraduates come through our present educational system retaining this hope. . . . [A student] is told the moment he arrives that his secret dream of greatness is a pipe dream, that it will be a long time before he makes a significant personal contribution—if ever."

* In late 1971 the company published the detailed results of its South African experiment, on the basis of which it has now decided to continue its business operations in that country.

Land then proposed, as a means of remedying the defects of the
existing approach to teaching, that a freshman upon entering the
university would immediately become a member of a small group
of perhaps about ten so that he could have intimate association
from the first with a mature scholar. In addition, he should be
started at once on his own research project—"to preserve his secret
dream of greatness and make it come true." His other suggestions
to reconstitute "the university of the future" were that it discard
the present grading system "in favor of one which would enable
the student to check his accomplishment but would not encumber
the relationship between the student and his professor." It should
introduce students to the several fields of science through courses
designed not to screen out nonspecialists but rather to give them
the essential insights and ideas in these fields, and it should preserve and multiply the best teaching of the best lecturers by the
greater use of motion pictures.

In the years since, he has provided MIT and Harvard University,
two institutions with which he has close contact, with substantial
funds to establish programs to implement his educational ideas. In
the case of Harvard, he has given several hundred thousand dollars to finance a program of freshman seminars which give students
close association with a faculty member and provide for independent, relatively unstructured study and research. There are no lectures, no exams, and no grades. For the benefit of MIT he has
created a charitable trust of $100 million—separate from the Land
foundation—the income of which is currently given to support the
Land Education Development Fund. Under its aegis some fifteen
experimental projects are being conducted, including one for undergraduate research opportunities, for unified science study, and
for research in new teaching methods. Thorough research on these
experiments has been done, the results of which indicate highly encouraging response by both faculty members and undergraduates
who have participated.

Edwin Land in the past has used his company and personal
charitable gifts as the means of applying his ideas about human
development, new teaching methods, and the enrichment of the industrial work environment. Now, in addition, he is beginning to

turn to the more structured instrument of his foundation. If he proves to be as able a foundation builder as he has been inventor and corporate innovator, he will render a major national service. For American philanthropy has not felt the buoyant force of a truly great donor for nearly half a century.

Part Three

PATTERNS, PROCESSES, AND PERFORMANCE

15.

A Profile of Big Philanthropy

HAVING DRAWN the individual portraits of the major foundations, we are able now to trace a profile of their general features. The dimensions of this profile include the *programmatic*, their patterns of behavior in grant-making and the nature of their programs; the *financial*, the interrelationships between the foundations and the bodies of wealth from which they emanate, as well as their practices in managing that wealth; and the *evolutionary*, the patterns of change which are observable in their external linkages, programs, and general behavior with the passage of time.

The Programmatic Dimension

Most of the big foundations were conceived as traditional family-style charities, not as professionalized institutions. The enormous prestige of the Rockefeller Foundation, with its proclaimed objectives of getting at the causes of human problems rather than treating merely the symptoms and of advancing the frontiers of knowledge, has helped to create the impression that its lofty standards characterize the larger foundations as a group. Similarly, some of the better and more articulate foundations, such as Carnegie, Ford, and Danforth have frequently spoken of "mounting systematic attacks on major problems," "mapping out long-term program strategies," and "exploring through creative experimentation and demonstration new solutions to the critical dilemmas of our society," thereby reinforcing a common impression that the large foundations in general are sophisticated, energetic, and innovative.

Unfortunately, they are not. The majority are unprofessional, passive, ameliorative institutions: they basically offer the multitude of useful nonprofit organizations in American life which depend on contributions "another door to knock on" in meeting their current operating needs and capital requirements.

Their preferred fields of activity are located squarely in the center of a spectrum ranging from the older forms of charity and individual relief at one extreme to advanced social and scientific experimentation at the other. They are primarily attracted to education and secondarily to medical sciences and health. The Foundation Library Center, in its review of foundation activities for 1968, gave a rough division of major fields in which grants of $10,000 or more were reported by foundations of all sizes (see Table 3).

Table 3

The Fields of Foundation Activity

Fields	1967		1968	
	Amount (millions)	Percent	Amount (millions)	Percent
Education	$191	33	$308	41
Sciences	79	13	106	14
International activities	84	15	93	12
Health	81	14	77	10
Welfare	82	14	74	10
Humanities	39	7	72	10
Religion	24	4	23	3
Total	$580	100	$753	100

Source: Foundation News, January 1969.

For the year 1968 the Peterson Commission asked a representative sample of foundations to classify their grants by fields. It found that education, health, medicine, and general welfare received more than 65 percent of all grants; education received 31 percent of the total, medicine 21 percent, and general welfare 14 percent.[1] The major exception to the traditionality of the grant patterns is the limited concern with religion. Only a handful of the large foundations make religious institutions and activities a major part of their programs, and several avoid the field entirely.

The big foundations, as well as the smaller ones, have a strong preference for making their gifts to established, reputable institutions which are offically certified as tax-exempt. The Peterson Commission found that 94 percent of all foundation grants were allocated to such recipients. Of the remainder, 3 percent of their outlays went to individuals in the form of scholarships and fellowships; another 3 percent went to newly established nonprofit bodies within the United States which had not yet received a U.S. Treasury ruling of tax exemption, or to foreign organizations.[2]

In education, the "alma mater factor" is conspicuously present and many of the grants to universities are designated for buildings and equipment. In the sciences, medical research is overwhelmingly the largest subcategory; the social sciences receive relatively little. Under the rubric of health, hospitals and medical schools receive nearly three-quarters of the total. In the welfare field, "community funds" are the prime recipients. Cultural activities and institutions are of interest to many of the larger foundations; the largest individual gifts are for physical facilities and general support for museums, libraries, and art centers.

In their grant-making procedures, most of the big foundations are more reactive than active, relying upon the initiatives of others. Because most donors have envisioned their foundations as vehicles for the simple distribution of charitable gifts, relatively few employed competent professionals at the beginning and, at present, only about one-third have fully developed and qualified staffs. Because of this lack, they seldom attempt to take the lead in identifying and filling institutional gaps in society or in launching new experimental programs. The majority of them can be compared to bankers, waiting for loan applications to be presented; and like any careful banker, they tend to give preference to the applicants who are familiar, who can present good credentials, and who are generally "sound."

In the geographical scope of their programs, most of them are essentially local institutions. Some largely confine their work to a single city—the Astor Foundation to New York, the Mott Foundation to Flint, the Houston Endowment to Houston, the Moody Foundation to Galveston, and the Haas Community Fund (formerly the Phoebe Waterman Foundation) to Philadelphia. Several

confine their activities to certain states—the Duke Endowment to
North and South Carolina, the Kaiser Foundation to San Francisco
and California, the Lilly Endowment to the region around Indianapolis, R. K. Mellon and Scaife to Pittsburgh and western Pennsylvania, the Nemours Foundation to Florida and Delaware, the Irvine Foundation to California, and the Fleischmann Foundation to
Nevada and California.

Several others are not primarily local, but place strong emphasis
in their programs on particular areas: the Rockefeller Brothers
Fund on New York City, A. W. Mellon on New York and Virginia,
Kettering on Ohio, Danforth on St. Louis, the Pew Memorial on
Philadelphia, the Surdna Foundation on Yonkers, Woodruff on Atlanta and Georgia, Longwood on Delaware and an adjacent locality in Pennsylvania. The Kresge Foundation has until recently
been interested primarily in Detroit and the northeastern region of
the United States, where most of the company's stores are located.
Relatively few of the big foundations see themselves as national institutions; only a small minority—Carnegie, Commonwealth, Ford,
Kellogg, and Rockefeller—have any important commitment to international programs.

There is much to be said, of course, for this concentration in a
given locality, even though it tends to deprive those areas of the
United States which are relatively lacking in large foundations—
notably the Rocky Mountain region and the Northwest—of access
to philanthropic funds. But if some localities are without large
foundations, others, such as Flint and Houston may be smothering
in them. Thus many of the big foundations, though pluralistic factors in American life in one sense, are powerful monolithic influ-
ences in the cultural and educational affairs of particular cities and
areas.

Finally, contrary to a widespread popular belief, the programs of
the big foundations are not on the whole reformist, nor are they
slanted to the far Right or the far Left. With few exceptions, their
basic approach is benign and benevolent, not ideological. A clear
and consistent radicalism—either in defense of or in opposition to
the *status quo*—is the last charge of which big foundations can be
found guilty.

The Financial Dimension:
Administrative Costs

The sumptuous quarters from which a few of the big foundations operate have created a strong suspicion that they are extravagant in their spending. But, in fact, most of them would do well to spend more, not less, on staff and administration. Some indeed are wasteful, but in general high administrative costs and vigorous programs seem to be correlated, as do low costs and poor programs.

The qualifications to this judgment, however, must be specified. First, foundation accounting practices are so diverse and lacking in cost consciousness that no precise comparisons can be made. It is not even possible to distinguish clearly in many cases between administrative costs in the general overhead sense and those that are related to the operation of "in house" projects and programs such as laboratories, clinics, and study commissions.°

Second, there does appear to be a greater sense of administrative thriftiness on the part of the family-style foundations, particularly while the donor is still alive, than among the independent, professionalized institutions. The former tend to operate from simple, even spartan offices; the latter from premises which are not only handsome but sometimes palatial. Salaries of foundation professionals are not as high as those of corporation executives, but they are usually well above those of their academic and government counterparts. (The upper limit is marked by the $130,000 salary paid to the chairman of the Kellogg Foundation board.) In addition to salary, foundation staff enjoy exceptionally generous perquisites in the form of insurance and retirement benefits as well as travel and entertainment allowances. It is not the style of the most

---

° The Peterson Commission estimated "administrative costs" to have averaged less than 3 percent of grants in 1968. (See its Report, p. 87). However, Representative Patman estimated them for the largest foundations the same year at 16.9 percent of grants. (See U.S. Congress, Staff Report of the Subcommittee on Domestic Finance of the Committee on Banking and Currency, *The Fifteen Largest U.S. Foundations: Financial Structure and the Impact of the Tax Reform Act of 1969*, 92C1 / July 15, 1971 / p. 15.)

prominent big foundations, therefore, to live in rags—as more than one impecunious professor has resentfully noted after being told that his request for a small grant had to be rejected "for budgetary reasons."

Third, the margin of possible waste in certain cases does not negate the fact that the major portion of "administrative costs" of the professionalized foundations goes into staff research and planning—the indispensable ingredient if foundations are to be more than simple check-writing operations. Thus the low expenses of the typical family-style foundation can be highly deceptive, obscuring the possibly high costs to society of a foundation that makes little purposeful use of its resources or that serves its own private interests more than those of charity. Paradoxically, therefore, the seemingly low-cost foundations are frequently very high cost in social terms, and vice versa.*

FINANCIAL TIES

Foundation annual reports habitually observe a discreet silence on the continuing relationship between philanthropy and the wealth from which it springs; it is as if foundations were created by some process resembling Immaculate Conception, and that once born their purity remains unstained by contact with the sordid

---

* Dr. Amitai Etzioni has elaborated a general theory by which one can gauge the professional quality of an institution's program by the ratio of resources invested "in the cybernetic overlay—which guides, reviews, and revises—and the action underlay." See his *The Active Society* (New York, Free Press, 1968), ch. 5. He proposes the development of a set of expenditure ratios for foundations, including the following divisions:

a) $\dfrac{\text{in-house}}{\text{total expenditures}}$ and b) $\dfrac{\text{in-house: professional}}{\text{in-house: administrative}}$

For example, when ratio (a) is very low, the foundation could be called a *conduit* foundations, serving essentially to transfer resources from donor to grantee. When it is relatively high, and when most of the in-house expenditures are for administration, this might identify the *self-serving* foundation. When the ratio is relatively high but most of the expenditures are for professional functions (in-house research, project development and guidance, and assistance to grantees), this might sort out the *guiding* foundation. Before such distinctions can be meaningfully made, however, foundations will have to improve their reporting practices greatly and adopt more uniform accounting procedures.

world of private economic interest. Such, of course, is hardly the case. Foundations derive from, and generally have remained intimately involved with, specific corporations or, in some cases, specific assets in the form of land, buildings, or mineral rights.

Among the big foundations there are only a few cases where a donor's resources have been transferred to an independent philanthropic institution not heavily influenced by his descendants or interconnected with his company or companies. Where this has occurred, as with Carnegie, Commonwealth, Fleischmann, and Sloan, it seems to have resulted from the childlessness of the donor and from his ownership either of diverse securities or of a relatively minor percentage of a gigantic enterprise, such as General Motors.° The typical situation is one in which the donor has children as well as other relatives, and in which he has been the dominant shareholder of one or at most a few enterprises, the control of which upon his death passes to his foundation or to his family or to a combination of both. This results in a triple interlinkage which is both intimate and enduring.

Of the big foundations almost two-thirds are closely connected with donor families through representation on their boards, and with associated companies through their own stockholdings and the holdings of trustees who are family members.† The triangular relationship is sometimes reinforced by the presence of officers of the associated company on the foundation's board. There are three cases—Hartford, Irvine, and Kellogg—where the family as such

° Of the donors of the thirty-three major foundations, ten were childless— Vincent Astor, Herman Brown, A. G. Bush, Stephen Harkness, Max Fleischmann, John A. Hartford, Jesse Jones, Pierre S. du Pont, Sid W. Richardson, and Alfred P. Sloan. In addition, Richard King Mellon's four children were all adopted; Mrs. Ailsa Mellon Bruce died childless, her only daughter having been killed in an accident; and Alfred A. du Pont, at the time he established his Nemours Foundation, was estranged from his children by an earlier marriage.

† For example, Brown, Bush, Danforth, Duke, Haas (Waterman), Houston, Kaiser, Kresge, Land, Lilly, Longwood, A. W. Mellon, Moody, Mott, Nemours, Pew, Richardson, Rockefeller, Scaife, Surdna, and Woodruff. Company-foundation links in the case of Bush have now been severed by court order; family participation in the case of Duke is limited, but company ties are very strong; the connection between A. W. Mellon and several family-controlled companies is being reduced.

has disappeared or almost disappeared from the picture, but where the foundation is clamped in a strong bilateral relationship through stockholdings and cross-membership of boards with an associated company.

Of the thirty-three only four can be said to be without significant donor-family or corporate ties—Carnegie, Commonwealth, Fleischmann, and Sloan. In addition, five have special family or company connections, but they are limited or attenuated, so that terms such as domination or control are inappropriate: the Rockefeller Foundation includes two family members on its board of twenty-one. Thirty-eight percent of its assets are in Standard Oil of New Jersey and Standard Oil of Indiana shares, but its holdings constitute less than 2 percent of the total shares of each of these large publicly held companies. The Rockefeller Brothers Fund is under family control but does not have controlling shareholdings in any particular company or companies. Ford and Kettering have family representation on their boards, but as small minorities in strong and diversified groups of trustees. The stockholdings of Kettering, which are concentrated in General Motors shares, have never constituted a significant fraction of the total outstanding, and investment diversification has now begun. In the case of Ford, cross-influence between the management of the foundation and the company has now been greatly reduced. A considerable part of the foundation's assets is still in the form of Ford stock, but its shares are nonvoting and a program of relatively rapid diversification is under way. The Astor Foundation is directed by the donor's widow, but the majority of the board is nonfamily and the foundation has no specific company ties.

The close foundation–family–company linkages that characterize most of the big foundations are normally of a direct and visible nature: the donor's wealth derived from one or two companies; he created only one major foundation; his family has not been massively wealthy for any long period; and his direct descendants are not particularly numerous. But none of these conditions apply to the three great dynasties of wealth in the United States—the du Ponts, the Mellons, and the Rockefellers. As a result, these triangular interconnections are less visible and more intricate. Because of the scale of their holdings, their involvement in the direction or control of numerous major corporations, the number of their foundations, and their numerous offspring after several generations, highly refined devices such as personal trusts, holding companies, investment trusts, and special groups of management and investment advisers have been established through which the circuits of power and influence pass.

What the role of the Mellon National Bank and Trust Company and of T. Mellon and Sons has been, in coordinating the investment policies of the various Mellon foundations and in providing general management for them, is not known. Neither can it be determined just what role Christiana Securities, one of the principal du Pont family holding companies, may play in coordinating the investment policies of the numerous du Pont foundations. Nor is it known to what extent the grant-making of the various Rockefeller foundations is coordinated, or how the members of the family, their various holding companies and trusts, and their several foundations coordinate their voting power when necessary to deal with a critical policy problem in a company in which they have an important interest. But it would be naive not to recognize both the existence and the potential power of foundation–family–company linkages, indirect though they may be. With the passage of time these close ties diminish, but slowly. The instinct on the part of family members and other trustees has been to perpetuate, not to sever them. (See for confirmation the conclusions of Ralph L. Nelson, who found that as of 1960 only ten of the forty-five largest foundations could be considered widely diversified.) [3]

In the case of four of the big foundations the question of voluntary diversification did not arise: Vincent Astor, the Harknesses, and Max Fleischmann bequeathed relatively diversified portfolios of securities, and Andrew Carnegie left his Carnegie Corporation an endowment in the form of bonds of the U.S. Steel Corporation which were redeemed by the company, after which the proceeds had to be reinvested.[*]

The endowments of the other twenty-nine, however, were in the

---

[*] A variant of the Carnegie situation on a more limited scale is the Rockefeller Brothers Fund, which received a gift of $57.7 million in 1952 in the form of a noninterest-bearing note of Rockefeller Center, Inc. As the note was paid off, the proceeds were reinvested in a wide selection of stocks and bonds.

form of concentrated holdings of property or securities which, alone or in combination with the holdings of the donor family, represented strong influence upon, if not control over, the management of one or more companies. Four donors—James Duke, James Irvine, Otto Haas, and John Hartford—strongly emphasized that the property they gave to their foundations should be kept intact. Most of the remainder, although they did not leave explicit instructions, made it clear to their trustees that they intended that their descendants, company, and foundation should remain in close association. As a result, investment diversification is a decision that most of the big foundations have been reluctant to face.

The Ford Foundation is probably the outstanding example of diversification on a major scale: twenty years ago its holdings were entirely in the form of Ford Motor Company shares, of which it owned 88 percent of the total outstanding. In the years since, Ford has disposed of 65 percent of its shares and its diversification continues. The Rockefeller foundations have diversified their holdings to some extent over the years, although their largest individual holdings still tend to be in Rockefeller-related companies. Kresge and Sloan have made significant initial moves toward diversification. In 1963, the Duke trustees sought court permission to depart from the terms of the donor's will and to diversify, but permission was refused. Two of the Mellon foundations, R. K. Mellon and Sarah Mellon Scaife, have retained their concentrated holdings while two others, Avalon and Old Dominion, had begun to diversify when they were consolidated into the A. W. Mellon Foundation.

But the du Ponts, except to the extent necessary to comply with court orders, have not diversified. Similarly, most of the other major foundations with highly concentrated holdings—Brown, Bush, Danforth, Hartford, Irvine, Kaiser, Land, Lilly, Mott, Pew, Richardson, Waterman, and Woodruff—made no move until the passage of the 1969 Tax Reform Act to break up their holdings.° In all, more than half have been adamant against diversification, and

° The Kellogg Foundation Trust, which holds about eight-ninths of the assets of the foundation, has not diversified; the foundation itself has diversified the one-ninth it owns directly.

during the 1969 tax bill hearings several of them argued fiercely against any mandatory divestiture provisions.°

It must be emphasized that until 1969 the law did not prohibit or even discourage a concentration of assets. But Treasury experts, Representative Patman, and others have long believed that such concentration has led to abuses: "self-dealing" between the foundation and the donor or the associated corporation; unfair competitive advantage for the corporation associated with a foundation; and inadequate or delayed benefits to charity.†

In regard to self-dealing—the sale of property or the lending of money between a foundation and the donor family or an associated corporation—the big foundations have a good, though not impeccable, record. The $2.1-million payment by the Bush Foundation to the widow of the donor for the maintenance of her Florida estate has been publicly questioned; so has the charging of certain personal and household expenses to the Moody Foundation by a daughter of the donor. Family trustees of the Houston Endowment and the Sid W. Richardson Foundation have reportedly acquired on a noncompetitive basis properties owned by their foundations. A member of the Irvine family has repeatedly accused trustees of the Irvine Foundation of self-dealing between themselves and the Irvine Ranch Company. Financial transactions between the Kresge Foundation and the Kresge Company, the Duke Foundation and the Duke Power Company, and the Kellogg Foundation Trust and the Kellogg Foundation have also provoked criticism from time to time in years past.‡

° Since 1969, such efforts having failed, they have sought to persuade Congress and the Nixon administration to ease or delay application of the new requirements. Commenting on these attempts, Representative Patman on July 15, 1971 stated: "It is . . . apparent that many foundations and charitable trusts are attempting to avoid the effects of the Act. There is mounting pressure on the Internal Revenue Service to weaken the law and hold it inapplicable to thousands of foundations and charitable trusts. This must not be allowed to happen."

† Nor are all of the many problems of conflict of interest strictly economic in nature. See, for example, the discussion in chapter 9 of the relationships between the Houston Endowment and the Houston *Chronicle*.

‡ Before the huge holdings of the Ford Foundation in the Ford Motor Company—which were nonvoting—could be offered for public sale, it was felt

But apart from occasional lapses and a few examples of insufficient fastidiousness, the big foundations do not appear to have been guilty of the kinds of self-dealing and self-aggrandizement that have come to light in the case of some medium-sized and smaller foundations.

As to the charge of giving unfair competitive advantage to the corporations with which they are linked, the big foundations are, on the whole, again relatively guiltless. There have been occasional examples of efforts to take a "public relations" advantage of the existence of a foundation by an associated company. S. S. Kresge at one time exploited the grants of his foundation to give favorable publicity to his stores; more recently a company controlled by the Sid W. Richardson Foundation did the same kind of thing. There also was a time when some local Ford dealers attempted to use the prestige of the Ford Foundation for the benefit of their automobile sales, but more frequently the foundation's grants have aroused local criticism that Ford dealers have regarded as a handicap to their business.°

On the other hand, the Lilly Endowment has scrupulously stayed out of the field of medicine and health because Eli Lilly & Company is a pharmaceutical manufacturer. Nor is there evidence that the Coca-Cola Company has attempted to use the Woodruff Foundation for any commercial purposes. The same is true of the Atlantic & Pacific Tea Company and the Purina Company, both of which are in the field of retail merchandising, where conceivably

---

that the shares had to be given voting rights. This in turn necessitated negotiations with members of the Ford family, who at the time held control of all of the "Class B," or voting, stock. The "price" paid to the family for diluting its voting control as a result of these negotiations constituted the largest single transaction between a foundation and a donor family to date. These negotiations, however, were conducted with the full knowledge of the Securities and Exchange Commission and the Treasury Department and in accordance with the advice of reputable legal and investment counsel. Moreover, the full details of the transaction were promptly made public.

° In two instances, major stockholders of companies controlled by big foundations have charged that the interlinkage has been to the competitive *disadvantage* of the company and that foundation control has meant sluggish management and low profitability. See the attacks of Mrs. Joan Irvine Smith mentioned in chapter 7 and of Huntington Hartford mentioned in chapter 10.

some advantage might be taken of the company's association with a major foundation. But in the case of the large foundations, the danger of competitive advantage is reduced by the fact that their associated companies operate on a national or even international basis, whereas most of the foundations operate in a more restricted area, so that any public relations benefits would at best be limited. The flagrant exception is the Alfred I. du Pont estate and the Nemours Foundation (see chapter 8). This is a scandalous example of the exploitation of a philanthropic façade to give unfair competititve advantage to associated banks and other profit-making corporations.

The most serious charge of financial abuse which has been made, namely, inadequate and delayed benefits to charity, is far more difficult to analyze, and the record of guilt or innocence is far more mixed.

One part of this complex issue at least can readily be disposed of —the complaint that the big foundations have "unreasonably" accumulated income. They have not. Danforth, at one time when its staff and program were in the process of being organized, was so accused by the federal tax authorities, but the problem was resolved as the foundation's program expanded; in recent years, moreover, Danforth has been conspicuous among the big foundations in giving away substantially more than its current income, invading capital to make up the difference. Ford Foundation officials in the early 1950s were troubled when the income from its motor company shares began to increase so rapidly that program expenditures had difficulty keeping pace. But its huge "one shot" package of grants to four-year colleges, hospitals, and medical schools in 1956 eliminated the problem. The grants of the Moody Foundation for a period also lagged behind income but have now been greatly increased.

Apart from such uncommon and temporary instances, the large foundations distribute the income they receive promptly and fully. The grant level of at least a third of them in recent years has exceeded their income.* The real problem, therefore, turns not on

* For the period 1951–60, Ralph Nelson found that the overall expenditures of the fifty largest foundations equaled 119 percent of their investment in-

whether they have been paying out the income they receive but, rather, on whether the big foundations have been receiving an "adequate" or "normal" income on their investments. But what measure should be used in formulating a judgment? Should it be the percentage of return on the market value of assets? Or the long-term growth in the capital value of assets? Or both? Financial experts would give one answer if they anticipated continued growth or inflation in the national economy and if their goal was to maximize the total return—current interest and dividends plus long-term capital growth—for a client with no immediate need of current income. But a trustee of an institution, such as a college, hospital, or foundation, seeking to protect its assets against erosion and at the same time to generate sufficient current income to sustain its programs, would obviously give another.

The premise on which federal tax legislation gives a donor current tax deduction for the full value of his contribution to a foundation requires that active charitable operations derive a reasonably adequate level of current benefit as a result. If a foundation, after the donor or his estate has had the full tax benefit of his gift, follows an investment policy that results in a long or indefinite deferral of charitable benefits in order to build up the foundation's corpus, it violates the spirit (and since 1969 the letter) of tax exemption. What, then, have been the actual investment practices of the big foundations, and what have been their financial and other consequences?

The data are somewhat conflicting. The first careful study of the investment policies of the big foundations was that of Ralph L. Nelson, based largely on 1960 financial information. He found that many foundations are in effect "one stock" institutions. He then analyzed the performance of the eighteen stocks constituting some three-quarters of the assets of the fifty-two large foundations on which his study concentrated. In the ten-year period 1951–60 these

_____

come. The biggest "over-spender" in that decade was the Ford Foundation. (Nelson, *Investment Policies of Foundations*, p. 33) For 1969, seventeen of the thirty-three in this study overspent: among the leaders, Kaiser's outlays were 345 percent of income (which was very low); Danforth 292 percent; Bush 198 percent; and Ford 190 percent.

stocks in terms of growth in value had a considerably better record than did stocks in general. For the eight-year period 1957–64 they did less well but still had a better record of growth in value than a broader list of stocks. On the other hand, cash dividends received by foundations on the eighteen stocks were lower than for common stocks in general. Nelson concluded that, on balance, the foundations in question probably would have better served the cause of charity if they had diversified.[4]

Another study of foundation investment practices in the same period by Thomas Troyer, a former Treasury official, rendered a far more critical judgment. His findings were based on the 1962 dividend yields of the concentrated investment holdings of a sample of roughly 1,300 foundations, including all of those with total assets of more than $10 million:

Here one finds a surprising quantity of goose eggs—not of the golden variety. Of the 213 business holdings of 20 percent or larger, 107, almost precisely half—had no yield whatever in 1962. Even among the holdings of the large foundations, where one would expect much better performance to follow from larger and more stable businesses, the figures are hardly less striking. Of the total of 87, 36 produced no dividends at all in 1962. . . . Interestingly enough the lack of current productivity was most pronounced among the interests which were most concentrated. Looking only at the 50% or larger interests—situations in which the foundations were not only involved in the business, but ordinarily in clear control of it—one finds 83 cases of zero yield for a total of 118 interests. Here the foundations were most completely masters of their own fortune: and here more than 70% of their interests produced no dividends at all for charity during the survey period.[5]

Troyer also examined whether the exceedingly unfavorable current performance was counterbalanced by exceptional growth in the overall asset value of the investments. A Treasury report in 1965 had found that the growth in value of foundation assets in the years after World War II was in line with the general growth of stock values but not significantly higher. His own conclusion was that data supplied by the foundations to the Treasury were far from definitive but that if "the large business interests of foundations possess abnormally great capital gains potentiality, the evidence supplied by the foundations themselves failed to disclose it."

More recently, two other critical reviews of foundation investment practices and performance have been made. *The Institutional Investor* of November 1968 (a year that proved to be the crest of a period of sustained increase in stock prices) published an article attacking the overly cautious investment practices of foundations. Among its breezily stated conclusions:

Is there a place as yet untouched by the revolution in money management? Where the winds of performance are not felt, where the opportuning cries of ambitious brokers are not heard, a last redoubt so quiet the clocks can be heard ticking? . . . The performance syndrome, which has blustered even such insulated havens as university endowment funds and union pension funds, has produced only the most gossamer of ruffles at the foundations. Indeed, it is safe to say that of all forms of institutional money, foundation funds are managed with just about the most resolute, unswerving dedication to the traditions of yesteryear. . . . It is all a somewhat paradoxical spectacle. Foundations built on the fortunes of ruthlessly capitalistic entrepreneurs now turn away in horror from the slightest investment risk . . . they have devised an abundantly topheavy system of committees, policies, and procedures that, good markets and bad, keeps often 40 percent or more of their assets locked in fixed income securities, ensuring annual spendable yields (including capital gains) of under 4 percent.

The publication's sweeping judgments were, however, so flimsily documented that they were impossible to evaluate. The following year, the Peterson Commission made a more serious analysis—but again using 1968 data—and came to equally harsh conclusions. It commissioned the Arthur Andersen Company, a well-known public accounting firm, to examine a sample of the tax returns of foundations of various sizes (forms which it stressed were infrequently audited by the Internal Revenue Service and in any event were too incomplete in a number of fundamental respects to permit a precise analysis or evaluation). The findings:

In 1968, the average performance of U.S. mutual funds was a 15.3 percent total return (interest, dividends, realized and unrealized capital gains) for a so-called common stock mutual fund, and 14.9 percent return for a balanced fund of stocks and bonds. In contrast, foundations' returns on their portfolios were as follows:

Asset size	1968 Total Investment Return (Median)
Under $200,000	4.7%
$200,000 to $1 million	6.7
$1 million to $10 million	6.0
$10 million to $100 million	7.7
$100 million and over	8.5

In the case of fourteen selected large foundations, the Commission took independent measures to confirm the accuracy of the total return data: the results again showed 8.5 percent total return for the big foundations against 15 percent for the balanced funds.

The commission stated, "every indicator it studied pointed to the conclusion that the investment performance of the foundations was significantly below par. This was not something to be lightly dismissed. It is clearly in the public interest to regain for use on charitable objects the hundreds of millions of dollars that are annually being lost to philanthropy because of a below-par investment performance by the foundations." [6]

For the thirty-three big foundations, which hold assets worth more than $10 billion, each percent loss of return amounts to $100 million annually. The deficiency of 7 percent in their total investment return for 1968, on the basis of the Peterson data, therefore, would have amounted to $700 million lost to charity for that year alone.

If this were typical of investment performance by foundations over a span of years, it would have staggering implications of incompetence or knavery, or both, on the part of their trustees. But since 1968, stock prices have suffered a marked decline, and the question arises whether foundation portfolios which lagged in growth during a period of rapidly rising market prices may have, on the other hand, fallen less than the market during the subsequent period of declining prices.

An analysis of the period 1967–69 shows that the big foundations' record of portfolio movement, though mediocre, is not as disastrous as the Peterson results suggest. Their assets produced a total return only slightly poorer than the market in general. (Scope, methodology, and detailed results are presented in the Appendix.)

The implications of the foregoing studies can be read in various ways, and because of the wide variations in economic linkages and investment practices among the large foundations any general conclusions must be drawn with great care. But the evidence *in toto* strongly suggests that: the excessive concentration of foundation assets has generally resulted in diminished income for charity; and if commonly accepted measures of performance are applied to foundation portfolio management, the returns achieved have not been superior to what a totally random selection of securities would have produced.

Manifestly, various private interest considerations have influenced the investment decisions of a good many of the large foundations. These may consist of the sentimental attachment of the donor's family and other trustees to a particular profit-making company or the desire of company officers who are also trustees to maintain the security of their employment by resisting diversification. Such intentions and others that can readily be imagined are of differing degrees of dubiety. But they all cast their shadow over the face of big philanthropy as it functions today. Foundation investment policies may not be serving the selfish interests of those who control them, but in far too many instances they appear to be.

The Evolutionary Dimension

Compared to churches, universities, and many welfare organizations the thirty-three big foundations are very young institutions, hardly out of their formative phase. The oldest is just over sixty, the majority are less than thirty years old. Their evolution is therefore still at an early stage.

Many of the changes which have so far occurred have been the result of a sudden transforming event such as the death of a donor, the succession of a willful executive head, or the election of an unusually able and energetic trustee. These eventualities have repeatedly altered the course of a foundation's development, as demon-

strated in a number of cases: the appointment of Merrimon
Cuninggim as head of Danforth Foundation; the successive appointments of Paul Hoffman, Henry Heald, and McGeorge Bundy
as presidents of the Ford Foundation; the death of Alfred P. Sloan,
donor of the Sloan Foundation; the appointment of Richard Bennett to head the Waterman Foundation; and the election of Walter
Orr Roberts as a trustee of the Kettering Foundation. In the cases
of Moody and Bush, the intercession of a state attorney-general
into their affairs proved to be another kind of transforming event.

Looking to the future—even the near future—important changes
in a number of other large foundations can be anticipated or are
already under way: the death of key figures in Mott, Nemours, and
Woodruff, and the advent of new executive heads in the Bush,
Hartford, Kaiser, Land, and Rockefeller foundations, to cite a few.
(It used to be said about the New York *Times* that because no one
was ever fired, "God was the personnel manager." The same is true
of many of the large foundations. In most cases the personnel
changes that have critically affected them have been the result of
retirement or death.)

But quite apart from their susceptibility to abrupt and episodic
changes, the big foundations in general also show significant signs
of continuous evolution. The data will not sustain overly refined
computations because the number of cases is small and the individual variation is very great. But taking a few lines of movement
—staff development, investment diversification, sophisticated and
innovative programing, independence of donor and company, and
board diversification—as criteria pointing generally in the direction of more responsive and effective philanthropy, it is possible to
test the big foundations by them to see to what extent and at what
rate of speed institutional improvement occurs. Table 4 is a
graphic attempt to indicate the successive stages of evolutionary
change reached by the big foundations as of 1972.

In a number of instances it appears that the passing of the donor
has most clearly set the process of institutional development in
motion. Conversely, as long as he is alive basic improvements are
often blocked—and donors tend to live an exceptionally long time.
But however initiated, once the evolution begins the process is sus-

Table 4

Successive Stages of Evolutionary Change Reached by the Big Foundations as of 1972

	Age (1972)	Nucleus of staff	Fuller staff development	Development of defined programs; sophisticated grant-making	Significant investment diversification	Significant innovative programing	High degree of independence of donor family and company	High degree of board diversification
Astor	24	x			x			
Brown	21	x						
Bush	19	x					x°	x°
Carnegie	61	x	x	x	x	x	x	
Commonwealth	54	x	x	x	x	x	x	
Danforth	45	x	x	x		x		x
Duke	48	x	x	x				
Fleischmann	20		x	x	x	x	x	x
Ford	36	x	x	x	x	x	x	x
Haas (Waterman)	27	x	x	x		x		
Hartford	43	x						
Houston	35	x			x			
Irvine	35	x						
Kaiser	24	x						
Kellogg	42	x	x	x		x		
Kettering	45	x	x	x			x	x
Kresge	48	x			x			
Land	11							
Lilly	35	x	x	x				
Longwood	35	x						
A. W. Mellon †	32	x	x		x			

	Age†							
R. K. Mellon	25	x	x					x
Moody	30	x	x	x				
Mott	46	x	x	x	x			
Nemours	36							
Pew	24	x						
Richardson	25	x	x	x				
Rockefeller	59	x	x	x	x	x	x	x
Rockefeller Bros.	32	x	x	x	x	x	x	
Scaife	31	x						
Sloan	38	x	x	x	x	x	x	x
Surdna	55				x			
Woodruff	34	x*						
Totals		27	15	15	12	10	8	6

* By court order
† Age of component foundations merged in 1969

tained by internal forces which are then generated. As the donor's influence lessens, a foundation develops its own kind of institutional pride combined with a somewhat greater sense of public accountability. As it acquires staff and experience in grant-making, more careful thought is given to the nature of its role; its areas of program interest tend to be defined in a more explicit way; it becomes more knowledgeable about problems and institutions in its field of interest and its programs tend to be better rationalized, better coordinated, and more professionally executed.

In sum, the big foundations, with all their weaknesses, are nonetheless institutions in forward movement. But the pace is stately and dangerously slow.

16.

Public Reporting:
The Enclave Mentality

ON THE SUBJECT of public reporting by foundations, J. William Hinckley, president of the Research Corporation, a private foundation, has claimed that "It is the current practice of foundations to operate in a 'goldfish bowl,' a practice that they have assumed voluntarily." [1] Warren Weaver, an eminent scientist long associated with the Rockefeller and Sloan foundations, has written that while "further improvements in disclosure are possible . . . it is evident that the secrecy that some foundations attach to their financial characteristics in the past has been almost wholly removed in the case of the largest and most prominent foundations." [2]

Both of these statements are unfounded and wrong. The overwhelming majority of American foundations—including a good proportion of the largest ones—have had, and continue to maintain, an obsession for privacy. They have generally been unwilling to make information freely available about their purposes, the nature of their grants, and especially about their investments, their expenses, and their corporate interlinkages. The extent to which more information has become available in recent years has largely been due to governmental compulsion. Annual reports by foundations to the federal government were first required by administrative action of the Treasury Department in 1942 and by statutory authority in 1953. But a high proportion of foundations were resistant or negligent in complying with these requirements. This was well known to Treasury officials from the beginning. It became obvious to Representative Patman as soon as his staff began to study copies of the information returns filed in Washington with the Internal Revenue Service. And it has been obvious to anyone who has carefully read these reports after 1950, when portions were first made available for public inspection. Mrs. Wilmer Shields Rich, editor of the basic reference work, *American Foundations and Their Fields,* was among the first to scrutinize them:

Between 1951 and 1955 I had the interesting and enlightening experience of analyzing the returns of more than 6,000 foundations on forms 990-A and 1041-A. In the course of this study, I was confronted by incomplete returns, several hundred letters from foundation trustees resentful of the availability of information about their activities, and occasionally cessation of filing returns. The high proportion of returns which were inadequately filled out prompted me, in 1953, to report my findings to Norman Sugarman [then head] of the Bureau of Internal Revenue.

Nine years later, in the course of its second nation-wide analysis of foundation returns to the Treasury Department, the Foundation Library Center continued to find inadequate completion of Form 990-A.[3]

In 1965 another reputable student of philanthropy, Marion R. Fremont-Smith wrote, "The experience of State officials using Internal Revenue files in connection with the search for foundations in their jurisdictions has borne out these serious findings and also reaffirmed charges that many organizations do not even file forms."[4] In 1967 an assistant commissioner of the IRS said of the filed returns, "One-third have had to be rejected from the automatic data processing system because of errors and omissions."[5]

Many foundations have not only failed to meet their reporting requirements but do not even respond to public inquiries. In his remarks to the Twenty-first Conference of Southwest Foundations, Manning Pattillo of the Foundation Center said, "Perhaps the most serious complaint that the Foundation Center receives about foundations is that they don't answer mail." He cited the recent experience of a leading university which sent out letters signed by its president to 150 foundations. It received only two acknowledgements and total silence from 148 others.[6]

If foundations have been reluctant to comply with requirements for submitting informational returns to the government, they have been even more reluctant to issue reports to the general public. F. Emerson Andrews, in his authoritative *Philanthropic Foundations,* listed only 107 foundations of the 15,000 existing in 1956 known to issue public reports: of these, 76 published annually or biennially; 31 others reported only "occasionally." By 1965 the editor of *Foundation News*, J. Richard Taft, located 212 foundations issuing reports, of which only 116 could be classified as regular reporters.[7] A more recent compilation by the Foundation Center is summarized in Table 5, which indicates that not only has the percentage of foundations reporting been very small but until Congress acted in 1969 to require annual public reports, the situation was not improving.

Table 5

Foundations Known To Issue Annual or Biennial Reports by Asset Classes in 1956, 1959, and 1966

Asset Class °		Number Reporting	Number in Class	Percentage Reporting
1956	A	44	84	52.0
	B	22	659	3.0
	C	11	4,000	0.3
Total		77	4,743	2.0
1959	A	49	129	38.0
	B	43	655	6.6
	C	16	4,418	0.4
Total		108	5,202	2.1
1966	A	71	237	30.0
	B	50	1,227	4.1
	C	6	5,339	0.1
Total		127	6,803	1.9

Source: Based on information compiled by the Foundation Center. The number of foundations used in the tabulation includes only those giving $10,000 or more annually, or those with assets of at least $50,000 (in 1959) or $200,000 (in 1966).

° A = over $10 million
B = $1–$10 million
C = under $1 million

In 1968, the center checked the situation again. Seven of the ten largest foundations, but only about one-third of the 261 foundations with assets over $10 million, voluntarily published annual or biennial reports.[8]

The Special Case of the Big Foundations

The thirty-three big foundations have issued public reports with far greater frequency than other foundations. But their performance has not been uniform. Up to 1969, when they were first required by law to begin issuing reports, the following was their record: Eleven issued regular reports which were relatively complete and informative (Carnegie, Commonwealth, Danforth, Duke, Ford, Kellogg, Kettering, Rockefeller, Rockefeller Brothers, Sloan, and Phoebe Waterman). Nine issued regular reports which were only fairly complete and informative (Astor, Fleischmann, Hartford, Kresge, Lilly, A. W. Mellon, R. K. Mellon, Moody, and Scaife). Four issued reports which had major deficiencies (the Houston Endowment reported irregularly and incompletely; the Irvine, Mott, and Nemours foundations reported incompletely and misleadingly). Nine never issued public reports (Brown, Bush, Kaiser, Land, Longwood, Pew, Richardson, Surdna, and Woodruff).

In addition, many of the large foundations that have issued regular reports began to do so only after a long period of nonreporting: the Old Dominion and Avalon Foundations waited nearly twenty years to issue their first annual reports; Houston Endowment waited twenty-two years; the Moody Foundation twenty-five; the Irvine Foundation twenty-eight; the Kresge and Kettering foundations thirty-four. Rockefeller, Carnegie, Commonwealth, and Duke have reported publicly on their activities from the beginning. Thus, about half the big foundations for most of their existence have not voluntarily reported, and although two-thirds of them were doing so by 1969 this is a relatively recent development.

If there has been a quantitative lack in foundation reporting, there has been an even greater qualitative deficiency. The literary quality of institutional prose in the United States has long depressed many critics. The word "gobbledygook" was invented to describe the burdensome circumlocutions which afflict government documents. Dwight Macdonald has coined its philanthropic equivalent:

There is also an esoteric language, which might be called foundationese, for communication with the outside world, which is developed most fully in the Annual Report, a literary product which is somewhat more readable than the phone book and somewhat less so than the collected sermons of Henry Ward Beecher. This language is, like Latin, a dead language, written rather than spoken, and designed for ceremony rather than utility. Its function is magical and incantatory—not to give information or to communicate ideas or to express feelings but to reassure the reader that the situation is well in hand. Its cardinal principle is to accentuate the positive. . . . Another principle of foundationese is not to go to undue lengths—or, in fact, to any lengths at all—to avoid the obvious, since foundationese is committee language and is therefore ever seeking the lowest denominator that everybody will agree on. Sometimes this is well below sea level.[9]

Using the Ford Foundation report for 1954 as his point of take-off, Macdonald then conducted his readers on one of the most enjoyable excursions ever made through this particular literary wasteland. He commented on these examples of foundationese:

"The Foundation attempts to administer its funds in ways that strengthen its grantees and enhance their ability to accomplish the purposes for which the grants were made." (As against, presumably, foundations that try to weaken their grantees and lessen their ability to make good use of their grants.) Or, "The Trustees of the Ford Foundation believe [any sentence beginning this way is bound to be disappointing] that a healthy economy is essential if American democracy is to function effectively." Or "The Ford Foundation believes that the advancement of human welfare depends on the partnership in progress of all free men." The virtuosity of foundationese becomes apparent when one considers that not only do the last two sentences mean nothing as they stand (that is, without a lengthy explication of almost every term) but also the gist of them is reversible, like a trench coat, thus: "Democracy is essential if a healthy economy is to function effectively." And "The partnership in progress of all free men depends on the advancement of human welfare." Gives just as good wear either way.

Foundations repetitiously insist on the risky and experimental character of much of their work, and yet their reports suggest oddly enough that the risks almost never result in losses and the experiments never fail. An average example of this tendency is the following summary of the work of the Rockefeller Foundation from its annual report for 1968:

From the time of its establishment in 1913, the Rockefeller Foundation has been a thoroughly professional organization. It maintains a highly qualified staff of scientists, social scientists, and humanists, capable of dealing at home and abroad with precisely defined human concerns. . . . During the past five years there have been notable and even dramatic results arising from Foundation efforts, both at home and overseas. Most spectacular have been those growing out of the Foundation's worldwide Conquest of Hunger Program, which has contributed millions of tons of food grains to the world food budget and has added hundreds of millions of dollars to the gross national product of the countries involved. . . . The Equal Opportunity Program, begun in 1963, has grown substantially and is becoming increasingly diversified. . . . The total problem of minorities is vast, perplexing, and difficult. It is also challenging. While the Foundation can play only a small role in the total effort in terms of resources, it is clear that this role can be designed so as to be meaningful and constructive; over a period of time, such an effort could contribute significantly to patterns for improvement. . . .

But whereas the Rockefeller Foundation delicately compliments its own achievements, the Mott Foundation thumps its own back resoundingly, as in its projects report for 1967–68:

A review of the past year can be summed up in one word: Action! Action against war, against poverty. Action involving money, race, jobs, education, crime, urbanization. Never before has the status quo received such attack!

And never before have the people responded so forcefully—with Interaction! . . .

It is this action and interaction that characterize the Mott Foundation Projects. Initiating, cooperating, planning, coordinating, and supporting a wide range of effort—evaluating all—are its daily fare. . . .

Action, yes. The Mott Foundation has always been in the fore. . . .

PRESIDENTIAL PONTIFICATION

It has become the fashion in foundation reports for the president to lead off with a little essay presenting his own ruminations on almost any subject before the presumably more mundane information about grants and finances is listed. Dr. Henry F. Pritchett, the first head of the Carnegie Foundation for the Advancement of Teaching, began the practice in the early years of the century. His were rousing statements by a powerful and opinionated man, and for some reason it has mostly been men connected with Carnegie philanthropies in the years since who have been able to uphold Pritchett's high standards. Frederick Keppel's commentaries in the reports of the Carnegie Corporation during the 1920s and 1930s were stylish and much-quoted; and in the post World War II period, John Gardner and Alan Pifer, his successors as head of the corporation, have written a series of wide-ranging analyses of the problems of American society and philanthropy.* The presidential essays of Raymond Fosdick of the Rockefeller Foundation in the 1930s can also be ranked with the best of the Carnegie output.

But except for these few examples of excellence, most president's reviews are preachy, platitudinous, and pretentious. For example, the president of the Mott Foundation in 1968 writes: "The philosophical purpose of the Mott Foundation is to increase the strength and stature of character in individuals and thereby also strengthen our free enterprise system of society. . . . So we hope that the result of our objectives will be 'Strong and Self-Reliant Individuals dedicated to Useful Living, working together in a Free Enterprise Society.'"

The president of the Rockefeller Foundation in 1967 has delivered this demure example of self-congratulation: "Perhaps the principal purpose of these remarks is to suggest that over a period of years the general purpose foundations have acquired both experience and a degree of wisdom. They have found that to be most useful to society, they must choose their projects in anticipation of the problems of the future and deal with them in a way which will bring light rather than heat to bear upon them. Philanthropic funds should be used with forethought, care, and persistence to support causes, programs, and projects that are clearly demonstrable as fundamental to human progress." Then, resigning himself to the hazards of such a daring course, "An element of risk will assuredly appear in all such cases and will take a variety of forms.

* From the standpoint of intellectual substance, the Annual Reviews of Dr. Caryl Haskins during his years as head of the Carnegie Institution of Washington were in a class by themselves. His literate discussions of advanced developments in science and of the relationship of scientific developments to other social and cultural trends were major contributions to contemporary thought.

These risks cannot be avoided nor can they be permitted to become deterrents to action. On the contrary they must be faced squarely with full realization of their implications."

The head of the Lilly Endowment ended his personal review of the foundation's work in 1959 on this stirring note: "We face the future in this modern world with deep concern but unafraid, as thankful for our responsibilities as we are grateful for our 'rights.' Inspired by the ideals of its founder . . . the Endowment will continue to endeavor to preserve, strengthen, and further our own society and system with the hope that we may, in some small measure, contribute to making de Tocqueville's prophecy (that America seems marked by the will of Heaven to sway the destinies of half the globe) prove true throughout all the world in the years to come."

Frequently, the presidential front end of foundation reports does not appear to know where the reportorial back end is going. A persistent example of this was the biennial reports of the Sloan Foundation from 1938 until the early 1960s. During those years the foundation was the personal instrument of its highly egocentric donor. Its grants went mainly to a few institutions with which he had a personal or sentimental connection, particularly his alma mater, the Massachusetts Institute of Technology. The staff was weak and subordinated to his dictates, and the board, a small group of his close friends, was little more than a rubber stamp. But in his introduction to the foundation's report for 1947–48, Sloan declared that the proper terrain for foundation action was out "at the frontiers of knowledge" and that rather than merely perpetuate the work of ongoing institutions foundations should "underwrite new patterns of action." In his report for 1951 and 1952 he described foundations as "instruments of social progress, not social amelioration," and he deplored the fact that so many people "still regard foundations as merely sources of funds for traditional charitable purposes." Nor did he hesitate in his report for 1955 and 1956 to call on other foundations to equip themselves with competent staff and urged that they should strengthen their governing boards by recruiting members who are "leaders in their communities and in their respective professions and pursuits."

The discrepancy between presumptuous words and the actual

grants of the Sloan Foundation was perhaps more amusing than sinister. But in some other instances, one suspects a deliberate intention to mislead. The Irvine Foundation published no report of its activities in the 1940s or 1950s, and in 1961 its president stated that it was the policy of the trustees not to make information available about the foundation and its grants. But in 1964, evidently as a result of growing criticism, public relations counsel was retained and the foundation's first public report appeared the following year. Financial information was omitted but there was no lack of florid emphasis on the foundation's high purposes: "It fulfills its public trust by exercising its intrinsic advantages of independence and flexibility and by utilization of its capacity to provide timely financial assistance to the solution of critical problems and to relieve acute wants and needs of the people of California."

In 1969 the foundation published its second report, an even smoother example of Madison Avenue methodology, which displayed a still wider gap between grants and professed purposes. In explaining the great potentialities of private foundations the brochure said: "They are able to question the *status quo*, encourage experimentation and provide the 'seed money' for new institutions and new ideas. Foundations do an essential job which the government by nature cannot do. The Foundation is more than a mechanical alternative for government action. . . . The Foundation is an instrument for our citizens to transfer profit from the commercial sector and put it directly to work as risk capital for the general betterment of society."

But the partial grant list, which "singled out one phase of our work—assistance to the youth of our state—for special comment," consisted of a donation of $25,000 to the Orange County Children's Hospital to help furnish the third floor; $10,000 to the Orange County Society for Crippled Children and Adults; $5,000 to the Orange County Symphony Association; and $5,000 to the Boys Club of South San Francisco to help build a gymnasium. The Irvine Foundation is neither the first nor the only foundation to embellish its image with high-flown verbiage. But given the many grounds for suspicion surrounding all its operations, its public reports suggest deliberate deception.

The Nemours Foundation has matched the Irvine Foundation in

noninformative reporting. It regularly publishes a document ambiguously entitled "Report of the Alfred I. du Pont Institute and the Nemours Foundation," which describes only the activities of the institute, the facility for crippled children maintained by the foundation. It contains no financial data and has never explained the relationship of the estate to the foundation or of the foundation to the institute. On the other hand, it carefully presents statistics on the number of items washed in the institute's laundry as well as detailed calculations on the percentage of increase or decrease in the laundry's output from year to year.

A CASE OF CALCULATED RETICENCE

The reticence of foundations to report fully to the public on their purposes, grants, and finances can hardly be a case of oversight. Leading philanthropic spokesmen for more than half a century have repeatedly appealed to their colleagues to adopt the practice. They have buttressed these appeals with several arguments.

First, the concept of accountability: because American foundations are members of an open society and are by nature quasi-public, the public has a right to know what they are doing. Raymond B. Fosdick, former president of the Rockefeller Foundation, called this the "doctrine of public responsibility." As he put it in 1963, on the occasion of the fiftieth anniversary of the Rockefeller Foundation, "This doctrine is still valid today. Indeed with the proliferation of foundations, it has become an urgent aspect of policy. The public is entitled to know the facts—all the facts—about the operation of foundations."

Second, the notion of a *quid pro quo* between foundations and society: because of their tax privileges and relative freedom from governmental regulation, foundations must accept an obligation to account fully to the public on their operations. The Old Dominion Foundation in 1952 in its reply to a congressional inquiry expressed it in these words: "The public has a direct interest in tax-exempt foundations and comparable organizations for two principal reasons: The fields which foundations support, such as education, religion, and health, are themselves of direct interest to the public; and the public has an interest to see that the tax exemption granted by government is not abused."

Third, the practical notion of foundation self-interest and survival: if they are going to maintain the confidence of the public and safeguard their own privileges, foundations must provide the public with a factual basis for such confidence. Frederick Keppel, president of the Carnegie Corporation, wrote in 1939: "The public is most likely to become suspicious when it is uninformed; and if it should once lose confidence in the foundations as a social instrument, we could all be taxed out of existence, for there is nothing constitutional in the present exemption."

But these arguments were obviously not persuasive to the vast majority of foundations, and in 1969 as part of its Tax Reform Act, Congress imposed a requirement of public reporting on all private foundations. Because foundation spokesmen had come to place such enormous importance on voluntary public reporting as a test of the "public responsibility" of philanthropy, this congressional action appeared to be a judgment on both the ethics and the practical prudence of foundations. With passage of the new law, it might now be concluded that the question of voluntary public reporting has become irrelevant. On the contrary, however, the attitudes underlying traditional foundation resistance to public reporting remain largely intact and have ominous implications for future foundation behavior.

The Enclave Mentality

The reasons underlying the widespread foundation preference for privacy reveal a state of mind—an enclave mentality—which is central to the character of the institution.

The first relates to donors and donor families, and the association in their minds between foundation obligations and the rights of private property. The American system of encouragement for the creation of foundations, at least as it has worked in the past, has not broken this association. Donors in many instances tend to feel, even when their philanthropy has been motivated by tax advantages, that they have performed a charitable act and should not be subject to public accountability. The foundation and its assets continue to be "their money," to do with as they please, within the broad requirements of the law. In fact, in most cases, so long as the donors have been alive, their foundations have not issued public reports; those foundations which up to 1969 had never voluntarily issued public reports were without exception those in which donor and donor-family influence were predominant. A number of scholars have noted this phenomenon.[10] Edward C. Lindeman, as long ago as 1936, said, "In spite of the fact that these are semi-public institutions, and that their influence upon American civilization is one of profound proportions, officials of foundations are distinctly unwilling to furnish facts to investigators and thus to the public." [11] This proved, in his view, that "a sense of social responsibility is not a normal thought pattern of the rich men who have created foundations." *

Donor reluctance about public reporting is frequently reinforced by the conviction of staff and trustees that the exposure of their activities and the motives behind their grant actions may lead to inconvenience—even danger—without countervailing benefit.

An excellent statement of the case against this view was made by Richard Magat, head of public reporting for the Ford Foundation, at the Ninth Biennial Conference on Charitable Foundations held at New York University in 1969. He cited two special reasons for public reporting not usually heard: the first "flows from the engagement of so many foundations in intellectual commerce. The House of Intellect has its own common law, and one of its most sacred tenets is to state one's purposes, methods, and results. Nothing is supposed to be taken on faith or on the reputation of its source alone. If we are to traffic in ideas and work with scholars, scientists

---

* In the course of gathering data for this study some foundations, such as Ford, Rockefeller, Carnegie, Danforth, and others, have been fully cooperative in providing information, but about one-third have not. Two have refused to answer letters or phone calls; one felt obliged to convene a special board meeting to decide whether or not inquiries would be answered; several others, although they were willing to provide certain basic factual information, were flatly unwilling to discuss questions about financial ties, investment policy, and program rationale.

and intellectuals, we owe it to them to report on our ways." He also argued that foundations would benefit from and be invigorated by the feedback from their own communications with the public: "There is no surer safeguard of the integrity of an institution than exposure to the light of public opinion and discourse. . . . Isolation and indifference to the knowledge and opinion of the larger society encourage a climate in which mischief and abuse— even if unintended—may too easily occur. History is too full of fallen angels and of tragic flaws in otherwise honorable and well-intentioned institutions."

But Magat's arguments encounter entrenched resistance. There is the belief that too much publicity about a foundation's activities will subject it to a flood of unwanted applications for assistance. A deeper objection is that if a foundation reveals too much about what it is doing and especially if it exposes its reasoning in deciding program objectives and priorities, it will generate external criticism and pressures which will compromise its freedom of action. As one officer of a large foundation said: "Any public statement of rationale, if sufficiently specific to be useful to outsiders, would make a foundation a natural target for those people whose profession it is to argue such things. This in turn would require the foundation and its staff to dissipate energies in defending its policies— a not especially useful exercise—and would induce a new kind of conservatism or conformity. Each action of the foundation would be influenced by the expected reaction of the intellectual community and would in effect make the foundation a hostage of that particular segment of the community." [12]

Seldom articulated but nonetheless real is the anxiety felt by foundation staff members that to subject themselves and their programs to inquiry and criticism by their peers in the intellectual and scientific community would force them into a humiliating debate because they could not hold their own. In reporting on their own programs, therefore, they have developed to a fine art the contrivance of the statement which conceals more than it reveals.

Such views have been widely held and consequently there has never been much *will* on the part of foundations to report fully to the public. The passage of the 1969 Tax Reform Act has not al-

tered that state of mind. Their preference to live in a cocoon is neither casual nor accidental. Most of them like that kind of existence,
find positive values in it, and will attempt in so far as possible to
preserve it.

That being so, it is not likely that their reports in the future will
do much to build a base of public confidence in foundations or
subject them to the invigorating effect of knowledgeable criticism
by their peers. There are too many ways—as the techniques of
public reporting employed by many foundations already testify—
to communicate with the public uncommunicatively, to issue co-
pious reports which by their high-altitude abstractions, generality,
obscurity, and selectivity give the appearance of informing without
actually doing so. If that is the result, how serious will be the loss
to the public interest? Realistically, it will not in all likelihood be
very great. For those spokesmen who have long—and un-
successfully—appealed to all foundations to issue regular public
reports have probably overestimated their potential value and
effectiveness. Quite obviously, formal reports as such are inadequate to a) ensure the responsible behavior of foundations, or b)
build a base of public confidence in them, or c) save them from
stagnation and irrelevance.

To achieve the first of these objectives, much stricter official surveillance has now had to be imposed. For the second, nothing less
than fundamental structural reforms and generally improved performance will be necessary, and even that, as will be discussed
later, may not save them. And for the third—to prevent stagnation
—more effective methods than general reports will have to be
adopted to provide stimulative feedback, including specialized
technical reports on particular programs for distribution to specialized audiences, "visiting committees" of outside experts to review
and appraise foundation programs, and greater use of empirical
methods of program evaluation by independent researchers.

17.

The Determinant Internal Forces:
Donors, Trustees, and Staff

MORE THAN MOST major national institutions, foundations are "inner-directed." They are not subject to the stimulus and
discipline of customers, stockholders, voters, or student bodies. Nor
does government regulation, although more intrusive than in the
past, do much more than mark off the broad boundaries within
which foundations are free to operate. What they are, therefore,
and what they do, are essentially determined by the controlling
forces within them.

Power in any organization is, of course, a constantly shifting
equation. Its locus and the objectives to which it is harnessed
largely define the character of any institution. In foundations, it is
divided among donors and their descendants, trustees, and staffs,
in varying patterns which shift greatly, and sometimes suddenly,
over time.

The Donors

The men whose names are carried by the large American foundations were by definition all great fortune builders. But in every
other respect they were a diverse lot. Some were farsighted entrepreneurs; others were hardly more than grandiose gamblers, the
beneficiaries of chance, economic boom, and the tax loophole. In
personality, some were enthusiastic and articulate, like Andrew
Carnegie; others were severe, silent, and detached, like old John
D. Rockefeller. Some were ebullient, generous spirits, like William

Danforth; others were cold, hard men like Andrew Mellon and William Moody. Some were self-confident and blustery, like Charles Kettering and C. S. Mott; others were the reverse, like W. K. Kellogg, about whom his doctor once wrote that he was "deeply unhappy and frustrated. In my long practice of psychiatry I don't know of a more lonely, isolated individual." Some were the genteel inheritors of wealth, like Paul Mellon; others were hearty self-made men like Henry J. Kaiser and James B. Duke.

Most of them grew up in the late nineteenth and early twentieth centuries, when America was predominantly rural or small town, its mores Victorian, and its bywords Progress and Opportunity. Most of them were stereotypes—some almost caricatures—of the Protestant ethic. They believed in hard work, thrift, and the pioneer spirit—and not a few were militantly opposed to the use of tobacco and alcohol. Money was the primary object of their lives, but at the same time many felt an obligation, whether religious or ethical in origin, to turn back at least a portion of their wealth to help their less fortunate fellow man.

About a third of them were religious, being active churchgoers and contributors. Of these about half were affiliated with fundamentalist and evangelical sects and about half with Protestant churches of more liberal doctrine. An additional third, though not churchgoing themselves, were strong believers in it for other people. They included churches and religious organizations in their charitable giving partly out of their general acceptance of the principles of Christianity and partly because they believed strong churches were good insurance against social upheaval. Of the list of the thirty-three big donors, none is Catholic, one is Jewish, the rest are of Protestant affiliation or background.

In their economic and political philosophy, nearly all held a strong belief in individual responsibility, private enterprise, *laissez-faire* economics, and minimal government. The earliest group were practitioners of raw and unrestricted industrial capitalism, hostile to "radicalism," Populism, and trustbusting. A later generation was anti–New Deal. A still later generation was not only antigovernment and antilabor, but vocally anti-Communist.

On a political scale, they and their families have been pillars of conservatism. With few exceptions, however, their politics have been incidental; they have generally involved themselves in such matters only to the extent necessary to protect their properties and privileges, not out of a highly formulated ideological position.

THE PSYCHOPATHOLOGY OF DONORSHIP

The real motives that impelled the donors to create the large foundations are virtually unknowable, and the subject has therefore invited much loose speculation. Friendly biographers of some of the donors would have us believe that they were inspired by pure humanitarianism and spirituality. Others, such as the author John Steinbeck, have seen the "philanthropic streak" in Americans as a euphemism for selfishness:

Perhaps the most overrated virtue in our list of shoddy virtues is that of giving. Giving builds up the ego of the giver, makes him superior and higher and larger than the receiver. Nearly always, giving is a selfish pleasure, and in many cases is a downright destructive and evil thing. One has only to remember some of the wolfish financiers who spend two thirds of their lives clawing a fortune out of the guts of society and the latter third pushing it back. It is not enough to suppose that their philanthropy is a kind of frightened restitution, or that their natures change when they have enough. Such a nature never has enough and natures do not change that readily. I think that the impulse is the same in both cases. For giving can bring the same sense of superiority as getting does, and philanthropy may be another kind of spiritual avarice.[1]

To judge by their own statements and conduct, it would appear that very different impulses have been operative, from religious conviction and strong sense of social responsibility on the one hand, to the fact of childlessness and the desire to keep the money out of the hands of government on the other. But in between these extremes can be found the high humanitarianism of Mrs. Stephen Harkness and her son Edward, the resentments generated by family feuds upon the neurotic Alfred I. du Pont, the militant civic reformism of C. S. Mott, the spirit of *noblesse oblige* of Ailsa Mellon Bruce, and the virulent social hostility of the Pews. The one general and objective fact which can be established is that the advent of higher income and estate taxes in recent decades had made the desire for tax savings an increasingly important factor motivating donors in creating foundations. Indeed, there is now strong evidence to suggest that such fiscal considerations are now the primary factor.*

But whatever the motivation—simple or complex, admirable or questionable—the creation of a foundation is a particularly personal, even egotistical, act. It tends to be performed either by a person in middle age, riding the crest of financial success, or by someone at the end of a long and successful career, faced with death and destiny. The result becomes a mirror held up to the ultimate qualities and limitations of his intelligence, character, and social outlook. Not surprisingly, therefore, odd inconsistencies appear. Some of the toughest old brutes in business were openly sentimental when it came to philanthropy; some of those who were the most cynical in money matters were remarkably naive in their charities; and some of those who were broad and forward-looking in the direction of their corporations were narrow and old-fashioned in guiding their foundations.

That the usual forms of organizational rationality do not govern the intense and intimate step of creating a foundation is perhaps most graphically shown by an examination of the methods by which the donors of the large foundations went about it. With few exceptions, all were men with long and successful experience in establishing major enterprises. Logically, it might be assumed that the typical donor would seek sound advice, review the experience of other institutions, assemble a board and staff of proven competence in philanthropy, and define the program of his foundation on the basis of some study of social or scientific needs.

But instead, if he consults anyone it is usually his lawyer, accountant, or wife. He usually makes no study of the work of other foundations and defines no clear objectives for his own. He feels

* The Peterson Commission in 1969 found that only 4 percent of large private donors said their giving would be unaffected by the elimination of tax incentives. The remaining 96 percent indicated that such a move would reduce their giving, and the median reduction was 75 percent. (Commission Report, p. 34) For further comments on why foundations are established and why donors give, see Warren Weaver, *U.S. Philanthropic Foundations* (New York, Harper & Row, 1967); and Hearings/HR CWM/91C1/1969/Part 4/ pp. 1483 ff.

little need for professional staff, and chooses trustees not for their competence in charitable work but for their pliancy. In effect he ignores the lessons of his long experience in organization-building since his objective is not really to build an institution. Rather, as he sees it, he is merely creating a vehicle for his own giving, or if he is advanced in age, for perpetuating control over his financial empire and the privileges of his descendants.

As a result, although donors have often been remarkably farseeing and creative in their businesses, they generally have been shortsighted and inept in launching their foundations. Compare for instance the innovativeness of the Eli Lilly pharmaceutical company with the style of the Lilly Endowment; the drive of the Minnesota Mining and Manufacturing Company with the torpidity of the A. G. Bush Foundation; the scientific leadership and the global approach of the du Pont Company under Pierre du Pont with the quaintness of his Longwood Foundation; the sweep and vision of the General Motors Corporation under Alfred Sloan with the eccentric quality of his foundation; the expansive outlook of Jesse Jones in his public and private career with the localism of his foundation; and the dynamism of the Sun Oil Company with the anachronistic quality of the foundation controlled by the Pew family. Obviously, qualities that make for success in creating the one have relatively limited application to the other.

The record clearly suggests that half or more of the major donors were men of limited mind and spirit and were incapable of creating foundations whose goals and program conceptions were proportionate to their resources. This is a commentary with profound meaning for a society that has traditionally granted major responsibility for its development to its business and financial leaders.*

Trustees and Trusteeship

In the long term, the legitimacy of the institution of private philanthropy rests on the principle of trusteeship. Legally, the board

---

* *Fortune* magazine describes them, and its clientele, as "the men who manage change" in American life.

of trustees *is* the foundation; all of its corporate affairs are conducted by the board's authority and in its name. It is to this group of private persons that the donor "entrusts" his endowment, to be managed in accordance with his wishes, and in whom society places its "trust" that the institution will be managed for the public benefit.°

Under the American system, donors are free to choose virtually anyone they wish as their trustees; thereafter, boards of trustees have the widest latitude in setting their criteria for membership and in choosing their successors. In theory, this high degree of freedom is the essence of, and indispensable to, the idea of democratic pluralism; and underlying it is the assumption that trustees are persons of honor and integrity, motivated essentially by a desire to serve the public interest and free of conflicting interests or obligations that would interfere with their independence of judgment.

In making their initial board selections, donors reach out to a limited circle: members of their family, officers of their company, their legal and financial advisers, close business associates. Occasionally an educator or a clergyman is added. Implicitly, their criteria have been two: persons whom they have known personally and in whom they had confidence; and persons who could be relied on to carry out their intention of maintaining family control over the foundation and over their property.†

° Throughout this discussion, the term "trustee" is used so as to include the directors not only of charitable trusts but also of corporate foundations. The legal distinction between the responsibilities of "trustees" and "directors" is limited and now disappearing. Marion Fremont-Smith, for example, suggests that corporate foundation directors be called "quasi-trustees" since they possess the attributes of ordinary trustees but are not subject to some of the more stringent supervisory powers of the probate courts. (*Foundations and Government* [New York, Russell Sage Foundation, 1965], p. 130)

† Only two of the big foundations pay their trustees substantial fees. Each board member of the Duke Endowment receives $46,300 a year for his part-time service; the trustees of the Fleischmann Foundation receive $30,000. The board members of the Moody Foundation receive $10,000; those of the Ford Foundation receive $5,000 and at times have been given other perquisites, such as the use of Ford Motor Company vehicles and opportunities to travel abroad with their wives on foundation assignments. But the trustees of most of the big foundations serve without remuneration. This practice, commonly as-

If the donor's primary criterion in choosing his trustees is their willingness to comply with his financial as well as his charitable objectives, their own principal criterion in choosing their successors once the founder has passed from the scene is "collegiality." This term derives from the idea that a board to function efficiently should be composed of persons who share common values and whose fund of mutual confidence permits easy communication and ready decision. In plainer terms, collegiality in practice has meant that the members of a foundation board are normally drawn from the business, legal, financial, and social circles of the donor and his family since they can be counted on to have "sound" ideas and not to make trouble. The usual product of this selection method is a homogeneous group consisting of aging members of the upper socioeconomic class in American society.

In age, the typical foundation trustee is between fifty and seventy. The few who are in their thirties and forties are almost invariably descendants of the donor; those few in their eighties and nineties are usually donors or members of donor families. Because several of the major foundations now have a mandatory retirement age of seventy for trustees, there are not many beyond that age. The boards are made up almost entirely of men, the few women normally being from the donor family. In race, they are almost exclusively white. Virtually all trustees are college educated, most of them in private Ivy League colleges. The biggest single group are businessmen, followed by lawyers; together they make up a majority. The rest of them include educators, doctors, foundation officers, and mass media executives.

The majority are of British or Northern European origin; their religion is Protestant (usually Presbyterian or Episcopalian); and their politics are Republican. Geographically, they come from the immediate area in which the foundation is based, and since many of the big foundations are located in the East, most of the trustees are Easterners. With rare exception, they are American citizens.[2]

Those who are seldom represented on the boards of the big

_____

sumed to ensure honorable motivation, may principally have the effect of making it impossible for persons without means to serve on foundation boards in the unlikely event that they should be invited.

foundations include young people, females, nonwhites, Catholics, Jews, Democrats, and persons whose forebears came from such places as Ireland, Italy, Greece, or Poland. There are very few prominent intellectuals, artists, writers, or social reformers. There is a total exclusion of labor union officials. Since only "successful" people become trustees, there are no representatives of the poor or the dispossessed. Some trustees are possibly identified with the radical Right, but none are known to be affiliated with either communism or the New Left.

Big foundation boards are a microcosm of what has variously been called the Establishment, the power elite, or the American ruling class. In this respect, they are even more homogeneous than the governing boards of churches, universities, and civic and welfare organizations of various kinds, and they are more resistant to change.* As of 1970, only the boards of major American profit-making corporations are more consistently and uniformly white upper-income Anglo-Saxon-Protestant than the boards of the big foundations. Of the 3,182 senior officers and directors of the nation's top fifty corporations, according to a study in 1970, only three were black.[3]

The most obvious problem created by the incestuousness of foundation boards relates to conflicts of interest. Anyone qualified to serve as a foundation trustee almost of necessity has potential or actual conflicts of interest—for example, direct or indirect connections with institutions that are potential grantees, or ties with banks or corporations that might benefit from foundation investment decisions. Nonetheless, important distinctions can be made concerning the nature and degree of such conflicts.

---

* A study of the governing boards of American universities conducted by the Educational Testing Service in 1970, for example, reflects their changing composition. "Where once the boards of trustees were made up largely of elderly and white men, since 1968 a significant number of institutions have added Negroes, women, and persons under 40 years of age. . . . Negroes have become board members at 14 percent of the 500 predominantly white universities included in the survey. The total is six times the number of Blacks who previously had served on these boards. . . . Women have been added to about one in five of all coeducational or all male colleges. Nearly one-third of the institutions reported that one or more trustees under forty years of age had been added."

To avoid unrealistic fastidiousness, therefore, and to achieve greater precision, conflict of interest for purposes of this analysis is taken to mean: being a member of a donor family with major financial holdings in a company directly associated with or controlled by a foundation; employment as an officer of such an associated or controlled corporation; employment by the donor family or such associated company in the capacity of legal or investment counselor; ownership of a significant block of stock in an associated company whether or not the trustee is a member of the donor family or a present executive of the company; and affiliation as a major stockholder or senior executive of a bank with which the donor family or the associated company is also closely identified.

By this definition the boards of the big American foundations are currently ridden with conflicts of interest incompatible with their objective and exclusive devotion to philanthropic purposes and the public interest.

Only nine of them can be said to be independent and unconflicted: Astor, Carnegie, Commonwealth, Fleischmann, Ford, Kettering, Rockefeller, Rockefeller Brothers, and Sloan. In addition, the Bush Foundation, which formerly had an unsavory board situation until public authorities intervened, should now be added to this group. This categorization does not imply "purity" in a theoretical sense: family members sit on the Astor, Carnegie, Ford, Rockefeller, and Kettering boards and dominate the board of the Rockefeller Brothers Fund, for example. Other members of these boards are connected with major beneficiary institutions. But in practical terms, these conflicts of interest are here considered to be limited and incidental.

The boards of most of the other big foundations are heavily conflicted. The Woodruff Foundation has virtually all its assets in Coca-Cola Company stock. The dominant individual on its board is Robert Woodruff, son of the donor, who is also the dominant figure in the company. The other members of the board are all connected in one way or another with Coca-Cola or with Woodruff's business and banking interests.

The board of the Haas Community Fund (Waterman) is composed principally of members of the Haas family who are also executives or major shareholders in Rohm and Haas, the family-controlled company in which the assets of the foundation are held. The board of the Pew Memorial Trust, which conceals itself behind the facade of the Glenmede Trust Company, is composed predominantly of members of the Pew family, all of whom are executives or major shareholders in Sun Oil Company and Minerals Development Corporation, in which the assets of the foundation are held; both the foundation and the corporations are controlled by the Pew family.

A majority of the trustees of the Moody Foundation—though the board now includes three independent members forced upon it by public authority—are members of the Moody family and are also major shareholders in or beneficiaries of associated companies in which most of the assets of the foundation are still held. The Richard K. Mellon Foundation, like the other Mellon foundations, has a small board made up partly of family members and partly of executives of companies or institutions heavily influenced by Mellon shareholdings or benefactions. The Longwood Foundation, like most of the du Pont foundations, has a small board dominated by members of the family and executives of du Pont–controlled companies, in which the assets of the foundation are principally held. The board of the Lilly Endowment, with only one exception, is made up of members of the Lilly family and executives of Eli Lilly & Company, which is controlled by the family and in which the assets of the foundation are principally held. Several trustees of the Duke Endowment are past or present officers of the Duke Power Company in which the bulk of its assets are held, and two of them are members of a law firm which receives fees from the foundation.

The board of the Kellogg Foundation has heavy cross-membership with that of the related company, in which the assets of the trust from which the foundation derives its income are concentrated. The Hartford Foundation's board is dominated by men who serve or have served the Great Atlantic and Pacific Tea Company, in which the foundation's assets are held.

The kind of conflict of interest represented by individuals on foundation boards who are also responsible officers of major recipient institutions presents different but no less serious problems. If a foundation with major program interests in higher education, for example, does not include some university figures on its board it may deprive itself of an essential kind of experience and knowledgeability in making its decisions. But if it includes such a person it runs the risk of acquiring a "built-in grantee" and in effect being discriminatory against all unrepresented institutions of that category. On the whole, it would appear that university heads and officers of other nonprofit organizations serving as foundation trustees have been sensitive to this problem and have conducted themselves with restraint. But in some cases, certain trustees of Ford, Sloan, and Commonwealth, for example, have sometimes behaved as if their primary responsibility as trustees was to ensure that their school or institute got its proper "share" of the foundation's outlays.

There is no real evidence that the heavily conflicted boards of the big foundations have indulged in the cruder forms of self-aggrandizement. The record of their trustees in this respect is not impeccable, but it is very good.

But there is much troubling, though inconclusive, indication that they have been delinquent in fulfilling the broader obligations of their trusteeship. Consistently, foundations linked with the automobile industry have been reluctant to finance research and experimentation on car safety, for example. Foundations connected with the chemical industry have been equally reluctant to take action on problems of air and water pollution, as have foundations connected with the petroleum industry to study questions related to tax equity and the oil depletion allowance.

Likewise, in investment policy, the trustees of the big foundations repeatedly avow their obligation to act as "prudent men," but nonetheless they frequently acquiesce in keeping all or most of their foundations' investments tied to an associated company whenever the donor, the donor's family, or the company executives have wanted them to do so, even when the results have been substantially to diminish the benefits to charity.*

---

* Investment analysts generally, and the courts in a number of instances, have agreed that nondiversification of investments is inherently imprudent.

Fremont-Smith in *Foundations and Government*, p. 100, gives this summary

Quite obviously, the operative definition of the obligations of "trusteeship" has only incidental relevance to the ideas commonly stressed in philosophical and legal writing on the subject. Trustees accept appointment not out of simple and pure motivation to serve the public interest but also because service on a foundation board fits into the total pattern of their professional, economic and social interests. Once appointed, most of them, judging from their actual behavior, appear to feel that in regard to both philanthropic and financial policy they are primarily trustees of the donor and donor family, and only secondarily of society. So long as the donor is alive, they are fully responsive to his wishes, even his whims. After his death, it is their custom to honor his notions about the foundation's priorities and program and to give special respect to the preferences of any of his descendants on the board, who are curiously considered to be the inheritors of his special rights and prerogatives. His ghost in several cases has sat in the board room for decades after his death.

The extent to which the governing body of a private institution should be representative of or responsible to its staff, its constituency, or society at large is obviously a matter of intense national debate at the present time, particularly with respect to universities and corporations. There are those who still believe that there is no need for private institutions that serve democratic societies to be democratic in their own procedures or representative in their governance. They find no fault with the tradition of giving full author-

---

of judicial attitudes: "One aspect of the application of the prudent man rule to trust investments is the question of diversification of risk. Common sense dictates that it is not prudent to keep too many eggs in one basket. The question of diversification is particularly important to trustees of the many charitable foundations to which donors have contributed large amounts of stock of a closely held corporation. Unfortunately, the cases do not make clear how far a trustee is subject to liability for failure to diversify investments. The requirement of diversification has been specifically recognized by the courts in some jurisdictions and has been imposed by statute in others." Fremont-Smith cites Ind. Ann. Stat., sec. 31–507; Tenn. Code Ann., secs. 35–308, 35–309, 35–310; N.H. Rev. Stat. Ann., sec. 386; 16; S.C. Code Ann., sec. 67–58.

For a general discussion of investment powers, see Charles P. Curtis, *The Modern Prudent Investor* (Philadelphia, Joint Committee on Continuing Legal Education of the American Law Institute and the American Bar Association, 1961).

ity over a foundation's affairs to a self-selected group of trustees that is neither drawn from nor responsible to the individuals and institutions most directly affected by their decisions. Indeed, some claim positive advantages in it. In private, many donors and trustees of the large foundations will contend that an individual prepared to devote his wealth to philanthropic purposes has the unfettered "right"—a kind of corollary to his private property rights—to pick men who will distribute that wealth in accordance with his wishes. To compromise this "right" in any significant way would, in their view, ultimately extinguish the institution of private philanthropy. Many of them also would say—even though it smacks of ethnocentrism—that the Protestant ethic is a special kind of "civic conscience" that deserves to be protected. American philanthropy, it is claimed, is an outgrowth of it; the humanitarianism inspired by it has made a great contribution to the progress and decency of American life in the past and will be no less important in the future. To dilute the uniformity of foundation boards in order to achieve greater "representativeness" would in their view be an inappropriate application of a political concept to a nonpolitical institution.*

But today the legitimacy of traditional concepts of choosing directors and trustees is increasingly challenged. Institutions of all kinds have been impelled by the temper of the times to be increas-

---

* For a somewhat shrill version of the same argument, see Warren Weaver's *U.S. Philanthropic Foundations*. In his opinion, those (unspecified) foundations which "take a broad and serious view of their public responsibility . . . place the final authority for policy and for all major decisions with a group of absolutely top-flight persons—men of experience, of special talent, of wisdom, and of integrity. These men are in no sense representatives of the founder or the founding family. In no conceivable sense do they represent the industry identified with the fortune in question. . . .

"From time to time one hears suggestions that at least part of the board should "represent the public" and that these members should be chosen in some way by the public. . . . From a long knowledge of several of the most important self-perpetuating foundation boards, I assert that they do indeed represent the public interest; and I cannot conceive of a procedure of public selection that would produce boards more intelligent, unselfish, and dedicated than those which result under the existing procedures" (p. 107). In stating his argument, Weaver omits to make explicit his own definition of "the public interest."

ingly responsive to their constituents, consulting them more often and bringing them into their councils. In the universities, both faculty and students are actively seeking participation in their own governance. The old notion that American society can safely delegate to self-selected corporate boards or university trustees final responsibility for interpreting the public interest and for operating their institutions in a manner consistent with it is increasingly questioned, and not only by radical critics.[4] The issue at stake has its parallel in respect to the governance of foundations.

Thus far, the big foundations have taken only hesitant action to overhaul their policies on trusteeship. A few, such as Rockefeller, Ford, Kettering, and Danforth, have voluntarily broadened and enlarged their boards. Some have now introduced a limitation on the number of years nonfamily trustees can serve. Many have at least begun to ask themselves questions about the proper role of the board: whether it should confine itself to investment matters and the hiring and firing of the president or whether it should play a more active role in program administration and grant evaluation. If the responsibilities of the boards are expanded to include these functions, foundations will find it even more difficult to justify in the future their general habit of selecting elderly, prestigious, extremely busy, and generally nonintellectual and nonscientific persons as trustees.

In no other aspect of private philanthropy is the theory so venerable and refined as it is with respect to trusteeship; and in no other aspect is the reality so deficient, so confused, and so potentially threatening to the viability of the institution.

Foundation Staffs

A number of major institutions, from the Catholic Church to the French government, have sometimes been able to overcome defects in their structure of governance by the caliber and dedication of their professional staff. But this is not so among most of the big foundations simply because they have little or no such staff. About one-quarter employ no full-time professionals, operating with only an accountant or secretary: Brown, Fleischmann, Irvine, Longwood, Nemours, Pew, and Surdna. Another quarter operate with only one or two professionals, in some cases on less than a full-time basis: Astor, Houston, Kaiser, Kresge, Moody, Richardson, Scaife, and Woodruff. A few employ what could be called a professional nucleus: Hartford, Haas (Waterman), Lilly, A. W. Mellon, R. K. Mellon, and Mott. Only ten have reasonably well-developed and capable staffs: Carnegie, Commonwealth, Danforth, Duke, Ford, Kellogg, Kettering, Rockefeller, Rockefeller Brothers, and Sloan.

Within this last group, the range in staff size is considerable: the Ford Foundation has 611 professionals, Rockefeller 160, Carnegie 41, Duke 38, Sloan 30, Danforth 32, Kellogg 27, Rockefeller Brothers 17, and Commonwealth 12. Even the largest foundation staffs, however, are small compared to those of universities and are almost microscopic compared to large corporations and government agencies.

Why staff members of grant-making foundations enter the profession at all, or remain in it, is something of a mystery, for there is hardly another comparable field of activity that is subject to so much disparagement by its clientele. The general public may regard philanthropic work as relatively prestigious, but in the academic and scientific community foundation officers are often considered second-rate individuals whose credentials would not qualify them for the faculties and staffs of first-rate universities or research centers. Similarly, many figures in intellectual life and the creative arts tend to think of them as bureaucratic functionaries. Although many government officials view foundation employment at times with some envy, they also think of it as a refuge for people who have retired to the periphery of affairs.

To be sure, with few exceptions one does not find great scientific minds in the grant-making foundations, nor great scholars, writers, musicians, or painters. Neither does one find the great social innovators or teachers. But this is precisely as it should be. The role of the foundation executive is different from that of all these professions, and it requires its own specialized skills. Much of the surreptitious disrespect accorded him reflects little credit on the understanding or the generosity of spirit of those who feel superior.*

Foundations, of course, employ various kinds of persons on their staffs, including clerks, stenographers, accountants, investment counselors, and scientists. For the category of foundations that is the focus of this study, however, the key personnel are the "program officers," that is, those whose work is the analysis and assessment of grant proposals.

In many respects they resemble the boards of trustees. They are almost entirely white, from middle- and upper-class backgrounds, educated at the better private colleges, Protestant, and British or North European in ethnic origin. They are not in the same income bracket as the trustees, but their dress and their manners are similar. The working atmosphere in most of the large foundations is genteel; Jews, blacks, and women (as professional employees) have not generally been permitted to intrude.

But some distinctions have to be made. The above characterization is true of the majority of large foundations with small staffs. Those few that employ a relatively large number of professionals have accepted more diverse types, and in several cases a significant contrast between board and staff in terms of socioeconomic background and political and social values can be noted. Moreover, time is beginning to bring further changes. The WASP homogeneity is being diluted by the appointment of a small but growing number of blacks, of individuals from various lower-status ethnic

* Some psychologists believe that the root of much of the resentment of the academic, scientific, and scholarly community toward the foundation officer lies in the nature of his position, which requires him to be their judge and evaluator. When he rejects a proposal it is interpreted as an adverse ruling on both the applicant's idea and his capabilities. And since foundations have to decline more than 90 percent of all proposals, the foundation officer constantly increases the number of disappointed and resentful applicants. Nor are those who receive grants necessarily grateful or admiring. Most of them feel that they were merely given their due, or perhaps something less. Former Vice-President Alben Barkley of Kentucky used to say that any patronage job for a politician was simply a "device for manufacturing nine enemies and one ingrate." Foundation officers have often felt that their grant budget is the same kind of infernal machine.

Donors, Trustees, and Staff

males as staff professionals. But these appointments tend to be at
the specialist level, not at the general executive level. Consequently, in the foundations with the larger staffs a kind of "generation gap" exists between the lower and upper echelons in both
background and attitudes.

With that half of the big foundations with tiny staffs, employment commonly is the result of a personal association with the
donor or an influential trustee rather than educational or professional qualification. In earlier times the foundation officer tended
to be a former "private secretary" of the donor. More recently he
seems to be a lawyer who has served the donor or his company, a
junior executive of the company, or a retired educator, frequently
from the donor's alma mater.

For the foundations with larger staffs whose functions are of a
specialized character, appointment now depends less on personal
connections than on objective qualifications. Chief executives come
from backgrounds in law, academic life, or government; program
officers come from academic life, government service, or sometimes
other nonprofit organizations. Foundations that emphasize scientific research, notably Rockefeller, draw that portion of their staff
from universities or research institutions working in similar fields.
A few notable foundation officers have come from journalism, labor
organizations, politics, and the ministry. They enter philanthropy
for several reasons: salaries, compared at least with those in government and the university, are good; the perquisites are excellent;
and job security is unexcelled. There is range and diversity in the
problems one deals with and in the contacts one makes; and there
is the feeling that one is "doing good." The field has a particular
attraction for the well-educated, the idealistic, and perhaps the in-
secure. For the academic it appears to offer a chance to get out of
the ivory tower and into contact with more concrete problems. For
the government official it seems an escape from the burdens of bureaucracy or from the advent of a new and uncongenial administration. For both of them it has the special appeal of being at least
a worthwhile "interim career"—although only a few of those who
enter foundations intending to move on actually do.

The new young program officer of a grant-making foundation quickly finds that his work is markedly different from what he has done before. The ex-academic discovers that he not only does not teach, he does not do research or writing in a scholarly or scientific sense; the man from government discovers that he no longer administers much of anything, and the numbers he deals with—of both dollars and employees—are suddenly much smaller. In his new role he is the nonprofit equivalent of a junior partner in an investment bank: he listens to the endless stream of proposals brought to the foundation and tries to formulate judgments on the merit of the ideas and the capacity of the applicants to carry them out. In most cases his involvement in any given project is limited to appraising it and its sponsor and recommending that it be financed or rejected. Then he moves on to the next item of business.

At the beginning, one of the unexpected pleasures for a new foundation officer is a sense of being at the center of things. He suddenly finds himself the focus of attention at social and professional gatherings where persons of importance take him aside to talk to him about their current project. His words on almost any subject are listened to with unaccustomed respect; even his pauses are taken to be significant. He is touched, in short, by the aura of power which the vast wealth of his foundation creates. For a young man of previously modest position in academia or government, this is heady wine, and if he is naive and vulnerable, he may have difficulty learning to apply the necessary discount of skepticism to the flattery he receives. But later, for a good proportion of the able people who enter philanthropy, frustrations begin. The low professional visibility of the work and the anonymity troubles many. The sense of isolation, of being cut off from intellectual and scientific peers outside the foundation compound, troubles others. Younger officers, given the typically small size of foundation staffs, begin to be concerned by the lack of any ladder for long-term advancement. Those who have come from the government and are accustomed to its scale of activity sometimes begin to feel that philanthropy is only a small side show and its resources inconsequential. Those from academic life, on the other hand, begin to be discontented by the continuous pressure to make new grants and launch new projects, with the consequent impossibility of seriously reviewing and evaluating past activities.*

But there are also more insidious frustrations. One is the inevitable realization for a grant officer that although he may receive public flattery, he is commonly held in private disrespect by those with whom he has professional dealings and with whom he feels the greatest sense of intellectual affinity. This ambiguous position tends over time to undermine his own self-esteem and the savor of his work. Another burden on his spirit is the vicarious nature of his job satisfactions. In those instances where a grant he has arranged enables a scholar or scientist to go on to great achievement, he feels a sense of reward. But in most cases he knows that he had little to do with the origin of the idea, that he made little if any contribution to the substantive formulation of the project, and that he had even less to do with its execution. Quite often, too, the scientist or scholar directly responsible for the project fails to remember or to give any credit to the foundation officer for whatever part he may have played. As in any kind of work, the efforts of the foundation officer turn out to have mixed results. Some of the grants with which he has dealt prove to be poor, most of them mediocre, and only a few excellent. He gains little psychic income from the failures and the undistinguished ones and he is not able to get much satisfaction even from his successes.

The overprotected, competitionless environment of foundations also has a corrosive effect on morale. Because of the traditional secrecy of philanthropy, an officer's ideas are insulated from the shock and stimulation of the kind of criticism to which the scientist

---

* Frederick T. Gates, the picturesque genius who played so prominent a part in guiding the philanthropic activities of John D. Rockefeller Sr., used to say; "In this business you have to live the life of a recluse. Never make friends. Don't join clubs. Avoid knowing people intimately. Never put yourself in a position where your judgment is swayed by unconscious motives." But Raymond Fosdick, who headed the Rockefeller Foundation later, commented, "The sensitive antennae necessary to detect opportunity and need and to trace the changing urgencies in human effort are not apt to be the products of isolation." (*Chronicle of a Generation: An Autobiography* [New York, Harper, 1958], p. 251)

or scholar is normally exposed. The results of his work are often intangible or unmeasurable and in any event are evaluated, if at all, by himself or persons in the foundation's employ. Foundation boards are usually incapable of appraising the work of a staff officer on technical or intellectual grounds, and in most foundations with developed professional staffs, internal cross-criticism is not common. Instead, there frequently develops a kind of tacit nonaggression pact among the heads of various divisions: "You lay off my program and I'll lay off yours."

Some grant officers, of course, find a kind of relief in the insulation against harsh challenge. A few, but only a few, take positive satisfaction in the element of power that a foundation position gives. The most able and energetic ultimately come to feel that they are living in an unreal landscape where the hot sun never blazes, the cold winds never blow, and failure does not exist. Eventually, their enthusiasm and productivity fade.

There are some splendid exceptions. Abraham Flexner of the Carnegie and Rockefeller foundations and Warren Weaver of the Rockefeller and Sloan foundations found in philanthropy a deeply satisfying lifetime career. McNeil Lowry of the Ford Foundation and Robert Morison, formerly of Rockefeller, are highly esteemed by the leaders in their fields outside philanthropy. And the late William McPeak of the Ford Foundation took a combative pleasure in injecting honest self-criticism into the workings of what he felt was a stagnating institution.

To catalogue the frustrations afflicting foundation employees is not necessarily to suggest that their lot is a distinctively unhappy one. Clearly philanthropy has greater appeal to some individuals than to others. Moreover, its rewards vary greatly from foundation to foundation; they also vary according to the nature of an individual's responsibilities. On the whole, employees directly involved in research or the operation of projects seem to gain greater sustained satisfaction than those concerned only with grant-making. The scientist working in the laboratory of a large foundation, or the person who is part of a team at an agricultural experiment station, or the young man who is associated directly with a development project in a field office abroad tends to have a more positive attitude toward his work than the officer who sits in the home office talking to applicants and processing grant papers.

Finally, the attraction of foundation employment can vary from time to time. There have been periods when the exciting opportunities of government service have made philanthropy seem comparatively dull to those in a position to choose between them. Conversely, there have been other times when opportunities in government have seemed dismal compared to those in the more active foundations.

Interactions and the Shifting Locus of Power

Power in a foundation means final authority over investment decisions, program objectives, grant decisions, administrative policy, and the appointment and dismissal of executive officers. Over time it tends to migrate from donors and their descendants to the trustees. The influence of the third element, the professional staff, grows but rarely becomes decisive.

In its initial years, a foundation is usually under the complete domination of the donor. In the case of more than half the big foundations, they have had the benefit, or the handicap, of the donor's active involvement in their affairs for ten to more than forty years. Sometimes he runs it from his own desk, sometimes by broad delegation to trusted associates. But whatever his method of control, his personal influence normally becomes less and less constructive as he himself advances into old age.

Donors frequently live remarkably long; but they do eventually die, and when they do their influence with some degree of diminution generally passes to their descendants or relatives. But after the second generation, the intensity of the family's interest in philanthropy rapidly slopes down.* At this point, the board of trustees as such presumably moves into the controlling role.

* Only the Rockefeller family has so far been able to sustain a longer tradition, followed at some distance by the Mellons. An interesting variation of the pattern of declining interest in the family's principal foundation is the ten-

The degree and manner in which this occurs reflect the pattern common in the corporate sphere, from which so many foundation trustees come. In a few cases, such as Houston, Kresge, and Fleischmann, the board takes direct responsibility for all administrative and policy decisions, including grant making. But most commonly there is a division of authority between board and staff. The trustees tend to retain decision over investment matters, budget, and the hiring and firing of the executives, while they delegate or share authority over the substance of grants and program with the professional staff. In some, as in the Carnegie Corporation, the tradition is to accord to the president and staff wide latitude in program matters: the board rarely takes initiative and almost never rejects a project or program recommended by the officers. The Rockefeller board operates according to the same general principle but at times plays a somewhat more active role in the shaping of programs. The Ford Foundation board has at times been passive but in more recent years has insisted on its right to take initiatives and exercise rather firm direction over program priorities.

The question of staff power in foundations must be understood in this context. The staffs of most of the large foundations are in fact very small, and they tend to be located in communities where the donor family and the other trustees are overwhelming figures on the local scene. When the executive head of such foundations as Lilly, Brown, Richardson, Longwood, and Scaife, for example, meets with the chairman of the board in his hushed and handsome office, or in the paneled boardroom of the donor's great company, he is acutely aware of where authority lies and that he is indeed a servant in the household of the prince.

Among the better foundations with larger staffs, a different atmosphere prevails, and a different balance between boards and staffs results. In so far as power can be said sometimes to lie on the staff side, it centers in large degree on the person of the president. There have been occasional situations, as in the Rockefeller Foundation, for example, where a staff member other than the president

---

dency of some of the younger Rockefeller, Mellon, and Mott descendants to set up their own smaller foundations to pursue experimental, sometimes almost radical, programs.

enjoyed such eminence in his professional field that his program recommendations could not readily be questioned. But these situations are exceptional.

Although the more fully developed staffs of the large foundations may not have immediate decision-making power, they have an influence on the affairs of the institution that over the long run profoundly affects the character and shape of its program. Naturally, a foundation does not acquire a strong and well-developed staff unless the board desires it; but once this kind of staff exists, almost irreversible processes are set into motion that impel it still further to expand the scope and improve the technical quality of its programs. A kind of dynamic balance evolves between the board and the staff that can be enormously productive but cannot adequately be described as a simple sharing of power.

Conservative critics in recent times have warned that a dangerous kind of "managerial revolution" is sweeping through foundations, by which the staffs come to control programs and policies, displacing the boards and thereby exercising "irresponsible" authority. It is true that in a few foundations strong staffs have strong influence. It is also true that in two instances—Malcom Aldrich of the Commonwealth Fund and Ralph Burger of the Hartford Foundation—men who were originally staff employees were able, as a result of unusual circumstances, to "capture" those foundations and exercise a remarkable degree of authority over the investments, trustees, and programs. But these have been rarities. For the most part, where donor control is not the reality, trustees retain sovereign authority, including decision over the framework of program. Within that framework, staffs may enjoy wider or narrower discretion and they may, in time, through their expertise, play a role in reshaping the framework. But governance—in the sense of the final power to decide immediate issues of policy—in fact and in theory rests with the boards.

18.

Big Philanthropy and
the Race Question:
A Case Study of Performance

ONE WAY TO JUDGE the significance of philanthropic
programs for American society is to examine their relationship to the
great contemporary issues of social change. The vocabulary foundations have adopted to describe their work suggests that they en-
visage themselves as part of the innovative vanguard. But to determine the extent to which the big foundations address themselves to
urgent issues of social change and the kinds of actions they take in
trying to deal with them, it is necessary to go beyond generalities
and look at their actual performance on specific problems. None is
more instructive than that of racial discrimination in the United
States. It is the oldest, the most visible, and now, in the view of
many, the most ominous challenge facing American democracy.

By the time the first of the big foundations were established, the
American race problem already had a tangled three-hundred-year
history and had again reached a crisis. Despite emancipation after
the Civil War, the black remained at the bottom of the pyramid of
American life. A complete system of political, economic, and social
discrimination had been reimposed on him, sanctioned by decisions of the Supreme Court and enforced by the unrestrained violence of the Ku Klux Klan. He was not only segregated and power-
less, but it was generally assumed that he was inferior and
incapable of achieving higher skills.

Through World War I the racial climate did not change. The
federal government enacted no new civil rights legislation and

made little effort to enforce existing laws. As black migration toward the industrial cities increased, Jim Crowism began to creep northward; it was under President Woodrow Wilson that the facilities of the federal government were resegregated in the District of Columbia. General John J. Pershing continued the long tradition of discrimination against Negroes in the armed services by refusing to accept black combat units in the American Expeditionary Force. They went overseas nevertheless, but fought as French soldiers, wearing French uniforms, serving under French officers, and earned French decorations for their heroism. But despite the repressive atmosphere, some hopeful signs were seen. The first was the emergence of influential black spokesmen. At the turn of the century Booker T. Washington urged blacks to develop their agricultural and mechanical skills in order to achieve positions of responsibility in the mainstream of American life. His gradualist approach was subsequently challenged by others such as W. E. B. Du Bois, who argued for a direct attack on "all caste distinctions," and by the National Association for the Advancement of Colored People, which after its founding in 1909 organized a legal attack on disenfranchisement and all forms of segregation.

Buttressing the efforts of the black community itself, various religious groups (especially the Baptists and Methodists) as well as a few smaller educational foundations that had been created in the late nineteenth century (the Peabody Fund, the Slater Fund, and the Anna T. Jeanes Fund) were diligently at work in the South to provide educational opportunities for the blacks. Nevertheless, as the first of the big foundations was established, the black remained in extreme need of help; moreover, his predicament was worsening, not improving.

THE GENERAL EDUCATION BOARD

The first of the major philanthropists to concern himself with the black problem was John D. Rockefeller. He and his wife, Laura Spelman Rockefeller, came from a tradition of religious and humanitarian concern about slavery and racial discrimination. Before the Civil War, her father had helped runaway slaves to make their perilous journey to Canada; after the war, the Spelmans continued their interest in black welfare. Through his close ties with the Baptist Church, Rockefeller contributed to missionary and educational activities in the South as soon as his fortune began to grow. When he established his first major institutional philanthropy after the turn of the century his intention was to call it the Negro Education Board, but he was dissuaded from limiting its purpose in this way by Henry St. George Tucker, then president of Washington and Lee University, who argued: "If it is your idea to educate the Negro, you must have the White of the South with you. If the poor White sees the son of a Negro neighbor enjoying through your munificence benefits denied to his boy, it raises in him a feeling that will render futile all your work. You must lift up the 'poor White' and the Negro together if you would approach success."

In April 1902 Rockefeller created the *General* Education Board with the first of what was to be a succession of major gifts. (In all, these totaled $129.2 million between 1902 and 1921.) From then until World War I the GEB was the single largest source of philanthropic funds for the development of education and educational opportunities for the black in the South.

Andrew Carnegie during the same period made substantial personal gifts to a number of black schools and colleges, particularly to Hampton and Tuskegee institutes. After the Carnegie Corporation was organized in 1911, it continued to make regular grants to these colleges as well as to such organizations as the National Urban League, which had been formed a few years before to deal with the problems of social and economic adjustment of blacks moving from the rural areas of the South to northern industrial cities. But in comparison with Carnegie's other philanthropic interests and the scale of the Rockefeller commitment these were relatively minor efforts.

The composition of the General Education Board gives an interesting glimpse of racial attitudes at the time. The men appointed were all white businessmen, educators, and clergymen. They were mainly from the North, and they had all previously displayed a religious or humanitarian interest in the condition of the black man. But their outlook was "liberal" only according to the norms of 1900. One of them, William H. Baldwin Jr., a railroad executive from abolitionist Boston, said in 1899: "The Negro should not be educated out of his environment. Industrial work is his salvation; he must work . . . at trades and on the land. . . . Except in the rarest of instances, I am bitterly opposed to the so-called higher education of Negroes." [1] J. M. L. Curry, one of the leading Southern members of the board, wrote: "The White people are to be the leaders, to have the initiative, to have the directive control in all matters pertaining to civilization and the highest interests of our beloved land. History demonstrates that the Caucasian will rule. He ought to rule. This white supremacy does not mean hostility to the Negro, but friendship for him." [2] Even Dr. Wallace Buttrick, a former Baptist minister who became the first executive head of the GEB, told a meeting of Tennessee school superintendents a year after his appointment that "The Negro is an inferior race. . . . The Anglo-Saxon is superior. There cannot be any question about that." [3]

Not surprisingly the board based its program on two premises—that its only hope of success was to work within the framework of racial segregation to ameliorate conditions, and that the most effective aid was education, essentially basic education and training in vocational skills. Recognizing that the resources of philanthropy alone were insufficient to effect a major change in the availability of education, it sought to stimulate nothing less than the creation of universal, publicly supported systems of primary and secondary schools throughout the South. At the time education in the region was in an abysmal state. Even for whites, the schoolhouses were few and dilapidated, and teachers' salaries were a disgrace. There was no tradition of free public schools, and no compulsory school attendance laws. Except for private academies, which were available only to white students who could pay the fees, there were no high schools. For blacks, educational possibilities were even worse. The idea of secondary education for them was generally opposed by white public opinion and in many areas was legally forbidden.

In pursuit of its stated goals, the GEB developed an extraordinarily active program: it made grants at the primary level to improve the qualifications and the effectiveness of school supervisors;

it promoted the consolidation of one-room schools and encouraged the transportation of children to these schools, first by horse and wagon and later by truck; it was ingenious in infiltrating the official educational structure with its paid "missionary specialists"; and it made effective use of liberal and persuasive Southerners rather than "outsiders" to gain public and political acceptance for its objectives.

Later, recognizing that there would have to be a more adequate tax base if a system of publicly supported schools was to be developed, the board began to take increasing interest in the problems of rural poverty, which led it in turn to a range of new efforts: demonstrations of new farming techniques; attempts to improve the marketing system for farm products; and the encouragement of "corn clubs" and "canning clubs" for rural boys and girls.

Within a few years encouraging results were achieved. But as support for better public education grew, the benefits went largely to schools attended by white children. Even the farm demonstration program and the corn and canning clubs mostly involved whites. So far as blacks were concerned, the initial GEB programs produced little benefit, though some aid did trickle down to them. This deficiency drew increasing criticism. In 1910, Booker T. Washington wrote to Buttrick, "I very much fear if the General Education Board continues to employ people to encourage white high schools, and does nothing for Negro high schools, the Southern white people will take it for granted that the Negro is to have few if any high schools."

Oswald Garrison Villard, editor of the liberal New York *Evening Post,* charged that blacks believed the board was "indifferent to their needs"; he appealed directly to John D. Rockefeller Jr., who acted as the donor's alter ego in the board's activities, to do something about the matter. With typical understatement Rockefeller then wrote to Buttrick: "I have felt for some time that possibly the Board was not performing its full duty to the Negro and that we should consider the situation fully and seriously."

Discussions and conferences were followed by a spurt of renewed emphasis on the black problem. In 1912, the board offered to subsidize the appointment of special officials in state departments of education throughout the South who could devote full time to the improvement of black schools. Three years later, working through the Slater Fund, it began to encourage the development of black secondary schools; emphasizing vocational education and domestic science, they were disguised as "county training schools" to appease Southern opinion. But after a brief time the GEB, under tension from within and pressure from without, weakened in its determination to concentrate almost entirely on the controversial problems of public education, rural poverty, and black advancement in the South. As World War I ended, major changes in the GEB's program and priorities were clearly impending.

THE ROSENWALD FUND

From 1910 onward, the cause of black education was aided by another important American philanthropist, Julius Rosenwald, the son of a Jewish immigrant who had amassed a fortune out of his development of the Sears Roebuck mail-order merchandising company. Strongly influenced by the ideas of Booker T. Washington, he became increasingly involved in the problem of the black in the South, at first making a number of contributions to various black colleges. Then, in 1912, he gave Dr. Washington a small sum to help stimulate the building of six rural schools for blacks in Alabama. The results of this experiment were so satisfactory that he provided funds for another hundred. In 1915, the year of Washington's death, Rosenwald made a public offer to pay one-third of the cost of an additional 300 schoolhouses. In 1917, to handle the growing number of applications for his help, he created the Rosenwald Fund, which further expanded the rural school building program.

To be eligible for Rosenwald funds, each school had to represent a common effort by state and county authorities and by local black and white citizens. The state and county had to contribute the principal part of the cost of the building and agree to maintain it as a regular part of the cost of the public school system. In addition—a telltale mark of Washington's influence—each school had to be constructed to provide not only for academic studies but also for carpentry and home arts, and two acres of land had to be made available for a school garden.

Initially, the Rosenwald Fund operated with the same approach —and with some of the same advisers—adopted by the General Education Board; it accepted the fact of segregation and worked within that context to try to improve the black's educational position.

New Problems and Patterns: The 1920s and 1930s

During the war hundreds of thousands of blacks had moved from the South to seek employment and a better life in the cities of the North. After the war, these and other changes led to intensified racial tensions. More than twenty-four major riots occurred in the last six months of 1919, white mobs took over whole cities, and violence against blacks went unchecked. In the South the Klan flourished: cross burnings, terrorism, and lynchings became commonplace. The NAACP performed valiantly, providing legal defense for the victims and appealing through its influential publication, *Crisis* (edited by W. E. B. Du Bois), for the enforcement of the Fourteenth and Fifteenth amendments.

THE GEB AND OTHER ROCKEFELLER INTERESTS

In this dangerous atmosphere the Rosenwald Fund not only persisted in its concern for Negro education but began to deal directly with basic issues of race relations and racial justice. But the GEB noticeably drew back, shifting its emphasis from the South and the problems of "the plainest sort of people" to less controversial problems of educational development throughout the United States.

The board's departure from its original approach aroused considerable bitterness in some quarters and led to accusations that it had been in conspiracy with white segregationists from the beginning.[4] But a fairer assessment would be that it was guilty mostly of excessive caution and half-heartedness, withdrawing too readily from the arduous task it had begun. In any event, there was a strong shift in the board's emphasis, but not total abandonment of its interest in black education. It continued to support some of its earlier programs, such as maintaining state agents in the South to promote better black education, and it made selective general support grants to a number of Negro colleges and medical schools. Its major innovation after 1920 was a fellowship program to provide advanced training for Southern white and black educators, based on a conviction that before many of the most serious schooling problems could be attacked directly, local leaders had to be produced who could take the primary responsibility for them. By the time the program ended three decades later the board's directory of fellows included the names of almost every black college president and prominent black educator in the United States. It enabled well-qualified individuals to realize their potential, and it demonstrated conclusively to blacks themselves, as well as to Southern whites, the intellectual capabilities of the black man.

Two other important Rockefeller philanthropies—the Rockefeller Foundation and the Laura Spelman Rockefeller Memorial, established in 1918—were also active during the same period. The foundation itself, set up in 1913, concentrated its work very largely in the fields of medicine and scientific research. Beginning in the early 1920s the memorial, under the direction of Beardsley Ruml, conducted a broad program of research in the social sciences with strong emphasis on problems of interracial relations. It financed studies of black life and history; it made grants to various organizations studying and administering to the economic, welfare, and health needs of blacks; it supported teaching and research programs in sovial sciences and social welfare in black colleges and universities; and it made a succession of major grants to the work of the Commission on Interracial Cooperation. In 1928, the memorial was absorbed into the Rockefeller Foundation as part of a broad reorganization of the family's philanthropies. At that point much of its boldest work was extinguished.*

* During this period, the personal actions of John D. Rockefeller Jr. in behalf of the black were at least as important as the work of the family's institutional philanthropies. He had been exposed early in life to the realities of the black's predicament by a series of visits to the South; by the time he left col-

THE ROSENWALD FUND

As the commitment of the Rockefeller philanthropies began to falter during the 1920s and 1930s, that of Rosenwald became more impressive. His fund had encountered serious financial difficulties because of sharp fluctuations in the price of Sears Roebuck stock. But it consistently pursued its schoolhouse program through the 1920s; by the time it dissolved in 1932, 5,300 rural schools had been built in thirteen Southern states. Following the pattern of the GEB, the Rosenwald Fund made grants to leading black colleges, subsidized officials in Southern departments of education to work for improved rural schools, and supported an extensive fellowship program for advanced education for blacks. The Rosenwald fellowships were not confined to education, but included a number of other fields, particularly the arts.

In addition, beginning shortly after the war, the fund mounted an attack on the system of segregation itself. In 1919 it contributed to the creation of the Commission on Interracial Cooperation, whose purpose was to bring together leading white and black citizens of the South, community by community and region by region, to work on common problems. Many believe that the commission was the most successful single force in changing racial patterns in the South in that era. It aroused officials and citizens to the horrors of lynching; it pressed for more liberal legislation regarding blacks; and it kept the Southern press informed of developments in black life. The fund also supported a number of other organizations to promote interracial cooperation, among them the American Coun-

---

lege in 1897 and began his long career in philanthropy he was already imbued with a sense of mission about the needs of the black. During his life he made a large number of important personal gifts to black organizations and causes. He encouraged and assisted his most able and trusted associates to help organize fund-raising drives and to strengthen organizations of various kinds dealing with Negro problems. He also persistently encouraged his friends to take an interest. There is reason to believe that it was he who persuaded Alfred P. Sloan, for example, to begin to contribute to black causes. By the 1920s, through his own great prestige he had made interest in the black problem "respectable" in business and other circles.

cil on Race Relations and, after 1944, the Southern Regional Council (the legal successor to the commission), whose pioneering work
laid the basis for the partial dismantling of segregation in the
South that has now taken place.

By the late 1920s the fund had also become active in the health
field. With the backing of the American Medical Association, virtually all the nation's leading hospitals at that time excluded black
doctors and surgeons. The fund undertook to raise standards of
service in a group of hospitals in return for their agreement to
train black interns and doctors. Seventeen hospitals in both Northern and Southern states cooperated, of which Provident Hospital,
associated with the University of Chicago, was the most notable.
For the first time a great American university had taken direct responsibility for the education of black undergraduate and post-
graduate medical personnel and for the support of a black teaching
hospital. The fund also launched experimental health centers in six
major cities. Staffed with black doctors and nurses, the centers provided specially designed health services to ghetto residents.
Despite vigorous opposition from professional medical organizations, the fund sought new ways to lower the cost of medical care
for the poor. In New Orleans, for example, it set up a penny-a-day
insurance plan to bring hospitalization within reach of the city's
blacks.

As the depression continued, the fund expanded its interests to
include other needs. It paid for a number of conferences on the
subject of black poverty and financed studies of the impact of farm
tenancy and trade-union practices on the status of the blacks. It
cooperated actively with a number of New Deal agencies, placing
specialists with them to encourage their attention to the special
needs of the urban and rural black population. Its final project, just
before its resources were exhausted, was to sponsor an inquiry into
every aspect of segregation in Washington, D.C., the findings of
which were to have an important influence on later policy actions
of the executive branch and decisions of the Supreme Court.

Rosenwald was a vigorous opponent of foundations established
in perpetuity, and in accordance with his views, the fund closed

down in 1946, fourteen years after his death. In its final report it made this comment about its long and unremitting attempt to equalize opportunities among all groups of the American people:

In our earlier efforts to contribute to the basic needs of Negroes, we had to work through segregated schools and services. This was the system maintained by law in the Southern States where the overwhelming masses of Negroes then lived. It was the only public system existing in these states, and we recognized that public provisions were the only adequate means of reaching the masses of any people. . . . But we were never happy in having to work in a system that segregated any group of Americans from their fellows. We did what we could to bridge the gap.

NEW FOUNDATIONS

From 1900 until World War II, the General Education Board and the Rosenwald Fund were the only two large-scale American philanthropies with a dedication to black well-being.* But during these decades the number of other large foundations began to grow. Surdna and Commonwealth were established before 1920; Duke, Kresge, Danforth, Hartford, Kettering, and Kellogg were created by 1930; and several more came into existence before the war. Although most of them did not concern themselves in any way with the black problem—Kellogg, Hartford, Kresge, and Kettering, for example—a few made some contribution.

In the 1920s the Commonwealth Fund put considerable emphasis on the needs of the poor in urban slums, on juvenile delinquency, and on the delivery of medical services on a nonracial basis to the rural poor. But by the 1930s this emphasis had faded and it began to devote its resources almost entirely to medical education and international fellowships. The Duke Endowment, through its programs to improve hospitals and facilities for the care of orphans, provided some assistance to blacks in North and

* In total, the GEB from its inception in 1902 through 1960 distributed $324.2 million, of which, according to its breakdown, black education received $62.5 million. Of this sum $32 million was given for general support and physical facilities and slightly over $10 million for medical education and sciences. Programs to improve public education for blacks in the South received $11 million. The Rosenwald Fund's total expenditures from its inception until its demise in 1946 totaled over $20 million, almost all of which was devoted to programs concerned directly or indirectly with the blacks.

South Carolina and also made regular gifts to a black college in North Carolina. But on the whole there was no large or sustained interest in black problems on the part of the growing number of large foundations in the period up to the war, and by then the Rosenwald Fund was approaching its end.

Pearl Harbor to Little Rock

Big wars typically have produced big changes in the configuration of the American black problem, and World War II was no exception. Profound changes occurred in patterns of black migration, black employment, and not least in black attitudes. In 1941, as manpower shortages began to develop in the defense industries, A. Philip Randolph, president of the Brotherhood of Sleeping Car Porters, attacked the rigid antiblack employment policies then being pursued. By threatening to organize a march on Washington of 100,000 blacks, he forced President Roosevelt to create the first Fair Employment Practices Committee. In 1948, President Truman ordered the end of segregation in the armed services. His Fair Deal reform programs in housing and other fields also helped to alleviate the condition of blacks. By midcentury a generally more liberal climate toward blacks began to prevail. But as had happened during the depression and prewar years, it was the government, not private philanthropy, that took the major initiative in seeking to expand black rights and opportunities.

In the early 1950s the Supreme Court in a series of notable decisions outlawed discrimination against Negroes in higher education and in some public facilities; in 1954 in *Brown vs. Board of Education,* it declared segregated public schools "inherently unequal"; and in a second case a year later it called for integrated education throughout the country "with all deliberate speed." This momentous step marked the beginning of a new phase, a dramatic intensification of the struggle for racial equality in the United States.

Following the Court's ruling repercussions were quickly felt in the political and governmental sphere. In 1957 the first civil rights bill since 1875 was passed and a federal Civil Rights Commission

established. That same year, President Dwight D. Eisenhower had
to employ federal troops to enforce the Supreme Court's ruling on
school desegregation in Little Rock, Arkansas. In the same period,
militant black organizations emerged, such as CORE (the Congress of Racial Equality), which had begun experimenting with direct action techniques in the 1940s.

After the Court's ruling, CORE organized "freedom rides" to test
compliance with desegregation of public facilities. Dr. Martin Luther King Jr., an advocate of nonviolent direct action, rose to
national prominence after his leadership of a bus boycott in Mont-
gomery, Alabama, in 1955. His methods gained a popularity, and
sometimes a success, which older approaches through legal and
legislative action had failed to accomplish. It was a time of opti-
mism and movement, and the forces of racism seemed to be in retreat on many fronts.

But in this period of ferment the older large foundations, in contrast to some of the active medium-sized foundations such as Field
and the Stern Family Fund, were to a large extent only spectators.
Among the exceptions were the newly activated Ford Foundation
and the Rockefeller Brothers Fund. As they developed their initial
programs, they promptly began to make a number of useful grants
to black organizations and institutions. The Sloan Foundation
began to make larger and more frequent gifts to black colleges; the
Mellon philanthropies, through their involvement in the renewal of
downtown Pittsburgh, were beginning to affect the lives of blacks
in the ghettos, if only by moving them out of their homes; and the
Danforth Foundation in St. Louis began to organize a larger and
more systematic program of assistance to improve a number of
black colleges. The Rockefeller Foundation, after the *Brown* decision in 1954, also took the constructive step of giving the General
Education Board an additional lease on life with a grant of $10
million.

In general, the big foundations were at the trailing edge, not the
cutting edge, of change; and congressional attacks upon them in
the mid-1950s, particularly in the case of the Ford Foundation,
tended to discourage what little initiative they had been inclined
to take in regard to social and racial issues.

The Decade of the 1960s
and Accelerating Activism

As the decade of the 1960s opened, it became apparent that although some progress had been made, black demands were outstripping the changes taking place and the gap between goals and reality was steadily widening. A process of black revolt had been set into motion, and it was being accelerated by the convergence of several forces: the courts had struck down the principle of segregation and sanctioned the black demand for equality; the enforcement machinery of the federal government for the first time was facilitating black advancement; the mass media, especially television, were sensitizing blacks as well as the rest of the American public to wrongs not yet rectified. And yet black unemployment was disproportionately rising and progress in the desegregation of housing and schools was maddeningly slow. As a result the fuel of frustration was heaped on the fires of hope.

Insisting on their demands with increasing force, black organizations began to multiply, and then to divide. All of them agreed that the civil rights struggle would have to move beyond emphasis on equal legal status to a search for practical solutions to economic and social distress; they also agreed that the ultimate weapon in the struggle would have to be the political potential of the black masses. But rivalry among the proliferating organizations increased over matters of strategy (gradualism versus militancy); over tactics (nonviolent direct action versus confrontation); and even over eventual objectives (integration versus separatism). Impatience with the pace of desegregation culminated in the student sit-ins of 1960—a decisive turning away from the moderation of traditional tactics. In 1963 activism took more dramatic form and the protest movement assumed a new note of urgency in demands for "Freedom Now!" Early in that year A. Philip Randolph once more called for a march on Washington, this time to dramatize the need for jobs; and in August more than 200,000 people converged on the capital to call for federal action. The huge demonstration also gave impetus to what was to become the Civil Rights Act of 1964, by which time Lyndon B. Johnson had succeeded John F. Kennedy as president. In 1964 and 1965, with the help of the new law ensuring the blacks' right to vote, the Student Nonviolent Coordinating Committee, CORE, the NAACP, and the Southern Regional Council pressed voter registration drives throughout the South.

But faced with the intransigence of the Southern segregationists and the various institutional impediments to black economic progress, an increasing number of younger blacks began to abandon hope in the efficacy of peaceful processes and even in the possibility of racial coexistence in the United States. As their discouragement grew, the rhetoric as well as the methods of their protest became more violent. Malcolm X came to symbolize the growing belief that only organized black strength, not reliance upon the conscience of the whites, could bring basic change. The call for Black Power, which was increasingly heard beginning in 1966, even though it remained undefined and contradictory as a program, reflected the new mood: something more than appeals to the nation's sense of fair play, or legal action through the courts, or even the tactics of direct action would be required if black equality was to be achieved.

Then, in the summer of 1967, racial disorders exploded in more than a hundred American cities, and at the end of July, President Johnson set up the Kerner Commission to find out what had happened and why. On March 1, 1968, it reported its basic conclusion: "Our nation is moving toward two societies, one black, one white —separate and unequal."

That same year, because of the catastrophic failure of his Vietnam policy, President Johnson retired from public life, but in the field of domestic civil rights, his administration probably represented the historical high point in active federal support for the political, economic, and social advancement of the black. Ironically, it also represented the high point up to that time of racial unrest in the nation. His successor, Richard M. Nixon, elected by a troubled and fearful citizenry, attempted in both his domestic and foreign policies to ease the acute tensions. But to blacks his appeal for a "lowering of voices" seemed like a euphemism for a lessening of effective federal interest in their predicament.

As the 1970s opened, deep-running demographic, economic, political, and psychological forces continued to aggravate the problem. Blacks were still streaming out of the rural South to the cities of the industrial North, which were ill equipped to provide them with either employment or dignity. Frustration, irrationality, and despair, particularly among younger and better educated blacks, were spreading. Their heroes had changed in less than twenty years from Thurgood Marshall and Martin Luther King to Malcolm X and the Black Panthers.

GENERAL ASSESSMENT

The large American foundations had generally permitted the hopeful and relatively orderly initial period of progress on the Negro problem in the 1950s to pass them by.° What was their response to the darkening and more dangerous developments of the 1960s?

A good proportion—nearly half—have still displayed little or no concern. Most of the others, beginning five to ten years after the *Brown* decision and after violence and disorder had increased, have taken an interest in the problem; but only a handful can be said to be actively attempting to deal with its most urgent and critical aspects. The thirty-three big foundations can be grouped thus according to their present involvement:

1. Ten have never had any discernible special interest in the problem. These include Hartford, with its concentration on medical research, Kettering on scientific research and education, and Longwood on horticulture. Also, Irvine, Nemours, Richardson, Surdna, and the recently activated Brown, Bush, and Kaiser foundations.

2. Eight show a greater—but still limited—degree of interest, but their grants tend to be in the traditional form of general support for educational and welfare institutions or scholarship programs. These include the Duke Endowment, which has long helped support Johnson C. Smith University in North Carolina, as

° Far more orderly on the black than on the white side, incidentally. During those years, white mobs every September carried on "massive resistance" to school desegregation and there were literally hundreds of bombings and burnings and killings perpetrated against blacks.

well as hospitals and orphanages providing some services to blacks; and the Lilly Endowment, which in earlier times took an interest in housing for low-income families in Indianapolis. The group also includes Kellogg, Kresge, and Moody, which were inactive on black issues until very recently. Pew and Scaife intermittently make some gifts to black institutions or black-related projects, and A. W. Mellon (through its predecessor components) has given similar help, including timely assistance to some New York settlement houses and birth control clinics.

3. There are six foundations that have shown a relatively higher degree of interest in the condition of the black and have occasionally funded innovative projects. The Astor Foundation, with its special concerns for New York City children and the slums, has made a number of useful grants. The Houston Endowment, reflecting the interest of Jesse Jones, its donor, in black education, has made numerous gifts to black colleges and has supported special scholarship programs for black children.° The Richard King Mellon Foundation showed a strong interest initially in the physical rehabilitation of Pittsburgh and more recently in its social and economic problems, including housing of ghetto residents. The Fleischmann Foundation, through its interest in juvenile delinquency and the administration of justice, has supported projects directly related to the black and other racial minorities and has also funded special scholarship programs. The Commonwealth Fund, though neglectful of all social problems for many years, has recently begun to seek to reduce medical costs for the poor, including blacks; and the Woodruff Foundation, through its medical programs, institutional grants, and special inner-city projects has also shifted in the same direction.

Four of the large foundations have taken considerable interest in the black problem, although through relatively orthodox grants. The Danforth Foundation, beginning in the 1950s, helped some twenty-eight black colleges in the South with direct budgetary support to enable them to achieve full accreditation; by 1962 this

° During his lifetime he served as a trustee both of Tuskegee Institute in Alabama and of the George Peabody College for Teachers in Nashville, Tennessee.

well-conceived program had enabled twenty-six of them to achieve that status. The foundation then proceeded to underwrite the basic cost of a new program of the Southern Association of Colleges and Schools and the College Entrance Examination Board to strengthen educational opportunities for blacks in the South in other ways. In 1964–65, it extended its work in black education to the field of secondary schools, and in 1965–66 it granted $5 million to support a seven-year program to help a number of black colleges improve their faculties. Toward the end of the decade, Danforth expanded its interest from education to the interrelated problems of the city and made a substantial initial appropriation for a number of experimental projects in the metropolitan area of St. Louis in such fields as housing, employment, and racial reconciliation.

The Haas Community Fund (formerly the Phoebe Waterman Foundation), which concentrates its work in the Philadelphia area, gives heavy emphasis to scholarships for underprivileged children, to social welfare programs relating to blacks and the poor, and to housing for low-income groups. It has been actively concerned with problems of black employment and with the handling of juvenile offenders by the local courts. Of its professional staff of six, one is a black.

The Sloan Foundation, while the donor was alive, made a number of general contributions to black educational institutions. Since his death it has given much greater emphasis to scholarship programs to enable blacks to enter the professions. It recently announced its intention to develop a significant new program addressed to the urban crisis, including the special problems of blacks.

In 1967, after a special committee of the Rockefeller Foundation had completed a study of the foundation's performance in relation to the black problem, the trustees directed that greater emphasis be placed on the delivery of health care for low-income groups and the identification and development of leadership within the ghetto. Whereas its earlier "equal opportunity" program had attempted to work through white upper-class institutions and to relate to middle-class blacks and their children, it was now to be increasingly aimed at the development of local, often uneducated, lower-class leaders. As part of what it began to call its "new thrust," the foundation made various grants to organizations such as the National Urban League, the Urban Coalition, and the NAACP; it also made a few to less well-known groups. But most of its grants have been cautious rather than daring. Hence, although the level of its commitment to the black problem is growing, it cannot yet be ranked with the bellwether group.

As of 1970, only four foundations—Mott, Rockefeller Brothers Fund, Carnegie, and above all, Ford—have a high degree of interest in and an activist approach to the problems of blacks.

THE MOTT FOUNDATION

The Mott Foundation, whose program is focused on the industrial city of Flint, supports a program that primarily benefits the working class, including the blacks, of the city. Its varied projects cover the special educational problems of adults and school dropouts, children's health, juvenile crime, jobs, and better housing. The Mott Foundation also supports direct action projects to open up wider employment opportunities for young people in the slums and to stop discrimination in housing. There are those, including some blacks, who feel that its approach has been paternalistic. But Mott has been both energetic and purposeful in such efforts, even though only a small proportion of its outlays has been given to them.

THE ROCKEFELLER BROTHERS FUND

The Rockefeller Brothers Fund over the thirty years of its existence has carried on the notable tradition of the Rockefeller family in assisting the black. From the beginning, substantial grants were made to strengthen black educational institutions; among the largest in this long list was a gift of $1 million to Atlanta University in 1960, and another of $500,000 in 1965, in memory of the father of the five brothers. A second continuing interest has been support to leading black organizations, such as the National Urban League, which has received a series of grants for general support and for special projects. The fund's interest in the economic and welfare needs of the blacks—in addition to education—has been reflected by its aid to various community centers, settlement houses, and antipoverty groups, largely in the New York area.

A distinctive feature of the fund's activity has been its support of Afro-American cultural organizations and activist civil rights groups. Over the years it has helped the Harlem School of the Arts, the Museum of Negro and African Art in Washington, D.C., and the Studio Museum in Harlem for theatrical presentations, poetry programs, and the training of black artists. Moreover, beginning in the 1940s, together with a few other smaller foundations with an intense interest in racial equality, the fund has given help to the Southern Regional Council for its efforts in the field of racial reconciliation, its consulting services to communities undergoing educational integration, and its effective—and controversial—program for voter education and registration. The fund has also made important grants to the NAACP's Legal Defense and Educational Fund, to the Interracial Council for Business Opportunity, and other organizations concerned with black rights and advancement.

But the published list of its many grants is only a partial indication of the fund's readiness to respond to crises in the black community. Some of the most eminent leaders in the civil rights struggle have recounted in private conversations how the officers and trustees of the fund have repeatedly provided personal assistance to them and generated other financial contributions when emergencies arose.[5]

THE CARNEGIE CORPORATION

The Carnegie Corporation, the third of this group, has had a benign but fluctuating interest in the black through most of its sixty-year history. Andrew Carnegie gave substantial amounts to black colleges, and through the 1920s and 1930s his foundation continued to make periodic gifts. During the 1930s it also made a few grants relating to black history and art. In the 1940s it financed the Myrdal study. During the 1940s and 1950s Carnegie continued to make small but regular contributions to the National Urban League, the United Negro College Fund, and selected black colleges and universities. Its most unusual grants during that period were a series of three to the University of Louisville for a project to train police in the handling of racial problems. After the Supreme Court's desegregation decision, the level of the corporation's grants in this field moved upward, but it was not until 1963 that a major new step was taken. In that year a series of grants totaling $1.5 million was made to advance black higher education. The recipients included the United Negro College Fund as well as Tuskegee, Dillard, Hampton, and a few other well-known institutions. Through 1965, however, although the level of the foundation's interest in the black had increased, the focus of its program was still almost entirely in the area of higher education.

In 1966 and again in 1968, the foundation funded a program in Boston to bus school children from the inner city to suburban schools. In 1967 a major grant was made to the Center for Applied Linguistics to develop programs to help school teachers understand the "Negro language" in order to help them better communicate with black children. That same year, a research project was financed through the National Opinion Research Center on the politics of northern school desegregation. By 1968 Carnegie was moving still further into new aspects of the problem of black education as well as into noneducational areas. A major grant was made to the Urban League to seek out black dropouts and prepare them for college. Another was given to New York University to train more black lawyers to become active in the civil rights movement. Help was also given to the New York Legal Aid Society for community law offices in East Harlem, to the National Committee Against Discrimination in Housing, and to a medical care program in the heavily black south Bronx section of New York City.

Also in 1968, moving a step beyond its traditional areas of interest, the corporation, under Alan Pifer, set a staff task force to work to develop program ideas in the broad and interrelated fields of the urban crisis, poverty, and race relations. In November its recommendations were presented to the trustees and approved as a new and continuing aspect of the corporation's program. The process of change had been careful and slow, but it had come. And as the 1970s opened, Carnegie had become one of the most vigorous and effective of the socially oriented large foundations concerned with the needs of the blacks.

THE FORD FOUNDATION

Since World War II, Ford, among all the big foundations, has been by far the largest as well as the most controversial source of grants for blacks. Since its full activation in 1950 some $250 million of its total outlays have been committed to projects related directly to the problem of black rights or whose principal beneficiary (as in the case of grants to improve low-income housing) has been the black segment of the population. But in that period the foundation's level of concern regarding the race problem has fluctuated repeatedly, its emphasis has alternated from traditional to newer aspects, and its style has shifted from boldness to conservatism and back again.

In its statement of program plans in 1950, Ford seemed to be picking up where the Rosenwald Fund and the General Education Board had left off. The document stressed the issue of racial discrimination in America and its language carried some of the flavor, even the wording, of the final report of the Rosenwald Fund on the occasion of its demise two years earlier. Under the leadership of Paul Hoffman and Robert M. Hutchins, who had been a member of the Rosenwald board, the foundation quickly began to implement this statement of intention. The Fund for Adult Education launched a number of projects to improve interracial understanding through channels outside the formal education system. The foundation itself made a number of grants to the NAACP's Legal Defense and Educational Fund, the Southern Regional Council, the American Friends Service Committee, and other bodies for studies and action programs in the field of race relations. And in early 1953, at the height of the McCarthy period, it financed the Fund for the Republic with a $15 million grant to defend civil liberties in the United States, especially those of the blacks.

This was the last major action of its kind. For the next five years, partly as a result of congressional attacks and investigations, the foundation eased off in its activism, and even its concern. The subsidiary educational funds, however, as well as the Fund for the Republic, continued the programs they had undertaken as long as their resources lasted.

The huge "one-shot" package of grants distributed in 1956 to four-year colleges, medical schools, and hospitals throughout the country had an important incidental effect of providing funds—ranging from $70,000 to $500,000—to each of forty black institutions. The grants may not have derived from a special concern for them, but the assistance provided was nevertheless considerable. Under President Heald's repressive hand, little was done from 1957 to 1959 relating to the black problem, apart from the renewal of a substantial grant to the Southern Educational Reporting Service. The project had been initiated by the Fund for the Advancement of Education to provide news of current developments relating to the desegregation of southern schools. The reports were a source of valuable information and provided a stimulus for all agencies in the South working on the problem.

By 1960, through its program addressed to the problems of the nation's cities and metropolitan areas under the leadership of Paul Ylvisaker, who had wide contacts in the black community, the foundation became actively involved in problems of black welfare. Major grants were made for delinquency prevention in Chicago and other cities; at the same time the education programs of the foundation gave greater emphasis to the special needs of disadvantaged children in the ghettos. In 1961 these efforts were further extended and $2.5 million was granted for the initial phase of a comprehensive attack on the problems of the central cities. These were disguised under the bland title of "community development" projects, but in fact they involved a variety of new approaches to the problems of poverty and unemployment and the improvement of housing and education, largely for blacks. Most significant of all, they employed and encouraged organizations directed by ghetto residents themselves to carry out much of the work.

Ylvisaker assembled a lively group of "social change technicians," both black and white, to formulate project ideas; and to give his enterprise "political muscle" he put together a group of cooperating mayors (including John Collins of Boston, Richard Lee of New Haven, James Tate of Philadelphia, and John Houlihan of

Oakland) with whose help many of the projects were put into effect. This so-called "gray area" program spawned many of the ideas later incorporated into the Johnson administration's war on poverty.*

The long-term results of the Ylvisaker program are perhaps debatable: the vaunted war on poverty has now disintegrated; his bright group of experimenters has been dispersed; and most of the cooperating mayors have left office. But in its day, the gray areas program represented a courageous and highly creative departure. At a time when the generally favored solution to the problems of urban life was the bulldozer and downtown renewal, it brought forth an interrelated strategy for dealing with both the human and physical problems associated with urban decay.

The foundation's largest single grants relating to the black were still in the traditional form of institutional support: $5 million to the United Negro College Fund in 1963; $7 million to the National Merit Scholarship Corporation in 1964 for grants to "academically promising Negro youth"; and $15 million that same year for "faculty and staff development and student assistance" in ten black institutions. But by the time Heald resigned in 1965, the Ylvisaker program was generating increasingly strong reactions, favorable and unfavorable, and Heald found himself ironically and rather uncomfortably the head of an institution which had become aggressively involved in a struggle for black rights.

Shortly after Bundy's accession, he and Ylvisaker had disagreements over organizational matters and Ylvisaker left. Thereafter, program officers of the division reported directly to Bundy and a spurt of still more controversial activity ensued. With his encouragement the foundation began to pour an increasing percentage of its outlays into a comprehensive attack on racial discrimination, poverty, and urban decay. Not only were the grants more numerous and larger than before but they began to take on distinctive

---

* The term prompted Saul Alinsky, the sharp-tongued Chicago social reformer who organized the "Back of the Yards" neighborhood movement, to write in a memorandum to his staff: "The Gray in your gray area has nothing to do with the race of its inhabitants; there are no gray people except in foundations."

new characteristics. Eventually, Mitchell Sviridoff, then head of Mayor John V. Lindsay's human resources administration in New York City, was hired to run the program according to Bundy's new style.

Increasingly, grants were designed to stimulate direct action by blacks and active participation by ghetto groups in housing, employment, and education programs. There were grants to activist groups trying to do something about welfare needs, job opportunities, and health facilities; about school dropouts and family planning; about legal aid for the poor and reform in police practices. Some were made to well-known and established organizations such as NAACP, the Urban League, and CORE. But the foundation also helped street gangs and other untried bodies. At the same time funds were given specifically to train leadership cadres for these new organizations. Reinforced with Ford money, a good many of them promptly became more strident in their demands and more militant in their efforts.

A second new element in the pattern of Ford grants was a willingness to enter zones of activity directly adjacent to politics and lobbying. In addition to grants for black voter education and registration in the South and North, foundation money helped the American Friends Service Committee to aid blacks who had been harassed in exercising their voting rights; the Urban Affairs Foundation to provide "internships" for young blacks to work on the staffs of practicing minority group politicians; and the United States Conference of Mayors to "strengthen" the municipal administration in Gary, Indiana, where a black had just become mayor for the first time.

Skirting close to the boundary of permissible philanthropic action, the foundation brought the Center for Community Change into being in Washington, D.C., with a multimillion-dollar grant in 1968. The stated purpose of the center is "to enhance the voice of the poor in their own destiny" through formation of strong community organizations throughout the country. In turn, the center sponsored the creation of a separate but closely related lobbying organization, the Committee for Community Affairs, to provide legislative and other services for the center and its constituent organizations.

The third new type of foundation activity was the direct financing of experiments in structural changes in public education, specifically the decentralization of the New York City school system. In 1967, Bundy headed a panel appointed by Mayor Lindsay to make recommendations for school reform. Once the panel's report was published, the foundation gave support for two "demonstration districts" set up by the Board of Education in largely black areas, which in effect delegated authority over the schools in each district to newly formed community councils. The ensuing conflicts between the local councils, the Board of Education, and the teachers' union over questions of curricula and the right to hire and fire teachers led directly to the school strikes of 1968 and greatly exacerbated tensions between the black and Jewish communities. The role which the foundation, and Bundy in particular, had played in the whole affair drew great criticism. Albert Shanker, the head of the New York City teachers' union, even went on a nationwide speaking tour to warn other teachers' organizations of the threat to their position and power represented by "irresponsible intervention" of philanthropic organizations.

But the turmoil of the New York school situation was only one of several controversies in which the Ford Foundation found itself embroiled by 1969. Some of the community action groups it had encouraged strayed into unexpected byways. Its grants to Mexican-American groups in the Southwest resulted in explosive disturbances to local political establishments. In the South, the foundation's grants for black voter registration aroused the anger and concern of white politicians throughout the region. And in Cleveland, the ex-mayor attributed his defeat by black Carl Stokes to the Ford Foundation's activities. By 1969, Ford's actions had become a prime target of right-wing politicians and the conservative press. Populist Wright Patman of Texas on the floor of Congress asked accusingly, "Does the Ford Foundation have a grandiose design to bring vast political, economic, and social changes to the nation in the 1970s?"

In October 1971, the foundation resoundingly affirmed that its interest in the problems of blacks had not diminished by announcing a massive $100 million commitment to be paid over a six-year period to strengthen a selected group of the better black colleges.

The much-needed help was welcomed by most black leaders, but some of the more militant among them believed that the noncontroversial nature of the program signified a fundamental decision by the foundation to moderate its activism and seek a "lower profile."

Summation and Evaluation

Given the great number of opportunities confronting the big foundations and the inherent importance of their diversity of objectives, there is no reason to assume that all of them can or should devote their attention to the issue of racial discrimination in American life. But it deserves to be noted that the big foundations that have never concerned themselves with the black problem, when measured by almost every criterion, tend also to be the least competent, energetic, and distinguished of their class.

Of the majority that have shown some degree of interest, the common area of focus has been education, especially higher education. The most typical grant has been for buildings and general support to black schools and colleges, followed by scholarships and fellowships for black students. This pattern reflects the fact that philanthropic interest in the black derives from the long tradition of humanitarian concern for his "plight" rather than from an ideological commitment to the principle of racial equality. It also reflects practical considerations: education is a familiar field of action for most foundations, one in which they have demonstrated a degree of institutional competence. Trained and identifiable leadership is available at reputable institutions which are qualified to receive and administer grants. Even more important, education fits the conventional wisdom of philanthropy, which holds that nothing is more productive in the service of human welfare than investment in the education and training of human beings. Reminiscent of the ideas of Booker T. Washington, it is commonly believed that the most fruitful way to solve the problems of the blacks is to open educational opportunities to them: by climbing the rungs of the educational and occupational ladder, they will eventually achieve full economic, political, and social equality within the system. Moreover, once educational opportunities have been opened, the primary responsibility for his advancement rests upon the black man—on his own ambition, determination, and effort.

The premises of this approach, of course, are now seriously questioned. Many blacks as well as whites assert that education and individual effort alone are not enough, that the black will never be able to make significant progress until fundamental structural impediments in the system itself have been removed, and that a foundation evades the essential issues by continuing to address itself only to problems of educational facilities and opportunities.

Over the last twenty years, as the configuration of the problem has changed, as the crisis has worsened, and as the goals and tactics of blacks themselves have evolved, most of the major foundations have attempted in one way or another to respond. Some that were previously indifferent have begun to make a few black-related grants, others with little previous involvement have increased the degree of their interest, and a few have made major shifts in their program priorities and the nature of their grants. One path of evolution has been from exclusive concentration on education to interest in other fields, including the economic and social. A second path of evolution has been away from an emphasis on rural areas and the South to concentration on the interrelated racial, economic, and social problems of the urban ghettos throughout the country. A third and less common line of development has been away from relatively uncontroversial grants for general educational, research, and welfare programs to more activist projects, such as black voter education and registration or legal challenges to discrimination in housing and employment.

The reaction time of the large foundations in making program shifts varies greatly from one institution to another. The Danforth Foundation intensified its efforts to improve black higher education almost immediately after the Supreme Court's decision in the *Brown* case, but not until almost fifteen years later did it begin to recognize the economic and social problems of the urban Negro. The Carnegie Corporation waited eight years after the *Brown* decision before giving major attention to black education and the problems of desegregation, and still longer before recognizing the noneducational aspects of the problem in its grants. The Rockefeller Foundation promptly gave funds to the General Education Board to help facilitate desegregation after the *Brown* decision; but it did not set up its own "equal opportunity" program until ten years later and waited another three years before extending its activities beyond higher education. The Ford Foundation, after a spurt of interest in the early 1950s, did not resume direct involvement in the black problem until the turn of the 1960s.

Thus, even the most concerned and adaptable of the big foundations have lagged behind the pace of events in the racial crisis by five to ten years. Black leadership itself and government action have been well in advance of the big foundations, as have been a number of the smaller foundations, such as New World, Taconic, Field, and the Stern Family Fund.

This sluggish response is explainable in part by the fact that in the composition of their boards and staffs, the large majority of big foundations are glaring examples of "institutional racism." Only a handful of their trustees in 1970 were nonwhite, and although some blacks have begun to be employed in junior staff positions, very few of their elected officers are black and no major foundation is yet headed by a black. In this respect, they lag far behind government at the federal, state, and municipal levels and also behind American churches and universities. It is an ironic commentary on institutions that have long contended that education is the avenue by which blacks could move to a place of equality in the American system that they themselves have been generally unwilling to admit blacks to their own ranks—even though well-qualified blacks have been available for at least forty years, often as a result of foundation assistance.

In sum, the relationship of big philanthropy to the American race question has been commendable but not glorious. Most of the big foundations have taken a sympathetic but passive interest. They have given a fair amount of educational and other assistance, but they have not generally been prepared to join blacks and other liberal forces in uprooting discrimination in American life. Currently a larger percentage of them are modifying their programs.

But they are anxious about approaching a problem so great and turbulent and are unclear about their role. Their conservatism and caution are apparent, but so are their good intentions. More commitment and change can be expected of them in the future, but in all probability not much more, and not very fast. The race issue in all its complexity and intensity seems to lie largely beyond the outer boundaries of concern, self-confidence, and capability of the big foundations as they are now structured and staffed.

Part Four

FOUNDATIONS IN THE AMERICAN CONTEXT

19.

Government and Foundations: The Tightening Embrace of Regulation

FOUNDATIONS are surrounded by and to a large extent are the artifact of legal privileges. That governmental embrace has traditionally been a friendly one, encouraging but not intrusive. But it has now begun to tighten uncomfortably. Congressional skepticism has replaced cordiality. Tax inducements have been curtailed and restrictions upon even the program freedom of foundations have been introduced.

Foundations have long been aware of their political vulnerability. But with the characteristic insensitivity of aristocratic institutions to new social trends, they have consistently misconceived its basis. They have tended to attribute it to "public misunderstanding" of their good works or their "lack of a constituency," ignoring the fact that they are highly visible examples of special privilege accorded to the very rich by an inequitable tax system that is increasingly resented by the general public.[1] This resentment is continuously being fed from three sources.

The Federal Income Tax System

The transformation and deformation of the federal income tax system, especially since World War II, has spread from a narrow base to a broad base and now bears directly on large new segments of the citizenry. It is becoming increasingly burdensome because of the heavy costs of military and domestic programs, and its fundamental fairness has now broken down. Special groups, including farmers, doctors, and entrepreneurs, seem readily able to escape a good part of their tax obligations; others, notably the poor, the aged, and salaried members of the lower- and middle-income groups, are paying a disproportionate share of an increasing total.[2]

Even the basic premise of progressivity has been compromised. As several recent studies show, the effective rates paid by taxpayers up to the level of about $50,000 per year of actual income are progressive. But for taxpayers above this level, the upward movement of effective rates begins to flatten; and above $100,000 the effective rate *decreases*. Those with incomes of $1 million a year or more, for example, in general pay tax rates no higher than those in the $20,000- to $50,000-a-year group; and more than a few of them pay little or nothing in income tax. As one expert witness told the House Ways and Means Committee during its hearings on the 1969 tax bill:

The obvious departure from the ability to pay concept . . . is self-evident. . . . Whether a person is below the poverty line or whether he is in the group between $20,000 to $50,000, he is certainly warranted in feeling that the income tax is not working fairly.

Even within the group of high income individuals there are unfairnesses. Some of these individuals are paying high effective rates on actual income. Thus we find taxpayers whose effective rates run considerably above 50 percent and up to 65 percent and 70 percent. They likewise are justified, when they compare themselves with the fellow members of their group who are paying relatively little or no taxes, in believing that the system is not working fairly. . . .

One more statistic is needed: the Treasury studies show that high income individuals who pay little or no tax in one year are quite likely to be in the same position in other years—so that their escape from tax is no one-shot phenomenon.[3]

This violation of progressivity is largely caused by certain items which wealthy taxpayers can exclude in calculating their taxable income. Chief among these have been the excluded half of realized capital gains; interest on state and local bonds; accelerated depreciation, mainly on buildings; farm "tax losses"; the excess of percentage depletion over cost of investment in mining and mineral properties; intangible drilling expenses of oil wells; and—until 1969—unlimited deductibility for charitable contributions in specific cases (usually made in the form of appreciated securities whose gain in value was not taxed). For dozens of multimillionaires these exemptions, singly or in combination, have brought their effective tax to zero. New provisions in the 1969 tax act provide some relief for low-income taxpayers and impose a slight increase of burden for high-income taxpayers, but the rich are still in effect heavily favored.

The Indiscriminate Use of Tax Incentives

From the earliest days of the republic, preferential treatment under the law has been given to foster private activities for public benefit. Since the advent of the federal income tax more than half a century ago, "tax incentives" have become the most common means of encouraging this kind of "voluntarism." But their use has become increasingly indiscriminate—and in many cases their value to powerful special interest groups is much more obvious than their contribution to the public welfare.

At present, the size and number of these inducements—and their cost in terms of revenue loss to the federal government—are even greater than the public suspects. For example: special tax credits are given to industry to encourage the purchase of machinery and equipment; mortgage interest and local property taxes are deductible to encourage home ownership; an allowance for excessive bad debt reserves is provided to encourage the growth of savings and loan associations and mutual savings banks; a $25,000 corporate surtax exemption is intended to foster small business; and preferential tax treatment has been given to qualified pension plans to foster broader pension plan coverage. The list of such "special provisions" runs into the hundreds. Their total revenue cost to the government for 1968 has been estimated to total some $45 billion, which is why some analysts now prefer to call them "tax expenditures." [4]

Among the arguments made in favor of tax incentives are that they encourage the private sector to participate in social programs; they promote private rather than governmental decision-making; and they are simpler to enact and require less governmental supervision and bureaucracy than direct expenditure programs.

The impression has also been nurtured by their proponents that tax incentives are "cost free" to the government. Professor Henry Aaron of the Brookings Institution in Washington attributes their popularity to a special combination of political illusions and irrationalities, namely, that they derive "from a peculiar alliance among conservatives, who find attractive the alleged reduction in the role of government that would follow from extensive use of tax credits, and liberals anxious to solve social and economic problems —by whatever means—before it is too late." [5] Consequently, they have usually been relatively easy to pressure through the Congress, which has never seriously attempted to appraise their "cost effectiveness." But the disadvantages of tax incentives, though often neglected or obscured, are considerable. They keep tax rates high by eroding the revenue base. They can be highly inefficient in accomplishing any social purpose because they often permit windfalls by paying taxpayers for what they would do anyway. They introduce confusion and divided authority in the legislative and executive processes of government by adding to the difficulties of setting clear national priorities for allocating resources and of maintaining budgetary controls on the basis of them. Above all, they are inherently inequitable, being worth more to the high-income taxpayer than the low-income taxpayer.*

Tax incentives thus contribute to an erosion of confidence in the

---

* Aaron has suggested that the real impact of the additional $600 personal exemption for the aged, proposed during the 1969 tax reform hearings, might have been described in these terms: "Yesterday on the floor of the Congress, Senator Blimp introduced legislation to provide cash allowances for most of the aged. Senator Blimp's plan is unique, however, in that it excludes the poor. The largest benefits, $70 per month, are payable to aged couples whose real income exceeds $20,000 per year. The smallest benefits, $14 per month, would be payable to couples with incomes between $1,600 and $2,600. Widows, widowers and unmarried aged persons would receive half as much as couples. No benefits would be payable to those with very low incomes." (Aaron, p. 4)

entire tax system. They are regarded as handouts to powerful and preferred groups, and the seeming impossibility under the existing political processes of blocking their continuation and wider use has generated angry public frustration—as voluminous congressional mail in recent years attests.*

The Hodgepodge of Privileged
Nonprofit Organizations

Most of the existing mass of privileges built into the tax system benefit special categories of individually wealthy taxpayers and certain groups of profit-making entities. But one segment relates to nonprofit organizations and charitable activities. The original intent of these special tax benefits was to encourage education, science, culture, and humanitarianism, but loose practice has now turned a defensible concept into a third source of smoldering public objection. The number of nonprofit bodies now enjoying exemption has wildly proliferated. (In 1965 it was estimated that the Internal Revenue Service was monitoring the exemptions of 400,000 principal organizations plus 700,000 subsidiaries.) [6]

Apart from religious, educational, and philanthropic institutions, whose situation will be considered separately, three general types of nonprofit organizations are tax-exempt: nonprofit business organizations (such as trade and professional organizations); nonprofit social and fraternal groups; and "social welfare" organizations

---

* The proclivity of the executive branch as well as the Congress for distributing tax benefits was illustrated in early 1971 when the Nixon administration proposed to change the income tax rules for calculating depreciation of business assets by administrative order. The stated defense for this action was to stimulate business spending on new plant and equipment and thus speed up the sluggish economy. According to the Treasury's own estimate, the liberalized write off of capital assets, coupled with special allowances for repair, maintenance, rehabilitation, and improvement of eligible property would have resulted in a revenue loss of $3 billion in fiscal 1972 alone. Between 1972 and fiscal 1980 the total tax loss would have amounted to more than $36 billion, or almost twice the total accumulated assets of all American foundations as of 1968.

(such as labor unions, conservation associations, and the League of Women Voters).

In addition to the tax advantages which all receive, specific differentiations in their privileges are applied: some are prohibited from lobbying and political activities, others are not; some are subject to controls on their investment behavior, others are not; some are subject to taxation on income from business activities not related to their tax-exempt purpose, others are not; some are subject to special reporting requirements, others are not; some are subject to special sanctions and penalties for infractions of their obligations, others are not.

In terms of public benefit, the basic justification for granting special tax status to tens of thousands of these organizations is questionable, and the gradations in their privileges are not defensible by any consistent logic or explicit set of social criteria. A large number of cemetery associations, for example, have been exempted from income taxes even though many were merely screens for the miscellaneous profit-making activities of their promoters. Until 1969, a university or hospital which ran a public restaurant was taxed on the income, but a country club or lodge engaged in the same activity was not. Trade associations, which serve essentially to increase the business income of their members and to carry on lobbying activities in their own interest, are granted tax exemptions even though the benefit to the general public, if any, is obscure. Still more baffling is the fact that these trade and professional organizations are allowed to deduct the costs of lobbying and legislative activity if it is of "direct interest" to the members; but the costs of "grass roots" lobbying by an organization such as the Sierra Club, for example, in behalf of a broad social objective such as environmental protection are nondeductible.

As one leading tax authority has defined the problem:

[The issue] is not whether these are "good" or "bad" organizations. It is whether support of these organizations should retain priority over other pressing needs of society. Continuation of tax benefits year after year to an exempt organization requires no appropriation or other action by the Congress. This, in effect, gives it a priority position over other needs and claimants. For example, should tax support of social and country clubs continue to take precedence over support of better school playgrounds for our crowded cities? Or should tax support of private lodges, fraternal and veterans' organizations, take precedence over the need for more recreational centers for the poor or for expansion of medical treatment facilities for the aged? Do the thousands of Chambers of Commerce and other organizations of profit-making enterprises really need a tax subsidy when compared with the need for more training and employment services for the unemployed?" [7]

Again, the 1969 tax act has corrected some of the more flagrant inconsistencies and inequities, but many remain.

The Doubly Privileged Inner Circle

These deficiencies of the tax system and its administration have produced the inflamed context of public distrust and hostility in which the privileges of the most favored—the doubly privileged inner circle—of tax-exempt nonprofit bodies must be understood. Known as the 501(c)(3) group because of the relevant section of the Internal Revenue Code, these select beneficiaries—religious, educational, scientific, cultural, and charitable organizations, including foundations—are not only given tax exemption on their income, but in addition, individual contributions to them are deductible from the donor's taxable income.

This section of the law is a chaos of inconsistencies, making differentiations within the group according to highly debatable criteria. Over the past few years, and especially since 1969, these differentiations have become even more sharp.

Churches still enjoy overall the most favored tax position of the group—which not only creates a tax inequity between believers and nonbelievers, but also raises the question of whether the federal income tax laws do not amount to an unconstitutional "establishment" of religion under the American system of separation of church and state. Although some slight reduction of various special preferences to religious bodies has now been enacted (they must, beginning after 1975, pay tax on the income of wholly unrelated businesses which they own, such as laundries, theaters, and metalworking plants), the Congress still gives strong encouragement to private taxpayers to support them. It does the same with respect to most of the nonreligious organizations in the 501(c)(3) group—universities, hospitals, symphony orchestras, and medical research centers, for example. As their financial problems have worsened in recent years, Congress has increased the inducements to their contributors. But its indulgence toward foundations has been radically reduced.

The origins of the congressional shift in attitude can be traced back to the late 1940s when the dramatic increase in the number and size of foundations gave rise to a concern that their economic influence might be becoming dangerous. In addition, it had become apparent after the increase in tax rates during the preceding period that tax planners and lawyers were devising ever more complicated schemes for using the creation of foundations to serve private purposes. In 1950, after several scandalous cases of foundation tax abuse had been brought to light, the Congress enacted a series of new restrictions upon them—a tax upon their unrelated business income, a prohibition against unreasonable accumulation of income and deferral of benefits to charity, and a prohibition against specific kinds of financial transactions between foundations and their donors.

In 1964, further important changes were made in the revenue act, several of them signaling greater congressional favor for "publicly supported" charitable organizations than for private foundations. Prior to 1964, up to 20 percent of a taxpayer's adjusted gross income could be deducted for contributions to all 501(c)(3) organizations—and an additional 10 percent was allowed for contributions to churches, schools, hospitals, and medical research organizations. The 1964 act extended the availability of the additional 10 percent to charitable organizations which "receive a substantial part of their support from . . . direct or indirect contributions from the general public." In explaining why it did not make the additional 10 percent available to private foundations, the House Ways and Means Committee said that these "organizations frequently do not make contributions to the operating philanthropic organizations for extended periods of time and in the meantime use the funds for investments. The extra 10 percent deduction is intended to encourage immediately spendable receipts of contributions for charitable organizations." [8]

This differentiation foreshadowed more stringent things to come. The Congress asked the Treasury to prepare a report on the adequacy of the 1950 amendments to the tax code and to make recommendations for any needed further legislation. It was submitted in 1965. *All of the recommendations which the Treasury presented were specifically limited to organizations that did not qualify to receive the 30 percent contribution deduction which had by then been enacted, namely, private foundations.*

Two problems were given primary attention: excessive involvement of foundations in business, and the manipulation of foundations to serve various private purposes of the donors. The proposals for new legislation were aimed at: "self-dealing" and other kinds of financial transactions unrelated to charitable functions; undue delays in the flow of benefits to charity; the use of foundations to control corporate or other property; and the undue narrowness of foundation management. In urging the use of the Internal Revenue Service to deal with foundation "abuses," the Treasury at the same time strongly endorsed the principle that the tax laws should not be employed as a pretext for infringing upon the program freedom of foundations.

The 1965 recommendations were the basis of many, but not all, of the new provisions of the 1969 Tax Reform Act affecting foundations. Other provisions derived from the fear that foundations might be straying into politics and exercising undue influence upon the social and foreign policies of the government.

1969: Ejection from Eden

Nearly one-third of the 1969 Tax Reform Act was devoted to the subject of foundations. Many of the numerous new restrictions it imposed upon them were needed. The definition of "self-dealing" was made more comprehensive and precise, for example, and a series of graduated penalties was provided to make its prohibitions effective. Also, the provisions discouraging speculative investments and requiring annual public reporting of activity were unquestionably useful.

The requirement that the equivalent of 6 percent of a foundation's assets be given out annually was effectively designed to correct the problem of inadequate or excessively delayed benefits to charity and to force a dilution of excessively strong ties between foundations and their associated companies.* The law also attempts to deal with the sensitive problem of reducing excess business holdings of foundations and undue donor control by imposing divestiture requirements. Some of these may prove to be too complicated to administer and may have to be revised. But at least Congress attempted to address itself seriously to an area of dangerous misuse of the foundation device.

The Congress, however, went far beyond concrete corrective measures by radically widening the differentiation that had begun to appear in early legislation between "operating" philanthropic organizations and "private" foundations. Henceforth, foundations are not only split off from other 501(c)(3) organizations, but the foundation category itself is now divided into three subgroups. The so-called "private" foundation is now distinguished from two other kinds, called "publicly supported" and "operating." The former are defined as receiving their support primarily from a diversity of donors or members; the latter are those that spend substantially all of their income directly for the active conduct of their own programs. The significance of the new subdivision is that the "private" foundation is accorded markedly inferior tax treatment in comparison to the other two, namely:

First, contributions to "private" foundations are now relatively discouraged. In 1969 Congress added major inducements to donors to contribute directly to such nonprofit organizations as churches, universities, and hospitals and also to "publicly supported" and

---

* After passage of the 1969 act, the Kellogg and Pew foundations, among others, continued to lobby actively for the easing of these requirements. In late 1971 the Ways and Means Committee of the House reported out a bill cutting the pay-out requirements to 5 percent and extending to 1978 the date by which previously established foundations would have to reach that level of disbursements. Approval of the modifications by House and Senate was generally anticipated.

"operating" foundations. Up to 50 percent of an individual's taxable income can now be deducted for such gifts. In addition, gifts of appreciated property can be deducted at their full fair market value. On the other hand, contributions to "private" foundations are deductible only up to 20 percent of the donor's taxable income, with no carry-over for excess contributions. Gifts of appreciated property (including corporate stock) are deductible only to the extent of the donor's cost plus *one-half* of the appreciation.

Second, "private" foundations are subjected to a 4 percent "excise tax" on their net investment income—a crucial change from the tradition of full tax exemption for all charitable institutions.

Third, the program freedom of "private" foundations has been jeopardized by the elimination of a most important qualifying clause in the long-standing prohibition against "political and propaganda" activity by foundations. From its first enactment in 1934 the legislative requirement was that "no substantial part" of a foundation's grants could be made for such purposes.

The 1969 act eliminated the qualification of substantiality, replacing it with a flat prohibition against "political and propaganda activity" and "otherwise attempting to influence legislation, including attempting to affect public opinion or communicating with persons participating in the legislative process." The force of the change is greatly increased by heavy penalties against foundations and their "managers" for any violation. A doctrine of "expenditure responsibility" has also been elaborated: foundations are now required to ensure that their grants are used only for the specific purposes intended and they are penalized severely for any failure to do so. One of the most dubious results of these provisions is to put the Internal Revenue Service—a tax-collecting agency—in the decisive position of censor over the substance of a broad range of foundation activity.*

* During 1970, the initial efforts of the Internal Revenue Service to carry out its new policing and censorship assignments stirred fears of a new kind of administrative McCarthyism emerging in the guise of enforcement of the tax law. The IRS raised the specter of bankruptcy for a number of small intellectual and scholarly journals by its attempts to tax their advertising income. It appeared to scrutinize with extraordinary severity the editorial content of the undergraduate student newspaper of Columbia University, which had been

IMPLICATIONS OF THEIR FALL FROM GRACE

Quite possibly, Congress did not deliberately intend to wreak all the damage upon private foundations in 1969 that it did.° In retrospect, the worst of what happened seems to have been almost accidental. The House and Senate found themselves at that moment unexpectedly caught up in a rip tide of public protest about taxes and the tax system; they were influenced by a succession of inflammatory cases of abuse of philanthropic privilege, almost all relating to private foundations, which had been brought to light by

---

outspokenly critical of the Nixon administration's policies, to see if its tax exemption should be revoked. It reportedly threatened American universities with loss of their tax exemption if they should permit their students a holiday to work as volunteers in the 1970 election campaign. Similarly, it threatened to remove the tax exemption of a number of public interest nonprofit law firms, whose creation had been inspired by the consumer crusader Ralph Nader, if they pressed litigation against corporate polluters of the environment. It formulated a draft regulation to remove the tax exemption of "activist" organizations, specifically black civil rights and antiwar groups. Concurrently, Internal Revenue agents "auditing" the records of foundations in accordance with the terms of the 1969 tax act began to insist upon examining not only financial data but also confidential background memoranda relating to applicant organizations and grantees. In some cases, quantities of documents containing information about individual student organizers, academic specialists, and labor, black, and Mexican-American leaders who had been involved in foundation projects were Xeroxed and shipped to government files in Washington. Even religious bodies reported an increasing number of disquieting encounters with IRS. In December 1971 an organization of thirty Episcopal clergymen and Wall Street lawyers, the prestigious Guild of St. Ives, publicly accused the federal tax officials of overstepping their authority in restricting political activity by churches. They thus brought to the surface a simmering feeling among liberal churchmen throughout the nation that the Nixon administration has adopted a policy of "intimidation" by use of the threat of loss of tax exemption. (The New York *Times,* December 12, 1971)

° For example, a *Report Prepared by the Staff of the Joint Committee on Internal Revenue Taxation* to explain the 1969 act, issued on December 3, 1970, appeared to be an attempt in part to reassure foundations that despite the elimination of the "substantiality" qualification they could still "examine" broad social, economic and similar problems, could issue the results of "nonpartisan analysis, study, or research," and could respond to written requests of lawmakers for "technical advice or assistance." (See *General Explanation of the Tax Reform Act of 1969,* 91C2/H.R. 13270/Public Law 91-1972/1970/ pp. 48–49)

Congressman Patman; they were infuriated by a few politically colored grants in the period immediately preceding the hearings; they were deeply impressed by the growing financial needs of schools, hospitals, and other welfare institutions across the country; and they were offended by the supercilious attitude of some of the foundation spokesmen who appeared before them. In reaction to these diverse stimuli, an aroused and conservative Congress lashed out to punish the transgressors and the disturbers of the status quo —the private foundation—and at the same time to do something to help needy operating institutions.

Nevertheless, there is a definite pattern in the legislative enactments concerning private foundations passed over the last twenty-five years. The tax act of 1969 is consistent with a trend, the difference being essentially one of the degree of discrimination and severity of the penalties now imposed. The new law reflects a fundamentally new evaluation of the benefits and the hazards of private grant-making foundations to American society. It appears to rest on four premises:

First, that it is more beneficial to the public welfare to encourage direct individual contributions to such operating institutions as universities, churches, and hospitals than to foundations.

Second, that among the different categories of foundations, "operating foundations" (such as Longwood, which essentially maintains the Longwood Gardens) make a more valuable social contribution than grant-making foundations (such as Rockefeller, Carnegie, and Kellogg).

Third, that private foundations are less trustworthy in their devotion to the public interest than foundations that are "publicly supported." *

Fourth, that there is something questionable, if not downright

* This judgment, deriving from a theory originally put forward by the Treasury, is based on the idea that when a foundation has to depend upon public support and multiple contributions, there is a kind of automatic protection of the public interest; if the foundation abuses its position or its program becomes ineffective, its supporters either stop their contribution or otherwise force rectification. If this presumed mechanism works at all, it surely does not work perfectly, as the numerous fund-raising "rackets" that have been uncovered in recent years testify.

objectionable, about foundations that choose to work on social problems of great national urgency and controversy. (The foundations that have repeatedly been the object of congressional attack for twenty years have been those that attempted to work in such areas. In 1969, those that escaped congressional wrath, so long as their financial affairs were in order, had confined their work to the most traditional or inconsequential forms of charitable activity.)

If these are the governing premises of the new public policy toward private grant-making foundations, then it is hardly an exaggeration to say that the essential rationale of private philanthropy is now rejected by Congress. It no longer believes that independent private sources of maneuverable social capital, with broad and unfettered authority to determine its allocation, are of special value to a pluralistic society.

Nor is there any present prospect that Congress will reverse itself. The situation results in part from the failings of foundations themselves; in greater part it is a consequence of growing public resentment against inequitably distributed and growing tax burdens. It also reflects the current high degree of public tension over a whole range of social issues which has made various embattled ideological and interest groups apprehensive of the effect of the intrusion of "nonresponsible" elements such as foundations on the balance of political power in these arenas of conflict.

A fundamentally new and perhaps permanent circumstance may therefore now confront private foundations. Historically, they have flourished in the United States in an atmosphere of friendly encouragement; they may henceforth have to function in one of public skepticism and at least mild official surveillance. If this is the case, then they are going to have an especially difficult time in the years ahead reinvigorating themselves and at the same time rebuilding an eroded base of public confidence.

20.

Government and
Foundation Programs:
The Endless, Ambiguous Interface

IN THE AMERICAN CONTEXT, foundations were originally conceived of as integral elements of that eighteenth- and nineteenth-century structure of political and social concepts which saw the role of government as limited and which marked off not only religion but the broad areas of welfare, medicine, science, culture, and much of education as the domain of the private sector. Foundations, according to this tidy scheme, had a clear function: to perform "charitable works" in the extensive sense for which government did not and should not assume responsibility, and they had a largely unobstructed jurisdiction.

The reality, of course, was never as neat as the theory. Government and private philanthropy from the beginning kept meeting and overlapping. Nonetheless, through most of the nineteenth century the vision, or the illusion, of definable separation between the spheres of government and private charity remained largely intact, and certainly the inherent desirability of such an arrangement was generally unchallenged. But that simple and static model has now been shattered by the forces of social, economic, political, and ideological change. Since the beginning of the twentieth century the accepted definition of government responsibility for the public welfare has undergone sweeping transformation. Nor has the evolution reached its end, because public demand is growing, not receding, for its further extension.

The result is that except possibly in the constitutionally reserved area of religion, all the fields in which foundations operate are now also occupied by government. Foundations and government now represent parallel means of serving the social, educational, scientific, and cultural needs of American society. Government in this sense has become a giant foundation—or an aggregation of public foundations—working side by side with the private variety.*

The proliferation of government programs has at the same time been accompanied by a massive change in their scale relative to those of private agencies. Over the past forty years, as a result of sustained prosperity and changes in tax rates and other provisions of the tax code, all forms of private giving in the United States (of which foundation grants are only a small fraction) have risen from about 2 percent to 3 percent of the gross national product. During the same period the volume of "public philanthropy" through government outlays has increased from about 3 percent to more than 9 percent of GNP.[1] In specific fields, the increase in government expenditures has been even more dramatic. In education, for example, there was a time when foundation activity compared to that of the federal government was preponderant. In 1913, the federal contribution to higher education was about $5 million, mainly for the Land Grant colleges, which was less than the expenditures that year of the Carnegie Corporation alone. But by 1964 there had been a *four-hundredfold increase* in federal expenditures on education: its outlays that year totaled about $2 billion, while the Carnegie Corporation spent a little over $12 million. In research and development, government expenditures sixty years ago were in the

---

* Some analysts point out that not only do government and private philanthropy now work in the same areas but that private profit-making institutions are also present. Private hospitals, textbook publishers, "learning corporations," educational film producers and distributors, the radio and television networks, and industrial research and testing laboratories—to name a few of the more obvious examples—are in a sense competitive with and a possible alternative to some of the medical, educational, cultural, and research services provided by government or nonprofit organizations. This third dimension of the problem is one about which the private foundations are now increasingly aware, and although it has neither the scope nor significance of the government relationship, it produces some complications. See on this general subject Dr. Solomon Fabricant, "Philanthropy in the American Economy," *Foundation News*, September–October, 1969.

range of $10 million; by the 1960s they had reached $2 billion. Nor are these unrepresentative examples of what has generally occurred. In purely dollar terms, foundation programs have become almost trivial compared to those of government.

This huge shift has altered the general environment within which private philanthropy must function. It has also affected the character and needs of the vast majority of recipient organizations of foundation grants, many of which have become quasi-public in terms of the base of their financial support. Since a large percentage of the federal funds flowing into universities and research institutions has a military origin, special issues of scientific and educational freedom are also presented. The whole situation confronts foundations with a fundamental need to reexamine and redefine their relationship to government.

Historical Changes in Foundation–
Government Relationships

The operational alternatives available to foundations include ignoring government, collaborating with it, or criticizing and attempting to reform it.* All these choices, separately and in ingenious combinations, have been adopted by one or another of the big foundations at various times. The luxuriant variety of relationships between government and foundations and the wide historical swings between foundation aggressiveness and hesitancy over the past seventy years in dealing with government are striking.

To a startling degree, given the emphasis placed upon the desirability of limited government and the jurisdictional separation between private charity and government in the nineteenth century, the first of the large twentieth-century foundations began operation

---

* From the government perspective, precisely the same range of alternatives exists. Some official agencies are ignorant of or indifferent to the work of philanthropy in their fields of responsibility, some cooperate with private foundations, and some set up demonstration projects which they hope foundations will take over. The critical evaluation of foundations, however, has been left to the legislative branch and is seldom undertaken, publicly at least, by executive agencies.

by flaunting such notions. The Rockefeller and Carnegie philanthropies collaborated with and sought actively to influence government, and they rapidly developed techniques for doing so. They
and their donors assumed that foundations had to get "leverage" to
multiply the impact of their grants, and they recognized that the
most obvious way to do this was to draw in government support
for their pioneering projects. Andrew Carnegie made it a condition
of his gifts of library buildings that each community provide the
site and commit itself to the library's upkeep. In the end more than
2,500 agreed, and the principle of public responsibility for community library services was established.

The Rockefeller Sanitary Commission in its initial work on the
control of hookworm in 1910 committed itself to "working through
governments." In the view of Dr. Wickliffe Rose, the head of the
commission, unless its work in public health was done with the
support and cooperation of government, it could have no firm basis
nor permanence.

The General Education Board was even more unrestrained in its
approach to government. Its initial aim was to encourage a more
adequate system of public schools throughout the South. But a
base of popular support was lacking so the board decided "to support in every State, attached to the faculty of the State University,
a trained specialist in secondary education—a man who could inform, cultivate and guide professional, public and legislative
opinion." [2] These "missionary professors" lobbied for new legislation in the southern states and went on numerous speaking tours in
support of school bond issues. Beginning in 1914 in Delaware the
board jointly financed commissions to develop school reform plans
with a number of states, and as a result new laws were passed and
school budgets increased.

This period was the epic time of interventionism for the major
American foundations. The rapidity with which they discovered
the full array of means for influencing government and the lack
of inhibition with which they pursued their course is, even in retrospect, difficult to comprehend. In that era the major industrial figures were in the habit of using their influence freely upon administrative agencies of government as well as upon legislative bodies.

(A frequently heard remark, for example, was that Rockefeller's Standard Oil Company had done everything possible to the Pennsylvania legislature but refine it.) In that sense it is not surprising that their philanthropies should have felt the same freedom. Yet there were paradoxes. The principal spokesmen for American business at that time were vehemently opposed to the extension of government programs into new fields, but the big foundations were doing their utmost to drive the government precisely in that direction. Moreover, vocal elements of the public were highly suspicious both of the big capitalists and the foundations they had created, yet the intrusion of private philanthropy into the sphere of government was tolerated, for a number of years at least.

By the beginning of the 1920s a discernible change had taken place. The Carnegie Corporation, partly because of financial difficulties which it encountered after the death of its donor, shifted toward smaller grants and less ambitious projects. This development tended to carry it away from the problem areas in which government was active. The Rockefeller Foundation began to give increasing emphasis to scientific research, individual fellowship programs, and international programs which, by intent or not, had the same result. The General Education Board, by redirecting its program emphasis toward the support of medical schools and other institutions of higher learning throughout the country, principally private, in effect also drew back.*

* This change in view was a conscious one on the part of senior foundation leaders. Kiger gives this excellent summary:

"Keppel [then head of the Carnegie Corporation] said that prior to World War I, 'if any board were unanimous in regarding as socially desirable the spread of a given opinion, there was no hesitation in taking action in supporting this spread.' He notes, however, that gradually 'it is evident that the realization is coming that while deliberate propagation of opinion is a perfectly legitimate function for the individual, it is not the wisest way to use funds that are tax-exempt and therefore "affected with a public interest." '

[Kiger continues] "Illustrative of the earlier attitudes, in 1910 Russell Sage Foundation created a Division of Remedial Loans. The director of this Division lobbied in behalf of legislation designed to curb the activity of loan sharks. In some instances, he actually drew up the legislation that put them out of existence.

"Even where the motives were undoubtedly blameless, critics felt that the public questioned such action when it was so obviously partisan. Conse-

The 1920s and 1930s were a time for thinking small and safe, and most of the foundations created in that period cast their programs with modest objectives. The giants of the early years of the century—Rockefeller, Carnegie, and Rosenwald—had sought to deal with issues of national and international importance, to create or reshape whole categories of institutions, and to lead the evolution of governmental policy in new directions. But in the next generation of donors a diminution in caliber and courage occurred. Kresge, the Lillys, and others, scaled their philanthropies to deal primarily with the problems of localities and of specific institutions, generally avoiding governmental involvements.

But not all of the new interwar foundations (fifteen of the present list of the thirty-three large foundations were established during this period) withdrew. The major exceptions were the Duke Endowment, the Commonwealth Fund, and the W. K. Kellogg Foundation: they chose to deal with governmentally related problems and with government agencies, but at the local rather than at the national or international level. Duke through its programs in North and South Carolina for hospital development and the care of orphans used its grants to stimulate action by communities throughout the region. The Commonwealth Fund in its rural hospital experiments, its child guidance clinics, and its early health and housing programs for the poor of New York City, worked closely with local public agencies. The Kellogg Foundation in its initial program sought to reform the child welfare practices of a group of rural counties in Michigan. Some of the older foundations also held their ground, even though it overlapped or was directly adjacent to government program territory. The Rosenwald Fund continued its efforts in the 1920s and 1930s in the broad field of race relations, education in the South, and health services for the poor. Beginning in the early 1920s the Laura Spelman Rockefeller Memo-

---

quently, from World War I on, we find many statements in the annual reports of various foundations that they will not support propaganda or attempt to influence legislation. 'Surely,' said Keppel, 'the discovery and distribution of facts from which men and women may draw their own conclusions offers a field sufficiently wide and sufficiently vital to the welfare of humanity.'" (Joseph C. Kiger, *Operating Principles of the Large Foundations* [New York, Russell Sage Foundation, 1954], pp. 80–81)

rial addressed itself to a wide range of social problems and supported research in a number of fields, including public administration, which brought it directly into the area of governmental concerns. Through the 1930s the Carnegie Corporation and the Rockefeller Foundation, through grants to such organizations as the Social Science Research Council and the Public Administration Clearing House, also provided a continuing source of financing for scholars and institutions working on problems of government structure and programing.

During the New Deal, the federal government rapidly came to be the center of the arena of social action, and the large foundations, perhaps intimidated by the sheer magnitude of government programs, remained out, or were left out, of the mainstream of new social and economic developments. Nor was World War II one of their exceptionally productive periods. Indirectly, some of their earlier work in scientific research and advanced training was of great importance to the national war effort: the structure and grant-making methods of the Office of Scientific Research and Development were influenced by foundation precedents, and the Manhattan Project was in a sense an outgrowth of earlier foundation grants in nuclear research. However, their direct wartime contribution principally consisted of government service performed by research institutions they had helped to develop and individuals they had helped to train. Although it was a time of rapid scientific and technological development and of great social change, it was not characterized either by strong intellectual leadership by the large foundations or by close foundation–government cooperation.

After the war, government retained the initiative in many fields relevant to philanthropy, such as educational programs for returning G.I.'s, land reform in Asia, peacetime applications of atomic energy, and foreign economic aid and technical assistance. Rockefeller and Carnegie were in periods of transition under new leadership, and the Ford Foundation had not yet gotten fully under way. Philanthropy in general was in a period of low vitality. Also, government was taking over important functions that had formerly been supported by philanthropy: the World Health Organization, formed in 1950, largely assumed the work of the international

health division of the Rockefeller Foundation; the National Science
Foundation, established the same year, began to pour greatly increased funds into fellowships and research in fields in which other
divisions of the Rockefeller Foundation had theretofore concentrated; and the creation of the National Institutes of Health at the
same time deeply affected the programs of all those foundations
which had been supporting medical research. As a result, some
foundations closed down activities that they felt had become dupli-
cative and redirected their efforts. Simultaneously, the growth of
government programs in scientific research and advanced training
produced a noticeable increase in professional contact and communication between public agencies and the foundations. The relationship was not formally structured, but it was reasonably productive.

Collaboration in the area of social problems and social science
research grew less rapidly than in technological fields, and it suffered a further setback in the early 1950s as the result of Cold War
tensions and the rise of McCarthyism. The successive Cox and
Reece investigations in Congress brought forth charges by conservatives and anti-Communists that the large foundations had undermined the nation by the use of such occult arts as "empiricism"
and "social engineering" to infiltrate the government and unduly
influence its policies. But by the advent of the 1960s and the New
Frontier in Washington, the climate of distrust had dissipated and
a period of widened cooperation developed, facilitated by the fact
that a number of foundation officials had moved into high positions
in the White House, the Department of State, the Department of
Health, Education, and Welfare, and other agencies.

By the mid-1960s, a busy network of intercommunication between foundations and government had been established between
staffs dealing with scientific programs and also with a wide variety
of social programs—from housing and urban redevelopment to the
so-called War on Poverty. The directors of the large professionalized foundations had come to recognize the practical necessity of
keeping informed about the activities of their counterparts in government; by the same token, regular contact with the foundations
was welcomed by government agencies both on the domestic scene

and overseas. Exceptionally close cooperation developed between officers of the Ford and Rockefeller foundations and U.S. embassies abroad in the areas of agricultural research, population control, and economic development. Joint action between some of the foundations and government and the "mixing" of public and private funds in various projects had become so common that in some quarters, particularly the Ford Foundation, a need came to be felt for a broad review of the situation and possibly a more coordinated method of foundation–government contact.

At Ford's initiative, a cabinet level meeting was convened in Washington in April 1965, chaired by then Vice-President Hubert H. Humphrey. The discussion was wide-ranging, beginning with a review of the many existing manifestations of informal communication and cooperation between foundations and the federal establishment, as well as of some unhelpful instances of noncontact and noncoordination. Various possibilities of future cooperation in education, housing and urban redevelopment, cultural activities, the handling of foreign students in the United States, and poverty programs were explored. Some government participants appeared to favor closer and more formalized collaboration in the future: joint planning of programs and systematic "pretesting" of government programs by foundations. Other officials disagreed about the usefulness or even the propriety of relationships of this intimacy on grounds that they might endanger the independence of foundations. They also felt that the government had both the right and the responsibility for doing its own planning, pretesting, and experimentation. In the end it was tentatively agreed that an informal liaison arrangement between government and the Ford Foundation should be created at the level of top management in both, the official representative presumably to be the director of the Bureau of the Budget. But for several reasons, including the departure from government shortly thereafter of several men who had been involved in the conversations, this proposal was never acted upon.[3]

With the advent of the Nixon administration in the late 1960s, the cordiality of foundation–government relationships cooled. The tax hearings in 1969 did nothing to encourage foundations to try to work more closely with government, and the provisions of the act as finally passed created additional uncertainty about the appropriateness of more formal communication links.

Present Patterns of Foundation–
Government Relationships

Within these broad trends, the big foundations follow different practices and hold to different views regarding their relationship to governmental programs. Roughly one-third still give only those kinds of grants which involve little or no contact with government, such as capital gifts and operating funds to private colleges, hospitals, and churches. These include Brown, Bush, Hartford, Irvine, Kresge, Land, Lilly, Longwood, Moody, Nemours, Richardson, and Surdna. Another third—Astor, Duke, Haas (Waterman), Houston, Kaiser, Mott, R. K. Mellon, Scaife, and Woodruff—carry on programs that to some degree require cooperation with government agencies, primarily at the local or regional level. The rest, because of their interest in broad social and economic problems in which government is also involved, are in regular contact and some collaboration with government at the national level. In the case of Ford, Rockefeller, and Kellogg, this cooperation extends overseas.

Apart from the pragmatic accommodation some of them may have made to the fact of pervasive government presence in their fields of work, there is a distinct dichotomy of philosophy between the traditionalist and the modernist foundations about the private–public relationship. The former cling to the view that philanthropy should work only in the private sector, support only private institutions, and try to be as independent as possible of government activity and influence. The modernists (who in a sense are a throwback to the big philanthropists of the early years of the century) believe that philanthropy must not only recognize the preponderance of government in their working sphere but must attempt in some positive way to relate to it.

The two viewpoints are not equally influential, however, because there is a high correlation between foundations of the traditionalist view and institutional weakness. In effect, they seek to uphold the principle of separation essentially by confining their work to the nooks and crannies where government programs have not yet entered. As a result, most of those following this course have condemned themselves to inconsequence. The Alfred I. du Pont Institute for Crippled Children of the Nemours Foundation, the home for the elderly of the Surdna Foundation, or the grants of the Irvine Foundation to improve local hospital facilities in Orange County—though all useful projects—have little impact nationally or even regionally.

In contrast, the modernist foundations tend to have greater institutional vitality and staff resources. This has meant, for one thing, a better articulation of their attitude toward governmental relationships. In November 1965, Merrimon Cuninggim, head of the Danforth Foundation, told a meeting which his foundation had arranged in cooperation with the U.S. Office of Education: " 'Private' support must not be relegated to those things outside the purview of public funds or peripheral to essential concerns of education; yet duplication must be avoided wherever possible . . . federal money, like foundation money, is automatically neither an ogre nor an angel. We must learn to live with it creatively and to combine it with other resources to the benefit of all education."

The traditionalist outlook is hardly more than a rationalization for lethargy. The modernists on the other hand have high aspirations for philanthropy and would impose on it heavy responsibilities. But their vision constitutes a good deal less than a workable philosophy of foundation–government cooperation because it proceeds from faulty assumptions about the capabilities of foundations, it commonly relies on evasions and euphemisms which skirt serious intellectual dilemmas, and it implies a political role for foundations which may be untenable unless it is more precisely defined and effectively defended.

The modernist view holds that foundations must remain at the center of things, not at the edges, and that they must more than merely coexist with government—they must communicate and collaborate with it. In so doing, they are assumed to have the strength and special qualities to maintain their own independence and integrity and also to exercise a stimulative influence upon their gargantuan companion.

Foundation executives regularly tell one another that compared to government their institutions possess superior personnel, are less bureaucratic, more flexible, more concerned with excellence, and more innovative; also that their grants, compared to the outlays of government, are especially protective of the freedom and integrity of the recipients. But foundations would do well to question these possibly self-serving assumptions.

Superiority of personnel obviously cannot be claimed for that majority of big foundations which have little or no professional staff. For the rest, the claim may have been tenable with respect to some of their specialists in times past; but in more recent years, because of the general interchange of staff that now takes place between the better foundations and government, this contention has worn thin. The most distinguished secretary of health, education, and welfare of recent years had been president of the Carnegie Corporation; his colleague as secretary of state had been president of the Rockefeller Foundation; and the present head, the vice-president for international programs, and the vice-president for domestic programs of the Ford Foundation—all came directly from positions in government. At lower staff levels, a number of able foundation officers have gone into government, particularly during the Kennedy administration, while government has become one of the principal recruiting grounds in filling staff positions for the more professionalized foundations. The relative attractiveness of one or another point of the government–foundation–university triangle changes from time to time. But at any given moment there is some excellence and a fair amount of mediocrity in all of them. Any outstanding man is likely to be found at some period in his career in government, at another in philanthropy, and at another in a university.

The presumed flexibility of foundations also tends to be overstated in much foundation discourse. More than a few of the large ones have remained utterly frozen for years, or even decades, in their program patterns. Even among those with formulated programs and competent staff, the tendency for continuity in the face of changing circumstances is very strong. Examine, for example, the glacial response by the Commonwealth Fund in altering its medical programs to deal with the general breakdown of the American system of medical services in the past forty years, or the stately pace of the Carnegie Corporation in adapting to the problems of racial segregation and the ghettos, or the belated recognition of the urban crisis by the Danforth Foundation.

On the other hand, the flexibility of government programs at the federal, state, and local levels is evident from the annual outpouring of new legislative initiatives in health, science, education, welfare, and environmental protection in recent years. Often the problem seems not to be inflexibility but a tendency under strong public and political demand to leap into new programs without adequate preparation and without the administrative machinery and trained staff necessary to translate high intentions into effective programs.° If the foundations have an advantage of flexibility, it may be that the limited scale of their programs gives them a ready choice of capable grantee organizations to execute their projects when and if they choose to try something new. Government programs, because of their scale, often encounter a lag factor because they require the creation of major new administrative agencies, which is a time-consuming process.

Foundations, along with other private nonprofit institutions, might also be more self-critical in their claims to excellence. In higher education, it is no longer possible to draw any general qualitative distinction between the best of the tax-supported institutions and private colleges and universities. In medical research, government-supported institutions rather than private centers have now become the most fruitful and important source of new scientific discoveries and technical developments. In the physical and natural sciences, including the nuclear and space sciences, government-supported programs and government-created and -supported institutions are producing most of the advanced work. Even in the

° An assistant to former President Johnson, Joseph Califano, has cited 435 major new legislative programs prepared by that administration in the period 1963–68.

social sciences, the government-supported Office of Naval Research and the Rand Corporation, for example, have achievements to their credit which few private institutions can match.

In regard to urgent contemporary social problems, it is fair to say that the early identification of issues, the support of basic research on them, and the creation of new programs to cope with them can be credited in recent decades largely to the legislative bodies and administrative agencies of government, not to private foundations.°

The assertion that foundation grants, because they are from a private, nonpolitical source, involve less risk of interference with the freedom of grantees than government subsidies is also questionable. On this issue McGeorge Bundy, from his experience as dean of Harvard College and before he became head of the Ford Foundation, had some interesting things to say in an address to the annual meeting of the American Council on Education in 1962:

Of the propositions which, in my judgment, have been demonstrated beyond doubt, two are of high importance. The first is that Federal investment in the higher learning has been extraordinarily productive, both for the national security and for the quality of our civilization. The second is that the processes of this investment have, on the whole, been such as to

° Donald Young, former head of the Russell Sage Foundation, has written: "The foundations must inevitably expand their activity in social research, training, and application, in consequence of the path-breaking example set by the federal government. It has long been said that foundations have the advantage of freedom to pioneer with projects far too controversial or uncertain of results for support by tax money under political control. This has been important in the past and may be important again in the future, but does not seem so at present. Foundations have yielded leadership in such controversial areas as race relations, medical care, care of the economically and socially disadvantaged, prevention of unemployment and poverty, mental health, and others. In the physical and biological sciences the government is taking as great risks as any foundation ever did. In the social sciences the federal government is far in advance of the foundations in basic research, training, and application, not just in the number of dollars expended but, more importantly, also in dependence on professional peers of applicants in the selection of projects, institutions, and individuals for support, in the breadth of subject matter and method accepted for consideration, and in willingness to accept the fact that many projects must fail in order that the unpredictable one of significance may not be missed." (F. Emerson Andrews, ed., *Foundations: Twenty Viewpoints* [New York, Russell Sage Foundation, 1965], p. 47)

enhance the freedom and independent strength of American colleges and universities. . . . We are so accustomed to a nervous suspicion of "Federal control" that it is not easy to accept the notion that the Federal dollar may in fact be a reinforcement of freedom.

Even when we leave aside the cruder forms of attack upon freedom of inquiry, there is little reason to single out the Federal dollar for criticism. An unbalanced allocation of resources is more characteristic of alumni than of Government agencies, and the overadministered grant was invented by the large private foundation long before the government became a significant force in academic life. Indeed, my own experience as an academic administrator leads me to the view that on balance the Federal Government makes its grants and signs its contracts with a better perception of the real needs of the higher learning than one can find, on the average, in the major private foundations.

When we look at the overall pattern of higher education, the record of the Federal dollar is still less open to comparative attack. The Federal dollar has not been used, as State dollars have been, to support whole departments and majors in subjects that do not belong at the college or university level. The Federal dollar has not been used, as private gifts have been, for overly luxurious athletic facilities that are reminiscent more of the country club than of the academy. The Federal dollar has not been used for the subsidy of athletes or the construction of pretensious and egocentric memorial buildings.

In the best of our institutions, the Federal dollar has been, on the average, as good as any other—always excepting the wholly unrestricted gift. In American academic life as a whole the qualitative rating of Federal money would, in my considered conviction, be better than that of any other major class of income.

Every institution probably has the right to some amount of self-flattering mythology, if only to keep its spirits up and to fuel the oratory of speakers on ceremonial occasions. But in the case of philanthropy, the contrast between the assumptions held within the institution about its own superiority and the contrary opinion and evidence from the outside is extraordinary. One especially unfortunate consequence of this discrepancy is that it has become a major impediment to clear thinking about the relationship of foundations to government. If they are not able to match government in vigor, professional competence, and creativity, then in any collaboration with it they will not be able to exercise significant influence or preserve their independence. They will be little more than passengers on governmental trains. So long as the assumption of qualitative superiority is erroneous for most of the big foundations, the modernist view of the proper relationship to government may be an illusory, overambitious conception.

The second major inadequacy of the modernist view is that it calls for an activist role by foundations in guiding and shaping government programs, at the same time denying that foundations are political institutions. As one foundation officer, Anthony Brandt, has observed:

Foundations generally dislike the idea that the social purposes they entertain harbor political implications. They prefer their purposes to be clearly acceptable, without debate or controversy, to society. They look for consensus; they couch their purposes in vague laudable phrases—"to advance science," "to improve education," "to help mankind." These phrases are meaningless; no one admits to wanting to hurt mankind or worsen education. Or foundations try to find obvious social needs which everyone recognizes, which everyone agrees ought to be met, and ought to be met in certain obvious nondebatable ways.[4]

Francis X. Sutton of the Ford Foundation, one of the most discerning and thoughtful members of the present generation of foundation executives, has provided an excellent illustration of Brandt's allegation. Concerning the international activities of foundations, he has urged that in working abroad they should display "a disinterested regard for human welfare, one of the most creditable characteristics of American society." He then goes on:[5]

It is important that such activities not be seen as in the direct service of the American government or American foreign policy, and it seems clearly in the interest of the United States that a separation should exist between them and our direct, official representation abroad. Foundation activities abroad should have a genuine autonomy.

[Foundations] are, of course, committed by their charters to the disinterested service of some aspect of human welfare. Being private, they do not derive their purposes from some wider public responsibility or political purpose. . . . These are important characteristics for the international role of foundations. They mean that philanthropic purposes can be served in some detachment from national political purpose.°

° A special dimension of the problem of foundation–government relations exists when projects are conducted overseas. To what extent should a foundation's personnel sent abroad be "cleared" for security with official agencies and its projects be coordinated in advance with the State Department or the

Sutton and other modernist philanthropic spokesmen may well be right that there is such a thing as value-free, nonpolitical activity in the realms of domestic public affairs and international affairs where foundations should play an active, influential role. The logical proposition that there are only nonpolitical or political areas or political or nonpolitical institutions may be too neat and simplistic. It may be essential, if foundations are to be relevant and genuinely pluralistic factors, that they function in this twilight zone. But if so, then foundation leaders must be acutely aware that while they may feel there exists this appropriate intermediate area, there are many others, especially in the Congress, who will not be inclined to accept their "disinterestedness" simply on their assertion of it.

They must recognize that foundations exist by legal privilege in a democratic political environment. Historically, institutions that have operated too aggressively on aristocratic premises in a democratic context have often suffered because of it. They must map out more precisely the limits of this twilight zone where they believe they can and must be free to operate. (Failure to do this may have been one of the reasons for the Ford Foundation's transgressions after 1967, which produced such turmoil in Washington.) They must also be prepared, in the face of opposition, to make a far more forthright and persuasive argument for their freedom to deal with issues of high social tension than they have so far been able to do. They may even have to fight for a restoration of the right to involve themselves in political and governmental concerns.

---

foreign aid agencies? To what extent should the U.S. embassy in the foreign country where a foundation is active be kept regularly informed of its plans and problems? In effect, to what extent should a foundation be free to pursue its own foreign policy objectives? Another set of problems involves the relationship between a private American foundation and the host government. In Eastern Europe, can or should it attempt to act somewhat independently of the local Communist government, or in full subordination to it? In Africa, if it chooses to operate in South Africa or another of the white-minority–controlled areas, should a foundation attempt to oppose discriminatory racial laws or accommodate itself passively to them? Such questions were less difficult to answer when foundation activities were limited to relatively specialized and technical fields, such as malaria control. But as broader scientific, educational, and developmental objectives have been adopted, more complex problems of foundation–government relations at home and abroad arise.

At the moment, the leaders of the more activist foundations apparently do not consider the time ripe for such initiative. But some defenders of the rights of nonprofit organizations have already begun to speak up. Mortimer Caplin, former commissioner of Internal Revenue, has pointed out that since 1962 profit-making businesses have been permitted to claim income tax deductions—as "ordinary and necessary" business expenses—for financing legislative appearances and related lobbying activities which are closely connected with their business operations. The amendment to the Internal Revenue Code enacted at that time overruled the well-established case of *Cammarano* v. *U.S.* (385 US 498) which had previously denied income tax deduction for this type of lobbying. According to the Senate Finance Committee it was felt to be desirable "that taxpayers who have information bearing on the impact of present laws, or proposed legislation . . . not be discouraged in making this information available to the Members of Congress or legislators at other levels of Government."

Yet, Caplin asks, if this is true for business entities, why is it not equally valid for educational and charitable organizations? He proposed that Congress should reexamine the entire area of legislative activities of exempt organizations with a view to granting them a broader measure of freedom: "No sound policy reason exists for denying charitable and educational organizations latitude in the political field equal to that allowed to business organizations. . . . [They] are playing a larger role in achieving the social and economic goals of our nation. In the fields of their special experience and expertise, their voices should be heard and they should be free to give legislative bodies the benefit of their views." [6]

In 1969 the American Bar Association passed a resolution consistent with this view. And in early 1971, Senator Edmund S. Muskie introduced a bill to the Senate (S.1408) to permit public interest law firms, consumer and environmental groups, and other nonprofit organizations, including some foundations, to present their views to Congress without risking loss of their tax exemption. In presenting his bill the senator said: "The outstanding characteristic of these groups has been their representation of views of those who are underrepresented before governmental agencies, in the courts, and elsewhere. It is fundamental in our constitutional system that they should have equal access with business groups and others in presenting their views to Congress. . . . If we are to maintain a democratic form of government in a society of increasing complexity, and if the Congress is to reach reasoned judgment on the important issues before it, we must act to assure that lines of communications to every segment of our society are available and open equally." The bill died in Committee but the senator reintroduced it in the 1972 session as S.3063.

Misery's Plentiful Company

That they cannot present their views on many issues to legislative bodies is only one of the inhibitions under which foundations now operate. Not all of them are the result of legislative prohibition; most are the product of an inhospitable political atmosphere which has led to self-restriction by foundations. But whatever the cause, the effect is to discourage foundations generally from working in controversial areas and from playing the role of critic, goad, and pace-setter for government programs.

The ambiguity of their predicament is troublesome to many of the leaders of philanthropy, but their confusion is shared by other leaders from the private sector in American life who must also determine their course amid ever-changing relationships with government.

In the area of economics, the interpenetration between official programs and private business is such that the old vocabulary of Capitalism and Socialism has become worthless, but as yet there is nothing better to take its place. The relationship between government and higher education is equally complex, creating a whole new range of problems relating to academic freedom and the financial dependency upon government of presumably private institutions. The relationships between government and the scientific community have also proliferated, which as Don K. Price has brilliantly argued, contains profound implications both for the freedom of science and for the intelligent formation of government policy.[7] Even the boundaries between Church and State are becoming obscured with governmental funds now being given to sectarian schools, for example, in ways previously considered unconstitutional.

Business, academic, scientific, and religious groups are all struggling in their own fashion to preserve their independence of action, while at the same time relating themselves realistically to the advent of the full-blown Welfare State. To an even greater degree than these other elements of the private sector, foundations are confronted with the same problems. And to solve them, a wholly new philosophy of action is urgently needed. For here, along this vast and ambiguous interface between foundations and government, is where the question of the significance of private philanthropy in the American future will largely be answered.

21.

Summation and Assessment

WHAT, THEN, does it all add up to? What do foundations contribute to our society? What are the costs as well as the benefits? In the end, given the scope and range of the nation's urgent needs and the multiplicity of its instruments and institutions for dealing with them, what difference do foundations make?

Like all questions of social evaluation, these are impossible to answer with finality. Too many elements are immeasurable. They involve value weights about which there may be infinite disagreement. They require the analysis of the incredibly complex interactions between a given institution and the social matrix within which it operates. They imply assessments of alternative states of the social system beyond our capacity at present even to describe.

Even a meaningful cost-benefit analysis cannot be attempted because most of the required data are simply not available. But a modest effort can be made to describe on the basis of available evidence what role foundations serve, to weigh some of the obvious costs and negative effects of foundations against their achievements, and to make a gross estimate of the contribution of foundations to the nation's stability and progress in relation to that of other private and governmental agencies.

Let it be granted at the outset that foundations are useful. Over the years, and after the expenditure of considerable sums of money, foundations have a number of significant achievements to their credit. But the critical issue for public policy is not whether foundations have been useful in the past, but whether their current usefulness, on balance, justifies continued encouragement and special protection.

The Transfer Function:
A Quantitative Justification

No single statement can adequately describe the role foundations serve. Each of them typically performs not one but several functions, combined in a formula unique to itself. Some concentrate on making capital grants for physical facilities, some on the general support of operating welfare institutions, some on scholarships to individuals. Some perform their role primarily in behalf of education, others of scientific medicine and medical care, and others of the arts and humanities.

On the whole, the principal function that foundations now perform is to transfer funds to sustain reputable nonprofit organizations in the private sector. According to the Peterson Commission, more than 90 percent of their grants go to governmentally certified charitable organizations, that is, organizations to which an individual donor could himself make a deductible contribution—churches, schools and colleges, hospitals, and publicly supported charitable organizations.[1] Foundations are thus an integral part of the present American institutional establishment. By their contributions they help primarily to ensure the stability and continuity of the system.

This is, of course, a service to society not to be disdained. Millions of citizens are benefited and a wide range of activities of spiritual, cultural, and intellectual importance is maintained. In the view of some, this function alone is sufficient justification for the existence of private foundations.

In recent years, this role of financial sustenance to the so-called Third Sector has been emphasized because of the crisis which many nonprofit organizations are experiencing. As labor intensive operations, their costs have risen disproportionately in an inflationary period, while at the same time their normal sources of revenue have decreased. Their deficits are now so great that in many cases their lives are at stake. Foundation help is thus of great importance, at least during this transitional period, until fundamental solutions are found to their funding problems.

But the defenders of the "sustaining" role of foundations see social value in it that transcends its usefulness in the present emergency. Some political scientists argue that by feeding financial help to the private nonprofit sector, foundations are preserving the American tradition of voluntarism, by which private and governmental organizations have a parallel involvement and responsibility for public affairs. In turn, they feel that other important benefits flow from the maintenance of this dual system—the preservation of a degree of heterodoxy in American life, for example, and the protection of academic and cultural freedom. Some economists see "nonexchange" transfers of funds—such as foundation grants—as nothing less than an important survival mechanism for American capitalism.

That capitalism contains within itself the seeds of its own destruction is not only a premise of Marxist doctrine but is also a concept supported by the most eminent modern defender of the market economy system, the late Austro-American economist, Joseph Schumpeter.* In his *Capitalism, Socialism and Democracy* he analyzed the interrelatedness of private property, religious and ethical values, and democracy—the same ideological matrix from which private philanthropy has also sprung—and predicted the probable disintegration of both capitalism and democracy because of their inherent self-destructive tendencies.[2]

Schumpeter never quite conceded that democracy was incompatible with the unfettered functioning of capitalism. But the Anglo-American economist Kenneth Boulding, building on Schumpeter's ideas, has argued that capitalism, which organizes economic life primarily through exchange, is likely to be unstable because it does not generate the social and psychological conditions necessary for its continuance. Its indifference as a system to humane

* The most succinct statement of these views of Schumpeter was contained in his address, "The March into Socialism," which he gave before the American Economic Association in New York on December 30, 1949, shortly before his death.

concerns, if not compensated by ethical institutions, tends to cut away its own political base. He perceives that a "grants economy" operates in parallel with the "exchange economy" in modern capitalistic states, which provides for a substantial and increasing flow of net uncompensated transfers of goods and services by both government welfare programs and nonprofit private agencies to neglected segments of the population.

In his view, the "grants economy" is indispensable to the continued existence of a capitalist structure under modern conditions. Its necessity derives from the fact that "a true exchange economy would develop conditions which would be widely recognized as pathological. It would be deficient in public goods, it might easily produce distributions of income which will be widely regarded as unacceptable, and if carried to extreme it might destroy its own legitimacy, destroying that minimum sense of community and maintenance of order which is necessary to sustain exchange." [3]

However, justifications of private philanthropy that are premised on its function of funding other organizations raise two troublesome questions. First, how much difference does foundation help make to the many other organizations of the private nonprofit sector? And second, does the service justify the costs, attendant abuses, and other possible negative social effects?

In strictly quantitative terms the aid of foundations is marginal in scale. The Third Sector in the United States comprises hundreds of thousands of groups and organizations of every conceivable kind. The gifts they reported receiving in 1970 amounted to $18.3 billion. (In addition, they had the benefit of the voluntary services of some fifty to sixty million individual Americans, with an estimated money value of an additional $5 or $6 billion.) [4] Of this sum, living individuals gave $14.3 billion, or 78 percent of the total. Individual bequests accounted for an additional $1.4 billion and corporation gifts nearly $1 billion. Foundations as such contributed $1.7 billion, or about 9 percent—a not insignificant addition to the total, but still a minor part.

Comparing foundation outlays with relevant expenditures of government, the marginality of the foundation role is even more striking. In 1970, foundation grants were about 0.5 percent of the federal budget; and if the educational, welfare, and other "philan-thropic" activities of states and localities are added, the foundation proportion becomes insignificant. In effect, the survival of volun-tarism and the existing network of nonprofit institutions in the United States has depended in the past primarily upon income from their own endowments, annual gifts by individuals and corpo-rations, and user fees—not foundation grants. If their costs con-tinue to increase, their deficits will have to be made up either by an increase of individual contributions or by an indirect form of government subsidy, or both. What foundations can provide, even under the most favorable assumptions, cannot be more than a small fraction of their requirements.

If not only the Third Sector but American capitalism itself is going to survive—accepting the validity of the theses of Schumpe-ter and Boulding—the outcome will again be only slightly affected by the contribution of foundations. The determinant factor will be the volume of welfare, education, research, and cultural grants by government.

Whether the conduit function of foundations in passing funds to other nonprofit organizations is a service to society worth its costs —and its possibly negative side effects—is a more complicated issue. The statements of many foundation spokesmen suggest that the institution of private philanthropy is something of absolute value and that its advantages cannot be weighed against possible alternatives. But there are costs as well as benefits in the operation of any institution, and there are available alternatives to philan-thropy.

How can the costs which accompany the benefits of foundations be estimated? Some of them such as the administrative expenses incurred by foundations in distributing their grants, are relatively minor (see chapter 15). A second obvious cost or "inefficiency" of foundations until passage of the 1969 Tax Reform Act was the non-pay-out of income for philanthropic activities. Representative Pat-man has documented the fact that in 1968, grants paid out by the fifteen largest foundations averaged only 57 percent of gross re-ceipts. Thus 43 percent of their income (including realized capital gains) was either used for administrative expenses or was added to corpus. The average pay-out for these same foundations over the four-year period 1965-1968 was somewhat higher, 69.2 percent of gross receipts.[5] The investment policies of foundations produce a third "cost" in so far as they result in a deficient flow of current benefits to charity.[*] A fourth is the cost to government of keeping watch over foundations in order to discourage abuses and misconduct. In 1969 the Congress imposed a 4 percent fee on their income, which probably reflects an overestimation of the actual bureaucratic expenses of surveillance.

However, by far the most important social cost is one which is indirect and immeasurable, namely the destructive effect of continued special tax privileges to the very rich upon the public's confidence in the national tax system. Many tax experts are troubled by the signs of growing public resentment from the existing inequities, and they fear the consequences should there be a genuine collapse of confidence in the income tax laws. If foundation donors' privileges could be reduced or eliminated, and if the sustenance of nonprofit organizations could be assured by some means other than preferential tax incentives, many experts consider the change would be decidedly in the national interest.

One alternative to foundations in providing funds for the needs of operating nonprofit institutions would be, of course, to broaden the base of private giving by granting additional incentives to the *average* taxpayer, such as a limited direct deduction from his tax bill, not merely from his taxable income. This alternative, in the view of its advocates, would not only sustain but might greatly increase the flow of charitable funds to nonprofit organizations. By encouraging a mass of individual contributions, the national tradition of voluntarism might be invigorated as well as democratized.

To appraise the costs and benefits of foundations or to determine the relative advantage or disadvantage of alternative methods of financing the Third Sector cannot be done satisfactorily at the present primitive stage of the study of private philanthropy. But at

---

[*] In fairness, if foundation performance in portfolio management is measured against that of hospitals and universities, for example, it is not markedly inferior. No social gain would necessarily result by forcing future donors to give endowments directly to these operating institutions.

least one general conclusion can be drawn: If the justification for foundations in the United States rests on the financial transfer role which most of them serve, they could probably be replaced with only minor damage to voluntarism and nonprofit institutions generally. Alternative means of accomplishing this purpose can readily be devised which would do the job better and cheaper.

The Creative, Innovative Function: A Qualitative Justification

The stronger theoretical defense of foundations rests upon qualitative grounds, namely, that they serve a vital role as purposeful, creative, innovative agencies contributing to scientific discovery, institutional adaptation, and social change. John Gardner has articulated the classic defense of foundations from this point of view. It was written as he was leaving the presidency of the Carnegie Corporation in 1964:

The modern foundation . . . [is] designed to make money go à long way in the service of creativity and constructive change. It is one of the few institutions in our society that can keep itself free to act quickly and flexibly in support of the talented individual or the institution that wishes to undertake an experimental program. . . . It is not only an element in our pluralism; by supporting a wide variety of creative individuals it contributes to an even greater and more fruitful pluralism.[6]

Alan Pifer, his successor, elaborated and refined these ideas in the corporation's 1968 report:

If there is an evident lesson to be learned from the turbulence of the times in which we live, it is that the nation has no higher requirement today than a flexible capacity for rapid change in its social institutions. . . . In the light of this national imperative, every agency which can serve the common good by facilitating the processes of institutional change toward a more just, healthier, better educated, and more universally prosperous national and world society has a very special value, and perhaps none more so than foundations.

Such assessments stress the social more than the scientific role of foundations, their adaptive or even reformist influence, and their capacities for creativity and innovation. These are all terms of high subjective content. They are inherently impossible of exact estimation, and hard evidence on which to base any judgment is remarkably scarce.*

But there is impressive evidence of various kinds which contradicts these assessments and which suggests that the large foundations—their theoretical usefulness as creative forces and as change agents notwithstanding—are in fact overwhelmingly passive, conservative, and anchored to the *status quo*. They are agents of continuity, not of change. This is an unflattering estimation. It relates to what is perhaps the central question in dispute regarding the actual nature and role of the large foundations. The several bases for it must be carefully and fully presented.

FIRST: THEIR FRAMEWORK OF GOVERNING SOCIAL VALUES

The boards of the big foundations are controlled by members of the American business elite. Upon this incontestable fact the strict economic determinist of Marxist persuasion erects a tall and symmetrical syllogism: foundations are part of a class-structured society and are dominated by the same capitalistic elements that dominate that society, namely, the financial and corporate estab-

---

* The following discussion may be especially troubling to the fastidiously logical because the very term "social change" and the factors which influence it cannot be delimited. As John Simon, president of the Taconic Foundation, has said, "All kinds of change produce social change. Any modification in what people consume or what they learn, or in the condition of their homes or their bodies, affects ultimately—even immediately—their capacity to cope with their surroundings and therefore their capacity to cope with other men and other groups. For this reason, even those charitable activities which are merely ameliorative—which do not seek to change anything—have social change effects." (Remarks by John G. Simon at a luncheon meeting of foundation executives at the Harmonie Club in New York City on November 25, 1969)

But both the friends and the enemies of private philanthropy must have something more precise than this in mind in praising—or criticizing—large foundations so repetitiously as "agents of change." Presumably their intent is to suggest that it is the philosophy of those who control the important foundations to foster and facilitate social change; that they make it a primary rather than merely incidental objective of their efforts; and that they pursue it by means that are both vigorous and direct.

lishment. The foundations must therefore consistently serve the interests of that class. They must also be opposed to any basic reform in the existing system of privilege and exploitation. That they are or even could be "agents of change" in other than a purely cosmetic sense is *a priori* impossible.

In the iron grip of such dogma, there is little room for the untidiness of historical accident and of human shortcomings, and no place at all for assumptions of higher motivation other than material self-interest on the part of the ruling class.

But if the Marxist opponent of philanthropy asks acceptance of an ideology open to serious question, the more ardent defenders of philanthropy ask acceptance of a set of propositions which make no ideological sense at all. They argue that although foundations are created and controlled by the business and financial class, they are "free of pressures" upon their general policies, devoting themselves to "the public welfare" in some detached sense removed from all considerations of power, politics, or self-interest. In the words of F. Emerson Andrews, the renowned "foundation watcher":

They are the only important agencies in America free from the political controls of legislative appropriations and pressure groups, and free from the necessity of tempering programs to the judgments and the prejudices of current contributors. Because of this position of unusual freedom, they have an opportunity, and perhaps a special responsibility, to attack the longer-range, more difficult, and often controversial questions which face the nation and the world.[7]

Such a statement assumes that the internal forces determining foundation policies are neutral as regards social change and controversy. The evidence which can be found regarding the social and political biases of foundation donors and trustees does not support this overcredulous assumption.

The boards of the large foundations make up a partial political spectrum ranging from liberal-conservative to ultraconservative. It is marked at its liberal end by three foundations—Ford, Rockefeller, and Kettering—whose boards are significantly diversified in terms of social class and political identification, and on the Right by two—Pew and Lilly—which have a visible identification with ultraconservative organizations.* On the conservative side are also the du Pont, Mott, Moody, Irvine, Brown, and Surdna boards. On the liberal side are the boards of Carnegie, Danforth, and perhaps Land. Between the two lies a relatively narrow range of difference, but still one broad enough to present definite variations of approach to social issues such as welfare reform, race relations, foreign economic and social development, and the equitable distribution of medical services. Of the liberal boards, none goes so far as to include a trade unionist or a known Socialist. On the other hand, some of the rightist boards do have direct associations with extremist causes and organizations.

The Pew family, which composes the board of the Pew Memorial, has had a long history of right-wing ties (see chapter 7). The Lilly family of Indianapolis is also an active sympathizer and supporter of various right-wing causes (see chapter 10). Prominent individuals associated with several of the other large foundations have also had discernible ultraconservative sympathies. Alfred P. Sloan actively supported rightist organizations in the 1930s and 1940s and his foundation at that time made large grants to Harding College in Searcy, Arkansas, often called "the West Point of the ultra-right." Charles Stewart Mott for many years has been a steady supporter of such groups. Ed Ball, the dominant individual in the Alfred I. du Pont Estate–Nemours Foundation complex, is an avowed segregationist and anti-unionist. Herman Brown, donor of the Brown Foundation, was a lifelong and militant anti-unionist. A. G. Bush, William Moody, and James Irvine had strong conservative and antiliberal connections. Various members of the Mellon and du Pont families as well as individual board members of the Houston Endowment and the Surdna and Woodruff foundations are known to have had some involvement with rightist groups.[8]

About one-quarter of the large foundations include individuals sympathetic to the extreme Right in their governance structure.

---

* It is the belief of a number of students of right-wing groups and movements in the United States that a considerable proportion of their financing comes from certain medium and small-sized foundations. Those foundations are not, however, of the scale of the group here under study, and no evidence on this point has been gathered to confirm or deny the belief.

However, only a small portion of their grants have an ideological coloration. In 1969 the total grants of the Pew Memorial were $6.7 million. Of this a total of $45,000 went to rightist recipients such as the American Educational League, Americans for the Competitive Enterprise System, Freedoms Foundation at Valley Forge, Invest-in-America National Council, Inc., the campus program in New York of the National Strategy Information Center, and the Forum Program of Pepperdine College in Los Angeles.[9] Only a small fraction of the grants of the Lilly Endowment were given directly to similar organizations. In fact, with the exception of the substantial grants of the Sloan Foundation two decades ago to Harding College to produce propaganda materials in behalf of its Free Enterprise crusade, the general pattern has been one of small, symbolic grants, made as expressions of support. The 1968 tax return of the Mott Foundation, for example, reports these grants: the Freedoms Foundation at Valley Forge, $3,000; the American Economic Foundation, $1,500; the Robert A. Taft Institute of Government, $1,000; the Christian Anti-Communism Crusade, $1,000; and the Foundation for Economic Education, $1,000.

The rightist viewpoint represented on the boards of some of the large foundations seems principally to translate into a general preference for conservative traditionalist programs and institutions in their grant-making. For example, the Pew Memorial in 1969, as part of its religious program, donated nearly $500,000 to groups, seminaries, and individuals of a fundamentalist, evangelical bent. Similarly, about $800,000 of Pew's educational grants the same year went to a variety of small, mostly sectarian, fundamentalist colleges.

Almost all the other large foundations could be called "moderate conservatives," as indicated by numerous studies of the social and political attitudes of the business executive group which predominantly populates their boards. Their social viewpoint is essentially Lockean—with the protection of private property rights and resistance to the extension of governmental powers and responsibilities as its central values.[10] However, some experts detect a growing willingness on the part of this particular elite to give dissident groups and ideas some recognition and assistance, essentially out of fear that the stability of the society will be endangered if present social tensions are not reduced. Within the broad, loose, and often incoherent set of values they embody, they are increasingly receptive to limited initiatives for social change, some experimentation in institutional adaptation, and some criticism of the established order, including government itself—as the actual record of foundation grants gradually begins to show.

However, as economist Robert L. Heilbroner points out:

We must guard against the assumption that big business has now shifted *en masse* to a more liberal orientation. It would be more accurate I think to stress the existence of a considerable wide spectrum of business opinion and to balance the views of the "new" management with those of an older vintage. . . . The fervid political commitment of the ultraconservative is not congenial to most big businessmen, who, like most Americans, are not fundamentally ideological creatures. Oratory and table-thumping to the contrary notwithstanding, I think that what is noticeable among the majority of big businessmen in America is a striking absence of real political commitment. What is visible instead is a profound unwillingness to get embroiled in anything that might take them away from their jobs, or that might not look good in the newspapers, or that might displease their main customers or their boards.[11]

To claim that the foundations are free of bias in the social, economic, and political orientation of their programs is naive. To categorize them, influenced as heavily as they are by donor families and other business and corporate leaders, as committed to providing "the venture capital of society" is almost in the nature of a *non sequitur*. Their outlook can perhaps be best described by repeating Alexander Pope's couplet: "Be not the first by whom the new is tried, nor yet the last to cast the old aside."

SECOND: THEIR "INNOVATIVENESS" AND "CREATIVITY"

Foundation officials have long insisted on the special qualities of innovativeness and creativity in their grants. But it is relatively rare to find an intellectual or academic figure who shares that view. On the contrary, there is a considerable body of independent opinion that strongly doubts that foundation grants display these qualities in any distinctive degree. Dr. Merle Curti, professor of history at the University of Wisconsin, and Dr. George J. Stigler, professor of economics at the University of Chicago, both scholars of repute, are cases in point. Curti has made a special study of American philanthropy and Stigler's contribution to Warren Weaver's *U.S. Philanthropic Foundations*,[12] is widely regarded as the best single contribution to that collection of testimonial essays. Curti asserts that the "social inventiveness" of philanthropy is not impressive and may be in decline. After detailed examination of the grants of the Ford Foundation for 1961, he concluded that Ford's pattern of outlays "does not diverge from the observed pattern of following trends rather than initiating them. Or challenging them."

In respect of the grants of the Carnegie, Rockefeller, and Sloan foundations for the same year, Curti made this judgment:

Carnegie Corporation of New York made 1960–61 grants and allocations, within the United States, of $10 million ($8.9 million of this from current income). In many instances its grants for education could be interchanged with Ford's: $100,000 to study college mathematics programs; $75,000 for Saturday college courses for high-school students; $300,000 for "research on higher education"; $300,000 to study teacher education; $250,000 "research on academically talented students." A number of Carnegie Corporation's 1960–61 education grants do show serious concern with social invention (e.g., $58,300 for teaching prekindergarten children to read and write), but neither the quantity nor the quality lives up to the announced standards—whether those are social pioneering, or creative giving, or "venture capital" and "seed money."

Rockefeller Foundation appropriations, in 1960, were $32.8 million. Education was not a separately listed category, but a respectable portion of the Foundation's money went for by-now familiar causes: $1.5 million for Harvard Medical Center and its central library; $225,000 for the Association of American University Presses; $86,000 for pre-doctoral fellowships in legal and political philosophy. Finally, the Alfred P. Sloan Foundation, with 1959–60 commitments of $18.4 million, committed $2.4 million to its national scholarship program (4-year grants); gave grants to the Council for Financial Aid to Education, the Independent College Funds of America, and the Association of American Colleges; and sent its funds to a wide variety of educational institutions and for the support of a good many fellowship programs.

The list could be extended, in similar fashion, through the available reports of virtually all foundations: these were chosen almost at random. Nor is it enough to reply—though it is indeed true—that education and health, two of the major objects of philanthropy, are values inadequately implemented. To give for such causes, in such a fashion, is simply less a creative act of social inventiveness than it was a hundred or even fifty years ago.[13]

Professor Stigler comes to similar conclusions regarding the alleged innovativeness of foundation grants in the field of economic research:

First, the large foundations in general are staffed by men whose personal convictions on the proper type of research are fairly representative of the consensus of respectable professional opinion. It would be considered irresponsible or dangerous for a larger foundation to plunge on a large scale into an eccentric program, and men who seek to do this do not get on or stay on foundation staffs. This trait is probably due to the professionalization of the administration of large foundations and possibly also to their vulnerability to criticism.

Second, there is some competition among foundations, despite the fact that an economist accustomed to studying industrial concentration would say that there is excessive concentration of assets in a few of the largest foundations. The competition is in at least some part a competition for the projects of distinguished scholars, and to this degree increases the scholar's role in the formulation of projects.

Both the acceptance of general professional opinion and the competition for scholars' work tend to reduce the directive influence of the foundations. Their influence becomes secondary to the values and goals which the science itself produces.[14]

Personal opinions and appraisals do not, of course, "prove" a case against claims of foundation innovativeness. But when combined with such fragments of solid empirical data as can be found they do place the burden of proof upon the claimants. One of the most persuasive of these is the recent qualitative comparison of government and foundation grants in medical sociology by Gerald Gordon, Ann Parelius, and Sue Marquiz, "Public vs. Private Support of Science." [15]

The universe of their inquiry consisted of all projects which studied the social-psychological aspects of disease listed in the "Inventory of Social and Economic Research in Health" from 1954 to 1960. Detailed information was obtained by questionnaires and otherwise on 250 projects. A panel of 45 persons selected by over 600 researchers as the leading experts in medical sociology was used to evaluate the "innovation level" of each project examined.

As a guideline in making their ratings, the evaluators were asked: "How innovative do you feel the research is—the degree to which the research adds to our knowledge of illness through the development of new theory or findings not explicit or anticipated in previous theories or findings and/or adds to the development of new methods of research? The reference points for this rating should be what you feel is the general level of innovation for studies dealing with the social-psychological aspects of illness."

Roughly *twice* as many government-supported projects as privately supported were rated highly innovative (22 percent to 12 percent). Also, research sponsored by the federal government was more innovative than that funded by state and local governments. Table 6 shows the more specific findings.

Table 6

Territorial Scope and Type of Control of
Funding Agency Related to Innovation

Innovation Quintile	Territorial Scope					
	National		State		Local	
	public	private	public	private	public	private
	%	%	%	%	%	%
1 low	15	25	22	17	—	55
2	16	25	11	50	—	9
3	14	19	31	17	—	9
4	29	12	16	17	—	27
5 high	26	19	20	0	—	0
Number of cases	73	32	45	6	0	11

THIRD: THEIR PROPENSITY FOR
CONTROVERSY AND ACTIVISM

A third indicator of the innovative-reformist quality of foundations is their readiness—or reluctance—to engage in activity at those high stress points where pressures for and against social change intersect and which commonly generate controversy. Some conservative critics believe that much of what foundations support is not charity but rather disguised political and social activism. On the contrary, the facts indicate overwhelmingly that most foundations spend most of their funds on conventional charitable projects and according to traditional patterns of giving.

The Peterson Commission asked a sample of foundations of all types and sizes whether in the three years 1966–68 inclusive they had made any grants "which some people might consider controversial or undesirable" and also whether they had made any grants to projects "which *they* considered to be controversial or particularly unpopular." The replies made it plain that the dominant qualities of foundation grant-making are prudence, civility, and discretion rather than an eagerness to expose themselves to controversy (see Tables 7 and 8).

During the three-year period in question, only 1 percent of the foundations viewed *any* of their grants as controversial; such grants amounted only to 0.1 percent of the total of their outlays and were almost totally centered in the large foundations. Nor should the relative "activism" of the larger foundations be exaggerated.

In the case of the Ford Foundation, for example, often considered to be the large foundation most involved in controversial social experimentation, the great bulk of its outlays to date have consisted essentially of financial assistance to orthodox institutional and individual grantees. Two measures of this may be cited:

Following the 1969 tax reform hearings, the foundation made a careful scrutiny of its entire list of 1,500 active grants to see which of them might be vulnerable to accusations of lobbying, influencing legislation, or propagandistic activity. In a succession of screenings by program officers, a committee of foundation lawyers, and finally President Bundy himself, every case was examined in detail. The result was that only 4 of the 1,500 were judged to be potentially questionable under the new and more restrictive legislation and their terms were consequently modified.

Another indication of the degree of Ford's domestic social "activism" can be obtained by separating from its grant list all those expenditures which clearly have no direct relation to controversial domestic issues—foreign grants, individual fellowships and scholarships, and general support to "benign" organizations. After this reduction, a maximum of 8 percent of the foundation's grants to date could be called experimental or activist.

Table 7

Percentage of Foundation Grants, 1966–1968, for
Specified Purposes Considered Controversial by Some °

Specified Purposes	Foundation Grants (percent)
Voter registration and voter education	0.1
Studies of subjects directly related to public policy issues and for dissemination of such studies to the general public by publication or discussion	0.3
Community or neighborhood organizing of an ethnic, ghetto, or impoverished group	1.5
Grants to individuals employed by government or persons acting as assistants to government employees or related persons	†
Birth control	0.9
Sex education	†
Urban youth groups (including gangs)	1.3
Student organizations	0.8

Source: Peterson Commission, Foundations, Private Giving and Public Policy, p. 83.

° We also asked about grants for schools for potential political candidates and grants connected with a specific election. No foundation surveyed reported any expenditures for these purposes.

† Less than 0.05 percent.

Table 8

Percentage of Grants Considered Controversial
by the Grantors: 1966–1968

	Foundations Answering "Yes" (percent)	Grants (percent)
Foundations with assets:		
under $200,000	—	—
$200,000 to $1 million	—	—
$1 to $10 million	16	1
$10 to $100 million	5	°
over $100 million	38	3
Company foundations	—	—
Community foundations	16	1
Total, all foundations	1	0.1

Source: Peterson Commission, Foundations, Private Giving, and Public Policy, p. 84.

° Less than 0.5 percent.

For the thirty-four-year period, from its establishment in 1936 to 1970, Ford gave a total of $3.9 billion. Of this, $913 million, or 23 percent, was given to foreign institutions and to American universities for work abroad, most of it for technical assistance and economic development programs. The remainder, some $2.9 billion, was the total of all domestic grants. Of this, slightly more than $600 million, or about 21 percent of the grand total, was given for fellowships and the support of organizations administering such individual awards as the National Merit Scholarships. By far the largest part, $2 billion, or more than 50 percent of all Ford grants, went to fund established nonprofit institutions—universities, hospitals, symphony orchestras, art centers, and educational broadcasting stations. A small fraction of this institutional support, such as that given to the Brookings Institution in Washington, might be challenged as "policy oriented" and, therefore, potentially innovative or controversial. But most was given to universities to improve teachers' salaries or to assist their general fund-raising drives, or for general financial assistance to such recipients as the Lincoln Center for the Performing Arts in New York City.

Only about $300 million of a total of $3.9 billion, therefore, might be classified as "research, experimentation, and social action." But even in this reduced category the majority of the projects could hardly be judged controversial or activist even by the most conservative critics.*

A Look at the Outer Limits

Another means of estimating the strength of the impulse on the part of the large foundations to support social change is to look at the *limits beyond which they have not been willing to go* in their "activism." Two cases are especially illuminating in this respect.

* It should be noted, however, that according to the foundation's own Office of Reports, the percentage of its total outlays which might be considered to fall in the broad "social action-research" area has been increasing in recent years. In 1960, for example, $7 million of the foundation's outlays of $160.7 million was judged by the foundation to fall in this category. In 1970, on the other hand, $42 million of a total of $192.3 million in grants was so classified.

The first is that of the Richard King Mellon Foundation—representative of the majority of family-type foundations among the group under study—in connection with the so-called "Pittsburgh Renaissance," sometimes considered the most successful single instance of large-scale urban renewal in the United States. The second is that of the Ford Foundation and its grants to Mexican-American organizations in the American Southwest since 1965.

MELLONS IN ACTION

The renaissance in Pittsburgh was initiated in the 1940s by the business and professional elite of the city under the recognized leadership of Richard King Mellon. He in turn made significant use of the resources of his own foundation as well as other Mellon philanthropies in planning, organizing, and initiating the action that took place (see chapter 12). From the first years of the twentieth century, the Pennsylvania steel-making city had become the very symbol of deterioration of an urban environment as a result of rampant industrialization—deterioration not only in physical but also in human and social terms.*

The mutilation of the city and the neglect of its housing, health, and social welfare problems occurred when business leadership was decisive in the region, unchallenged by any significant countervailing power. Responsibility for the disastrous situation could therefore properly be laid at the doorstep of the city's industrial

---

* Some observers were even more distressed by the cultural blight. "The supreme crime in Pittsburgh," according to R. L. Duffus, was the "willful defiance of the little group of Scotch-Presbyterians who regard themselves as having been elected by Providence to be the city's masters, and who are, in fact, its masters. . . . The city would benefit immeasurably from one large and comprehensive funeral—it needs to bury John Calvin so deep that he will never get up again." ("Is Pittsburgh Civilized?" *Harper's Magazine*, October 1930)

Dwight Macdonald conjured up the same image of a "big-business culture at its crudest and most powerful," tempered by a "veneer of spirituality." Nowhere, he found, were the worldly needs of the average citizen more neglected, and nowhere was there a more "anxious concern" for his spiritual welfare. The response of Richard B. Mellon, brother of Secretary of the Treasury Andrew Mellon, to the "challenge of the depression in 1931" was "a gift of $4,000,000 to build the East Liberty Presbyterian Church." ("Pittsburgh: What a City Shouldn't Be," *Forum*, August 1938)

leaders, and of these none was more central than the Mellon family itself. Their philosophy was that the role of government should be severely limited to the protection of property and the enforcement of law. Specifically, intervention in environmental problems was held to be the exclusive prerogative of the private sector.*

But by 1939 the problems in the city of Pittsburgh had become so grave that they clearly threatened the economic viability of the entire area. Belatedly and only under the prod of a direct threat to its financial interests, the business community developed an active concern. At that point, Richard King Mellon took the lead in organizing a group whose objective was to "crystallize citizen effort behind a movement to stop depreciation of real estate values within the Golden Triangle" (the downtown business district). As the mood of impending crisis intensified during the next few years, the younger generation of business leadership came to believe that a basically different approach to the city's problems was needed. What then evolved has been described as the concept of a "reverse welfare state," a strategy of dramatically expanding public powers and expenditures to rehabilitate the city, but to harness these resources to plans laid down by the business leadership of the area to serve corporate and industrial objectives.[16]

The first step was to unify business support. The second was to achieve the active cooperation of the city-county Democratic political machine headed by Mayor David Lawrence. Both were accomplished by the full utilization of the prestige and power of Mellon and his associates. Checking the city's deterioration was a common interest, public officials accepted the priorities which had been laid down by the business group ("the values of the downtown must be preserved and strengthened before all else"), and an effective working relationship between the Lawrence administration and Richard Mellon was established.

The key agency through which the renaissance was to be planned and organized was the Allegheny Conference on Commu-

---

* Any dissent by local newspapers, academics, or political leaders was not lightly regarded by the controlling group. Instances of brutal suppression and retribution are on record. See, for example, Rose M. Stein, "Academic Cossacks in Pittsburgh," *Nation*, July 24, 1935, p. 105.

nity Development (ACCD), set up by Mellon in 1943 and composed of a number of the city's leading professionals and academics and a majority of top corporate executives. It was initially
financed by grants from the Richard King Mellon Foundation and
other Mellon philanthropies. The ACCD did not simply advocate
general policies: it sponsored concrete, detailed plans prepared by
engineers, architects, economists, and other experts of the highest
technical competence. At the same time, close liaison was established between various city and country agencies and the business
group.

The group then set in motion a skillful and highly successful
financing plan. The "front money" was a $4 million gift by three
Mellon foundations to develop a park in the center of the area to
be rehabilitated. Simultaneously, commitment of a substantial
amount of corporate investment for new construction and renovation was obtained. In turn, these moves triggered the allocation of
large public funds for major new infrastructure investments for
flood control, smoke control, and transportation.

In one highly visible respect, the result was a triumph: the sooty,
dilapidated center of the metropolitan area was transformed into a
handsome collection of new multistory commercial structures, com-
plemented by a fine new park. But some of the side effects were
less triumphant. Several thousand black and other low-income families suffered serious dislocation and received little or no benefit,
since low-cost housing was given little attention. As a result, they
began to vigorously assert their objections to "bulldozer redevelopment." They resolutely opposed any further large-scale clearance
and insisted upon a voice in the planning of major new projects,
particularly in the Lower Hill district, which was then threatened
by a proposed expressway through its center. As social protest
against the redevelopment plan grew in the 1950s, the ACCD was
forced to alter its initial priorities and began to give greater emphasis to the improvement of slum housing, the general social consequences of physical renewal, and even to the recognition of the
rights of affected neighborhood residents.

To cope with the new pressures, the Mellon group responded,
but in their own characteristic way: they seized the initiative by

utilizing another voluntary nonprofit organization, in this case AC-
TION-Housing Inc., to formulate plans, to draw in initial corporate financing, and to obtain large-scale public financing to execute
the plans. Money from the Mellon philanthropies was used to get
the organization under way, and direct leadership of it was taken
by one of Mellon's aides. Its primary objective was to improve
slum housing, but on the basis of a free enterprise philosophy and
by employing the profit-making approach: "To be perfectly pragmatic, in the long run this motivation offers the most potent stimulant for action on a massive scale. After all, our profit-motivated
system has proven itself to be the most prolific provider for human
needs and wants yet known to man." [17]

As in the case of ACCD, ACTION-Housing was able to tap the
full resources of the business community for its managerial and
professional expertise. According to Professor Roy Lubove of the
University of Pittsburgh, ACTION-Housing was quite "briskly
businesslike in its operations. Far removed from the realm of amateur humanitarianism, its administrative, research, and public relations methods resembled those of the corporation." [18] The agency
succeeded in persuading a good number of Pittsburgh corporations
and foundations to make financial commitments in behalf of its
programs, and it also generated some public financing. But the
profit-making stimulant on which its hopes so largely rested produced little action and few practical results. As a consequence,
ACTION-Housing then found itself in the awkward position of
trying to mediate between neighborhood interests it helped arouse
and the political and business leadership on which it depended for
support. In contrast to the initial success of the renaissance in the
Golden Triangle, the effort to do something about slum housing
became mired in the complex and interrelated problems of poverty, race, and demands for neighborhood participation.

In the late 1960s, after years of floundering attempts to reconcile
its free enterprise philosophy with new kinds of social demands,
ACTION-Housing (with the help of a substantial injection of Ford
Foundation assistance to supplement that of the Mellon foundations) formulated a new strategy which placed greater emphasis on
citizen participation. This represented a sharp shift from the Pitts-

burgh tradition of elite initiative in defining the goals of urban development. At present, the entire effort seems to have lost its momentum—because of the death of Mellon, a general loss of interest by the business community, and the sheer intractability of the social aspects of the renewal problem.

Over all, the experience of the renaissance to date suggests that a major foundation controlled by leaders of the business community can draw strength for its efforts by its collaboration with them, but its actions are severely hindered by the limited social vision of that group. Reliance upon business community initiative in dealing with the problems of a distressed city means that concern comes late; when it comes it is primarily directed to objectives of direct economic interest to the business community; and attention to broader social and noneconomic considerations has to be forced into the plans and programs by organized effort, sometimes by militancy and confrontation, by nonbusiness groups in the community.

THE FORD FOUNDATION AND LA RAZA

The role of the Ford Foundation in dealing with the problems of the Mexican-American community in the Southwest is an example of the most "radical" approach to a situation of friction and social change which any of the major American foundations has so far been willing to adopt.

Its grants relating to the problems of Mexican-Americans have been violently assailed from all sides. *Ramparts* magazine, expressing a view of the New Left, has strongly objected to the moderate approach of the program, calling it a scheme for undermining authentic radical Mexican-American leadership and replacing it with stooges—"a pacification program." [19] The attacks of the Right and Center have accused Ford of straying into partisan politics. This charge derived from the foundation's relationship to MAYO, a youth organization in San Antonio (which indirectly received a total of $8,527 of Ford Foundation funds). One of its young Mexican-American leaders, José Angel Gutierrez, while still on the payroll of one of the Ford projects, made a number of public charges in 1966 against local political figures and allegedly advocated racism and violence. In April 1969, Mario Campeon, another of the young founders of MAYO, ran against the incumbent mayor for his seat on the city council (in San Antonio the mayor is chosen by the council from among its membership) and MAYO, presumably using some of its Ford funds, actively campaigned in his behalf. Campeon came within a few hundred votes of forcing the mayor into a run-off.

As a result, Mayor Walter McAllister called the Ford Foundation, along with Vista, "the two most subversive organizations in the country." Congressman Henry B. Gonzales, a Democrat who has received high marks from such organizations as Americans for Democratic Action because of his liberal voting record, charged that the Mexican-American grants of the Ford Foundation had led "to the emergence of reverse racism in Texas," providing money to "militant and radical groups and leaders . . . who are at best irresponsible and who present a real danger to peace and safety and progress of the people of south and south-west Texas." [20]

Almost immediately, the foundation cut off funds to the offending youth organization and forced the "resignation" of Gutierrez as its chairman. Nevertheless, despite the small portion of its grants which had trickled into the political process, Ford's Mexican-American program acquired a sensational public reputation. The facts of the case are a great deal less colorful than the image.

Mexican-Americans, numbering some five million, constitute the nation's second largest deprived minority group. They are concentrated largely in California, Arizona, Colorado, New Mexico, and Texas. About 80 percent live in urban areas, usually in the *barrio*, the Mexican-American equivalent of the black ghetto. The two cities with the largest Mexican-American population are Los Angeles, with about a million, and San Antonio, with about 300,000. Historically, because of language problems and economic and social discrimination, they have suffered from poverty, unemployment, and poor education. In recent times the gap between them and other groups in the Southwest has steadily widened. More than one-third live below the generally accepted poverty line, and their unemployment rate is about double that for the "Anglo" (non-Mexican-American) population of the region. Their children typically complete only about half as many years of high school as do the children of other groups; the dropout rate is high. Few aspire to or reach the university. They are subjected to voting restrictions and are victimized by the gerrymandering of electoral districts. As a result, they tend to be unrepresented in city councils, state assemblies, and the Congress. Moreover, because of their poverty and their dispersion over the Southwest, Mexican-American groups have not been linked together in effective organization to coordinate their efforts to obtain redress for their grievances.

Ford took its first action to assist them in 1963, when a grant was made to the University of California at Los Angeles for a comprehensive study of their social, economic, and political status. Four years later, it made a second grant of $150,000 to the University of Denver to provide scholarships to enable Mexican-Americans to enter legal careers. But the foundation's active involvement in the affairs of La Raza (one of the terms by which Mexican-Americans call themselves) dates from 1968. In May of that year, $2.2 million was given to establish a Mexican-American Legal Defense and Education Fund (MALDEF), modeled generally after the NAACP's Legal Defense and Education Fund which, since 1939, has led the attack, through legal procedures, on discrimination against blacks. In announcing the grant, the foundation said, "In terms of legal enforcement of their civil rights, American citizens of Mexican descent are now where the Negro community was a quarter of a century ago. . . . Legal process alone will not secure civil rights, but without skillful, imaginative probes of the full potential of laws and regulations, the path to full opportunity will be harder and longer." [21] Subsequently, a number of other substantial related grants were made, which by 1970 totaled nearly $13 million. The major subdivisions of this amount are as follows:

1. About $1 million has gone for basic research on the problems of the Mexican-American community;
2. More than $2 million has been given for individual scholarships at established colleges and universities to train young Mexican-Americans;
3. Nearly $3 million has been spent for what the foundation calls "leadership development." A minor part of this touches

upon the political process (for example, a project to place interns in the offices of practicing politicians). But far heavier emphasis has been given to increasing the capabilities of *barrio* businessmen, implicitly because of a belief in and an endorsement of business leadership in organizing the Mexican-American community;

4. About $3.5 million has been spent for the rural development aspect of the program, which is based on the same free enterprise approach. The principal single project has been the financing of a feed-lot to help raise the income of Mexican-American cattle farmers;

5. Grants of nearly $1 million have been given in the area of housing, mainly to assist the development of Mexican-American community organizations to take advantage of federal programs to assist construction of low-income housing. But a substantial part has gone to help Mexican-American home owners—the middle class of the *barrio*—to improve their properties;

6. About $2.3 million has been given to legal service projects intended to help Mexican-Americans achieve their rights through the courts and established legal procedures.

The foundation calls the broad objective of the program "building the capacity of Mexican-Americans to deal with the American system, helping them achieve legal, economic, and political parity within the system." [22] It has attempted to do so mainly by providing educational help for individuals and by encouraging the development of Mexican-American leadership and organizations to press the claims of the group more effectively. In this respect, the program would seem as American as apple pie. Indeed a rather plausible case could be made that Ford has been guilty of an excessively cautious approach. It did little about the Mexican-American problem until the late 1960s, by which time organizations promoting black rights had been receiving foundation help for many years. Most of the funds it has given, which constitute only a tiny fraction of its outlays, have been given to established organizations and for relatively traditional activities, such as research and fellowships. Much of the remainder has gone for activities which, though less traditional by philanthropic standards, are still relatively non-controversial: rehabilitation and retraining of migrant farm workers; assistance to groups concerned with enforcing state health and safety codes and securing welfare and social security benefits for their members; and fostering the development of "brown capitalism."

What the foundation did that was out of the ordinary was to define a social objective and to take strong initiative in pursuing it. When necessary it created new organizations, composed in some cases of ardent and inexperienced young people, which created in turn the delicate problem of supervising their activities and their use of funds. The net effect of the foundation's program, even though it pursued its goals through accepted educational, legal, and economic avenues, has been to alter in a subtle way the balance of political forces in those areas where Mexican-Americans are concentrated. A formerly unorganized and inarticulate disadvantaged group has been helped to find its voice and to demand its rights. This development has disturbed various vested interests, created great local sensitivity, and generated most of the criticism of the foundation.

The case illustrates both the internal and external constraints which operate even on the largest and most powerful of the big foundations. It helps define the extreme limit of acceptable foundation action at the present time in the United States in an area of social tension and change—a boundary line well removed from anything that could seriously be termed revolutionary or even radical.

On the basis of the foregoing evidence—the governing social values of the large foundations, the degree of their innovativeness, the extent of their involvement in urgent social problems, and the rather narrow limits upon their "activism"—the conclusion would seem inescapable that the big foundations are far from the dynamic, creative, reformist institutions that some of their most eloquent defenders have claimed. Not one-tenth (probably not one-twentieth) of their grants have any measurable impact upon the major social problems confronting the nation at the present time.

The Case for a Further Gamble

Judged on the basis of its present actual performance, private philanthropy in the United States today is a sick, malfunctioning institution. As conduits of funds for the support of other nonprofit organizations, foundations serve a useful social function but hardly a vital one, given the limited scale of their contributions and their disutilities and inefficiencies. Their support of the tradition of voluntarism and sustenance of nonprofit institutions in general could probably be done as well, or better, by alternative means. In respect to creativity and social experimentation, the vast majority of foundations avoid taking any risk and even the most activist of the large foundations venture forth only hesitantly and infrequently.

In both quantitative and qualitative terms, private philanthropy as it now operates is not an institution of high productivity or crucial importance. On the basis of the record, it is difficult to insist that the public and the Congress should exert themselves excessively to defend and encourage foundations. And there are, of course, a considerable and growing number of Americans—the extreme left, extreme right, trade unionists, middle-class taxpayers, black militants and the new generation of educated white youth—who would prefer to see the special privileges of foundations reduced or gradually allowed to expire.

But if the foundations, particularly the larger ones, are judged by the performance of the best of them and if some of their great achievements of the past are kept in mind, it is obvious that private philanthropy has an enormous unrealized potential. This potential is so great and of such special value at this point in American history that it would be reckless imprudence to throw it away. The wisest course of public policy would appear to be to give them a further chance—for a reasonable but limited period of time —to begin to fulfill their possibilities.

This course involves a gamble, obviously. Many would argue that over the last seventy years foundations, despite certain minor improvements, have on the whole become less vigorous and effective and that they have by now conclusively demonstrated their unwillingness to revive themselves. But even if there is only a slim chance that the largest foundations can be prodded to come to life in the next few years, there is a decisive reason why the attempt should be made—namely, the nature of the current national crisis and the unique contribution which a set of concerned and creative large foundations could make toward easing it.

It is no longer mere rhetoric to say that the survival of the United States as a decent and progressive nation is today in jeopardy. It is under assault by an unprecedented combination of forces of change—technological, economic, military, social, and psychological—moving at unprecedented speed. The intense pressures so created encounter a set of institutions which have become rigid and unresponsive—including corporations, universities, the organized professions, the media, and the agencies of government. The result is a pervasive state of anxiety and growing friction. If some better answers are not found for adaptation and evolutionary progress, the nation might even see its bicentennial celebration in 1976 illuminated by the beginning fires of a new civil war.

An especially dangerous consequence is the decay of public confidence in the capacity of both private and governmental institutions to cope with the crisis. Faith in the social responsibility of *laissez-faire* capitalism, in the working of Adam Smith's concept of "the invisible hand," has long since disappeared, and at least since the 1930s the credibility of the business community and corporate leadership in dealing with larger social questions has been fractured and in recent years has almost disintegrated.

The collapse of the prestige of business leadership during the great depression was accompanied by a corresponding increase in public faith in government as an instrument of social advancement. But in the more complex crisis of the present, this faith has also begun to deteriorate. Official agencies have demonstrated that their policies can become as rigidified and dehumanized as those of the profit-making sector. It has almost come to be accepted as inevitable that local governments are corrupt, that state governments are feeble, that the structure of government is antiquated, that the military system is out of control, and that the political parties are almost useless as instruments of the popular will.

An even deeper concern exists about the fundamental adequacy of the democratic approach in resolving major contemporary problems. More and more, the vital issues of public policy—whether of nuclear weaponry, the health services system, the educational system, the tax system, trade policy, energy supply or communications —have moved beyond the technical competence and comprehension of the average citizen. Behind the ritual of democratic process, he increasingly suspects that the experts and the bureaucracy, if anyone, are in control of the central issues of public policy directly affecting his life. He senses that he does not even know what the issues are, let alone have a qualified opinion about them. He sees his government, like a great blind beast, stumbling about in the wreckage of its health, housing, education, and welfare programs, exhausting itself in military adventures and unable to provide him with safe streets, good schools, regular mail service, reasonable transportation, or even clean air.

Somehow, he instinctively understands that nothing is more important at this moment than to find some means to reestablish essential citizen control over the vast faceless forces of both corporate enterprise and government. Unless they can be effectively challenged, competently criticized, and held ultimately accountable—and unless means are found to generate new ideas and methods to ensure the responsiveness of their programs—he senses that the whole American dream may die and himself with it.

Hence, the recent resurgence of interest in the Third Sector—the venerable sphere of nonprofit, nongovernmental citizens' organizations and action. The sprouts of this new growth are becoming visible everywhere, from the movement for the appointment of ombudsmen to the formation of crusading political groups outside the traditional political structure, such as Common Cause, to Ralph Nader and his swelling movement of consumer advocates and public interest lawyers. The search is on for new organizational forms to cope with urgent new societal needs. In this context, the private foundation takes on new importance. Originally conceived as a vehicle for humanitarian and charitable purposes in the older sense, it can now be seen as an unusually well-adapted social mechanism for assisting processes of institutional and social change and for reinvigorating the concept of pluralism in the contemporary setting.

The private grant-making foundation, particularly if it is of sufficient scale, has unique possibilities: it can assemble and bring to bear specialized and disinterested competence to analyze complex issues, policies, and institutions; it can organize groups of influential private individuals to formulate knowledgeable appraisals of corporate and governmental programs; it can commission the preparation of well-grounded proposals for the reform of our archaic institutions; it has the resources to experiment with new programs and procedures—from the use of educational television, to the reorganization of community health services, to the overhauling of the criminally unjust bail system for criminal offenders. In the face of such needs, old-fashioned passive philanthropy is perhaps less socially important than ever before. But innovative philanthropy could be more important than ever before.

This is not to suggest that private foundations can be major sources of intellectual or artistic creativity, or that they can and should be sources of social and political leadership in American life. In the sphere of the fine arts and pure thought, talented and devoted individuals are the great generative forces—not institutions. In the sphere of social and political progress and reform, leadership lies in the hands of influential political figures operating through the processes of organized social and political groups, legal procedures, and processes of representative government. No technocratic, plutocratic factor such as private foundations can or should play this leadership role.

But foundations can play an important ancillary role and can perform some necessary and valuable services which otherwise would be accomplished only with great delay and difficulty. For the best of the things they do there is no readily available alternative. Who else in the 1920s and 1930s would have provided funds to give advanced training to a generation of black leaders? Who else would have helped initiate the early work on population control and family planning in the face of great public indifference and institutionalized hostility? Who else would have financed the Myrdal study on the American racial dilemma in the 1940s? And in recent years, what other funding could have been found to help organize the Mexican-American community to assert its rightful claims? Who else would have created a commission on public broadcasting, financed the Conant study of the American high school, and created the Kerr commission on higher education? Who else would have put up the money for *Sesame Street?*

Theoretically, other sources might have been found; but in fact they did not come forward, and it was one or another of the handful of modern major foundations which supplied the missing ingredients to initiate these and other extremely useful ventures.

If American society had available a number of well-funded institutions which could serve as "change agents" to help it through its present agonizing transition, then foundations might be dispensable. But it does not. In this respect foundations are unique, which must not be overlooked or underestimated in striking a wise balance in determining public policy in an area in which imponderables and uncertainties lie on every side. Experience may show that even with further encouragement, foundations do not contain within themselves the capacity to reform and energize themselves. Equally important, the American public, for all its need of the creative and innovative contribution which foundations might make, may not in the end tolerate their greater activism.

But the gamble of giving them greater encouragement still deserves to be taken. So long as there is a serious possibility—which there is—that foundations can become more vigorous and more independent institutions fully and exclusively devoted to public purposes, they should be given a further chance. If, after another decade, no significant improvement has occurred, then another hard look at public policy toward them should be taken. But if they now begin to face their problems, accept their responsibilities, and grasp their opportunities—if they begin to play their full part in the greening of the Third Sector—their contribution to humanizing and advancing American democracy, possibly even ensuring its survival, could be truly enormous.

22.

Epilogue: A Note on the Prospects for Self-Reform and Self-Renewal

MUCH OF WHAT can be done by legislation to force foundations to overcome their major and obvious debilities has already been done, and in certain respects overdone. What now remains can best be corrected by the foundations themselves—which raises tantalizing practical and theoretical problems relating to institutional self-reformation and self-renewal.

The crucial immediate question is, will they make the effort? The prospects are not excessively encouraging. One has only to look at their nonresponse to the challenges they have faced in recent decades to appreciate the almost limitless capacity of foundations to resist adaptation and self-improvement. Whether the problem was as blatant as financial self-dealing or as obvious as failure to issue public reports, foundations have commonly preferred to ignore the problem, or to react with righteous indignation to criticism, or to attribute the difficulty to "public misunderstanding," rather than to face their own faults and take individual and collective action.

Some thinkers have long contended that such rigidity is an inherent tendency of foundations. The French economist Turgot, in an article on the charitable perpetuity for Diderot's Encyclopaedia in the mid-eighteenth century, wrote that "it bears within itself an irremediable defect which belongs to its very nature—the impossibility of maintaining its fulfillment. Founders deceive themselves vastly if they imagine that their zeal can be communicated from age to age to persons employed to perpetuate its effects. There is no body that has not in the long run lost the spirit of its first origin."

More recently, Irving Kristol has argued that some private institutions, namely universities, are controlled by a configuration of internal vested interests that makes reform impossible except by governmental crackdown:

All of the groups—professors, administrators, and students—now engaged in this enterprise of "restructuring" are deficient in the will to do anything, or the power to do anything, or ideas about what might be done. . . . What faculty members of our universities fail to see is that any meaningful restructuring will not only have to be done *by* the faculty, but will also have to be done *to* the faculty. And to ask the American professoriat to restructure itself is as sensible as if one had asked Marie Antoinette to establish a Republican government in France. Whether or not it coincided with her long-term interest was immaterial; the poor woman couldn't even conceive of the possibility. . . . So the beginning of wisdom, in thinking about our universities, is to assume that the professors are affected with an interest in, and an implicit ideological commitment to, the *status quo* broadly defined, and that reform will have to be imposed upon them as upon everyone else. If any empirical proof were required of the validity of these assumptions, one need only cast a glance over the various proposals for university reform that have been made by faculty committees at Berkeley and elsewhere. These proposals have one distinguishing characteristic: at no point, and in no way, do they cost the faculty anything—not money, not time, not power over their conditions of employment. They liberally impose inconveniences upon the administration, upon the taxpayers, upon the secondary schools, upon the community. But they never inconvenience the faculty.

Nor is the administration going to "restructure" the university. It couldn't do it if it tried; and it is not going to try because it doesn't regard itself as competent even to think about the problem. . . . True, a determined administration can badger and bribe and blackmail the faculty into marginal revisions of the curriculum, just as a determined administration can have some influence over senior appointments. But most administrations are not all that determined—like everyone else, university administrators prefer an untroubled life. . . . As for the administration's power over students, that hardly seems worth discussing at a time when the issue being debated is the students' power over the administration. Suffice it to say that, where disciplinary power does exist on paper, it is rarely used; and it is now in the process of ceasing to exist even on paper.

And the students? They, alas, are indeed for the most part rebels without a cause—and without a hope of accomplishing anything except mischief and ruin. . . . To date most of the reforms sponsored by students have been in the direction of removing their obligation to get any kind of education at all.

From this acid analysis of the principal factors in the university equation, Kristol concluded: "So where are we? In an impasse, it would appear. Here we have a major social institution in a flagrant condition of crisis, and not one of the natural social forces involved with this institution can be relied upon to do any of the necessary work of reformation."[1] It is not difficult to apply Kristol's line of argument to the case of foundations.

The reforms which foundations most need all run directly against the grain of the thinking of most of the people who control them. From the perspective of the typical donor, diversifying the board and the portfolio and professionalizing the staff would mean depersonalizing his foundation, diluting his influence, and frustrating his dynastic ambitions. From the perspective of most trustees, such reforms would mean the ending of collegiality, the intrusion of unfamiliar people and alien ideas, the sharing of authority with nonbusiness professionals and intellectuals, and the commitment of the foundation to open dialogue and dispute. Their natural inclination has been, and presumably will be, to stand pat.

It might therefore seem that the only practical possibility of improvement is through further governmental compulsion. The difficulty with such a solution, however, is that although it may succeed in correcting certain weaknesses, it cannot constructively deal with most important ones, namely the lack of vitality and creativity of many foundations. Self-improvement remains a far better answer, both philosophically and practically.

But it can happen only if two conditions are met: first, if the members of the leadership class of American society, essentially the business class, who control the major foundations, have become sufficiently aroused by the dangers of the present situation to overcome their habitual inertia, and second, if the "public interest" movements such as Common Cause and Nader's Raiders will begin to generate sustained pressure upon foundations for reform. In effect, the best hope for progress rests largely upon a curious combination of forces—the ethic of social responsibility of the old Establishment and the militancy of some of the newer forms of expression of social discontent—working not necessarily in concert but at least on an object of common concern. If they can produce significant change among institutions as encapsulated as foundations, the omen for the chances of overhauling other categories of lethargic and outmoded American institutions would be exhilarating.

Appendix

A Note on Foundation Investment Performance°

THE COMMISSION on Foundations and Private Philanthropy, or Peterson Commission, examined the investment return on foundation portfolios of various sizes for the year 1968 (see discussion in chapter 15). This appendix extends those findings by presenting a more complete picture of the investment performance of the largest grant-making foundations for the three-year period 1967 through 1969. Annual measures of total return, including capital appreciation or depreciation, as well as dividend and interest yields are given. Foundation performance is also compared to that of the market in general (as measured by Standard and Poor's 500) as well as to that of public mutual funds (as measured by the Lipper index of balanced mutual funds). The following conclusions emerge:

First, for the three-year period, the big foundations did roughly as well as the mutual funds and did not perform significantly better or worse than the market. This is in sharp contrast to the Peterson findings, which indicated that for 1968 foundation investment performance was far inferior to market performance.

Second, foundations seem to have done slightly better than the mutual funds for the three-year period, although the difference is not substantial.

Third, when individual foundations have done markedly better than the market, it was generally not the result of astute portfolio

° The author wishes to acknowledge the able assistance of Frank J. Husic of the faculty of the Wharton School of the University of Pennsylvania in the preparation of this analysis.

management. Rather, it was most often due simply to continued holdings of a single security that performed exceptionally well over the period. There is little evidence, for example, of switching from stocks to bonds to take advantage of a period of high bond yields or of diversifying to limit risk exposure.*

Fourth, the fact that the investment performance of this group of very large foundations was comparable to that of the mutual funds and the market cannot be interpreted as an exoneration of foundation trustees in general from the charge of poor portfolio management. The Peterson data indicates that the medium and smaller foundations do much less well than the larger foundations. Moreover, in the sample on which the present study is based there is unquestionably a preselection bias. By concentrating on the largest foundations, it tends to include a disproportionate number of "single stock" foundations whose holdings happened to perform spectacularly well during the period; it also tends to exclude those whose holdings performed badly and fell in value, thereby dropping them out of the largest size category.

Scope and Sources

The original intent of this study was to evaluate the performance of the thirty-three general purpose foundations having assets greater than $100 million as of 1968. But because of data problems, some had to be eliminated from the analysis. The sources of information here used have been two: the annual reports of the foundations; and IRS-990A forms. For purposes of performance evaluation these data had several major drawbacks of which the most troublesome was the lack of uniformity with respect to reporting cycles. Over half the foundations in the sample report on a calendar year basis, but the remainder report on other fiscal year bases. These differences in reporting period during a time of rapid market fluc-

---

* Because of resource limitations, this study did not attempt a thorough examination of risk diversification and switching techniques and results. A far more comprehensive study of foundation investment performance is needed, which should include quantification of these phenomena.

tuations greatly complicate the problem of making valid comparisons.

A second difficulty was the presence of holdings other than negotiable securities in the portfolios of a number of the foundations. Assets such as real estate, buildings, oil wells, etc. present serious valuation problems. They also have such different risk and liquidity aspects as to make comparison to simple stock and bond portfolios meaningless. Moreover, in some cases the accounting methods used made separation of the liquid and nonliquid assets impossible, as well as any clear allocation of cash flows to different segments of the portfolio. This problem caused elimination of the Irvine Foundation and Houston Endowment from the sample.

Third, data were incomplete or unavailable in some cases. Three foundations in the sample (Longwood, Moody, and Waterman) began providing annual reports only as of 1968. Prior to that, they provided two-year reports. For these foundations, returns were computed only for the period 1968–1969. Lack of data also necessitated deletion of the A. W. Mellon Foundation from the study. It was formed in 1968 by a joining of two previously separate foundations, which had reported on different fiscal bases, making a consolidation of their reports impractical.

Finally, it was not possible to separate the affairs of the Alfred I. du Pont Estate and the Nemours Foundation on the basis of the information available, and the foundation had to be deleted.

Thus, the final data base consisted of information necessary to generate annual rates of return for each of three years for twenty-six foundations, plus data to produce return figures for each of two years for an additional three foundations.

Methodology

The rate of return measure employed is an approximation to what is commonly known as the internal rate of return.°

° For further explanation of this approach, see Peter O. Dietz, *Pension Funds—Measuring the Investment Performance*, (Glencoe, Ill., Free Press, 1966); and *Measuring the Performance of Pension Funds for Purposes of Interfund Comparisons* (Park Ridge, Ill., Bank Administration Institute, 1968).

Mathematically, the measure is:

$$V = \frac{M_2 - M_1 - C^\circ}{M_1 + \frac{1}{2}C}$$

where V = rate of return for the period
M_1 = market value at start of the period
M_2 = market value at end of the period
C = net cash flow during the period

To make interfoundation comparisons possible despite different reporting cycles, a performance ratio has been calculated, which can be defined as the return on a foundation portfolio divided by the return on the market for the equivalent time period.

Results

Table A1 presents internal rates of return for individual foundations for each year in the period covered; and cumulative performance for the three years taken together. Foundations are grouped by reporting cycles with the relevant S & P 500 and Lipper index performance given for each group. It also provides the following information:

° Returns for each year are linked to form a cumulative return. If R is the cumulative performance for three years,

$$R = (1 + V_1) \times (1 + V_2) \times (1 + V_3)$$

where V_1 = annual return for 1967
V_2 = annual return for 1968
V_3 = annual return for 1969

By linking, the annual internal rates become an estimate of the time-weighted rate of return for a foundation. Time-weighted rates measure the change in unit price of the portfolios rather than change in total dollar value. For a more detailed discussion see the Bank Administration Institute study, pp. 102–5. Both Dietz and the institute in their work point out that a useful method of presenting time-weighted rates is to form the geometric average of annual rates of return. Thus, if V_1, V_2, and V_3 are internal rates of return for 1967, 1968, and 1969 derived by our earlier formula, the average time-weighted rate V_T is:

$$V_T = \sqrt[3]{(1 + V_1)(1 + V_2)(1 + V_3)}$$

1. A simple unweighted average *yield* for all foundations reporting in each period.

2. Value-weighted average *yield* for all foundations reporting in the period, the weights being the market values of portfolios.

3. A simple unweighted average *return* for all foundations reporting in the period. This average gives equal weight to each foundation return, regardless of portfolio size, and corrects to a degree for the preponderant influence of Ford in any weighted average.

4. A value-weighted average *return* for all foundations reporting on a given fiscal year basis. The weights are the average market values during the year.*

5. *Return* on the S & P 500 for the equivalent period. Since the return estimates for the foundations take into account total cash flow including dividends, the S & P 500 price index was adjusted for income by adding the appropriate annual yield of the S & P 500.

6. *Return* on balanced funds contained in the Lipper balanced fund index. This is presented where available. Before 1969, it was computed on a calendar year basis only.

Table A2 gives a size distribution of foundation portfolios in the sample.

Tables A3 and A4 present performance ratios to permit comparisons and consolidations as discussed earlier. Table A3 gives the value-weighted ratio for each of the groupings of Table A1. Table A4 gives the corresponding unweighted ratios. Linking annual ratios to form a cumulative expression, the results are mixed. The cumulated simple unweighted average of the ratios is 1.087. This implies that allowing each foundation performance ratio equal weight, the foundations do slightly better than the market. However, when the ratios are weighted by the value of the foundations'

---

* In accordance with standard usage, "yield" comprises interest and dividend income of a portfolio; "return" includes yield plus capital appreciation or depreciation.

portfolios, the market does somewhat better (.005) than the foundations.

Table A5 compares performance ratios for the foundations and the Lipper index wherever the latter is available. It indicates that the foundations included in the sample had slightly higher returns than the balanced funds included in the Lipper index.

Table A6 presents average time-weighted rates of return for the foundations on an unweighted and value-weighted basis. It also presents performance ratios computed as the ratio of time-weighted return of the foundations to time-weighted rate of return of the market.

The mixed results of Tables A3 and A4 reappear as expected. By the simple unweighted average, foundations again slightly outperform the market (1.015) while by the value-weighted average they lag (.997).

Table A1

Total Annual Returns for Individual Foundation Portfolios
(portfolios are grouped by fiscal year end)

Fiscal Year End: December 31	1967	1968	1969	Cumulative Performance
Eli Lilly	17.51%	45.62%	33.10%	127.71%
Hartford	13.39	28.17	− 17.54	19.84
Kresge	82.33	23.61	24.70	181.05
Rockefeller	14.79	15.90	− 10.54	19.01
Duke	− 5.04	5.45	− 15.77	− 15.65
Woodruff	46.84	10.83	14.57	86.45
Kaiser	111.85	2.12	8.59	134.93
Astor	12.96	5.10	− 3.84	14.16
Scaife	32.88	17.00	− 23.85	18.39
Rockefeller Bros.	11.14	14.05	− 6.82	18.11
Richardson	40.57	34.54	2.13	93.14
Pew	46.59	25.95	− 31.05	27.31
Mott	21.84	12.43	− 8.67	25.12
Mellon	16.55	16.65	− 10.49	21.69
Sloan	22.72	4.26	− 3.42	23.57
Unweighted average yield	3.22	2.98	3.07	—
Value-weighted average yield	3.35	3.09	3.06	—
Unweighted average return	32.46	17.45	− 3.26	50.50
Value-weighted average return	20.49	17.98	− 4.24	36.11
S & P return	23.34	10.91	− 7.21	26.94
Lipper Balanced Fund Index return	20.85	15.98	− 11.25	24.39

(Table continues)

Table A1 (continued)

	1967	1968	1969	Cumulative Performance
Fiscal Year End: May 31				
Danforth	21.92	−9.52	6.69	17.70
Yield	1.81	2.30	2.36	—
S & P return	6.68	14.03	8.09	31.48
Lipper Balanced Fund Index return	n.a.	n.a.	7.51	—
Fiscal Year End: June 30				
Surdna	17.20	1.27	−21.50	− 6.83
Brown	17.56	26.32	1.22	50.3
Fleischmann	7.22	7.78	1.60	17.42
Commonwealth	0.61	7.82	6.08	15.10
Unweighted average yield	3.93	3.90	4.11	—
Value-weighted average yield	3.97	3.96	4.18	—
Unweighted average return	10.65	10.80	− 3.15	18.73
Value-weighted average return	8.82	9.52	− 2.45	16.26
S & P return	10.21	13.11	1.37	26.38
Lipper Balanced Fund Index return	n.a.	n.a.	− 1.36	—
Fiscal Year End: August 30				
Kettering	21.16	1.21	− 0.88	21.55
Kellogg	19.71	13.22	− 2.27	32.47
Unweighted average yield	4.15	3.96	4.37	—
Value-weighted average yield	3.81	3.64	4.07	—
Unweighted average return	20.44	7.22	− 1.58	27.09
Value-weighted average return	20.02	10.69	− 2.01	30.19
S & P return	24.70	8.82	0.14	35.52
Lipper Balanced Fund Index return	n.a.	n.a.	− 3.41	—

Fiscal Year End: September 30

Ford	22.90	9.73	− 11.16	19.82
Carnegie	21.36	4.19	− 5.66	19.29
Unweighted average yield	4.52	4.15	4.44	—
Value-weighted average yield	4.75	4.30	4.55	—
Unweighted average return	22.13	6.96	− 8.41	19.65
Value-weighted average return	22.77	9.24	− 10.68	19.79
S & P return	29.57	9.41	− 6.05	33.19
Lipper Balanced Fund Index return	n.a.	n.a.	− 8.38	—

Fiscal Yar End: November 30

Land	15.39	33.61	11.89	72.49
Bush	15.62	84.40	20.43	156.76
Unweighted average yield	1.79	1.06	.95	—
Value-weighted average yield	1.89	1.04	.95	—
Unweighted average return	15.50	59.00	16.16	113.33
Value-weighted average return	15.61	55.89	16.05	109.17
S & P return	20.09	18.53	− 10.16	27.89
Lipper Balanced Fund Index return	n.a.	n.a.	− 11.77	—

Table A2

Size Distribution of Foundation Portfolios—Average Market Value
Aggregated by Fiscal Year End
(value in millions of dollars)

Fiscal Year End	Number of Foundations	1967 average market value	1967 percent of total	1968 average market value	1968 percent of total	1969 average market value	1969 percent of total	Average Percentage 1967–1969
December 31	15	$4125.88	46.78%	$4779.19	49.54%	$4945.62	49.88%	48.73%
May 31	1	188.04	2.13	188.30	1.95	172.85	1.74	1.94
June 30	4	408.03	4.63	431.39	4.47	429.51	4.33	4.48
August 31	2	471.58	5.35	521.47	5.41	522.40	5.27	5.34
September 30	2	3606.46	40.89	3603.57	37.36	3581.44	36.12	38.12
November 30	2	19.08	0.22	122.47	1.27	263.44	2.66	1.38

Table A3

Performance Ratios (Foundation Return:Market Return)
Using Value-Weighted Average Returns

Fiscal Year End	1967	1968	1969	Cumulative Performance
December 31	.977	1.064	1.031	1.071
May 31	1.14	.793	.987	.892
June 30	.987	.968	.858	.920
August 31	.962	1.017	.981	.960
September 30	.948	.998	.951	.90
November 30	.963	1.315	1.292	1.64
Value-weighted average performance ratio	.968	1.030	.998	.995

Table A4

Performance Ratios (Foundation Return:Market Return)
Using Unweighted Average Returns

Fiscal Year End	1967	1968	1969	Cumulative Performance
December 31	1.074	1.059	1.043	1.186
May 31	1.14	.793	.987	.892
June 30	1.004	.980	.955	.939
August 31	.966	.985	.996	.938
September 30	.943	.978	.974	.898
November 30	.962	1.340	1.293	1.670
Unweighted average performance ratio	1.015	1.023	1.041	1.087

Table A5

Value-Weighted Performance Ratios for Foundations
Compared to Lipper Index

Fiscal Year End	Performance Ratio			Cumulative Performance
	1967	1968	1969	
December 31	.977	1.064	1.031	1.071
Lipper Index	.979	1.046	.956	.979
May 31			.987	.987
Lipper Index	n.a.	n.a.	.995	.995
June 30			.858	.858
Lipper Index	n.a.	n.a.	.868	.868
August 31			.981	.981
Lipper Index	n.a.	n.a.	.967	.967
September 30			.951	.951
Lipper Index	n.a.	n.a.	.975	.975
November 30			1.292	1.292
Lipper Index	n.a.	n.a.	.982	.982

Value-weighted average ratios:
  Foundations   .998
  Lipper Index   .957

Appendix

447

Table A6

Average Time-Weighted Rates of Return and Comparison to
Market Performance (foundations grouped by fiscal year end)

	Unweighted Average Return	Value-Weighted Average Return	Performance Ratio
December 31			
(a) 15 foundations	14.58	10.81	1.023
(b) S & P 500		8.28	
May 31			
(a) 1 foundation	5.36	5.36	.962
(b) S & P 500		9.55	
June 30			
(a) 4 foundations	5.88	5.14	.973
(b) S & P 500		8.11	
August 31			
(a) 2 foundations	8.31	9.18	.987
(b) S & P 500		10.66	
September 30			
(a) 2 foundations	6.16	6.20	.965
(b) S & P 500		10.02	
November 30			
(a) 2 foundations	28.70	27.86	1.178
(b) S & P 500		8.55	
Value-weighted average ratio			.997
Unweighted average ratio			1.015

Notes

CHAPTER 1. PHILANTHROPY UNDER FIRE

1. Report of the U.S. Commission on Industrial Relations, 1915, pp. 118–19, 125.

2. Ferdinand Lundberg, *The Rich and the Super-Rich* (New York, Lyle Stuart, 1968), p. 394.

3. René A. Wormser, *Foundations: Their Power and Influence* (New York, Devin-Adair, 1968).

4. David Horowitz and David Kolodney, "The Foundations [Charity Begins at Home]," *Ramparts*, April 1969.

5. U.S. Congress, House, *Hearings Before the Committee on Ways and Means on the Subject of Tax Reform*, 91C1/1969/Part I, p. 10.

6. *Ibid.*, Part I, pp. 231–32.

7. *Ibid.*, Part IV, p. 1573.

8. Peterson Commission, *Foundations, Private Giving, and Public Policy: Report and Recommendations of the Commission on Foundations and Private Philanthropies* (Chicago and London, University of Chicago Press, 1971).

9. *Congressional Record*, December 5, 1969, p. S15759.

10. *Ibid.*, p. S15757.

11. *Ibid.*, p. S15756.

12. U.S. Congress, Staff Report of the Subcommittee on Domestic Finance of the Committee on Banking and Currency, *The Fifteen Largest U.S. Foundations: Financial Structure and the Impact of the Tax Reform Act of 1969*, 92C1/July 15, 1971/p. iv.

CHAPTER 3. CARNEGIE: EMERGENCE FROM ELITISM

1. Kathleen Fidler, *The Man Who Gave Away Millions: The Story of Andrew Carnegie* (London, Lutterworth, 1955), p. 113.

2. Abraham Flexner, *Pritchett* (New York, Columbia University Press, 1943), pp. 140–41.

3. Carnegie Corporation of New York, *Annual Report, 1938*, p. 19.

4. *Appreciation of Frederick Paul Keppel by Some of His Friends* (New York, Columbia University Press, 1951), p. 59.

5. Author's interview with Flexner, May 16, 1959.

CHAPTER 4. THE FORMIDABLE ROCKEFELLER FLEET

1. See, for example, C. Joseph Pusateri, "Re-Evaluating a 'Robber Baron'— the Case for John D. Rockefeller," *Carroll Business Bulletin* (June 1969).
2. Raymond B. Fosdick, *The Story of the Rockefeller Foundation* (New York, Harpers, 1952), p. 141.
3. Abraham Flexner, with Esther S. Bailey, *Funds and Foundations* (New York, Harpers, 1952), p. 77 ff.
4. Fosdick, p. 239.
5. New York *Times*, March 13, 1966.

CHAPTER 5. COMING OF AGE IN THE FORD FOUNDATION

1. *Time* (July 20, 1970), p. 66.

CHAPTER 6. DANFORTH AND KELLOGG: FINE BUT FLAWED

1. Gordon M. Philpott, *Daring Venture: The Life Story of William H. Danforth* (New York, Random House, 1960), p. 86.

CHAPTER 7. SURDNA, BUSH, PEW, AND IRVINE:
UNDERACHIEVERS AND DELINQUENTS

1. Interview with Philadelphia banker unwilling to be identified.
2. Los Angeles *Times*, May 14, 1969.
3. Ed Reid, *The Grim Reaper: Anatomy of Organized Crime in America* (New York, Bantam Books, 1970), pp. 227–28.
4. Los Angeles *Times*, May 19, 1969.
5. U.S. Congress, House, Subcommittee Chairman's Report to Subcommittee No. 1, Select Committee on Small Business, *Tax-Exempt Foundations and Charitable Trusts: Their Impact on Our Economy*, 90C1/April 28, 1967/1127 pp.

CHAPTER 8. THE DUCAL DU PONTS

1. William H. A. Carr, *The du Ponts of Delaware* (New York, Dodd, Mead, 1964), p. 256.
2. *Ibid.*, p. 262.
3. American Guide Series, *Delaware* (1955 ed.; New York, Hastings House).
4. New York *Times*, June 13, 1971.
5. Interview with a senior du Pont foundation executive unwilling to be identified.

CHAPTER 9. TEXAS: RICH LAND, POOR LAND
MOODY, HOUSTON, RICHARDSON, AND BROWN

1. Galveston (Texas) *News*, December 10, 1958.
2. Denny Walsh, "Investigative Report: A Two-Faced Crime Fight in St. Louis," *Life* (May 29, 1970), p. 25.

3. For extensive details on the questionable financial dealings of the foundation, the trust, and the associated family companies, see the New York *Times,* February 6, 1972.

4. New York *Times,* September 4, 1965.

CHAPTER 10. LILLY, HARTFORD, AND DUKE:
BIRDS IN GILDED CAGES

1. New York *Times,* June 23, 1968.
2. "The A & P Saga, Part 1," *Progressive Grocer* (February 1970), p. 73.
3. New York *Times,* April 3, 1969.
4. *Annual Report, 1958,* p. 5.
5. Warren Weaver, *U.S. Philanthropic Foundations* (New York, Harper and Row, 1967), p. 272.
6. John Wilbur Jenkins, *James B. Duke: Master Builder* (New York, Doran, 1927), p. 54.
7. *Ibid.,* p. 81.
8. Two university deans and two full professors interviewed, unwilling to be identified.

CHAPTER 11. SLOAN, KETTERING, AND MOTT:
GM'S PHILANTHROPIC OFFSPRING

1. Report of the Sloan Commission on Cable Communications, *On the Cable: The Television of Abundance* (New York, McGraw Hill, 1971).
2. Studs Terkel, *Hard Times: An Oral History of the Great Depression in America* (New York, Pantheon Books, 1970), p. 135.

CHAPTER 12. THE MIDDLING MELLONS

1. Harvey O'Connor, *Mellon's Millions: The Biography of a Fortune* (New York, Blue Ribbon Books, 1933), p. 13. For a kinder treatment of the Mellons, see Philip H. Love, *Andrew W. Mellon* (Baltimore, Heath Coggins, 1929).
2. O'Connor, p. 16.
3. *Ibid.,* p. 20.
4. *Ibid.,* pp. 113–14.
5. See Arthur M. Schlesinger Jr., *The Coming of the New Deal* (Boston, Houghton Mifflin, 1958), p. 569.
6. O'Connor, p. 236.
7. *Ibid.,* pp. 209, 211, 364.
8. S. N. Behrman, *Duveen* (New York, Random House, 1951).
9. *Ibid.,* p. 158. See also Schlesinger, p. 569.
10. A. W. Mellon Educational and Charitable Trust, *Report 1930–55,* p. 17.
11. 1968 federal tax returns.
12. New York *Times,* August 26, 1969.

CHAPTER 13. ASTOR, WOODRUFF, KRESGE,
WATERMAN, AND KAISER:
PHILANTHROPY FAMILY STYLE

1. Interview with Coca-Cola official unwilling to be identified.
2. Interview with Atlanta educator unwilling to be identified.
3. Floyd Hunter, *Community Power Structure: A Study of Decision-Makers* (Chapel Hill, University of North Carolina Press, 1953), pp. 100–1.
4. See Ferdinand Lundberg, *America's 60 Families* (New York, Vanguard Press, 1937).
5. New York *Times*, October 19, 1966.
6. Interview with business associate unwilling to be identified.
7. Interview with Rohm & Haas Company official unwilling to be identified.

CHAPTER 14. FLEISCHMANN AND COMMONWEALTH:
TWO INTRIGUING ABERRATIONS
LAND: A GLEAM OF HOPE

1. Interview with a trustee unwilling to be identified.
2. Interview with a trustee unwilling to be identified.
3. *The Commonwealth Fund: Historical Sketch, 1918–1962*, p. 39.
4. "The Future of Industrial Research," address given at the Standard Oil Development Company Forum, Waldorf Astoria Hotel, New York City, October 5, 1944.
5. Report in the files of the Polaroid Company.
6. *Ibid.*
7. *Ibid.*

CHAPTER 15. A PROFILE OF BIG PHILANTHROPY

1. Peterson Commission, *Foundations, Private Giving, and Public Policy: Report and Recommendations of the Commission on Foundations and Private Philanthropy* (Chicago, University of Chicago Press, 1970), p. 79.
2. *Ibid.*, p. 78.
3. Ralph L. Nelson, *The Investment Policies of Foundations* (New York, Russell Sage Foundation, 1967), p. 12.
4. *Ibid.*, pp. 16–17, 72.
5. Thomas A. Troyer, "The Treasury Department Report on Private Foundations: A Response to Some Criticism," *UCLA Law Review*, 13:965 ff.
6. Peterson Commission, *Foundations, Private Giving and Public Policy*, p. 13.

CHAPTER 16. PUBLIC REPORTING: THE ENCLAVE MENTALITY

1. J. William Hinckley, *Annual Report 1962* (New York, The Research Corporation), p. 11.
2. Warren Weaver, *U.S. Philanthropic Foundations* (New York, Harper and Row, 1967), p. 134.

3. Memorandum to the Members of the National Council on Community Foundations, Inc., September 5, 1962.

4. Marion R. Fremont-Smith, *Foundations and Government* (New York, Russell Sage Foundation, 1965), p. 388.

5. Frank M. Chapper, "Disclosure and Reporting: Present Requirements and Forms," *Proceedings of the Eighth Biennial Conference on Charitable Foundations*, ed. Henry Sellin (New York, Matthew Bender, 1967), p. 192.

6. *Foundation News*, Vol. 10, No. 4 (July–August 1969), p. 142.

7. *Foundation News*, Vol. 6, No. 5 (September 1965).

8. Foundation Center, *Annual Report 1968*, p. 13.

9. Dwight Macdonald, *The Ford Foundation: The Men and the Millions* (New York, Reynal, 1956), p. 102.

10. Harold C. Cofman, *American Foundations: A Study of Their Role in the Child Welfare Movement* (New York, Association Press, 1936), p. 7.

11. Edward C. Lindeman, *Wealth and Culture* (New York, Harcourt, Brace & World, 1936), pp. 5–6.

12. Interview with officer of the Rockefeller Foundation unwilling to be identified.

CHAPTER 17. THE DETERMINANT INTERNAL FORCES:
DONORS, TRUSTEES, AND STAFF

1. Quoted in Scott M. Cutlip, *Fund-Raising in the United States: Its Role in America's Philanthropy* (New Brunswick, Rutgers University Press, 1965), pp. 526–27.

2. For more detailed data, see Edward C. Lindeman, *Wealth and Culture* (New York, Harcourt, Brace and World, 1936); F. Emerson Andrews, *Philanthropic Foundations* (New York, Russell Sage Foundation, 1956); Donald R. Young and Wilbert E. Moore, *Trusteeship and Management of Foundations* (New York, Russell Sage Foundation, 1969). See also Suzanne Keller, "The Social Origins and Career lines of Three Generations of American Business Leaders" (unpublished Ph.D. dissertation, Department of Sociology, Columbia University, 1953); C. Wright Mills, "The New American Business Elite: A Collective Portrait," *Journal of Economic History*, Vol. IV, No. 4, Supplement 5 (December 1945), pp. 20–44; and Osborn Elliott, *Men at the Top* (New York, Harpers, 1959).

3. New York *Times*, October 1, 1970.

4. See, for example, the excellent special report on corporate boards in *Business Week*, May 22, 1971, and the various writings of Myles L. Mace, of the Harvard Business School.

CHAPTER 18. BIG PHILANTHROPY AND THE RACE QUESTION:
A CASE STUDY OF PERFORMANCE

1. Raymond B. Fosdick, *Adventure in Giving* (New York, Harper and Row, 1962), p. 11 (quoted from *Southern Workman and Hampton School Record*, 1899).

2. Fosdick, p. 11 (quoted from Charles William Dabney, *Universal Educa-*

tion in the South [Chapel Hill, University of North Carolina Press, 1936], II, 534).

3. Fosdick, p. 11 (quoted from *Proceedings of the Conference of Tennessee School Superintendents at Nashville, April 8–9, 1903* [Chapel Hill, University of North Carolina], Southern Education Collection).

4. Fosdick, pp. 323–24.

5. Interviews with Martin Luther King Jr., Whitney M. Young Jr., and Bayard Rustin.

CHAPTER 19. GOVERNMENT AND FOUNDATIONS:
THE TIGHTENING EMBRACE OF REGULATION

1. Louis Harris Survey, in *Life*, August 15, 1969.

2. Philip M. Stern, *The Great Treasury Raid* (New York, Random House, 1964).

3. Stanley S. Surrey, quoted in U.S. Congress, House, *Hearings Before the Committee on Ways and Means*, 91C1/1969/Part IV, p. 1611.

4. For a fuller discussion see Stanley S. Surrey, "Tax Incentives as a Device for Implementing Government Policy," *Harvard Law Review*, Vol. 83, No. 4, (February 1970), pp. 709–11.

5. Henry Aaron, "Tax Exemptions—The Artful Dodge," *Transaction* (March 1969), pp. 4–6.

6. Marion Fremont-Smith, *Foundations and Governments* (New York, Russell Sage Foundation, 1965), p. 407.

7. Lawrence M. Stone, quoted in U.S. Congress, House, *Hearings Before the Committee on Ways and Means*, 91C1/1969/Part I, pp. 147–48.

8. U.S. Congress, House, *House Report 749*, 88C1/1963/p. 53.

CHAPTER 20. GOVERNMENT AND FOUNDATION PROGRAMS:
THE ENDLESS, AMBIGUOUS INTERFACE

1. National Bureau of Economic Research, *The Changing Position of Philanthropy in the American Economy* (New York, Columbia University Press, 1970). Also Mary Hamilton, *Philanthropy and the Economy*, Appendix V of the Peterson Commission, *Foundations, Private Giving, and Public Policy: Report and Recommendations of the Commission on Foundations and Private Philanthropy* (Chicago, University of Chicago Press, 1970).

2. General Education Board, *Final Report, 1964*, p. 5.

3. Ford Foundation files, unpublished summary of Ford Foundation and government meeting, Sheraton Carlton Hotel, Washington, D.C., April 7, 1965.

4. Anthony S. Brandt, *Foundation News* (May–June 1969), p. 107.

5. "American Foundations and U.S. Public Diplomacy," presented to a subcommittee of the House Committee on Foreign Affairs, July 22, 1958, reprinted by the Ford Foundation.

6. George Webster, ed., "Tax Problems of Non-Profit Organizations," *Journal of Taxation* (New York, 1968), p. 31.

7. Don K. Price, *Government and Science* (New York, New York University Press, 1954) and *The Scientific Estate* (Cambridge, the Belknap Press of Harvard University Press, 1965).

CHAPTER 21. SUMMATION AND ASSESSMENT

1. Peterson Commission, *Foundations, Private Giving, and Public Policy: Report and Recommendations of the Commission on Foundations and Private Philanthropy* (Chicago, Chicago University Press, 1970), p. 77.

2. Joseph A. Schumpeter, *Capitalism, Socialism, and Democracy* (New York, Harpers, 1950).

3. Unpublished paper prepared for the Kettering Foundation, "Towards a Pure Theory of Foundations," November 1970.

4. From *Giving, U.S.A., 1970*, based on data compiled by the American Association of Fund Raising Counsel, Inc., New York.

5. U.S. Congress, Staff Report of the Subcommittee on Domestic Finance of the Committee on Banking and Currency, *The Fifteen Largest U.S. Foundations: Financial Structure and the Impact of the Tax Reform Act of 1969*, 92C1/July 15, 1971/p. 9 ff.

6. John Gardner, *Carnegie Corporation Annual Report 1964*, p. 12.

7. F. Emerson Andrews, ed., *Twenty Viewpoints* (New York, Russell Sage Foundation, 1965), p. 6.

8. For detailed references to the rightist activities of various individuals and families associated with some of the larger foundations, see Richard Dudman, *Men of the Far Right* (New York, Pyramid Books, 1962) and D. Janson and B. Eisman, *The Far Right* (New York, McGraw Hill, 1963).

9. For a full listing of organizations on the extreme right see the 1962 edition of *The First National Directory of "Rightist" Groups, Publications, and Some Individuals in the United States (and Some Foreign Countries)* (Los Angeles), compiled "for and by right wingers"—which named nearly 2,000; the 1963 supplement added another thousand.

10. See "A Self Portrait of the Chief Executive," *Fortune* (May 1970), p. 181; "The Executive as Social Activist," *Time* (July 20, 1970), p. 62; see also chapter 17.

11. Robert L. Heilbroner, *The Limits of American Capitalism* (New York, Harper and Row, 1966), p. 38.

12. Merle Curti, *American Philanthropy Abroad: A History* (New Brunswick, Rutgers University Press, 1963); Warren Weaver, "The Foundation and Economics," *U.S. Philanthropic Foundations* (New York, Harper and Row, 1967), pp. 276 ff.

13. *Foundation News* (November 1962), p. 7 ff.

14. Weaver, p. 283.

15. *The American Behavioral Scientist* (May 1967), pp. 29–32.

16. Roy Lubove, *Twentieth-Century Philanthropy* (New York, Wiley, 1969), pp. 106–7.

17. ACTION-Housing, *Proposal for the Creation of the Allegheny Housing Rehabilitation Corporation*, June 1967.

18. Lubove, p. 145.

19. Rees Lloyd and Peter Montague, "Ford and La Raza: They Stole Our Land and Gave Us Powdered Milk," *Ramparts*, September 1970.

20. *Arizona Daily Star*, May 23, 1969.

21. "News from the Ford Foundation," May 1, 1968.

22. Interview with Mitchell Sviridoff, vice-president of the Ford Foundation.

CHAPTER 22. EPILOGUE: A NOTE ON THE PROSPECTS
WFOR SELF-REFORM AND SELF-RENEWAL

1. "A Different Way to Restructure the University," *New York Times Magazine*, December 8, 1969; reprinted in Daniel Bell and Irving Kristol, eds., *Confrontation: The Student Rebellion in the Universities* (New York, Basic Books, 1969), pp. 145 ff.

Index

Aaron, Henry: quoted, 368
Academy of Natural Sciences, Philadelphia, 242
Accountability, public, 304
Acklin, Arthur, 231
ACTION-Housing, Inc., 420
Activisim, *see* Social action programs
Administration costs, 277-78
Africa, 75-76, 88-89n
Ages and aging: grants, 90, 147, 237, 389
Agriculture: grants, 57, 62, 66, 67-68, 93, 114, 142, 252, 336, 387, 424
Alcoa Foundation, 23
Aldrich, Malcolm P., 257, 258-61, 331
Alinsky, Saul, 355n
Allegheny Conference on Community Development, 216-17, 418-20
Allen, Ivan, Jr., 233
Alley Theatre, Houston, Tex., 160
Aluminium Company of America, 209, 212
American Bar Association, 174, 396
American Council on Race Relations, 341
American Dilemma, An (Myrdal), 39-40, 351, 430
American Economic Association, 174
American Economic Foundation, 409
American Educational League, 125, 409
American Foundations and Their Fields (ed. Rich): quoted, 296
American Friends Service Committee, 353, 356

American Medical Association, 256, 341
American National Insurance Company: and Moody Foundation, 151, 155, 157
American Public Welfare Organization, 60
American Red Cross, 125
Americans for the Competitive Enterprise System, 125, 409
American Tobacco Company, 183
Andelot Foundation, 138
Andrews, F. Emerson: *Philanthropic Foundations*, quoted, 296-97; *Foundations: Twenty Viewpoints*, quoted, 392n, 407
Andrus, John, 119-20
Andrus Memorial, Julia Dyckman, 120
Angell, James R., 36
Anti-Communism: grants, 123, 124, 173, 174-75, 409
Antioch College, 198
Appalachia, 104
Area programs, *see* Geographical areas
Arts programs: grants, 23, 33, 38, 41, 56, 59-60, 62, 63, 65, 71, 75, 90, 93, 95, 96 (*table*), 143, 160, 179n, 214-15, 220, 222, 223, 224, 232, 237, 241, 275, 351, 416
Asian studies: grants, 47n, 74
Assets, foundation, 22 (*table*), 24n, 25, 51, 52, 72, 74, 76, 79, 120, 121, 122, 124, 127, 139, 142, 145, 152, 157, 158-59, 163, 164, 167, 171, 183, 184,

Assets (*Continued*)
   192, 215, 217, 218, 220, 222, 224, 228, 231, 236, 238*n*, 240, 247, 252, 253, 263, 289, 444
Association of American Colleges, 411
Association of American University Presses, 411
Astor, Brooke (Mrs. Vincent), 228-29
Astor, John Jacob, 227-28
Astor, Vincent, 228, 279*n*, 281
Astor Foundation, Vincent, 22, 227-30, 275, 280, 292 (*table*), 298, 317, 323, 348, 388, 441
Athens, Ga., 256
Atlanta, Ga., 231-34, 276
Atlanta Arts Alliance, 233
Atlanta University, 233, 350
Atomic energy: grants, 62
Austin, Paul, 231
Avalon Foundation, 22, 222-23, 282, 298
Avon Products, Inc., 24

Babcock Foundation, Mary Reynolds, 189
Baker, William O., 224
Baldwin, William H., 236, 238
Baldwin, William H., Jr.: quoted, 334-35
Ball, Edward, 144, 147, 148-49, 408
Baptist Church, 333-34
Barnard, Chester I., 63-64
Barr, David P., 258-59
Barr, Joseph W., 9
Bass, Perry, 163*n*, 164
Battelle Institute, 21
Battle Creek, Mich., 111, 113
Beck, Paul, 133
Behavioral sciences: grants, 82, 90
Bell, Allyn R., 124, 126
Bell, David E., 94, 96
Benedict, Mrs. Helen A., 120
Bennett, Harry, 78-79
Bennett, Richard K., 240, 291
Berelson, Bernard, 82
Berry, George P., 258
Betts, Allen W., 229, 230

Bible Study House (Philadelphia), 125
Big Brothers, 204
Biology: grants, 59, 61-62, 180, 196, 199
Bishop Estate, Bernice P., 23
Blackerby, Philip E., 115
Blacks: civil rights movement, grants, 11, 16, 20, 75, 77, 92, 226*n*, 232, 345-47, 351, 352-53, 356-57; education grants, 11, 34, 45, 46, 69, 104, 105, 113, 115, 160, 172, 223, 224, 238, 384; colleges and universities, grants, 23, 43-44, 68, 104, 105, 115, 142, 160, 165, 172, 223, 224, 233, 339, 340, 343, 344, 348-49, 350, 351-52, 354, 355, 357-58; *An American Dilemma* (Myrdal), 39-40, 351, 430; grants, general, 43, 35, 68, 71, 75, 92, 196, 218, 223, 229, 232, 243, 248, 265-66, 333-61 *passim*, 429; on foundation staffs, 95, 324-25, 349, 360; "A Better Answer than Extremism" (Blackerby), 115; foundations and, 333-61; health services, grants, 341, 342, 349, 352, 354, 384; medical programs, grants, 341, 347, 348, 352, 353; hospitals, grants, 341, 348, 354; grants, summary, 347-58
Blind: grants, 223
Boards of trustees, *see* Trustees
Bollingen Foundation, 224*n*
Borlaug, Norman, 67
Boston, Mass., 352
Boulding, Kenneth, 401-2, 403
Bowles, Chester, 67
Boys, Inc., 163-64*n*
Boy Scouts of America, 134, 142, 165, 231, 251
Brandt, Anthony: quoted, 394
Bredin Foundation, 138
Breech, Ernest R., 79
Brookings Institution, 60, 416
Brooks, Ernest, Jr., 224
Brown, Herman, 165-67, 279*n*, 408
Brown, Kenneth I., 102-3
Brown Foundation, Inc., 22, 165-68, 279*n*, 282, 292 (*table*), 298, 323, 330, 347, 388, 408, 442

Bruce, Ailsa Mellon, 209, 215, 221, 222, 279n, 311
Bruce, David K. E., 221
Buchanan, Norman, 65
Bundy, McGeorge, 10-12, 14, 93-97, 291, 355, 357; quoted, 17-18, 392-93
Burger, Ralph W., 177-78, 179, 331
Bush, Archibald G., 121, 279n, 408
Bush, Mrs. Archibald G., 121, 122, 283
Bush Foundation, A. G., 22, 121-23, 279n, 282, 283, 286n, 292 (table), 298, 313, 317, 347, 388, 443; Minnesota court and, 122, 291
Bush Institute, A. G., 121, 122
Buttrick, Wallace, 49, 57, 58; quoted, 335
Byrnes, John W: quoted, 12

California, 124-25, 133, 251, 276, 303
California, University of, 113n, relations with Irvine Foundation, 131-33; at Los Angeles, 423
Camp Fire Girls, 252
Cancer: grants, 8n, 16, 125, 193, 194, 198
Caplin, Mortimer: quoted, 396
Carnegie, Andrew, 25n, 31-34, 45, 46, 263, 309; philanthropies, 33-34, 334, 351, 382
Carnegie Corporation of New York, 17, 22, 31, 35-46, 64, 262, 273, 276, 280, 281, 292 (table), 298, 301, 305, 317, 323, 325, 328, 330, 334, 351-53, 359-60, 377, 380, 382, 383, 385, 390, 391, 411, 443
Carnegie Endowment for International Peace, 34
Carnegie Foundation for the Advancement of Teaching, 34, 37, 40, 44n, 55, 300-1
Carnegie Hero Fund, 34
Carnegie Institute of Pittsburgh, 33
Carnegie Institute of Technology (Carnegie-Mellon University), 33
Carnegie Institution of Washington, D.C., 23, 34, 301n
Carnegie Trust for Universities of Scotland, 33

Carolinas, 183-84, 189-90, 276, 342-43, 347, 384
Carpenter Foundation, 138
Carroll, Thomas, 85
Carter, Amon, 163
Carter, Edward W., 130, 131n, 132
Case, Clifford, 84-85
Case, Everett, 195
Center for Advance Study in the Behavioral Sciences, 82, 90
Center for Applied Linguistics, 352
Center for Community Change, 356
Charitable Foundations, Conference on, 306-7
Chicago, University of, 48-49, 341
Children, grants: crippled, 146, 232, 303, 304, 389; cerebral-palsied, 158; orphans, 185, 354, 384
Children's Television Workshop, 45
Child welfare: grants, 111-12, 114, 146, 156, 165, 172, 185, 187, 203-4, 228, 229, 232, 241, 242-43, 255-56, 303, 354, 384
China, 54-55
China Medical Board, 53
Christiana Foundation, 138
Christian Anti-Communism Crusade, 124, 409
Christiana Securities, 137, 142, 281
Churches, see Religious bodies and churches
Church foundations, 4
Cities, grants to, see Localities, grants to
Citizens for Decent Literature, Inc., 125
Civil liberties: grants, 84, 226n, 232, 353, 424
Civil rights movement: grants, 11, 16, 20, 75, 77, 92, 226n, 232, 345-47, 351, 352-53, 356-57
Claremont Colleges, 134
Clark Foundation, Edna McConnell, 24
Cleveland Foundation, 23
Coca-Cola Company: relation to Woodruff Foundation, 230-31, 232, 233, 234, 284, 317

Cohen, Edwin, 15
Cohn, Roy, 155
College Entrance Examination Board, 104, 349
Colleges, see Universities and colleges
Collins, John, 354
Colorado, University of, 45
Colorado Fuel and Iron Company, 53
Commission on Cable Communications, 197
Commission on Educational Television, 44n
Commission on Foundations and Private Philanthropies (Peterson Commission), 15, 274-75, 277n, 288-89, 312n, 400, 414-16 (tables), 435, 436
Commission on Interracial Cooperation, 339, 340
Committee for Community Affairs, 356
Common Cause, 428, 433
Commonwealth Fund, 22, 254-62, 276, 280, 292 (table), 298, 317, 323, 331, 343, 348, 384, 391, 442
Communications: grants, 197
Community development and services, 202-4, 417-21; grants, 216-17, 218, 220, 223, 229, 233, 238, 242-43, 248, 252, 256, 275, 340, 351, 354, 356, 415; see also Rural development
Community foundations, 23, 453
Compton, Karl, 79
Conant, James B., 44, 45, 430
Congressional investigations: Patman Committee, 6, 7-8, 130, 277n, 295-96; Cox Committee, 6, 82, 386; Walsh Committee, 53-54; Reece Committee, 85, 86, 91, 386
Congress of Racial Equality, 11, 344 346, 356
Connally, John B., 163n
Connor, Ralph, 239, 240
Controversial programs, 11, 19-20, 46, 75-76, 98, 195-96, 230, 353-58, 413-16 (tables), 416-26; see also Blacks; Mexican-Americans; Race problems

Copeland Foundation, 138
Corporate foundations, 23, 178
Corporation for Public Broadcasting, 44n
Corpus Christi (Tex.) Symphony Orchestra, 157
Council for Financial Aid to Education, 411
Council of Southern Universities, 105
Cox, Eugene, 82
Cox Committee, 6, 82, 386
Creekman, J. Howard, 159
Creel, Dana, 73; quoted, 77
Crime Prevention Association of Philadelphia, 125
Crime problem: grants, 204, 233, 248, 253; see also Juvenile delinquency; Law and courts
Cunninggim, Merrimon, 103, 291; quoted, 389
Curry, J. M. L.: quoted, 335
Curti, Merle, 410-11; quoted, 411-12

Danforth, Donald, 101
Danforth, William, 99, 100-1
Danforth, William H., 103n, 104
Danforth Foundation, 22, 99, 100-7, 273, 276, 279, 282, 285, 286n, 291, 292 (table), 298, 322, 323, 342, 344, 348-49, 359, 391, 442; difficulties with Internal Revenue Service, 102, 285; attacks on, 105
David, Donald K., 83, 87
Davidson College, 185, 188
Davis, Chester A., 81, 84
Day, Edmund, 59
Delaware, 141, 145, 276, 382
Delaware, University of, 143
Delaware Federation of Garden Clubs, 142
Denahy, Claire F., 133
Dentistry: grants, 114
Denver, University of, 423
Detroit, Mich., 238, 276
Dillard University, 352
Dillon, Douglas, 66
Dilworth, J. Richardson, 73

Divestiture of stocks, 87-88, 117-18, 282-83, 285, 374

Doermann, Humphrey, 123

Dollard, Charles, 41

Donner, Frank J.: quoted, 84-85

Donner, Frederick, 197

Donors, 309-13; control by, 279-84, 291, 306, 329; effect of death upon foundations, 291, 294, 306, 329; high degree of independence of, 292-93 (table); attitude toward public reporting, 305-6; characteristics of, 309-11; religions of, 310; motives of, 311-13

Douglas, William O., 13

DuBois, W. E. B., 333, 338

Duke, James B., 182-85, 282, 310

Duke Endowment, 22, 25n, 182-90, 276, 279n, 282, 283, 292 (table), 298, 314n, 318, 323, 342, 347, 384, 388, 441

Duke Power Company, 183; relation to Duke Endowment, 184, 189, 190, 283, 318

Duke University, 184, 185, 186, 188-89

Duling, Harold, 171

du Pont, Alfred I., 138, 139-41, 144, 279n, 311

du Pont, Henry A., 140

du Pont, Henry Francis, 143

du Pont, Irenée, 139

du Pont, Mrs. Jessie Ball, 140, 144, 145-46; gifts, 146n; Religious, Educational and Charitable Fund, 146n

du Pont, Lammot, 139

du Pont, Pierre S., 139, 140-41, 279n, 313

du Pont, Pierre S., 4th, 136, 137

du Pont, Pierre Samuel, 135, 145

du Pont, T. Coleman, 139, 140

du Pont de Nemours and Company, E. I., 135, 137, 142, 143, 313

du Pont Estate, Alfred I., 22, 26, 138n, 147-49; income, 25, 145-46; assets, 139, 147; relation to Nemours Foundation, 144-45; as a bank holding company, 147-48; House investigation of, 148-49

du Pont family, 25n, 135-38, 139-41, 206, 280, 281, 408; criticisms of, 137-38; foundations, 138, 318

du Pont Institute, Alfred I., 145, 146, 304

Dutton, Frederick, 132

Duveen, Joseph, 213-15

Ecology, see Environment and conservation

Economic development; grants, 75-76, 82, 387, 416

Economic principles: grants, 193

Economics: grants for research, 59, 60, 70

Edison Institute, 79

Educational Testing Service, 41

Education Commission of the States, 44n, 105

Education Facilities Laboratory, 93

Education grants, 11, 16, 23, 34, 35, 42, 45, 49, 81-82, 85, 90, 96 (table), 102-3, 114, 115, 125, 134, 156, 159, 171, 172, 176, 185, 186, 196, 198-99, 220, 222, 223, 231-32, 237, 241, 248, 252, 268; blacks, 11, 34, 45, 46, 69, 104, 105, 113, 115, 160, 172, 223, 224, 248, 333-61 passim, 382, 411; teachers, 34, 42, 90, 102, 103, 174, 204, 223; medical, 34, 47n, 53, 54-55, 56, 57, 61, 88, 114, 180, 186, 196, 215, 217, 220, 222, 231, 241-42, 257, 258-59, 275, 285, 339, 355, 383; adult, 38, 41, 81, 85, 113, 114, 203, 205, 350, 353; secondary, 42, 45, 104, 114, 141, 165, 199, 204, 238, 255, 347, 349, 382, 411, 430; theological, 47n, 103, 125, 172; women, 77; community schools, 203, 204, 205; grants, $10,000 or more, 1967 and 1968, 274 (table); percent of total grants, 1968, 274; see also Scholarships and fellowships; School buildings and equipment; Universities and colleges

Ehrgott, John, 182
Eleutherian Mills-Hagley Foundation, 142-43
El Pomar Foundation, 24n
Emory University, 231-32
Engineering: grant, 196; biomedical, 179-80
Environment and conservation: grants, 69, 220, 222, 223, 242, 252, 253; pollution, 199
Establishment of foundations: dates, 22 (table), 31, 34, 52, 73, 79, 101, 111, 116, 119, 121, 124, 127, 138, 141, 145, 151, 158, 163, 167, 171, 177, 183, 193, 198, 203, 214, 217, 222, 228, 235, 236, 239, 247, 254, 263, 312-13, 342, 384; by incorporation, 35, 52, 124, 144, 158, 163, 177; by special legislative enactment, 52; by endowments, 116, 120, 127, 152, 167, 171, 183, 203, 214, 222, 228, 231, 236, 247, 281-82; see also Foundations, subhead Purposes
Etzioni, Amitai: The Active Society, quoted, 278n
Europe, 82, 96, 114
Evangelical Foundation, Inc., 125
Evans Foundation, Lettie Tate, 232
Eye research: grant, 237n

Fabricant, Solomon: quoted, 380
Fahs, Charles B., 65
Family foundations: relations to corporations, 279-84
Family trusts, 25, 26, 120, 124
Fargo, N.D., 256
Farrand, Max, 255
Fellowship Corporation (Kellogg), 111
Fellowships, see Scholarships and fellowships
Field Foundation, 344, 360
Fifteen Largest U.S. Foundations, report, 278n
Films, grants, 62, 193
Financial aspects, 278-90; administrative costs, 277-78, 403; corporation shares, 279-80, 286-97; family rela-
tions with corporations, 279-84, 291; "self-dealing" (between foundation, donors, and corporations), 283-84, 373; see also Assets; Divestiture; Income; Investments
Finch, Robert, 15
Fleischmann, Max C., 250-51, 279n, 281
Fleischmann, Sara Hamilton, 252
Fleischmann Foundation, Max C., 22, 250-54, 276, 280, 292 (table), 298, 314n, 317, 323, 330, 348, 442
Flexner, Abraham, 34, 42, 55, 57, 328
Flexner, Simon, 49, 57
Flint, Mich., 202-4, 275, 276, 350
Florida, 276
Food supply, world: grants, 62, 67-68, 69, 90, 113, 300
Ford, Edsel, 25n
Ford, Mrs, Edsel, 78-79
Ford, Henry, 25n, 78-79
Ford, Henry, 2d, 78-79, 81, 83, 88, 98
Ford Foundation, 22, 24-25n, 78-98, 273, 276, 280, 284, 295-86n, 291, 292, (table), 298, 299, 314n, 317, 322, 323, 328, 330, 344, 353-58, 360, 387, 388, 390, 407, 416, 421-25, 443; and 1969 tax hearings, 10-12, 17-18, 97; attacks on, 82-83, 84, 85-86, 88-89n, 97, 344, 353, 357, 395, 421-22; sale of company shares, 87-88, 282, 283-84n, 285
Ford Hospital, Henry, 79
Ford Motor Company: relation to Ford Foundation, 78, 79, 83, 84, 88, 96-97, 280, 281, 314n; sale of Foundation shares, 86-87, 282, 283-84n, 285
Foreign programs and studies, grants, 41, 47n, 54-55
Forestry: grants, 57, 186
Fortas, Abe, 13
Fortune, quoted, 24n, 313n
Fosdick, Raymond B., 61-63, 301, 305; quoted, 63, 327n
Foundation Center, 274, 296, 297 (table)

Foundation Directory, 24n

Foundation for Economic Education, 409

Foundation News, 297

Foundations: history, 3-5, 379; criticisms of and attacks on, 5-7, 9-17, 75-76, 82-83, 84, 85-86, 88-89n, 97, 105, 130-33, 137-38, 195, 344, 353, 357, 376-78, 381n, 394, 395, 421-22; and Tax Reform Act of *1969*, 9-20, 25n, 86, 102, 120, 130, 131, 138n, 148, 190, 233, 285-86, 372, 371 (*see also* Tax Reform Act); total, *1968*, 21; general purpose, with assets of over $100 million or more, by rank order of size, 22 (*table*); new, to be possibly established, 24; number controlling 90 percent of all assets, 24n; with assets approaching $100 million, 24n; with resources of over $10 million each, 24n; size changes, *1968* and *1969*, 24-25n; impact, diversity, scope of interests and operations, and leadership, 26-27; purposes of, 35, 41, 45, 46, 50, 54, 57-59, 60, 73, 74-75, 80-81, 103-4, 111-13, 124, 141, 145, 158, 178-79, 183-84, 193, 195, 205, 236, 237-38, 240n, 253, 295, 307; growth of and change patterns, 273, 290-94 (*table*); age of, *1972*, 292-93 (*table*); internal forces, 309-31; power shifts, 329-31; views on, traditional vs. modernist, 388-97; role, functions, and contributions to society, 399-430; funding other organizations, conduit function of, 401-5, 426; creativity and innovativeness, 405-6, 410-13; role in social change, 405-10, 413-26; roles of, 405-25; future of, 426-30; reforms, 431-34

"Foundations at the Service of the Public" (Pifer), 45

"Foundations, Private Giving, and Public Policy, Report and Recommendations of the Commission on Foundations and Private Philan-

thropies" (Peterson Commission), 15

Freedoms Foundation, 125, 409

Fremont-Smith, Marion, *Foundations and Government*, quoted, 296, 314n, 319-20n

Fund for Adult Education, 81-82, 85, 353

Fund for the Advancement of Education, 81-82, 85, 355

Fund for the Republic, 84-85, 353

Funds and Foundations (Flexner), 57

Furman University, 185, 188

Gaither, H. Rowan, 79-80, 81, 83, 84-89

Galveston, Tex., 152, 156-57, 275

Gardner, John W., 41-44, 45, 301; quoted, 405

Gates, Frederick T., 48, 50, 52, 58, 71; quoted, 55, 327n

General Education Board, 23, 49, 52n, 55, 56, 57, 141, 382, 383; grants to black schools and colleges, 333-37, 342, 344, 360

General Motors Corporation, 147, 280, 313; stock owned by du Pont family, 137, 147; foundations formed by officers, 191-206

Geographical areas: grants to, 104, 105, 115, 116, 119, 120, 123, 141, 142, 145, 165, 171, 172, 183-84, 189-90, 198, 223-24, 228-30, 231-34, 237, 238, 240-43, 251, 252, 256, 275-76, 382; *see also* Locations, grants to

George, Harry B., 182

Georgia, 231-34, 256, 276

Getty, J. Paul, 24

Glazer, Robert, 262

Glenmede Trust Company, 124, 318

Gonzales, Henry B., 422

Gordon, Kermit, 95

Gordon College, 125

Gore, Albert, 17

"Gospel of Wealth" (Carnegie), 32-33

Government: grants for study of, 75, 196; programs, 379-81, 391-92; co-

Government (*Continued*)
  operative programs with foundations, 385-88
Government, foundations and, 304-5, 365-98; reporting and disclosure, 18, 233, 263, 295-96, 298, 305, 307-8, 372, 374, 376n; legislation, 50-52, 373, 396, 431 (*see also* Tax Reform Act); pay-out requirement, 86, 102, 120, 285-86, 374, 403-4; limitation on administration expenditures, 277-78; foundations and donors, financial transactions between, 283-84, 372; taxation of unrelated business income, 372; manipulation of foundations to serve private purposes of donors, 373; involvement in business, excessive, prohibition of, 373, 374; penalties for violations, 373, 375, 377; relationships, historical changes in, 381-88; relationships, current pattern, 388-97; *see also* Congressional investigations; Internal Revenue Service; Treasury Department, U.S.
Graham Evangelistic Association, Billy, 124, 165
Grant-making: policies and procedures, 39-40, 41, 45, 53, 55-60, 67, 73, 91-92, 103-4, 106, 113, 115-16, 120, 122, 124-25, 133-34, 142-43, 156-57, 167, 175-76, 181-82, 184-85, 187, 194-95, 198-99, 202-3, 215, 218, 222, 229, 237, 253-54, 255-56, 273-76, 291, 294, 307, 324n, 326-27, 335-36; development of, 292-93 (*table*); *see also* Programs
Grants, 11, 35, 36, 38, 40, 41, 45, 52, 54, 55, 57, 60, 62, 73, 74, 75-76, 76-77, 81, 84, 85, 86, 87-88, 92, 94, 98, 102, 105-6, 113, 114, 115, 116, 120, 122-23, 124-25, 133, 134, 142-43, 145, 146-47, 156-57, 159-60, 164-65, 167, 171-72, 174-75, 179-81, 185, 193, 198-99, 204, 206, 215-16, 217-18, 220, 222-23, 224, 229-30, 231-32, 236-38, 241-43,

248, 250, 252-54, 255-56, 257, 263, 275-76, 295, 303; matching, 92, 232; major fields, $10,000 or more, *1967* and *1968*, 274 (*table*), *see also* subjects and names of organizations
Great Atlantic and Pacific Tea Company, 176-77; relation to Hartford Foundation, 177-78, 182, 284, 318
Greater St. Paul United Fund, 122
Green, Percy, 105
Greer, Marcus, 154, 155
Gregg, Alan, 61, 65
Gulf Oil Company, 209, 220, 225
Gutierrez, José Angel, 422, 423

Hass, John C., 239, 240, 241
Haas, Otto, 239, 282; Charitable Trusts No. 1 and 2, 240-41
Haas, Paul R., 155
Haas Charitable Trust, Phoebe W., 240-41
Haas Community Funds, 22, 241, 275, 279n, 292 (*table*), 317, 323, 349, 388; *see also* Waterman Foundation, Phoebe
Haas family trusts, 240-41, 317-18
Hahnemann Medical College and Hospital, Philadelphia, 241-42
Hampton Institute, 223, 224, 334, 352
Harding College, 195-96, 408, 409
Harkness, Edward, 254-55, 256-57, 262, 281, 311
Harkness, Mrs. Rebekah, 254-55, 311
Harkness, Stephen V., 254, 279n
Harlem School of the Arts, 351
Harper, William Rainey, 49n
Harrar, George A., 62, 66-70
Hartford, George, 176-77
Harford, Huntington, 178, 284n
Hartford, John A., 176-77, 279n, 282
Hartford Foundation, John A., 22, 176-82, 279, 282, 291, 292 (*table*), 298, 318, 323, 331, 342, 347, 388, 441; relation to Great Atlantic and Pacific Tea Company, 177-78, 182

Harvard University, 41, 223, 268, 411

Haskins, Caryl, 301n

Hayden Foundation, Charles, 24n

Heald, Henry T., 89-93, 291, 354, 355

Health services: grants, 8n, 16, 49, 53, 61, 64, 65, 73, 113, 114, 115, 125, 156, 172, 181, 187, 204, 222-23, 231-32, 237, 242, 248, 256, 275, 350; percent of total grants, 1968, 274; grants, $10,000 or more, 1967 and 1968, 274 (table); see also Hospitals; Public health

Heart attack victims: grants, 242

Heilbronner, Robert L.: quoted, 410

Henderson, Vivian, 95

Hinckley, J. William: quoted, 295

Historical sites, preservation of: grants, 75, 143, 220

Hitch, Charles J., 131n

Hoffman, Paul, 81-83, 85, 291, 353

Hollins College, 146

Hookworm control: grants, 53, 54, 382

Horowitz, David and David Kolodney: quoted, 7

Horticulture: grants, 142, 347

Hospitals: grants, 17, 75, 88, 113, 115, 125, 134, 142, 143, 145, 146, 156, 164, 167, 180, 181, 184, 185, 186, 187, 204, 218, 222n, 228, 232-33, 237, 241, 242, 245-46, 252, 256, 257, 275, 303, 384, 388, 389

Houlihan, John, 354

House Banking Committee: investigation of Alfred I. du Pont Estate, 148-49

House Small Business Committee, 8

House Ways and Means Committee: hearings on 1969 Tax Reform Act, 9-13, 366, 372-73, 374n

Housing: grants, 239, 241, 242, 248, 348, 349, 350, 352, 353, 354, 356, 384, 424

Houston, Tex., 159-60, 275, 276

Houston Endowment, 22, 157-62, 275, 279n, 283, 292 (table), 298, 313, 323, 330, 348, 388, 408; Hous-

ton Chronicle and, 158, 160-61, 283n

Hoving, Thomas P. F., 229

Hughes Medical Center, Howard, 23

Humanities programs: grants, 59-60, 62, 63, 65, 69, 70, 90, 95, 96 (table); 143, 156, 171, 223, 241, 275; grants, $10,000 or more, 1967 and 1968, 274 (table)

Hunt, H. L., 24

Hunter, Floyd: quoted, 233-34

Hunterdon Medical Center (N.J.), 258

Hurwitz, Laurence, 155

Hutchins, Robert M., 81-82, 83, 85, 353

Hutchins, William J., 101-2

Income, 37, 86-87, 94, 102, 107, 116-18, 120, 122, 133, 142, 145-46, 147, 152, 157, 164, 184, 185, 285-86; pay-out requirement, 86, 102, 120, 285-86, 403-4; distribution of, 285-86; overspending of, 285-86n; excise tax on, 375

Income tax, federal, 365-67; loopholes, 9, 13, 366; deductions for contributions to charity, 19, 372-73, 374-75, 377, 380, 400; Mellon plan, 210-11; evasion of, Mellon, 214-15; tax incentives, 367-69

Independent College Funds of America, 411

India, 65, 82, 103

Indiana, 171, 172

Indianapolis, Ind., 171, 172, 176, 276, 348

Indiana University, 172

Industrial relations: grants, 53-54

Institute for Cancer Research, 125

Institute for Development of Educational Activities, 199, 200

Institute for the Future, 199

Institutional Investor: quoted, 288

Inter-Collegiate Society of Individualists, 174

Internal Revenue Service: foundations and, 8, 15, 161, 163n, 164, 283n, surveillance tax, 18, 19, 405;

Internal Revenue Service (*Continued*)
review of reports and tax returns,
20, 288, 295-96, 376*n*, 405, 436;
pay-out requirements, 86, 102, 120,
285-86, 372, 374, 403-4
International Education Board, 56
International Health Board, 53, 54
International programs, 256, 276,
383, 385, 386, 388, 394-95*n;* grants
to, 34, 41, 44, 54-55, 59, 61, 64, 65,
82, 92, 94, 96 (*table*), 416; grants,
$10,000 or more, *1967* and *1968*,
274 (*table*)
Interracial Council for Business Opportunity, 351
Invest-in-America National Council,
Inc., 409
Investments, 18, 52*n*, 73, 95, 97, 107,
142, 159, 204, 229, 252, 286, 295,
319, 373; diversification, 281-82,
286-87, 291, 292-93 (*table*), 319-
20*n;* income return from stocks,
286-90, 319; performance, *1967-
1969,* 435-45 (*tables*)
Irvine, James, 126-27, 282, 408
Irvine, James, 2d, 127
Irvine, Myford, 128-29
Irvine Foundation, 22, 126-34, 276,
279, 282, 292 (*table*), 298, 303,
323, 347, 388, 389, 408; and 1969
tax hearings, 129*n;* internal difficulties, 129-30, 283; charges of political intervention, 130-31; relations
with University of California regents, 131-33
Irvine Ranch Company: relation to
Irvine Foundation, 127, 129, 134,
283; and University of California,
131-33

Jackson Hole Preserve, Inc., 47*n*
James, Henry: quoted, 38-39
JDR 3d Fund (Rockefeller), 47*n*
Jeanes Fund, Anna T., 333
Jessup, Walter A., 40
John Birch Society, 173, 196
Johnson Foundation, Robert Wood,
23-24

Jones, Boisfeuillet, 231, 233
Jones, Jesse H., 157-58, 279*n*, 313,
348
Jones, Joseph, 231
Jonsson, John Erik, 24
Jordan, W. K.: quoted, 4
Josephs, Devereaux, 40-41
Juvenile delinquency, prevention of:
grants, 204, 233, 253, 256, 342,
348, 349, 350, 354

Kaiser, Edgar, 247-48
Kaiser, Henry J., 244-47, 310
Kaiser Family Foundation, Henry J.,
22, 244-49, 262*n*, 276, 279*n*, 282,
286*n*, 291, 292 (*table*), 298, 323,
347, 388, 441
Kaiser Foundation Medical Care Pro-
gram, 245-47, 248
Kaiser Hospital Foundation, 246
Kaiser Industries Corporation, 244-
45; relation to Kaiser Family Foun-
dation, 247, 248
Katz, Milton, 81, 84
Kellogg, John Harvey, 108-9
Kellogg, John L., 110
Kellogg, John L., Jr., 110
Kellogg, W. K., 99, 107-11, 310
Kellogg Company, 109-10; relation to
Kellogg Foundation, 116-18, 318
Kellogg Foundation, W. K., 22, 99,
107-18, 276, 277, 279, 283, 292
(*table*), 298, 318, 323, 342, 348,
274*n*, 377, 384, 388, 442; and 1969
tax hearings, 117-18; question of di-
vestiture of company stocks, 117-18
Kellogg Foundation Trust, W. K., 25,
116-17, 283
Kenan Foundation, William R., 24*n*
Kennedy, David M., 15
Keppel, Frederick P., 36-40, 42, 45,
301; quoted, 304, 384*n*
Kerr, Clark, 44*n*, 45, 430
Kettering, Charles F., 197-98
Kettering, Eugene, 198, 199
Kettering Foundation, Charles F., 22,
197-200, 276, 280, 291, 292 (*table*),
298, 317, 322, 323, 342, 407, 442

Kettering Research Laboratory, 198, 199
Kiger, Joseph C.: quoted, 383-84n
Kimball, Philip J., 143
King, Martin Luther, Jr., 75, 90, 344, 347
King, W. L. Mackenzie, 53, 57
Knowles, John H., 70
Kohler, William, 240
Kreidler, Robert, 196
Kresge, Sebastian S., 235-36
Kresge Company, S. S., 235; relation to Kresge Foundation, 238, 283, 284
Kresge Foundation, 22, 235-38, 276, 279n, 282, 283, 292 (table), 298, 323, 330, 342, 348, 384, 388, 441
Kristol, Irving: quoted, 432-33

Land, Edwin H., 263-68
Land Education Development Fund, 268
Land Foundation, Edwin H. and Helen M., 22, 262-69, 279n, 282, 291, 292 (table), 298, 443
Landis, Kenesaw Mountain, 51
Latin America, 62, 65, 66, 74, 113
Law and courts: grants, 115, 125, 186, 253, 348, 349, 352, 423, 424
Lawrence, David, 418
Lawrence, Ernest O., 62
Leach, Sales, 155
Ledyard, Elizabeth, 164
Lee, Richard, 354
Lesesne Foundation, 138
Lewis, Fulton, Jr., 84
Liberty League, 136
Libraries: grants, 275; public, 33, 35, 41, 218, 382; college and university, 42, 134, 164, 165, 167, 223, 411; school, 114; rural, 252
Lilly, Eli, 171, 313
Lilly, J. K., 2d, 171, 173-74
Lilly, J. K., 3d, 171
Lilly and Company, Eli, 170-71, 318
Lilly Endowment, 22, 25n, 170-76, 276, 279n, 282, 284, 292 (table),
298, 302, 313, 318, 323, 330, 348, 384, 388, 408, 441
Lilly family: politics of, 174-75, 407, 408
Lincoln Center for the Performing Arts, 75, 179n, 416
Lincoln University, 142
Lindeman, Edward C.: quoted, 306
Localities: grants to, 105, 111, 113, 124-25, 133, 141, 145, 152, 156-57, 159-60, 171, 172, 176, 183-84, 189-90, 198, 202-4, 212-13, 215-16, 217-18, 219-21, 222, 228-30, 231-34, 238, 240-43, 248, 251, 256, 258, 276-76, 303, 352; see also Geographical areas
Lombard, Richard, 199-200
Longwood Foundation, 22, 141-43, 276, 279n, 292 (table), 298, 313, 318, 323, 347, 377, 388
Longwood Foundation, Inc., 138n
Longwood Gardens, Inc., 138n, 377
Louisville, University of, 40, 352
Lowry, W. McNeil, 90, 328
Lubove, Roy: quoted, 420
Luce Foundation, Henry F., 24n
Ludwig, Daniel K., 24
Lundberg, Ferdinand: quoted, 6
Lykes, James M., Jr., 154
Lynn, John S., 173, 175

McAllister, Walter, 422
McCloy, John J., 93
Macdonald, Dwight: quoted, 299, 417n
McFadden, A. J., 134
McGinnis, Richard R., 173
McLaren, N. Loyall, 127, 129, 130
McNamara, Robert, 95
McPeak, William, 85, 88, 328
Magat, Richard: quoted, 306-7
Malaria control: grant, 54
Manly, Basil: quoted, 5-6
Maple Corporation, 242
March, Cecil C., 121, 122
Marion County, Ore., 256
Markel Foundation, 180
Mason, Max, 59

Massachusetts Institute of Technology, 268, 302

Matching grants, 92, 232

Mathematical sciences: grants, 55, 411

Mauzé, Mrs. Abbie Rockefeller, 77

Mayfield, Carey, 155

Mecom, John W., 161

Medical Education in the United States and Canada (Flexner), 34, 55

Medical programs and research: grants, 8n, 23, 24, 47n, 49, 53, 57, 59, 61, 65, 114, 120, 125, 164, 179-81, 198, 222-23, 237, 241, 248, 256, 257, 258-62, 339, 341, 347, 348, 352, 391, 412-13; for poor, 45, 61, 348, 352; percent of total grants, *1968*, 274; *see also* Education, *subhead* medical; Health; Hospitals; Public health

Mellon, Ailsa (Mrs. David Bruce), 290, 215, 221, 222, 279n, 311

Mellon, Andrew, 209-15, 221, 311; as U.S. secretary of the treasury, 210-11; income tax evasion suit, 214-15

Mellon, Paul, 209, 215, 221-22, 223, 224, 226, 310

Mellon, Richard King, 213, 216-17, 218, 279n, 417-19

Mellon, Thomas, 207-8

Mellon Educational and Charitable Trust, A. W., 23, 214-16, 222, 276, 279n, 348

Mellon family, 206-26, 280, 318, 329-30n, 408, 418-21

Mellon Foundation, Andrew W., 22, 222, 224-25, 292 (*table*), 298, 323

Mellon Foundation, Richard King, 22, 217-18, 276, 282, 293, 298, 318, 323, 348, 388, 417-21, 441

Mellon Institute, 213, 217

Mellon National Bank and Trust Company, 209, 211n; relation to Mellon foundations, 216, 217, 281, 318

Mental health: grants, 90, 223

Merriwether, Duncan, 240

Methodist Church, 152, 333; in North Carolina, 185, 187

Mexican-American Legal Defense and Education Fund, 423

Mexican-Americans (La Raza), 11, 252, 357, 376n, 421-25, 430

Mexico, 62, 66

Michigan, 115, 116, 237, 384

Michigan, University of, 204

Michigan State University, 204, 237

Mills, Wilbur, 9, 17

Minerals Development Corporation, 124, 318

Minnesota, University of, 123

Minnesota Mining and Manufacturing Company, 121, 313; relation to Bush Foundation, 121, 122

Minnesota Orchestral Association, 123

Minorities, 252-53, 300, 357, 376n; *see also* Blacks; Mexican-Americans

Mission Information on Drugs and Narcotics Project, 157

Mondale, Walter F., 16

Moody, Shearn, Jr., 153, 154n, 155-56

Moody, William L., Jr., 151-52, 408

Moody, William L., 3d, 152-53, 310

Moody Foundation, 22, 151-57, 275, 279n, 283, 285, 293 (*table*), 298, 300, 314n, 318, 323, 348, 388, 408; family disputes, 152-55, 156, 157; investigation of by Texas House of Representatives, 155, 291

Moody National Bank, 151; relation to Moody Foundation, 155, 318

Moody Trust, Libbie Shearn, 25, 152, 155, 157

Morality in Media, Inc., 125

Morehouse College, 223

Morgan, John P., 32

Morison, Robert S., 65, 329

Morris, Emory W., 117

Mott, Charles Stewart, 201-2, 310, 311, 408

Mott, Stewart, 202n, 330n

Mott Foundation, Charles Stewart, 22, 201-6, 275, 279n, 282, 291, 293 (*table*), 298, 301, 323, 350, 388, 408, 409, 441

Murphy, George, 130-31

Museum of Modern Art, 62, 74

Museums: grants, 17, 23, 33, 62, 143, 167, 214-15, 220, 224, 232, 251, 275, 351

Music: grants, 17, 47n, 63, 96 (table), 123, 125, 157, 220, 223, 303

Muskie, Edmund S., 396

Mustard Seed, Inc., 175

Myrdal, Gunnar, An American Dilemma, 39-40, 45, 351, 430

Nader, Ralph, 376n, 428, 433; attack on du Pont family, 137-38

Narcotic drug control: grant, 157

National affairs: grants, 96 (table)

National Association for the Advancement of Colored People, 333, 338, 346, 350, 356; Legal Defense and Educational Fund, 351, 353, 423

National Association of Evangelicals: World Relief Commission, Inc., Biafra Relief Program, 125

National Bureau of Economic Research, 70

National College of State Trial Judges, 115

National Committee Against Discrimination in Housing, 352

National Council on Community Foundations, Inc., 453

National Education Program, 195-96

National Gallery, 23, 214-15

National Institutes of Health, 65, 180, 181, 386

National Merit Scholarships, 17, 355, 411, 416

National Opinion Research Center, 352

National Science Foundation, 64-65, 386

National Strategy Information Center, 409

National Urban League, 75, 334, 350, 351, 352, 356

National Vigilance Committee for Prohibition Enforcement, 235-36

Negroes, see Blacks

Nelson, Ralph L.: Investment Policies of Foundations, quoted, 281, 285-86n, 286-87

Nemours Foundation, 22, 144-49, 227, 276, 279n, 291, 293 (table), 298, 303-4, 323, 347, 388, 389, 408; income from du Pont Estate, 25-26, 145-46, 147; control of by trustees of du Pont Estate, 144-45; relation to du Pont Estate, 147-49, 285

Nevada, 251, 252, 276

Nevada, University of, 252

New Detroit Committee, 238

Newman, J. V., 130

New Orleans, La., 341

Newsom, Earl, 79

Newton, J. Quigg, 259-60, 261-62

New World Foundation, 360

New York City, 11, 75, 179n, 228-30, 275, 348, 351, 357, 384, 416

New York Hospital-Cornell Medical Center, 259

New York Legal Aid Society, 352

New York University, 352

Nobel prize winners, 67

Nonprofit organizations: taxation and, 369-71, 375-76n, 377, 404; foundations and, 396, 400, 401-5, 426; gifts to by public, 402, 404

North Dakota, 256

Northen, Mrs. Mary Moody, 154, 283

Nursing: grants, 47n, 114, 222, 232

Nutrition: grant, 113

Ohio, 198, 276

Old Dominion Foundation, 22, 223-25, 282, 298, 304-5

Omnibus, 82

"Operating" foundations, 19, 21, 23, 374, 377-78

Operating Principles of the Large Foundations (Kiger), quoted, 383-84n

Orange County, Calif., 130, 134, 303, 389

Oregon, 256

Parks: grants, 217, 224, 229, 419

Parran, Thomas W., 215

Parvin Foundation, 13

Patman, Wright, 6, 7, 18, 127, 177n, 211n, 277n, 283, 295, 357, 377, 403; quoted, 9-10, 20, 127, 283n

Patman Committee, 6, 7-8, 130, 277n, 295-96

Pattillo, Manning: quoted, 296

Pauley, Edwin W., 131n

Peabody Fund, 333

Peace, international, 34

Pegler, Westbrook, 84

Peking Union Medical College, 54-55

Pennsylvania, 142, 276

People-to-People Health Foundation, 125

Pepperdine College, 125, 409

Percy, Charles H., 16

Perkins, James A., 42

Personnel, see Staff

Peterson, Peter J., 15

Peterson Commission, see Commission on Foundations and Private Philanthropies

Pew, J. Howard, 123, 126

Pew, Joseph N., 123

Pew family, 311, 313, 318; politics of, 123-24, 408

Pew Freedom Trust, J. Howard, 123-24

Pew Memorial Trust, 22, 25n, 124-26, 276, 279n, 282, 293 (table), 298, 313, 318, 323, 348, 374n, 407, 441

Philadelphia, Pa., 240-43, 275, 349

Philadelphia Council for Community Advancement, 243

Philadelphia Lyric Opera, 125

Philanthropy: "The Gospel of Wealth" (Carnegie), 32-33; "Private Initiative for the Public Good" (Gardner), 43; "Foundations in the Service of the Public" (Pifer), 45; Kellogg's definition of philanthropist, 111n; Sloan's idea of, 193; John Steinbeck on, 311; views on, traditional vs. modernist, 388-97

Photosynthesis: grants, 198, 199

Pifer, Alan, 44-46, 301, 352n; quoted, 17, 405

Pittsburgh, Pa., 33, 212-13, 215-16, 217-18, 219-21, 222, 344, 348, 417-21

Pittsburgh, University of, 213, 215-16, 217-18, 220

Planned Parenthood Federation, 223

Polaroid Company, 262-66; see also Land Foundation

Political parties: contributions to, 123, 130, 228

Politics: and foundations, 3-5, 7, 10, 11, 124, 130-31, 161, 163, 173-74, 196, 356; federal prohibition of political or propagandistic activity by foundations, 19, 161, 373, 375; and churches, 376n

Population problems: grants, 16, 67, 68, 69, 71, 74, 90, 95, 96 (table), 115, 387, 429

Pornography, elimination of: grant, 125

Portugal: government attack on Ford Foundation, 88-89

Poverty and the poor: grants for, 43-44, 45, 46, 73, 77, 93, 104, 160, 199, 204, 218, 220, 223, 229, 242, 248, 255, 336, 341, 342, 344, 348, 349-50, 351, 352, 354, 356, 384, 415

Presbyterian University of Pennsylvania Medical Center: Eye Institute, 125

Presidents, 35, 36, 40, 41, 44, 46, 52, 54, 59, 61, 63, 64, 66, 70, 73, 81, 83, 89, 93, 102, 103, 111n, 115, 116, 120, 123, 128, 129, 159, 177, 182, 195, 196, 198, 199, 224, 229, 236, 255, 257, 258, 260, 262n, 291, 330; and foundation reports, 300-4

Price, Don K., 85, 397

Princeton University, 34

Pritchett, Henry F., 35n, 36, 300-1

"Private" foundations, 8, 374-75, 377-78

Programs, 60, 66-67, 69-70, 90-92, 96, 97, 103-4, 106, 111-13, 114,

115, 124, 178-79, 186-89, 195, 196-97, 198-200, 202-4, 229-30, 231-32, 237-38, 241, 254, 291, 307; defined, development of, 292-93 (*table*); analysis of in reports, 299-300, 301-2; *see also* Grant-making policies and procedures

Public administration: grants, 59, 196, 385

Public health: grants, 8*n*, 49, 53, 54, 59, 61, 64-65, 73, 75, 113, 114, 215-16, 220, 232, 255-56, 258, 382

Public Health Foundation for Cancer and Blood Pressure Research, 8*n*

Public Health Service, U.S., 232

Public interest, foundations and, 43, 45, 304-5, 308, 321*n*, 377*n*

Public opinion: grant for study of, 352

Race problems and relations: grants, 19, 40, 43, 46, 47*n*, 75, 92, 116, 232, 240, 338, 339, 340, 353-58, 384; foundations and, 333-61 *passim*, 391, 430; *see also* Blacks; Mexican-Americans; Minorities

Radio: grants, 62, 82, 174; du Pont awards program, 146

Radio Free Europe, 174

Ralston Purina Company: relation to Danforth Foundation, 100-1, 103, 106-7, 284

Rand, James H., Jr., 8*n*

Randolph, A. Philip, 345

Reagan, Ronald, 130, 132-33

Reece, Carroll, 85, 91

Reece Committee, 85, 86, 91, 386

Regional Planning Association on New York, 223

Religious bodies and churches: grants, 34, 125, 152, 156, 159, 164, 165, 171, 172, 176, 185, 186, 187, 237, 252, 272, 310, 388, 409, 417*n*; grants, $10,000 or more, *1967* and *1968*, 274 (*table*); tax exemption of, 371-72, 376*n*

Rencourt Foundation, 138

Reports, annual, 17-18, 37, 38, 39, 41, 42-43, 67*n*, 104, 114, 115, 146, 156,

159, 171, 174-75, 179, 180, 186-87, 194, 197, 199, 218, 229, 233, 236, 237, 238, 241, 252, 255, 261-62, 263, 436, 437; government requirement of, 18, 233, 263, 295-96, 298, 305, 307-8; number of foundations issuing, *1956*, *1959*, and *1966*, 297 (*table*); prose of, 298-304; of big foundations, 298-305; analysis of programs and projects in, 299-300, 301-2; presidents and, 300-4; lack of information in, 304-5; foundation preference for privacy, 305-8

Revie, Norman, 155

Reynolds Foundation, Z. Smith, 24*n*, 189

Rice Research Institute, 93

Rice University, 167

Rich, Mrs. Wilmer Shields: quoted, 296

Richardson, Sid W., 162-63, 279*n*

Richardson Foundation, Sid W., 22, 162-65, 279*n*, 282, 283, 284, 293 (*table*), 298, 323, 330, 347, 388, 441

Richmond Foundation, Frederick W., 10

Roberts, Walter Orr, 291

Rochester (N.Y.) Regional Hospital Council, 258

Rockefeller, David, 74

Rockefeller, John D., Sr., 47*n*, 48-49, 56, 71, 263, 309, 327*n*, 333

Rockefeller, John D., Jr., 49, 52, 54, 71, 73-74, 339-40*n*

Rockefeller, John D., 3d, 12-13, 15, 64, 68, 71, 74, 90

Rockefeller, John D., 4th, 72

Rockefeller, Laura Spelman, 56, 333

Rockefeller, Laurance, 74; quoted, 76

Rockefeller, Nelson, 74

Rockefeller, Winthrop, 74

Rockefeller Brothers Fund, 22, 47, 72-77, 276, 280, 281*n*, 282, 291, 293 (*table*), 298, 317, 323, 344, 350-51, 441; attacks on, 75-76

Rockefeller family, 71-77, 280, 329-30*n*

Rockefeller Family Fund, 47n
Rockefeller Foundation, 22, 50-70, 90, 273, 276, 279n, 282, 291, 293 (*table*), 298, 299-300, 301-2, 317, 322, 323, 328, 330-31, 333-37, 339, 344, 349-50, 360, 377, 382, 383, 385, 388, 391, 407, 411, 441; and 1969 tax hearings, 12, 15, 76-77; investigation by U.S. Commission of Industrial Relations, 53-54; reorganization, 56-60; family involvement in, 71-72
Rockefeller Fund (JDR 3d Fund), 47n
Rockefeller Fund for Music, Martha Baird, 47n
Rockefeller Institute for Medical Research, 49; assets, 52n
Rockefeller Memorial, Laura Spelman, 56, 57, 339, 384-85; assets, 52n
Rockefeller Sanitary Commission, 49, 53, 382
Rockefeller University, 47n
Rohm and Haas Company, 239, 240, 318
Rollins College, 123
Rooney, John J., 10
Root, Elihu, 34
Rose, Wickliffe, 49, 53, 57, 58, 382; quoted, 55-56
Rosenwald, Julius, 263, 337, 341-42; quoted, 342
Rosenwald Fund, 23, 337-38, 340-42, 384
Rovere, Richard: quoted, 16n
Ruml, Beardsley, 57-58, 60, 339
Rural development: grants, 114, 115, 116, 185, 252, 255, 257, 336, 340, 359, 384, 424
Rusk, Dean, 65-66
Russell, John M.: quoted, 36-37
Russian Research Center, Harvard University, 41
Rutherford County, Tenn., 256

Sage Foundation, Russell, 383n
St. John's College, 223
St. Louis, Mo., 105, 276, 349

St. Louis University, 106
St. Paul, Minn., 122
St. Thomas, University of, 167
San Antonio, Tex., 421-22
San Francisco, Calif.: Bay Area, 248, 276, 303
Santa Ana (Calif.) Community Hospital, 134
Santa Barbara, Calif., 251
Scaife, Sarah Mellon, 218-19, 221
Scaife Foundation, Sarah Mellon, 22, 218-20, 276, 279n, 282, 293 (*table*), 298, 323, 330, 348, 388, 441
Schmidt, Adolph A., 224
Scholarships and fellowships: grants, 54, 55, 62, 69, 90, 97, 101, 102-3, 104n, 105, 134, 142, 143, 146, 157, 160, 165, 198, 224, 241, 248, 256, 257, 258, 275, 339, 348, 349, 358, 383, 411, 416, 423
School buildings and equipment: grants, 93, 120, 134, 157, 160, 164, 165, 167, 198, 204, 223, 232, 248, 275, 337, 340, 358
Schools, *see* Education; Universities and colleges
Schumpeter, Joseph, 401, 403
Science programs: grants, 34, 47, 55, 56, 57, 59, 61-62, 156, 196, 198, 268, 275, 339, 347, 383; grants, $10,000 or more, *1967* and *1968*, 274 (*table*)
Scotland, 33
Sealantic Fund, 47n
Sears Roebuck Company, 337, 340
Selman, A. C., 111n
Senate, U.S.: and Charter of Rockefeller Foundation, 50-52
Senate Finance Committee, 396; hearings on 1969 Tax Reform Act, 15-17, 278n
Sesame Street, 45, 430
Shanker, Albert, 357
Shenker, Morris, 155
Sibley, James, 231
Sibley, John A., 231
Simon, John: quoted, 406n
Simon, Norton, 132-33

Slater Fund, 333, 337

Sloan, Alfred P., 191-95, 196, 279n, 291, 313, 340n, 408

Sloan, Harold, 193

Sloan Foundation, Alfred P., 22, 191-97, 280, 282, 291, 293 (*table*), 298, 302-3, 317, 323, 328, 344, 349, 411, 441; attacks on, 195-96

Sloan-Kettering Institute, 193, 194

Smith, Barry C., 255, 258

Smith, Mrs. Joan Irvine: attack on Irvine Foundation, 129-30, 133n, 283, 284n

Smith, William French, 132

Smith University, Johnson C., 185, 188, 347

Social action programs: grants for, 11, 16, 45, 62, 67, 69, 75, 97, 173, 196, 199, 200, 344-47, 392, 413-26; *see also* Controversial programs

Social issues, foundations and, 44, 45, 68, 106, 115, 196, 378, 392; Keppel quoted on, 39-40; *see also* Blacks; Race problems

Social Science Research Council, 60, 62, 70, 384

Social sciences: grants, 59, 62-63, 65, 70, 171, 275, 339

Social welfare: grants, 112-13, 204, 217, 218, 223, 241, 242-43, 248, 255, 275, 339, 349, 354, 385; grants, $10,000 or more, *1967* and *1968*, 274 (*table*); percent of total grants, *1968*, 274

Sokolsky, George, 84

South, University of the, 146n

Southern Association of Colleges and Schools, 104, 349

Southern Education Reporting Service, 354

Southern Regional Council, 11, 75, 341, 351, 353

Southwestern University, 167

Southwest Foundations, Conference on, 296

Spelman Fund, 56

Staff of foundations, 36, 63-65, 66, 68, 82, 94, 115-16, 133, 156, 164, 175, 181, 189, 196, 200, 204, 222, 243, 255, 259, 275, 277-78, 291, 292 (*table*), 294, 307; number of, 323; motives of employment, 323-24; characteristics of, 324-25, 390; qualifications of, 325-26; satisfactions and frustrations, 326-29; and power shifts, 329-31

Standard Oil Company of Indiana, 72, 280

Standard Oil Company of New Jersey, 48, 49, 50, 51-52, 72, 280, 382

Stanford University, 134, 174

States, grants to, *see* Geographical areas, grants to

Steinbeck, John: quoted, 311

Steiner School, Rudolf, 125

Stern Family Fund, 344, 360

Steven, William T., 160-61

Stevens, David H., 59

Stevens, Stoddard M., 224

Stigler, George J.: quoted, 412

Stokes, Carl, 357

Stone, Lawrence M.: quoted, 370-71

Stratton, Julius, 93

Studio Museum, New York City, 351

Sugarman, Norman, 296

Sun Oil Company, 123, 124, 313, 318

Surdna Foundation, 22, 119-20, 227, 276, 279n, 293 (*table*), 298, 323, 342, 347, 388, 389, 408, 442

Surveillance tax, 18, 19, 405

Sutton, Francis X.: quoted, 395

Sviridoff, Mitchell, 96, 356

Swarthmore College, 142

Taconic Foundation, 226, 360

Taft, J. Richard, 297

Taft Institute of Government, Robert A., 409

Tarbell, Ida, 48

Tate, James, 354

Tax exemption: individuals, 13-14, 366, 404; foundations, 102, 117-18, 286, 304, 312n, 371, 376n, 396; of recipient institutions, 275

Tax Reform Act (1969), foundations and, 9-20, 370, 373-78; hearings,

Tax Reform Act (*Continued*)
9-17, 76-77, 97, 117-18, 240*n*, 276-
77, 287-88; program restrictions,
11, 19-20, 373, 376*n;* reports requirement, 18, 233, 263, 295-96,
298, 305, 307-8, 372, 374, 376*n;*
prohibition of political or propagandistic activity, 19, 161, 373,
375; pay-out provisions, 86, 102,
120, 285-86, 372, 374, 403-4;
"special interest" amendment, proposed, 131; *Fifteen Largest U.S.
Foundations: Financial Structure
and Impact of the Tax Reform
Act of 1969*, staff report, 278*n;* divestiture provisions, 282-83, 374;
penalties for violations, 373, 375,
377; Joint Committee on Internal
Revenue Taxation, report, 376*n;*
benefit and hazards of private foundations, summary, 377-78

Teachers: grants, 34, 42, 90, 102, 103,
174, 204, 223

Teachers Insurance and Annuity Association, 34, 37, 40

Television grants: educational, 16,
44*n*, 45, 90, 96 (*table*); commercial,
82

Tennessee, 256

Texas, foundations in, 150-69; House
of Representatives investigation of
Moody Foundation, 155, 291

Texas Christian University, 165

Texas Southern University, 160

Texas Wesleyan University, 165

Theano Foundation, 138

Thomas, Charles S., 130

"Time for Decision in Higher Education" (Gardner), 41-42

Treasury Department, U.S.: *Report
on Private Foundations* (1965), 8;
and 1969 Tax Reform Act, 9, 14-
16, 373, 377; requirements of annual reports, 18, 233, 263, 295-96,
298, 305, 307-8, 372, 374, 376*n;*
study of asset value of investments,
287

Trebor Foundation, 232

Trefethen, E. E. Jr., 247

Trinity College, 184-85*n*

Troyer, Thomas, 287-88

Trustees, 46, 50, 54, 279-80, 283, 290,
296, 313-22; relation to donors, 35,
52*n*, 71, 152, 189-90, 204, 229;
meetings, 35, 153, 255, 260; selection and appointment of, 36, 74,
80, 85-86, 105, 253, 313, 314-15,
321-22; policy-making, 58, 70, 106,
112-13, 198-99, 200, 252, 320-21,
329-30, 408-10; representation of
donor families and company personnel, 72, 76-77, 117, 120, 121-
22, 128, 142, 154, 155, 156, 158,
159, 162, 164, 171, 188-89, 190,
193, 204, 217, 219, 222, 224, 229,
231, 236, 240, 243, 247-48, 262,
263, 279-80, 291, 292-93 (*table*),
314; backgrounds of, 72, 77, 95,
315-16, 406-7; conflict on interests
in, 116-17, 124, 142, 154-56, 173,
177-78, 189-90, 221, 224, 231,
240-41, 316-19; duties, 133, 158,
178, 314, 330; payment of, 154,
184, 252, 314-15*n;* high degree of
diversification, 292-93 (*table*); al-
ternate terms for, 314*n;* ages of,
315; politics of, 407-10

Tucker, Henry St. George: quoted,
334

Tuskegee Institute, 224, 334, 352

Underdeveloped countries: grants, 65,
66, 67, 97

United Fund of Philadelphia, 125

United Negro College Fund, 115, 165,
172, 224, 351, 352, 355

U.S. Commission on Industrial Relations, 53-54

U.S. Conference of Mayors, 356

U.S. Steel Corporation, 32, 281

Universities: governing boards of,
316, 322; restructuring of, 432-33

Universities and colleges: black grants
to, 23, 43-44, 68, 104, 105, 115,
142, 160, 165, 172, 223, 224, 233,
339, 340, 343, 344, 348-49, 350,

351-52, 354, 355, 357-58, 383, 388, 425, 430; grants, 33, 34, 41-42, 44-45n, 47, 48-49, 67, 77, 85, 86-87, 92, 102, 104, 105-6, 114, 120, 123, 134, 142, 143, 164, 167, 172, 180, 184, 185, 186, 187-88, 193, 198, 204, 213, 215-16, 217, 218, 222, 223, 231, 237, 241, 248, 252, 268, 285; "Time for Decision in Higher Education" (Gardner), 41-42
Urban Affairs Foundation, 357
Urban Coalition, 115, 350
Urban problems: grants, 19, 45, 46, 47n, 74, 77, 90, 93, 105, 115, 116, 160, 196, 202-4, 216-18, 220, 228-29, 231-32, 233, 238, 248, 255, 341, 342, 344, 348, 349, 352, 354, 356, 359, 391, 415, 417-21

Vanderbilt University, 174
Villard, Oswald Garrison, 336
Vincent, George E., 54, 57, 58, 59
Virginia, 223-24, 276
Voorhies, Paul W., 236

Wallace, Mr. and Mrs. De Witt, 24
Wallace, Henry A., 62
Walsh, Frank T., 53-54
Washington, Booker T., 333, 337, 358; quoted, 336
Washington, D.C., 341, 351
Washington and Lee University, 146
Washington College, Mary, 146n
Washington University, 105, 107n
Waterman Foundation, Phoebe, 22, 239-43, 275, 279n, 282, 291, 292 (table), 298, 317, 323, 388; see also Haas Community Fund
Watson, Thomas J., 24
Wayne State University, 204, 237n
Weaver, Warren, 59, 65, 328; quoted, 194n; U.S. Philanthropic Foundations, quoted, 295, 321n, 411-12

Welch Foundation, Robert A., 24n
Weltner, Philip, 231
Wesleyan University, 120
Wessel, Nils Y., 196
Western Reserve University, 259
Wheeler, Mrs. Charles S., 130
Wheeler, Sessions S., 253
Whitehead Foundation, Joseph B., 232
Whitehead Foundation, Lettie Tate, 232
Wildlife protection: grant, 253
Wilkins, Roy, 90
Williamsburg, Va., restoration of, 75
Willits, Joseph H., 65
Winterthur Foundation, 138
Wolfson Family Foundation, 13
Woodruff, Ernest, 230
Woodruff, George, 231
Woodruff, Robert, 230-34, 317
Woodruff Foundation, Emily and Ernest, 22, 230-34, 276, 279n, 282, 284, 291, 293 (table), 298, 317, 348, 408, 441
Woods, George D., 247-48
World Health Organization, 65, 385
World War I: relief grants, 52
Wormser, René: quoted, 6

Yale University, 65, 223
Yellow fever vaccine, 61
Yerkes Regional Primate Research Center, 232
Ylvisaker, Paul, 90, 96, 354-55
YMCA, 134, 142
Yonkers, N.Y., 119, 120, 276
Young, Donald: quoted, 392n
Young, Whitney M., Jr.: quoted, 18-19n
Youth programs: grants, 90, 160, 163-64n, 203, 205, 222, 229, 237, 241, 242-43, 355, 356, 415, 421-22

Zoos: grants, 220, 230